American Beginnings

American

Exploration, Culture, and

Edited by Emerson W. Baker, Edwin A. Churchill, Richard D'Abate, Kristine L. Jones, Victor A. Konrad, and Harald E. L. Prins

UNIVERSITY OF NEBRASKA PRESS
Lincoln and London

Beginnings

Cartography in the Land of Norumbega

Publication of this book was assisted by a grant from the National
Endowment for the Humanities.

The paper in this book meets the minimum requirements of
American National Standard for Information Sciences—Permanence
of Paper for Printed Library Materials, ANSI Z39.48-1984.

Library of Congress Cataloging-in-Publication Data
American beginnings: exploration, culture, and cartography in the
land of Norumbega / edited by Emerson W. Baker . . . [et al.].
p.   cm.
Includes bibliographical references and index.
ISBN 0-8032-4554-8 (alk. paper)
1. Indians of North America—Maine—History.   2. Indians of North
America—History.   3. United States—Discovery and exploration.
4. Cartography—Europe—History.   I. Baker, Emerson W.
E78.M2A74   1994
974.1'01—dc20   94-4380
                                                                    CIP

Contents

Illustrations

Figures

Plates

Following page 158

Preface

In 1986 the University of Southern Maine received an extraordinary collection of rare maps, atlases, and globes donated by
Lawrence M. C. and Eleanor Houston Smith. It was knowledge of the private donation to the university of this gift, rich
in material on the early explorations of America, that inspired
the Maine Humanities Council in 1987 to undertake an award-
winning project called the "Land of Norumbega." From this seed
grew a traveling high-security museum exhibition and a host
of related activities that focused public attention on the exploration, culture, and cartography of the northern part of the New
World. The exhibition opened at the Portland Museum of Art on
November 15, 1988, and traveled to the Hudson Museum at the
University of Maine in the spring of 1989. The Smith Collection
had become a star, even before there was a permanent home to
house it. Connected to the exhibition was an international conference, held in Portland on December 2–3, 1988, which offered
new ways to understand the topic of exploration, encounter, and
settlement and revealed the exciting interpretive dimensions of
maps. The papers from the conference, in turn, now serve as

the basis for *American Beginnings*. The conference presenters and others have supplemented this core work with several new papers as well as revised versions of two previously published works.

An important element of the Norumbega exhibition was a series of maps loaned from the private collection of Dr. Harold L. and Peggy L. Osher. When the Oshers donated their collection to the University of Southern Maine in 1989, two remarkable collections were brought together. The Smith and Osher materials chronicle the expansion of the Old World into the New in a collection of over twenty thousand maps, as separate sheets or bound in over six hundred rare books and atlases. Although the collections have a global nature, the exploration and discovery of North America spanning the years between the early 1500s and the 1800s is a particular strength. These materials will be housed in the Osher Map Library, an integral part of the new University of Southern Maine Library. The Osher Map Library will contain exhibition areas, as well as space for research and study, so that scholars, students, and the public will all have the opportunity to learn from these maps. The publication of *American Beginnings* is envisioned as an integral part of the university's commitment to this new cartographic resource.

The "Land of Norumbega" activities and the publication of this book have also provided an important platform for the dissemination of new insights gained in recent historical, anthropological, and archaeological research on northern New England and the Maritime Provinces. The 1970s and 1980s saw a tremendous increase in scholarly interest in the history of native peoples of the region. A growing number of professional archaeologists have unearthed a tremendous amount of data on the prehistoric peoples of Maine. Historians and anthropologists have added to the contributions of archaeologists in several monographs, dissertations, and numerous articles in journals and other publications. Much of this work appears in new interpretive frameworks in *American Beginnings*.

The editorial board of this multiauthored volume could not have been graced with more gracious or supportive assistance at all stages of the project. Dorothy Schwartz, Executive Director of the Maine Humanities Council, lent her considerable expertise and unwavering support, nurturing the project at all stages. Deborah Zorach provided able administrative assistance, not to mention her own living room for occasional editorial board meetings. Marcia Carlisle served as the project coordinator for the initial planning and implementation of the "Land of Norumbega" public humanities projects that led to this publication. Advisers to the project included Richard Candee, Joseph Conforti, Richard Emerick, Robert French, Elizabeth Miller, Neil Rolde, Robert Rothschild, Martha Severens, Karan Sheldon, and David Weiss. The efforts of Ingrid Monk, the conference coordinator, were greatly missed following her serious injury in a tragic automobile accident.

American Beginnings has been shaped by many scholars. The "Land of Norumbega" conference featured many fascinating speakers, not all of whose work could be included here. Their contributions sparked an intense reexamination of the early history of the North Atlantic among all of the participants and informed subsequent revisions in the works included here. Speakers included David Buisseret, Nathan Hamilton, Alison Quinn, Andrew Wahll, and James Welu. The editorial board is particularly grateful for the gracious assistance and cooperation of four conference speakers whose contributions will be or have been published elsewhere: Susan Danforth, Curator of Maps and Prints at John Carter Brown Library, Brown University; John Wolter, Chief, Geography and Map Division, Library of Congress; Andrea Bear Nicholas, Native Historian, Maliseet Indian Reserve, Tobique, New Brunswick; and Edward Dahl, Early Cartography Specialist, Public Archives of Canada, who also provided critical guidance for obtaining reprint permissions.

The scholarly community was greatly saddened by the death of Roger Howell, Kenan Professor of History, Bowdoin College. His untimely death prevented his inclusion in this volume. The death of J. B. Harley, Professor of Geography at the University of Wisconsin at Milwaukee, was also keenly felt by the scholarly community. We are honored to be able to publish his contribution posthumously.

Neither the "Land of Norumbega" project nor this publication would have been possible without the firm financial support of the National Endowment for the Humanities. The institutional support provided by the University of Southern Maine was ensured by the friendly direction of David Davis, Dean of the College of Arts and Sciences, and by the helpful and prompt attentions of Sharmon Toner and Jan Limpert. Gene Pranger and Lawrence Waxman of the university's Office of Sponsored Research administered the grant. The assistance of Dr. Harold and Peggy Osher, patrons of the Cartographic Center of the University of Southern Maine Library, as well as University Librarian George Parks and Cartographic Librarian Yolanda Theunissen, facilitated the editorial work of this illustrated volume. Many individuals and organizations are responsible for providing the illustrations for this book. In particular, thanks are due to photographers Jay York, John Tanabe, and David Mishkin. William Barry provided advice on illustrations, and Kerry O'Brien supplied logistical support.

The managing editors are especially grateful for the professional, prompt, and friendly cooperation of the editorial board and the goodwill of all the contributors. Finally, without the professional editorial assistance of Ann Binder, the research abilities of Ken Weisbrode, and the word-processing magic of Carol Fritzson, this work could not have been completed.

EMERSON W. BAKER
KRISTINE L. JONES

General Introduction

Richard D'Abate
and Victor A. Konrad

The name "America" was probably created in 1507 by the German cartographer Martin Waldseemüller. He used it to designate the new discoveries being made by Amerigo Vespucci, Christopher Columbus, and others in the western ocean. Realizing that these discoveries were not part of the Indies, as many thought, but were an entirely new continental object located between Asia and Europe, Waldseemüller drew in an ungainly but unmistakable landmass and called it America. To Europeans, America became the New World, an object of consciousness made all the more startling for the presence of its native inhabitants, the so-called Indians, who intrigued, frightened, taught, and battled the Europeans at every turn and who everywhere died in the track of the European invasion. To the natives, obviously, there was nothing new about this America; it had been their home for thousands of years. What was new was the presence of these white strangers who one day sailed into view and began to work their will and would never again leave. In this sense, "America" is the name of the beginning of an unheralded experience for both the European and the Indian. America *is* a new world: the place where two formerly separate histories intersect and begin, however unequally, to implicate each other.

In the United States, the popular imagination of American beginnings usually reduces to a few archetypal moments of U.S. history: the arrival of Columbus in 1492, the founding of Virginia in 1607, or the first thanksgiving at Plymouth in 1621. Like the friezes that symbolize these moments in the rotunda of the Capitol building in Washington, D.C., these are miraculous, ahistorical moments—stations in the sacred pageant of national identity. They are not meant to teach the complexity of history but rather to symbolically reinforce an explanation of who Americans are as a people. The reality of American beginnings, however, is that they lasted for nearly two centuries— the time it took for Europeans to consolidate their presence in the New World—and extended geographically to every point of contact throughout North and South America. For each of these points—whether in present-day Brazil, the West Indies, Mexico, California, Florida, Virginia, New England, Newfoundland, or Quebec—there is a potential historical narrative of exploration, cultural encounter, and colonial struggle. Though each of these narratives is the locus of a regional history, all are aspects of the new train of events set in motion in America. The point of this book is to present one of the northern chapters of this history as it played out in a region known in the sixteenth century as the Land of Norumbega.

The Northern Orientation

As Fernand Braudel and more recently Donald Meinig have amply demonstrated, in the age of exploration Europe exchanged its Mediterranean orientation for an Atlantic outlook.[1] This change came about slowly, pressured by the need to find new routes to the trading capitals of the East, facilitated by technological advances in navigation, such as the compass, the astrolabe, and sea charts, and prompted by ancient myths of paradisiacal islands beyond the Pillars of Hercules. The Portuguese were the first to venture out, and much of Columbus's belief that there were opportunities for discovery, trade, and gain in the western ocean can be attributed to their pathbreaking activities throughout the fifteenth century, especially the discovery and settlement of the Azores by the mid 1400s, and their regular voyages deep into the North Atlantic to conduct trade with Iceland. Columbus, in fact, sailed on one of the Iceland voyages in the 1470s. By the 1480s the English, who were involved with the Portuguese in the Iceland trade, were attempting to expand farther into the Atlantic in an effort to establish new fisheries. Some interesting evidence (a letter sent to Columbus, in fact) suggests that Bristol seamen may have reached Newfoundland in this early period, searching for a mythical land called the Isle of Brazil. The general point, however, is that England and Portugal had turned their prows to the west and the north well before 1492. This explains why Columbus's discoveries in the West Indies, once the news was out, could be so quickly matched in the North Atlantic. John Cabot officially discovered Newfoundland for England in 1497 and was soon followed by the Portuguese Corte-Real brothers in 1500-1501. As a result of these and other voyages, fishing expeditions and reconnaissance missions to and from these northernmost parts of North America became commonplace throughout the sixteenth century.

There were, then, not one but two geopolitical poles around which the greater European community organized its early understanding of the New World in the Atlantic: the West Indian, established by Columbus and expanded by Spain, and the northern, established by Cabot for England but variously claimed and expanded by other European powers. Though some studies of early European exploration make little or no mention of this northern sphere of interest, one can find English flags on the Juan de la Cosa map of 1500, the earliest surviving world map to show the new discoveries. Giovanni da Verrazzano's voyage for France along the eastern seaboard in 1524 was in fact deliberately organized to go between these two well-understood but presumably unconnected geopolitical entities. His hope had been to find a water passage to the riches of the Indies—the famous Northwest Passage—that would make the arduous southern route around Cape Horn unnecessary. What he found instead—from the Carolinas to Maine—was another unbroken continental seaboard, stunningly beautiful and fertile. Many others followed Verrazzano's path, continuing to poke into the new continental landmass in search of a northwest passage. These efforts led to the creation of a new territorial concept, linked to the first northern discoveries in the Newfoundland region but in a slightly more temperate clime, south of Cape Breton Island. This was the "Land of Norumbega"—the name sixteenth-century Europeans gave to the territory that for the most part is known today as New England.

Beginning with the voyage of Verrazzano in 1524, the European concept of a place or region known as Norumbega took about fifty years to elaborate and had an active geopolitical significance for perhaps another forty or fifty years. It was the product of a limited number of actual explorations, a great deal of speculation and mythical projection, and an admirably developed but self-repeating cartographic record. But to understand what Norumbega signified—to understand the importance of the geographical realities it seemed to describe and the dreams of abundance attached to them—one must consider the area in the context of Europe's response to the earlier discoveries in the northeastern parts of the New World.

Our understanding of the early exploration of the Northeast remains imperfect, but it is fairly certain that even though the offshore banks of Labrador, Newfoundland, and Cape Breton were fished heavily starting in the early fifteenth century, the land itself remained virtually unexplored and unsettled for over a century. Clearly, initial sightings and landfalls on these shores proved there was little to induce settlement or even temporary stays. Carl Sauer has eloquently described the harsh and uninviting shorelands that loomed before Europeans as they approached these rugged and isolated coastal regions.[2] It remains unclear who saw the land first, for landing was not important nor was it necessary. As David Quinn points out, "It did not greatly matter whether men from Bristol or men from Terceira [Azores] first saw land in the west, so long as they did not align their sovereigns behind them to obtain exclusive rights and thus manipulate discovery and control exploitation in these areas."[3] The attractive resource was offshore, and it was a resource shared in a nonterritorial sea. Unlike today, the abundant fish of the northern waters did not attract sovereign attention. Primarily for this reason, the land was not acknowledged. Preoccupation with the fishery partly accounts for the lack of exploration initially, but it does not explain why the first tentative explorations were not followed by more concentrated efforts during the sixteenth century. The lack of any apparent land-based resources may help to explain this neglect: accounts of northeastern shores provide little inducement for any settlement or even resource exploitation. Then again, a majority of exploratory voyages were being diverted northward to Davis Strait, Baffin Bay, and Hudson Bay in an almost frantic effort to discover the Northwest Passage. The Northeast coast sheltering the Gulf of St. Lawrence was being characterized as a glacially scoured, windblown, sparsely vegetated wasteland. There simply was nothing there worthy of more exploration.

It is in contrast with the inhospitable conditions in these northern parts—regions deemed unworthy of further consideration—that the Land of Norumbega, often approached by explorers from the north and the east, as Donald Meinig clearly shows, took on both geographical and economic meaning (fig. 1). Environmentally speaking, the difference is obvious. It was and is a region characterized by a south-facing coast swept by the ameliorating effects of the warm Gulf Stream currents. These conditions, coupled with more substantial soil cover in the southern reaches of continental glaciation, supported deciduous forests with higher carrying capacities for animal and human life. Agriculture was possible on the land; and in the adjacent Bay of Fundy and Gulf of Maine, current mixing and immense tidal amplitude supported a diverse richness of sea life unrivaled along the Atlantic shore. The salt marshes of these protected shores remain global leaders in biomass production. In contrast to the rock-bound and forbidding coasts facing the North Atlantic, Norumbega was a rich and abundant land—the beginning of a truly New World.

Although a modern environmental analysis cannot tell us how sixteenth-century Europeans felt and thought about a particular piece of the world's geography, the historical record, though ambiguous in many ways, seems to concur. In the sixteenth century, the idea of Norumbega was firmly fixed to the image of abundance: it was portrayed as an especially welcoming land of mineral wealth, navigable waters, agricultural fertility, plentiful game, and pliant natives. The documentary evidence consists of a few experiential accounts, passages of recorded hearsay, fabrications, political manifestos, and, above all, maps. Throughout the sixteenth century, mapmakers speculated on, embroidered, and manipulated a small store of observed geographical information about the Northeast. It is especially on the sixteenth-century map, a wonderfully flexible and rapidly evolving cartographic device, that the image of Norumbega—part imagined, part real—persists and develops.

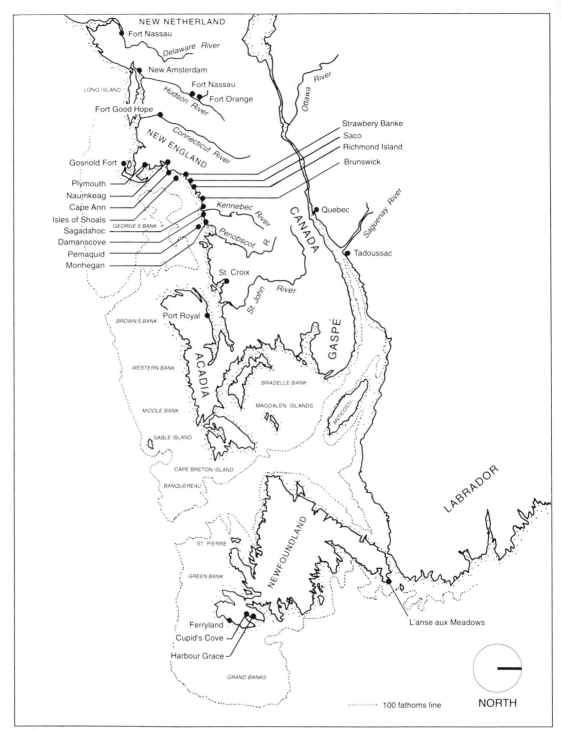

NEW NETHERLAND

Fort Nassau

Delaware River

New Amsterdam

LONG ISLAND

Fort Nassau

Fort Orange

Hudson River

Fort Good Hope

Ottawa River

Connecticut River

NEW ENGLAND

Strawbery Banke
Saco
Richmond Island

Brunswick

Gosnold Fort

Plymouth
Naumkeag
Cape Ann
Isles of Shoals
Sagadahoc
Damariscove
Pemaquid
Monhegan

GEORGES BANK

Kennebec River

Penobscot R.

CANADA

Quebec

Saguenay River

Tadoussac

St. Croix

St. John River

BROWNS BANK

Port Royal

WESTERN BANK

ACADIA

GASPÉ

BRADELLE BANK

MIDDLE BANK

MAGDALEN ISLANDS

ANTICOSTI

SABLE ISLAND

CAPE BRETON ISLAND

BANQUEREAU

LABRADOR

ST. PIERRE

NEWFOUNDLAND

GREEN BANK

L'anse aux Meadows

Ferryland
Cupid's Cove

Harbour Grace

GRAND BANKS

·········· 100 fathoms line

NORTH

1. Northeast North
America viewed from
the east, after Donald
Meinig, *The Shaping
of America*, 1986, p. 34.

The Land of Norumbega

Although the extent of Norumbega varied from map to map, its focal point—one of the most unmistakable features in New World geography—was the Penobscot River in what is now Maine. This part of the world was first coasted and described in a famous letter by Verrazzano in 1524, but the Penobscot itself—the only major northeastern estuary penetrated before 1529—was probably first explored in 1525 by Estevan Gomes, who expected its wide mouth to be the longed-for northern passage to the Indies. Its immediate appearance on two influential maps—a deep "V" dotted with islands—assured it a long-lasting and disproportionate geographical prominence. This image was soon conflated with information from Verrazzano's voyage: a place marked "Oranbega" on one of his brother's maps and an idyllic native encampment ravishingly described in his letter. These early identifications, boosted to some extent by Jacques Cartier's voyages to Canada in the 1530s, helped keep the concept of Norumbega alive in the European mind throughout the mid-sixteenth century, when the apparent lack of a northern sea route had dissuaded new explorations. Little more was needed, however, to feed Europe's New World, mythmaking machinery. Like El Dorado, Norumbega became an alluring imaginative possibility—a paradisiacal Indian kingdom waiting seductively at the head of the Penobscot with untold riches.

The kingdom of Norumbega soon began to take shape with a more or less consistent location and with identifiable dimensions, features, and attributes. Pierre Crignon, in his 1545 discourse on Jean Parmentier, a sea captain from Dieppe, wrote: "Beyond Cape Breton is a land contiguous to that cape, the coast of which travels south-southwestward, toward the land called Florida, and for a good 500 leagues. . . . The inhabitants of this country are docile, friendly and peaceful. The land overflows with every kind of fruit; there grow the wholesome orange and the almond, and many sorts of sweet-smelling trees. The country is called by its people Norumbega."[4] Jean Alfonce, Roberval's pilot, extended the description in his *La Cosmographie:* "Fifteen leagues within this river [the Penobscot] there is a city called Norombegue with clever inhabitants and a mass of peltries of all kinds of beasts. The citizens dress in furs, wearing sable cloaks. . . . The people

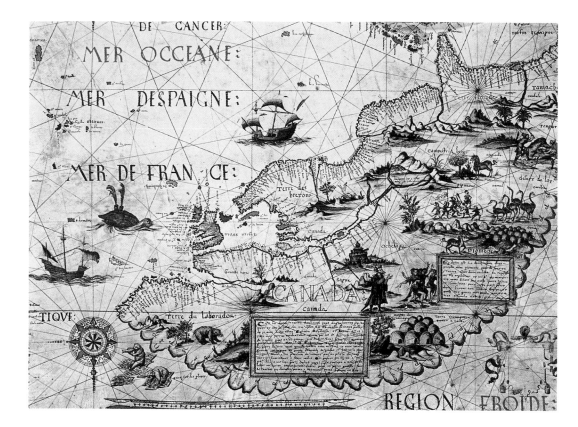

2. Portion of Pierre Desceliers, *Plani-sphere,* 1550. Courtesy of National Archives of Canada. By permission of the British Library, Add. Ms. 4065.

use many words which sound like Latin and worship the sun, and they are fair people and tall."[5]

Although he dismisses Norumbega as a myth in his seminal work *The European Discovery of America,* Samuel Eliot Morison confirms that it appears with strong regularity and consistent co-ordinates on the French maps based on Cartier's voyages and soon thereafter on other European maps. "Like Cartier's Canada, it is at once a region and a place."[6] On Pierre Descelier's delight-fully illustrated map of 1550, for instance, Norumbega appears as the first inhabited region beyond "Terre des bretons" (fig. 2). The distinctive estuarine notch dotted with islands identifies the Norumbega region, and a drawing of trees and dwellings indi-cates the presence of settlement. Though fanciful, the drawings may point to substantive French knowledge of greater resources and population existing south and inland from the Laurentian gateway to Canada. At this point in the development of car-tographic knowledge of the Northeast coast, the Bay of Fundy is not known, and Norumbega appears contiguous with what is now recognized as peninsular Nova Scotia. Giacomo Gastaldi's *La Nuova Francia* gives Norumbega an expanded regional presence, encompassing New England and perhaps the lower part of Atlantic Canada (fig. 3). This map, published by Giovanni Ramusio in 1556, also illustrates Norumbega as a peopled and hospitable land, in contrast to the lands associated with the fishing banks to the northeast.

In his *Cosmographie universelle* (1575), Andre Thevet, a monk who traveled widely in the New World during the sixteenth century, places Norumbegue only one degree south of the entrance to the Penobscot, and he describes in rich detail the features of the land and its people, though he may not have seen either. At about this time, maps of the Northeast begin to establish consistently that Norumbega is both a settlement and a region. This image is clearly depicted on Gerardus Mercator's map of 1569 and repeated on Cornelius de Jode's map of 1593 (fig. 4) and Cornelius Wytfliet's map of 1597. In all instances, Norumbega, its southern aspect well defined, lies astride the Penobscot and below its forks, a peopled region with an established capital. Mercator is explicit in situating the settlement at the head of the estuary and defining the region as inclusive of all the lands from the height of the Appalachians to the coast. This regional definition is repeated by de Jode in a rendition with a few more familiar landmarks to confirm the New England–wide extent of Norumbega. In Wytfliet's map, which identifies Chesapeake Bay, Cape Cod, and the Gulf of Maine, Norumbega stretches from present-day Nova Scotia to New York. By the end of the sixteenth century, Norumbega had gained substantial dimensions as the only territory identified directly south of New France. The geographical underpinnings of the myth were in place.

The image of Norumbega was also embellished by an alleged visitor. David Ingram, a member of the slaver John Hawkins's crew in an ill-fated voyage to the Caribbean in 1567, was shipwrecked along the Gulf of Mexico. He and two companions said that they walked northeast across the continent until they were finally rescued in Maritime Canada. Ingram expanded the Norumbega legend, claiming that he had seen "a towne half a myle longe" which "hath many streets farr broader than any street in London."[7] He described the inhabitants as adorned with gold, silver, and jewels, but he reported as well an excellent description of moose, which are common in the region. The intertwin-

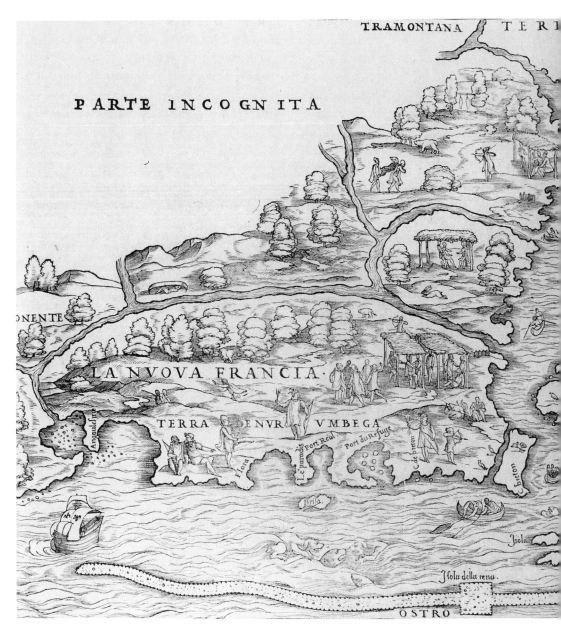

TRAMONTANA TERI

PARTE INCOGNITA

LA NVOVA FRANCIA.

TERRA DE NVR   VMBEGA

ONENTE

Angoulef

Iloia

Le paradis Port Real.

Port du Refuge

C. de breton

Breton

Brisa

Jsola

Jsola della rena

OSTRO

3. Giacomo Gastaldi,
La Nuovo Francia, in
Giovanni Battista
Ramusio, *Terzo Volume
delle Navigationi et
Viaggi*, 1556. Courtesy
of Smith Cartographic
Collection, University
of Southern Maine.

ing of factual and fanciful elements is well developed in Ingram's testimony. This blend of truth and fiction, combined with a substantial accumulation of geographical fact from earlier explorers' maps, led Elizabethan expansionists to again explore the land of Norumbega.

In addition to the lure of new wealth and hopes of finding the Northwest Passage, the English, under the direction of Sir Humphrey Gilbert, planned to build a naval station from which the Spanish West Indies might be harassed and to establish in Norumbega a settlement modeled on the manorial landholding patterns of the west country of England. The scheme never materialized because of Gilbert's pompous and inept leadership: after leaving Newfoundland, his fleet turned back without ever reaching Norumbega. Gilbert was lost at sea in 1583 on the return voyage. When his half-brother, Sir Walter Raleigh, revived English interest in planting a North American outpost in the late 1580s, the focus was on latitudes south of New England.[8]

In the late sixteenth century, both France and England reconsidered the economic potential of Norumbega—France above the Penobscot, England below. The maps available at the time, by Desceliers, Gastaldi, Mercator, and others illustrated in this volume, all delineated an insular region south of the great Laurentian entry into the New World and bounded by eastern and western waters. A ridge of mountains ran like a spine from west to east across this region separating French claims to the north from Norumbega's south-facing lands characterized by coves and islands. In 1579 and 1580, English voyages by John Walker and Simon Fernandez were commissioned to find the fabled Norumbega. Walker and Fernandez returned with reports of a less magical but still fair land, and this prompted Richard Hakluyt's *A Discourse on the Western Planting* (London, 1584), written at Raleigh's request to promote settlement and exploitation of the Norumbega region. The work has been called the most comprehensive statement of English colonial theory and intent. Intentions became practice when James I chartered dual colonial companies in 1606. We can see how their destinations defined the two poles of England's geohistorical memory: the London Company went to Jamestown, Virginia, following Raleigh's earlier ventures there, and three months later the Plymouth Company founded the Popham Colony in Maine, where the first American ocean-trading vessel was later built. The French too, guided by Samuel de Champlain, made colonizing efforts as early as 1602, returning to the region that Verrazzano had long ago mapped for their king.

As European settlements were established in the region at the beginning of the seventeenth century, the image of Norumbega began to fade. Champlain, perhaps the most accomplished and meticulous cartographer of northeastern North America, was quick to deemphasize and then to delete the mythical kingdom from his maps.[9] Based on personal reconnaissance and meticulous documentation, Champlain's maps were the best of his day. A map drawn in 1607 retained a reference to Norumbega, which was repeated on his maps of 1612 and 1613. One of his best and most beautiful maps, the *Carte Geographique de la Nouvelle Franse* (1612) (fig. 5), defined Norumbega merely as a native settlement on the Penobscot. Norumbega reemerged in somewhat broader regional representation on one of his later maps (1616), completed by Pierre Du Val in 1653 and titled *Le Canada*. Du Val incorporated other elements from earlier maps as well, and this rendition must be interpreted with caution. On the maps Champlain

4. Cornelius de Jode, *Americai Pias Borealis, Florida, Baccalaos, Canada, Corterealis,* 1593. Courtesy of Smith Cartographic Collection, University of Southern Maine.

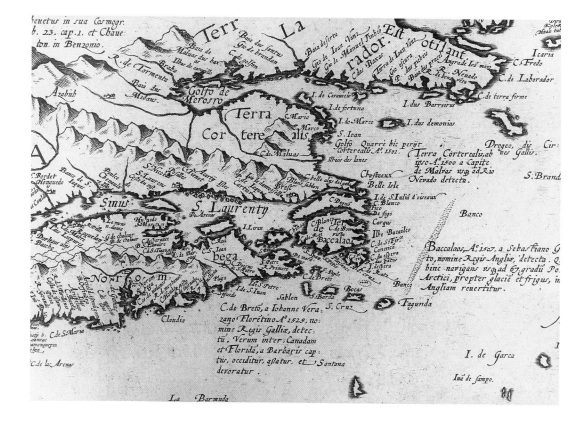

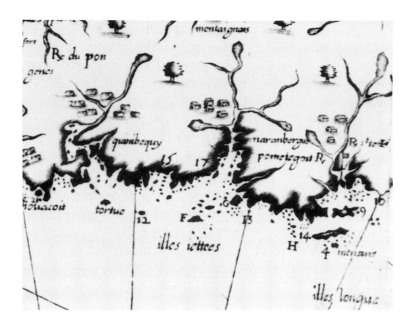

5. Detail showing
Norumbega from
Samuel de Champlain,
*Carte Geographique
de la Nouvelle Franse,*
1612. Courtesy of John
Carter Brown Library
at Brown University.

completed after 1616, the name "Norumbega" was applied only
to the Penobscot River. An image, once powerful and alluring,
had been reduced, transferred, and anchored to a well-defined
geographical feature.

The Present Volume

Part 1 of this book, "'There Appeared a New Land': European
Discovery, Exploration, and Cartography," concerns itself with
the European approach to the Norumbega region: the ancient
framework of geographical theory that stimulated and guided
their northern explorations; the voyages and the cartographic
representations they produced; and the gradual conceptualization
of Norumbega as both an imaginative and a geographical fact. In
beginning with these subjects, we recognize that it is European
history that has given weight and substance to our topic. Though
there is still some question whether the name Norumbega referred to any pre-European Indian reality, it is clear that Norumbega starts for us as a European construct. Establishing such
a priority represents the bias of our vision as well as our method.
We are riding in Europe's boat. Once arrived onshore, however,
we find our responsibilities clearly indicated. Part 2 of this work,
"'Wenooch': or, Who Are These Strangers? Native Americans
and the European Encounter," tries to restore some substance

to the native historical reality and point of view. The Indians of Norumbega—whom the Europeans met, learned from, profited by, feared, and killed—were the Wabanakis, the ancestors of the present-day Abenaki, Penobscot, Passamaquoddy, Maliseet, and Micmac tribes of Maine and the Canadian Maritimes.[10]

The effort to give Wabanaki life and thought a vitality independent of European perception is problematic, as it is for all the native tribes who figured in the history of American beginnings. Because they did not historicize themselves in writings as the Europeans did, it has always been hard to imagine how the white man's behavior was interpreted in the framework of native belief and expectation. And yet there is every reason to believe that when the Europeans came to America, they were stepping into a native social and cultural system that was as real, coherently organized, and complexly differentiated as their own—though in different ways. Too much has been learned from the investigations of anthropologists, archaeologists, and ethnohistorians, and from the mythological histories and oral tales of the natives themselves, to ever again discount their status in the cultural encounter. On the other hand, we know that the transforming power of contact began to immediately change Wabanaki life and history in complicated ways, forcing new cultural adaptations and contingencies, just as it had all the other aboriginal societies in America. In part 2 the authors open a window on the remote complexity of the Wabanaki world: a probable reconstruction of cultural similarities among the tribes; the function of narrative myths in the scheme of tribal identity; religious cosmology and social behavior; a review of early contacts with Europeans; and a look at their adaptive role in the trade systems that ultimately helped foster European settlement.

The myth of Norumbega as a northern paradise functioned as a lure, much as the legend of the Seven Cities of Cíbola had done in the Southwest in the earlier part of the century. The countries of Europe with northern interests needed an attraction that would rival, at least imaginatively, Spain's real golden discoveries to the south. Rumors about Norumbega were, in fact, directly promoted by England and France as a kind of advertising campaign to help stimulate colonial ambition in the later half of the sixteenth century. Part 3 of this book, " 'Planting, Ruling, Ordering and Governing': European Colonization and Settlement," examines the results of that campaign: French and English at-

tempts to develop colonies in the Norumbega region. The process
had begun well before the Pilgrims landed at Plymouth in 1620,
but it was still, by 1700, a very uncertain experiment, especially in
the northern parts of New England. The authors look at a number of important issues: the geopolitics of settlement; cultural
differences and adaptive strategies on the frontier; early efforts
to establish commercial operations in trade and the fisheries; the
omnipresence of the Wabanakis in colonial life; and especially
the manipulation of Wabanaki bitterness into the intracolonial
wars that devastated Norumbega for more than a century.

It will be evident that the history of cartography plays a central role throughout this volume. Maps, along with voyage narratives, are obviously the key historical records of the exploration
and settlement period, as well as important guides to the historical geography of America. Maps are not, however, simply
objective indices to physical places on earth; they are complex
representations of human knowledge, and nowhere is this more
obvious than in the European discovery of America. As a number of essays show, exploration proceeds through the interaction
of real and imaginative geographies—empirical experiences of
the land understood and interpreted in the light of expectations,
desires, preconceptions, and cultural attitudes. The one cannot
exist without the other, and neither is realized without finding
a fixed cartographic form. The map is thus a text in which the
image of the world is constituted and reconstituted through mul-
tiple acts of observation and interpretation. To attend to early
maps and the history of their making and use is to reconstruct
a momentous act of knowledge: the European mind—with all
its powers, suppositions, and traditions—moving to encompass
a new and startling object.

The realization that maps are instruments of interpretation,
however, also implies a recognition that they are neither value-
neutral nor necessarily benign but are capable of representing a
whole range of persuasive intentions regarding the configuration
and apportionment of land. The final part of this book, "Victims
of a Map," examines the implicit politics of the European map.
The particular concern is the means by which native claims to
the territory of Norumbega—and hence to their own identity—
are unobtrusively but systematically dismantled in a number of
famous maps that seem to be guided only by the aims of objective
representation. The use of empty space, the control of nomen-

clature, and the manipulation of iconography all play a role in asserting European dominance and native subordination in the new American world.

It is important to realize that more than one history, more than one reality, is at play in American beginnings. There are some who feel that the European victimization of the Indians, whose claims to priority in this hemisphere are unassailable, was so morally outrageous as to justify a total condemnation of the European colonial enterprise and all that it has meant in the subsequent history of this country. In a way this is a rebuttal to the sometimes insensitive and univocal intoning of our national narrative—the one that marches archetypally across the Capitol rotunda—in which the transfer of European cultural values (sometimes called civilization) takes precedence over any prior aboriginal claims. And yet, the demands of moral justice and symbolic nationalism notwithstanding, both the colonial reality and the native reality, as well as the peculiar power of the European mind, must be equally accounted for in a comprehensive history. If we accept the opening premise—that "America" is the name of a place where two separate human histories first began their unequal but continuing dialectic—then only a simultaneous, plural, complex vision will be adequate to the job of understanding how we began, who we are, and what we will become.

"There Appeared a New Land"

Europeans Discovery, Exploration,
and Cartography

Introduction

Richard D'Abate

In 1524 Giovanni da Verrazzano's explorations made the eastern seaboard of today's United States a startling geographical fact. In a letter he described the voyage: "We continued on our westerly course, keeping rather to the north. In another 25 days we sailed more than 400 leagues, where there appeared a new land which had never been seen before by any man, either ancient or modern."[1]

In truth, Verrazzano was disappointed. By keeping to the north of Spain's recent discoveries in Florida, yet south of England's long-recognized claims in Newfoundland, he had hoped to sail right through to the Indies. Ancient cosmological ideas had prepared the European mind to expect such an opening toward the top of the world, and the most up-to-date maps and theories of New World geography in the early sixteenth century were careful to leave room for the possibility. This was the Northwest Passage —the short route to the riches of the East—which continued to be a stimulus to European exploration well into the seventeenth century. The lure of the passage drew attention to the northern

lands, which in turn themselves became objects of desire, speculation, and investigation—became, in fact, Norumbega.

In chapter 1, "The Indrawing Sea," John L. Allen reviews the
history of the idea of a Northwest Passage and its impact on
exploration. As Allen notes, beliefs about the geography of the
world have always developed through the interplay of experience
and imagination—the world as tested and the world as hypothe-
sized. Renaissance theorists, such as Peter Martyr, interpreted
actual observations from the earliest northern voyages in the
light of ancient Greek and medieval Christian theories of land
and water distribution. The resulting belief in a broad strait that
split the North American continent in two laid the groundwork
for a series of European voyages near Norumbega throughout
the sixteenth and early seventeenth centuries. Allen examines
the tenacity of the passage theory in the face of growing contradictory evidence and shows how both were mediated in the rich
cartographical record.

Though the extent of the land of Norumbega varied greatly, its
geographical focus was always the coast of present-day Maine. In
chapter 2, "The Early Cartography of Maine," David B. Quinn
looks in detail at the early voyages that contributed significantly
to the cartographic description of northeastern North America.
Each major voyage—from the first reconnaissance missions of
Verrazzano and Estevan Gomes in the 1520s to the increasingly
careful surveys of Samuel de Champlain and Captain John Smith
in the early 1600s—is examined in terms of the politics that set
it in motion, its probable sightings and landings in the land of
Norumbega, and the maps and traditions of maps that it created.
In this way Quinn traces the method and growth of Europe's
geographical understanding of one region of America.

Through most of the sixteenth century, however, that understanding remained rudimentary, especially in regard to Norumbega. In the absence of a steady flow of information from the
New World, as Richard D'Abate shows in chapter 3, "On the
Meaning of a Name," the texts that had been produced by
the early explorers—the narratives of their voyages, the maps,
and other sorts of imagery—took on a life of their own in the
European mind. Perhaps most important for the Norumbega
concept was Verrazzano's description of an idyllic American holi-
day in the company of strikingly beautiful and civilized northern

natives. D'Abate shows how this account was recombined with a series of shifting signs—names and cartographical features especially—to produce the idea of Norumbega: a seemingly real geographical place that was also a mirror of English and French desires for a golden paradise of their own in the New World.

CHAPTER ONE

The Indrawing Sea
Imagination and Experience in the Search for the Northwest Passage, 1497–1632

John L. Allen

In the opening years of the nineteenth century, America's national exploratory epic unfolded as Meriwether Lewis and William Clark traversed the continent from the mouth of the Missouri River to the mouth of the Columbia River and back in the years 1804–6. As described in the instructions that Thomas Jefferson gave to Lewis in 1803, the goal of this exploration was to locate, via the rivers of western North America, whatever stream might "offer the most direct & practicable water communication across this continent for the purposes of commerce."[1] Lewis and Clark sought the Northwest Passage, a water communication across North America, which had been the goal of continental exploration for centuries.

If we examine the "geosophy," or geographical images, of North America before the early nineteenth century, we find that the conception of a Northwest Passage did not begin with the European contacts with the areas west of the Mississippi River in the late seventeenth century. It is true that Jefferson based his instructions to Lewis largely on the comment of Father Jacques Marquette, who, on discovering the Missouri River in 1673, con-

cluded that following the Missouri to the northwest would lead
to a lake out of which another river flowed westward to fall into
the sea. "I have hardly any doubt," wrote Marquette in his journal, "that this is the Vermillion Sea [the Gulf of California], and
I do not despair of discovering it some day."[2] It is also true that
during the centuries between Marquette and Lewis and Clark,
this dominant geographical idea of a commercial water passageway across North America kept reappearing in the literature and
on the maps of the North American continent. But if we probe
for the antecedents of Marquette's and, subsequently, Jefferson's
faith in the Passage, we find ourselves involved not just in the literature of North American continental exploration in the seventeenth and eighteenth centuries but in the literature of North
American exploration dating back to the first European contacts
with North America.

Marquette, it turns out, had described the Passage in its final
and most realistic form: a simple and very short portage between the navigable waters flowing to the Atlantic and some
great river that flowed toward the setting sun. It was this version of the Passage that was sought by Lewis and Clark. But
explorers before them had visualized and searched for eastward-
flowing streams that mingled their waters with streams flowing
west to the Pacific Ocean. And before that version of the Passage, geographers and explorers had envisaged vast interior lakes
out of which rivers flowed in both directions, to the Atlantic and
the Pacific. Retreating still further into the past, a search for the
origins of the idea of a water communication across the continent reveals a concept of sea-level saltwater straits that formed a
corridor between the seas of the North or Atlantic and the South
or Pacific. This bit of imaginary geography was the Passage in its
original form, developed after exploration had revealed the New
World as a barrier lying athwart Europe's path to the Orient.
But even this original conceptualization of the Passage had its
origins further in the past—in the geographical imagination of
Renaissance, medieval, and even classical geographical theorists.
The early developmental history of this idea of a Northwest Passage—one of the most powerful geographical ideas of all time—
is the theme of this chapter. It must be noted that this inquiry
into the origins of imaginary geography represents the planting
of soil that has already been well tilled by David Quinn and many
others. My attempt here is to concentrate on the evolution of a

geographical idea and to indicate its relationship to an exploratory process that was so important for increasing geographical knowledge of lands in and around Norumbega in the sixteenth and seventeenth centuries. In doing so, I hope to illustrate something more basic: the relationship between imagination and experience in the development of geographical images.

Ever since the pioneering work of John K. Wright[3] and Ralph Hall Brown[4] in the 1940s, students of geosophy have come to the belief that this combination of imagination and experience is how people have always developed their images or patterns of belief about the world or any of its regions. The Greek philosopher Strabo, one of the first thinkers to inquire into the process of how geographical images are formed, wrote that man is informed of the nature and content of his world "through perception and experience alike."[5] But even for Strabo and his contemporaries, "perception and experience" were necessarily combined with theory and imagination. Strabo's worldview was not confined to his recognized *oikoumene,* or "known world," but included images of unexplored regions that, for Strabo at least, were similar to places well known and carefully studied. Hence both imagination and experience played a role in the creation of the Greek worldview. For those of us who attempt to merge the study of geosophy with the history of discovery, the combination of imagination (the system of developing man's understanding of his world through the application of theoretical reasoning and creativity) and experience (the process of developing understanding through experience and the direct perception of geographic reality) has been particularly important for interpreting that process that we call exploration.[6] For in the exploratory process, theory and reality often merge to condition the objectives of exploration, to determine the nature of exploratory behavior during the course of an expedition, and to modulate the consequences of an exploration for geographical knowledge. Let us trace, then, the relationship between imagination and experience in the search for the Northwest Passage between the time of the voyages of John and Sebastian Cabot, who began the search for the Passage in the last decade of the fifteenth century and the first decade of the sixteenth, and the explorations of Luke Fox in 1632, whose voyages concluded the early phase of the maritime search for the Passage.

The Origins of the Concept of the Northwest Passage

One of the first recorded references to a Northwest Passage (although it was not yet called by that name) appeared in 1516. In that year, Peter Martyr d'Anghiera, dean of Granada cathedral, published the first three "Decades" of his *De Orbe Novo* (Decades of the New World), in which he related the latest information on the exciting discoveries that were being made in the western Atlantic.[7] In writing of the voyages of one Sebastian Cabot, near what would later be called "The Land of Norumbega," Martyr noted that Cabot had discovered a new continent lying where he had not expected "to find any other land but that of *Cataia*, and from thence to come in to *India*." The discovery of this new continent was, in Cabot's own words, "a great displeasure."[8] We are not certain exactly where Cabot made his landfall on his voyage of 1508–9; it may have been anywhere from Maine to southeast Newfoundland, although the best guess is that it was somewhere around the forty-fifth degree north latitude.[9] Nor do we know how far along the coast he proceeded to the north and to the south before turning east for England, although the optimum range would have him coasting the Atlantic shores from as far north as the Arctic Circle to as far south as Florida. More important than the actual extent of the voyage, however, was the fact that as Cabot sailed along the coast of the land he had discovered, he found what he described as a "course of the waters toward the West, but the same running more soft and gently than the swift waters which the *Spaniards* found in the Navigation Southward."[10] To Cabot and Martyr, this "course of the waters" was evidence of the presence of a passageway through what Europeans were just beginning to realize was a continent that barred the easy path to the Orient. Martyr expressed the theoretical construction of this passage: "[It] is not onely more like to be true, but ought also of necessity to be concluded, that betweene both the Lands hitherto unknowne [Martyr is talking about the lands discovered by Columbus to the south and those discovered by English sailors to the north] there should be certaine great open places, whereby the waters continually passe from the East to the West. Which waters I suppose to be driven about the Globe of the Earth by the incessant Motion and impulsion of the Heavens . . . because they see the Sea by increase and decrease to ebbe and flow."[11]

In this statement of Martyr's may be found a classic example of the relationship between imagination and experience in the development of a geographical idea. Cabot may have seen or experienced what he believed to be a strait that would lead through the land he had discovered to that portion of the all-encircling ocean whose waves washed the shores of Cathay and Cipangu. Martyr had theorized or imagined his "passage for the waters flowing from east to west," a construction called for in his worldview, which included a comprehension of global oceanic circulation based in current geographical theory. For the next century and a half, and even beyond, these methodologies of the imagination and experience would continue to clash as explorers experienced the geographical reality of the North American coastline and as theoreticians attempted to fit those experiences into patterns of rational explanation of global or regional geography.

When Martyr described the straits that Cabot had supposedly discovered as a geographical feature that provided "a passage for the waters flowing from east to west," he was articulating a geographical theory that had its roots in classical, medieval, and Renaissance cosmography. He was also attempting to find, in that cosmography, a solution to the "great displeasure" that Cabot had expressed on finding that his way to the Orient was impeded by a continental barrier. To begin with, it must be noted that the twin bases of Martyr's assumptions regarding the "passage for the waters" were (1) knowledge that the earth was a spherical body and (2) awareness of the variable distribution of land and water. Both of these bases were viewed by Martyr (and other cosmographers of the period) as factors that controlled the circulation of ocean waters; it was this circulation that Martyr deemed necessary to create a passage between the Atlantic and the seas adjacent to Asia. The remnants of classical geography that medieval times had inherited provided for this argument, as did such medieval and Renaissance works as the *Navigationi Sancti Brendani*, the *Descriptio Insularum Aquilonis*, the *Inventio Fortunata*, and the *Imago Mundi*.

The earth was envisaged by classical geographers as a sphere; although some early opinions had held that the earth was disk-shaped, this notion was discarded by the Pythagoreans and by Plato and was no longer operative after their time. And although some of the reasons the ancients gave for their belief in the earth's sphericity were based in speculation and philosophy rather than physical or experimental demonstration, the doctrine of a spherical earth was well known and often cited in medieval times, in spite of some theoretical objections. In such works as those mentioned above, the earth's spherical shape was also cited as a logical proof that the East could be reached by sailing west.[12]

Of the distribution of land and water, which conditioned oceanic circulation on the spherical earth, no such nice agreement prevailed. Many classical writers believed that the earth was divided into several zones, that waters circulated within a zone, and that passage between them was impossible because of extremes of heat and cold.[13] But those classical theorists whose works were of most importance to the late medieval European worldview—writers such as Aristotle, Pliny the Elder, Ambrosius Macrobius, and Martianus Capella—set forth the notions that the *oikoumene* was surrounded by an ocean, a fact that would obviously facilitate travel around the globe.[14] This belief was apparently common to many early cosmographers and may be traced in literature back to Homer and his world-encircling Ocean Stream. The Greek mathematician and geographer Eratosthenes might have derived his oceanic hypothesis from the writings of Homer; envisaging the ocean as encircling the entire globe, Eratosthenes used that notion to conclude that it would be no great problem to sail between Spain and India.[15]

None of these views, however, gained the degree of ascendancy over the minds of medieval theorists as did the Cratesian theory, first held by the Pythagoreans and worked out in detail by Crates of Milos.[16] According to this theory, the *oikoumene* was only one of four similar bodies of land on the surface of the earth. Crates and others imagined an impassable fiery ocean girdling the globe in an east-west direction and a meridional or north-south ocean reaching from pole to pole; these oceans divided the world into four habitable zones between which the ocean waters circulated freely. Some clerical scholars rejected this notion on the grounds that it invoked the doctrine of the Antipodes, lands forever beyond the reach of Christianity and therefore unthinkable. But others cited Crates in substantiating the possibility of circumnavigating the globe. The opposing theory of the encircling landmass—as expounded by Ptolemy and Herodotus—discredited the notion of circumferential oceans, bringing the continents of Africa and Asia together in the far southeast and making the Indian Ocean a landlocked sea.[17] But like the Antipodean arguments, this theory was less important for the simple reason that Ptolemy's *La Geographia* was not widely read in Christian Europe until the fifteenth century and the works of Herodotus were not known at all to medieval Europeans. For Martyr and many others, the teaching of Crates, Aristotle, and Eratosthenes remained foremost, and the emerging theoretical explanation of Martyr's "great straits" found its primary base in them.

Important as the theories of classical geography were in determining the medieval scholars' conception of lands beyond the *oikoumene* and of the passage thither, they were not the only sources of information or conjecture regarding the western Atlantic. In addition to the conceptual geography that grew out of the logic and literature of the past, the late medieval geographer was confronted with the information and misinformation from voyages of exploration — planned or accidental, real or apocryphal — in which men were supposed to have discovered lands beyond the borders of the known world. It is uncertain when the first sailors ventured courageously (or were blown off course) through the Pillars of Hercules and thence across the sea to the west; thus the beginnings of man's conquest of the Atlantic are as shadows lost in the darkness of the "Ocean Sea." Yet these shadows were not without substance, for they were cast on the European worldview.[18]

Some of the earliest venturings of the Celtic peoples into that portion of the North Atlantic that separates the British Isles from Iceland came into medieval geography in the forms of the *Navigationi Sancti Brendani*, and the fourteenth-century *Inventio Fortunata* also contained references to voyages westward from Britain.[19] More importantly, perhaps, the *Inventio Fortunata* also seems to have been based on the Scandinavian geographical concepts that emerged from the Greenland and Vinland voyages. Whatever the source, both of these pieces of literature evoked the crucial image of islands in the North that were separated by channels or "indrawing seas," which poured their waters into the polar ocean. The *Inventio Fortunata* spoke of these seas as "dividing all countries as they flow into the circle of the world from the outer oceans . . . the indrawing seas which divide the north."[20] This concept was given visual expression on Martin Behaim's famous globe of 1492 (fig. 6) and was certainly used by Martyr as

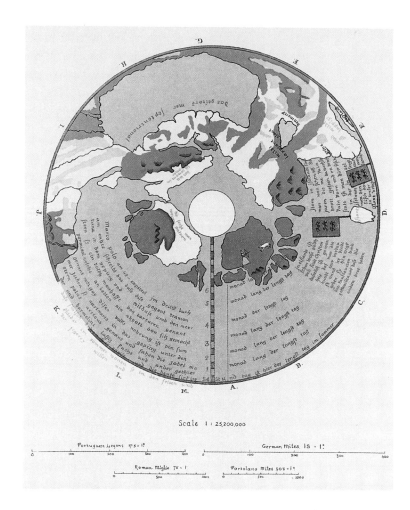

6. Polar projection
from Martin Behaim,
Globe, 1492. Facsimile
of 1908 courtesy of
Smith Cartographic
Collection, University
of Southern Maine.

proof of his view of the geography of the northwestern Atlantic: islands or continents, divided by channels or "indrawing seas," which poured into or from the polar ocean.

Aside from these literary sources, one other means by which the Celtic and Scandinavian geographical concepts might have been transmitted to the rest of Europe must be mentioned. This was the traffic of ideas that took place between Iceland and the English seaport of Bristol, the principal terminus of English trade with the western Atlantic.[21] Begun as early as 1411, the Bristol-Icelandic merchant trade had been flourishing since 1424, and at about the same time, Bristol fishermen began frequenting the Icelandic fishing grounds. Since Iceland was the repository for the folktales dealing with Norse exploration westward, the Bristol merchants and fishermen might well have learned of the

Norse concepts of the "indrawing seas" at the Atlantic's western edge. These sailors of Bristol, in turn, might have imparted their information to contacts in the Mediterranean, bridging the gap of knowledge between the earlier Norse discoveries and the coming age of exploration. There is even some arguable evidence that Bristol sailors actually sailed westward in search of the legendary medieval Isle of Brazil and made contact with what may have been the North American mainland nearly a decade before the landfall of Christopher Columbus in 1492.[22]

Whether or not the English discovery of the New World predated the initial Columbian voyage probably does not matter a great deal. But it may be significant that the first readily documented European exploratory response to Columbus's 1492 voyage was carried out by Sebastian Cabot's father, John Cabot (or Giovanni Caboto), an Italian mariner then living in Bristol.[23] Spurred by the news of the discoveries of Columbus to the south, John Cabot petitioned Henry VII for letters of patent that would grant him the right to sail toward the northwest, where he "would come to India by a shorter route."[24] It seems that John Cabot believed that by sailing the old Vinland course of the Greenlanders, he would reach the northwestern sections of Asia and that by sailing southeast, down the coast, he would reach Cipangu and from there make his way to India.

Martyr's discussion of the voyage of John Cabot's son, Sebastian, reports that the discovery of a new continent was "a great displeasure," since that landmass barred Europe's commercial route to the East. A displeasure it might have been, but perhaps not really a surprise. For according to the full chronicles of the Cabot voyages contained in the *Navigationi et Viaggi* by Giovanni Ramusio, it would appear that John Cabot's interpretation of the location of Asia put it far westward of Columbus's initial sighting of land. Moreover, according to Ramusio, Asia could be reached easiest by sailing "to the northwest, expecting to pass through to go to Cathay, and from thence turn toward India."[25] The natural question is, "to pass through" what? Sebastian Cabot may have already been thinking, before his 1508–9 voyage, of a route via the great straits or indrawing seas of classical and medieval imagination and of Norse experience. He may have learned of the existence of such straits either through existing literature or from actual exploratory contact, since it appears he accompanied his father on the elder Cabot's 1497 journey to

North American shores and could possibly have seen the Gulf of St. Lawrence and interpreted it as the "indrawing sea." He also could have had access to Martin Waldseemüller's world map of 1507, which showed a continental-sized landmass east of Asia with passages around it to both the northwest and the southwest. He could even have had knowledge of the futile Portuguese attempts, led by the brothers Gaspar and Miguel Côrte-Real in 1501 and 1502, to pursue the indications, given by John Cabot's 1497 journey, that a northwest passage might provide a short way to Asia.[26] The Corte-Reals did not discover any such passage, but their explorations did seem to confirm the existence of a western continent rather than the island archipelago of medieval maps. They themselves indicated a belief that the land they discovered was "mainland" and that it joined "another land which was discovered last year in the north" (perhaps a reference to John Cabot's discovery). The Corte-Reals also thought that this land was "connected with the Antilles, which were discovered by the sovereigns of Spain" (a reference to Columbus's discoveries).[27] But whether or not Sebastian Cabot's geographical knowledge of the lands of the western Atlantic was precise, or whether he believed in the existence of a passageway through a continental barrier to the seas adjacent to Asia, makes little difference. For Martyr, in reporting on Cabot's voyage, definitely expressed such an opinion. And in his commentaries on Cabot's discoveries, Martyr combined the logic of the Cratesian theory and other classical notions on the all-encircling ocean with the geography of the Norse and with the exploratory experience of the Cabots, both father and son, to create the conceptual geography of a continental landmass separated by great straits in the western Atlantic. This concept was to find cartographic expression in the works of Gerardus Mercator.[28] It was to be cited authoritatively by Richard Hakluyt in his *Navigations*, by John Dee in his mathematical essays, and by Sir Humphrey Gilbert in his *Discourse on a New Passage to Cathay*. It was to become the foundation for the exploratory objectives that conditioned maritime exploration in the northwestern Atlantic well into the seventeenth century.

The Early Attempts on the Passage

It is impossible to report here on each and every voyage that touched on the question of the "indrawing seas" or the Northwest Passage between John Cabot in 1497 and Luke Fox in 1632. And it is impossible to fully discuss the cartography and theoretical geography that both grew out of exploration and contributed to further westward searches. But what one can do is attempt to focus on the most significant explorers and theoreticians as we continue to examine the evolution of this geographical concept.

For nearly four decades after John Cabot's seminal discoveries, most of the important exploration of the western borderlands of the North Atlantic were carried out by France and Spain, rather than by the English (to whom credit must be given for the initial exploration). The Spanish had, early in the sixteenth century, sought a passage through the Caribbean, recognizing that the great current that flows into that sea along the north coast of South America had a westerly set and was identified by no less than Columbus himself as a possible passage to the Pacific.[29] This current encouraged a belief that North and South America were separate landmasses, on the grounds that such a volume of water must have an outlet. By the 1520s, however, Spanish and Portuguese exploration to the south had proven the existence of two major continental landmasses—North and South America—joined by a narrow isthmus, which Vasco Núñez de Balboa had crossed in 1513 and where he had climbed a peak "from which he myght se the other sea so longe looked for, and never seen before by any man comynge owte of owre worlde."[30] The discoveries of Balboa and others had shown the true position and form of the Atlantic coasts of Central and South America and of the gulf coast of North America. The explorations of Juan Ponce de León and of Alonso Alvarez de Pineda had proved that the Gulf of Mexico contained "no strait there by which ships could reach Asia."[31] Knowledge of the northern continent in the opening years of the 1520s, on the other hand, was still inexact and speculative—as was any additional information regarding the "indrawing seas" of higher latitudes (fig. 7).

After Cabot, the first major attempt on the passage north of the Caribbean began in 1523 when the French officially entered the race toward Asia, with Francis I's dispatch of an exploring expedition under the leadership of the Florentine navigator Giovanni da Verrazzano.[32] Verrazzano's stated intention in this voyage was "to reach Cathay and the extreme east of Asia, not expecting to find such an obstacle of new land as [he] found." He added: "And if for some reason I expected to find it, I thought it

7. Sebastian Munster, *Typus Cosmographicus Universalis,* in his *Novus Orbis Regionum,* 1532. Courtesy of Osher Cartographic Collection, University of Southern Maine.

not to be without some strait to penetrate to the Eastern Ocean. And this has been the opinion of all the ancients, believing certainly our Western Ocean to be one with the Eastern Ocean of India without interposition of land. This Aristotle affirms, arguing by many similitudes, which opinion is very contrary to the moderns and according to experience untrue."[33] Sailing from the Madeiras, Verrazzano made his landfall on the American coast in latitude thirty-four degrees north and coasted both north and south of that landfall "with the continual hope of finding some strait or true promontory at which the land would end toward

the north in order to be able to penetrate to those blessed shores of Cathay."[34]

Although Verrazzano failed to find a passage through the northern continent, his exploration made significant contributions to geographical knowledge in that he filled the gap, more or less, between the Spanish ventures to the south and the English and Portuguese enterprises to the north.[35] In so doing, he bolstered the conviction that North America was a continent, albeit one that was penetrable to the "Eastern Ocean" via a sea-level strait. Most important, perhaps, Verrazzano's conjectural geography included a narrow isthmus of land around the thirty-fourth parallel, beyond which lay the South Sea or Pacific. This isthmus mirrored that discovered by Balboa farther south and suggested that if a sea-level strait could be found through it, the passage to the Pacific would be a short one. Verrazzano's discoveries played a major role in the geographical interpretations of North America by English and other geographers. And even though the voyage of Estevan Gomes, sailing for Spain in 1525 and having "no other thing in charge than to search out whether any passage to the great Chan, from out the diuers windings and vast compassings of this our Ocean were to be founde,"[36] proved there was no strait south of the forty-fifth parallel, Verrazzano's geographical data—including representations of great straits through the North American continent—would haunt theoretical geography and cartography for a century (fig. 8).

The second significant French explorations in search of the Passage—and the last French efforts for many years—were those led by Jacques Cartier and Jean Roberval from 1534 to 1543. The first Cartier voyage of 1534 was essentially a reconnaissance around the Gulf of St. Lawrence. "By reason of the great depth and breadth of the gulfe," Cartier commented, "we conceived hope that we should finde a passage."[37] Henceforth, French explorations would be focused on the area in and around the Gulf of St. Lawrence and up the great river, which offered a key to the geography of the interior. On his second voyage of 1535 Cartier entered the St. Lawrence proper "because he would know if between the lands any passage might be discovered."[38] He sailed up the river as far as the Indian town called "Hochelaga" on the site of present-day Montreal before determining that the river was not a sea-level strait. But he did learn that the river "went so farre upwards, that they never heard of any man who had gone to the end therof."[39] He also learned of a huge lake or inland sea that lay many days' journey to the west and another great river "which commeth from the West."[40] Cartier's second voyage was the first noteworthy continental penetration of North America north of Mexico, and it set the feet of French explorers on a different path than that taken by other European nations. After Cartier, the French search for the Passage would focus on the river and lake systems of the continental interior, thereby providing both a theoretical and an experiential basis for much of North American exploration well into the nineteenth century.[41] But Cartier's travels also reinforced much existing geographical information, which continued to support the geographical proximity of North America and Asia and the theory of a passage from Atlantic to Pacific waters around the northern end of the newfound lands. A Portuguese report on the preparations for Cartier's third voyage of 1541–42 referred to Cartier's conjecture that the lands above Hochelega contained "many mines of gold and silver in

8. Sebastian Munster, *Die Newen Inseln,* in Claudius Ptolemy, *Geographia,* 1540–44. Courtesy of Osher Cartographic Collection, University of Southern Maine.

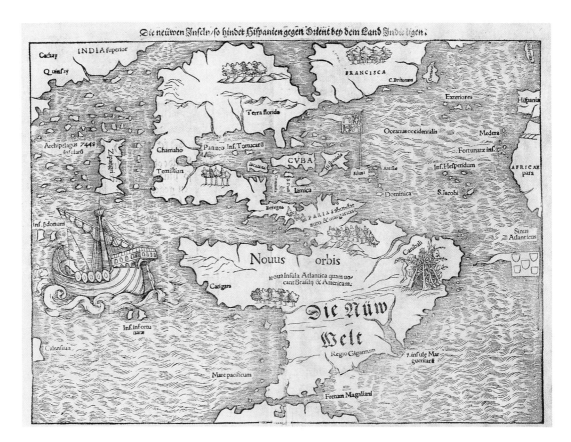

9. Detail from Diogo Homen [*North America and the North Atlantic*], 1558. By permission of the British Library.

great abundance . . . and [an] abundance of clove, nutmeg, and pepper."[42] And another Portuguese report of Cartier's third expedition (which was devoted primarily to an attempt to found, in conjunction with Roberval's party, a French settlement) notes that the great river entered by Cartier "is very long . . . and that on the other side it empties itself into a great sea"[43] (fig. 9). In spite of the seemingly optimistic assessment of the chances to discover the passage to the Sea of Cathay, the French made no further attempts until the early years of the seventeenth century—and when those attempts were made, they were toward the continental interior. After Cartier, the torch that lit the way to the Orient by way of the indrawing sea was passed to the English, and the story of attempts to find a Northwest Passage in the remainder of the sixteenth and into the seventeenth centuries is largely a story of English seamen.

Indeed, the English had begun attempts to locate the indrawing sea even before the Cartier explorations. As early as 1517 there was an abortive attempt at western exploration by an English lawyer named John Rastell, who was, not so coincidentally, also Sir Thomas More's brother-in-law.[44] Although Rastell's expedition never got past Waterford, Ireland, he wrote, after his return, a document entitled (in modern English) "Interlude of the Four Elements," which illumines for us the early-sixteenth-century English geographical understanding of, among other things, the passage to India. Rastell discussed "certeyn poyntes of cosmography . . . of the cause of the ebbe and flode of the see," which suggests, at least, an English belief in the indrawing sea configuration described in more detail by Martyr.[45] That Martyr's ideas, as derived from Sebastian Cabot, were current in England at this time is substantiated by a visit made by Cabot to England in 1521 and a subsequent attempt to obtain support from English merchants to finance a Northwest Passage voyage.[46] The attempt failed, largely because the London merchants were unwilling to risk ships and funds on the strength of Sebastian Cabot's word that the indrawing seas existed. "It is said among maryners in an olde proverbe," concluded the merchants, "[that] he salys not surely that salys by an other mannys compas."[47]

The necessity of a voyage in search of the indrawing sea, however, derived further impetus from the knowledge, obtained in 1522, of Ferdinand Magellan's passage of Cape Horn and entry into the Pacific in 1519. This passage, in the eyes of some Englishmen, conferred considerable trading advantages on Spain, and the hope of a passage by sea through or to the north of the northern continent—a passage that would be easier than Magellan's tortured passing of the cape—was renewed. In 1527 John Rut left England "to make a certaine exploration toward the north, between Labrador and Newfoundland, in the belief that in that region there was a strait through which to pass to Tartary."[48] Rut's voyage carried him to Labrador, Newfoundland, and down the Atlantic coast to the West Indies, in order "to go and discover the land of the Great Khan,"[49] and would seem to have been based not only on the indrawing seas concept of Martyr and Cabot but also on Verrazzano's belief in a narrow isthmus somewhere around the thirty-fourth parallel of latitude.[50] Neither the passage to the north nor a sea-level strait near Verrazzano's supposed isthmus was found; one of Rut's ships was lost near the fifty-third parallel of north latitude, and after proceeding some ten more futile degrees northward, Rut broke off the attempt and returned to England.

By the time of Rut's exploration, some twenty years of exploratory experience had accumulated without any valid or objective sighting of the indrawing sea, a fact that had not diminished the strength of imaginary geography. In the same year as Rut's voyage, an English merchant named Robert Thorne produced an elaborate theoretical justification for the continued belief in a passage to the Spice Islands around the northern end of North America. Addressing his statement to King Henry VII, Thorne wrote, "There is left one way to discover, which is into the North; for that of the foure partes of the worlde [a reference to the Cratesian world view?], it seemeth three parts [a reference to routes to the Pacific across the Isthmus of Panama and around Cape Horn, and to the Indian Ocean around the Cape of Good Hope] are discovered by other Princes."[51]

In addition to waxing enthusiastic over the riches to be obtained by the English discovery of such a northern route, Thorne laid out his belief that the strait leading to Asia could best be found by sailing directly over the North Pole—this would be the shortest distance, and in Thorne's opinion, there was "no sea unnavigable."[52] Establishing by geometry that the shortest route to the "Spiceries" lay "over or across the Pole," Thorne concluded, "If from the sayd New found lands the Sea be navigable there is no doubt, but sayling Northward and passing the Pole, descending to the Equinoctial line, we shall hit these Islands, and it should be a much shorter way, than either the Spaniards or the Portingals have."[53] Thorne's theoretical geography was supported by Roger Barlowe, an Englishman living in Spain who had accompanied Sebastian Cabot on a voyage to South America in 1526–28. In his "Briefe Summe of Geographie,"[54] Barlowe repeated Thorne's sailing directions for an English route via the strait or indrawing sea that would lead to and across the North Pole. He climaxed his argument, "And beside all this yet, the comoditie of this navigation by this waie is of so grete advantage over the other navigations in shorting of half the waie, for the other must saile by grete circuites and compasses and thes shal saile by streit wais and lines."[55]

Thorne's cosmography may also have prompted a mysterious and obscure voyage by Captain Richard Hore of London, described as "a man of goodly stature and great courage, and given to the studie of cosmographie . . . who encouraged divers Gentlemen and others to accompany him in a voyage of discoverie upon the Northwest parts of America."[56] With two ships, Hore left England in 1536 and sailed to Cape Breton and then to Newfoundland in search of the Passage. But in high latitudes, so high that "they sawe mightie Islands of yce in the sommer season,"[57] his company's food supply ran low, and the expedition was forced to return to England without having discovered the indrawing sea or strait to Asia. This voyage marked the end, for several decades, of serious English attempts to locate the indrawing sea and the passage to Cathay. The first round of English efforts to circumvent the continent had died out in the ice fields, and the English gave up, for a time, the discovery of the short route to Asia by the northwest.

Theoretical Development of the Northwest Passage Concept

The fact that the English endeavors to locate a passage were halted for a while meant only that there was a pause in the accumulation of empirically based geographical lore. The other side of geographical knowledge—that obtained through speculation and imagination and theory—received tremendous stimulus from the work of several commanding English intellectuals during the hiatus in exploration. By far the most important of these was the Welsh-born Elizabethan mathematician and cosmographer John Dee.[58] Alone among English geographers, Dee numbered among his teachers such great continental geographers as Gemma Frisius, Gerardus Mercator, and Abraham Ortelius, from whom he learned not only mathematical geography but much about the probability of a Northwest Passage as well. Frisius, for example, had produced a map on which the passage to Cathay was clearly indicated, marked as *Fretum Trium Fratum* (The Straits of the Three Brethren), a reference to the indrawing sea or straits mentioned in the narratives of either the Cabots or the Côrte-Reals. Ortelius showed a similar great northern strait on a number of maps produced during the 1560s and 1570s (plate 1). And the inset of the Arctic on Mercator's world map of 1569 illustrated a classic example of the "indrawing seas" concept from the *Inventio Fortunata*, probably through Martyr (fig. 10). In England, Dee served as friend and adviser

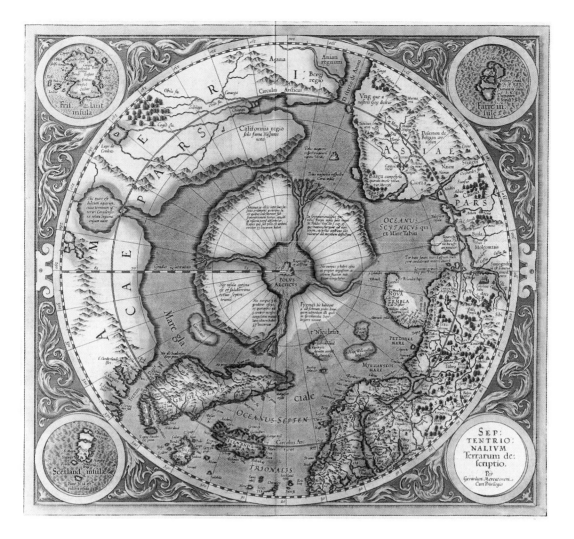

10. Gerardus Mercator, the arctic from his *World Map,* 1633 edition. Courtesy of Osher Cartographic Collection, University of Southern Maine.

to the other great practitioners of the geographer's art and science in Tudor England—men such as the Richard Hakluyts (elder and younger), Leonard and Thomas Digges, Michael Lok, and Thomas Harriot. He was also a technical adviser and confidant of the great figures of Elizabethan exploration—men like Humphrey Gilbert, Martin Frobisher, John Davis, Walter Raleigh, and Francis Drake. His views on the Passage exerted tremendous influence over the course of exploration when, in the 1570s, the English renewed their efforts to discover the indrawing sea or *fretum trium fratum*, which was, as Richard Eden noted in his 1553 preface to *Treatyse of the Newe India,* "sufficiently known to such as have any skill in geography."[59]

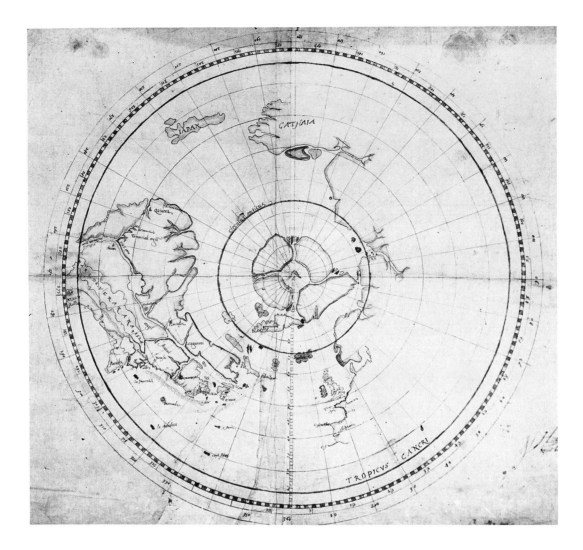

11. John Dee,
*Humfray Gylbert
knight his charte*
(chart of the Arctic),
ca. 1582. Courtesy of
Rare Book Library,
Free Library of
Philadelphia.

During the time that Dee was acting as an instructor in the science of mathematical navigation and the art of geographical imagining, there were a number of possible interpretations as to the actual configuration of the great straits that nearly all geographical authorities agreed would lead to the shores of Cathay. Dee's interpretation, shown on a map he drew in 1582 (fig. 11) and the one that would come to dominate theoretical geography in England, had North America detached from the Asian mainland and separated from it by a lengthy sea-level passageway that had its eastern opening somewhere near the sixtieth parallel of latitude and trended somewhat southwest to terminate in the Pacific near the fortieth parallel of latitude. South of this great passageway lay North America; north of the passage lay either polar lands or Tartaria, seen by Dee as separate from Cathay. There are two essential facts in this imaginary geography: the first is that the worldview of geographers was still much more clearly grounded in ancient theory than in empirical knowledge; the second is that in this imaginary geography, the way to Cathay lay open from the Atlantic and thus from England. Dee's conceptualization of the strait found expression in the worldview of Richard Hakluyt and, through Hakluyt, in the geographical writings of Elizabethan England's most eloquent spokesman for the discovery of the Northwest Passage, Sir Humphrey Gilbert.[60]

During the decades of the 1560s and 1570s, speculative geography on the Northwest Passage received considerable stimulus through the efforts of Gilbert, Dee, Lok, and others. As early as 1565, for example, Gilbert was enthusiastically promoting the possibility of finding a passage to Cathay by way of the northwest. In a petition to Queen Elizabeth, Gilbert noted that since "of longe tyme, there hath bin nothinge saide or donne concerning the discoveringe of a passage by the Northe to go to Cataia, & all other east parts of the worlde," he wished to "make tryall thereof."[61] In the following year, 1566, Gilbert wrote his theoretical exposition of the Northwest Passage: *A Discourse of a Discoverie for a New Passage to Cataia*[62] (fig. 12). The *Dis-*

12. Sir Humphrey Gilbert, map illustrating *A Discourse of a Discoverie for a New Passage to Cataia,* 1566 (published 1576). Courtesy of New York Public Library.

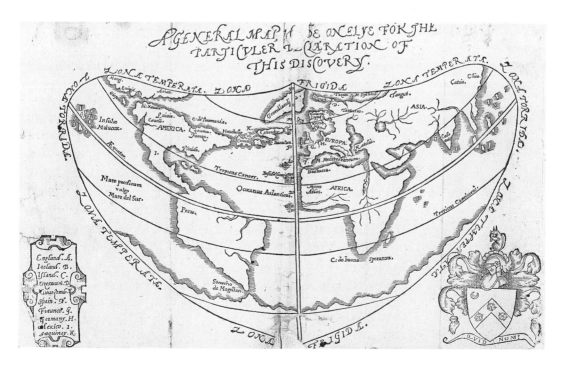

course was a remarkable document for a variety of reasons: it illustrates the degree to which geographical thinkers of the time relied on the cosmographical interpretations of classical authorities; it portrays the state of geographical knowledge of America and thus the worldview of geographical science in the last quarter of the sixteenth century; and it reveals the degree to which geographical thinkers of the time relied on the skimpy exploratory experiences of travelers since Columbus and John Cabot. In essence, Gilbert's *Discourse* was an extraordinary combination of the geography of the imagination, based in theory (and what Gilbert called "reason"), and the geography of what was perceived to be reality, based on empirical evidence from exploration. In summary, Gilbert asserted the following: (1) that America was detached from the Asian mainland and was the "fourth parte" of the world as defined in Cratesian theory, as demonstrated by the logic of classical writers, and as understood by contemporary European geographers; (2) that the passage around the northern end of America was required by cosmographical theory, which in turn required the presence of indrawing seas to allow the circulation of the ocean waters from east to west; (3) that the eastern entrance to the passage was well known through the efforts of explorers such as Sebastian Cabot; and (4) that strong evidence existed of the actual traversing of the passage by "3 brethren . . . whereof it tooke the name, of Fretum trium fratrum."[63]

Gilbert's thinking, along with general interest in the subject of a Northwest Passage, stimulated other geographical theorists to set down their ideas regarding the location and configuration of the indrawing seas. Lok and Dee, for example, in 1576 compared their notes and found that they agreed on the "conjectures and probabilities" through which Gilbert and they had "conceived of a passage by sea unto the same sea of East India by that way of the northwest from England."[64] But Gilbert did more than incite other geographical theorists to offer, through reason and logic, their views on the Passage. Dee himself notes in the preface to his *Memorials* that he carefully examined Gilbert's *Discourse* and, on the basis of that examination, laid out "Articles of Consideration" for "him or them, whom he should deem apt or desirous to further the said Discovery."[65] And William Bourne, one of the most influential Elizabethan authorities on navigation, even gave explicit sailing directions based on the *Discourse* to those who would attempt "to go unto *Cattay* by the Norwest."[66] In spite of the fact that Gilbert himself was diverted from his interest in the Passage to an all-consuming passion for a colonial enterprise in America (resulting ultimately in his death at sea) and even gave up his letters of patent to discoveries north of the fiftieth parallel to Dee in 1578, Gilbert's ideas provided the spark for the beginning of a new series of explorations in search of the indrawing sea, and the geography of the imagination would begin to give way, at least partially and for a time, to a geography based on experience.

The Resumption of Exploration

The first of the many fruits that sprouted from the seeds planted by Gilbert, Dee, Lok, and others was the series of voyages to the Northwest by Martin Frobisher between 1576 and 1578. On his first voyage, Frobisher reached Baffin Island and entered Frobisher Bay, where "a great mayne or continent" was found on either hand: the one on the right as he sailed westward Frobisher "judged to be the continent of Asia" because it was inhabited by people "like to Tartars"; on his left was "the firme of America," separated from Asia by the waters he plied.[67] Having entered what he assumed was the indrawing sea and having confirmed Dee's view of a passage between America to the south and "Tartaria" to the north, Frobisher returned to England with reports of a successful journey. On the strength of his reports of the Passage and the supposed discovery of gold on the shores of Frobisher Strait, his financial backers (the Cathay Company) supported a second and third voyage in 1577 and 1578. The efforts of these latter two expeditions were devoted more to the search for gold than to the search for the Passage. Yet on his third voyage Frobisher did enter Hudson's Strait, where he found a surprisingly strong current, adding credence to the conceptual indrawing sea that passed ocean waters from east to west,[68] and the map of the world that accompanied George Best's *True Discourse* showed a mighty "Frobishers Straightes" linking the Atlantic and the Pacific.[69] Experience seemed to have confirmed theory, and even though Frobisher's gold turned out to be worthless, the passage to Cathay still beckoned (fig. 13).

Although some geographers (Dee among them) were temporarily diverted to the speculative geography of a Northeast Passage following Frobisher, the bulk of English theoretical geography continued to focus on the northeastern sections of North

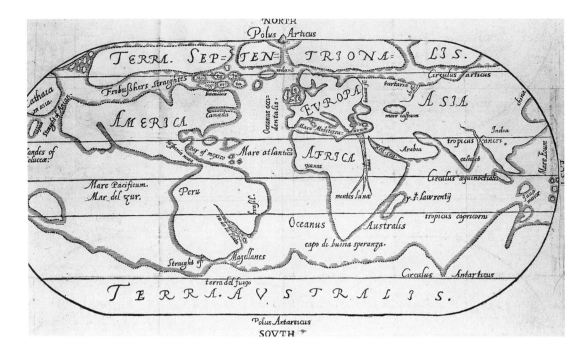

13. *World Map* (probably by James Beare), in George Best, *A True Discourse of the Late Voyages of Discoverie*, 1578. Courtesy of New York Public Library.

America in the 1580s. The publication of the younger Richard Hakluyt's *Divers Voyages* in 1582 provides an example. Hakluyt began his work with a printing of Henry VII's letters of patent to John Cabot and worked into his text Ramusio's description of Sebastian Cabot's attempts on the Northwest Passage, Thorne's theoretical treatise on the polar passage, and Verrazzano's letter to the king of France describing his voyage and the possibilities of a passage. In 1584 Hakluyt produced *A Discourse on the Westerne Planting*, which incorporated among its listed objectives for an English colonization on North America "that hardy perennial, to discover the Northwest Passage."[70] Also in 1583, Dee met with Adrian Gilbert (younger brother of Humphrey) and an English sea captain, John Davis, at his home, where "talk was begone of the Northwest Straights discovery."[71] And, in 1584, a patent was issued to Adrian Gilbert to "discover a Passage unto China and the Iles of the Moluccas by the Northwestward."[72] Between 1585 and 1587, three voyages were made under this patent, all of them commanded by Captain John Davis and all of them focusing on the area between Greenland to the east and Labrador and Baffin Island on the west as the logical place to look for the indrawing sea.[73]

The voyages of Davis were important for several reasons. He

added considerably to knowledge of the eastern Canadian Arctic and discovered the straits that now bear his name and open into Baffin Bay; of Davis Strait he wrote, "By this last discovery it seemed most manifest that the passage was free & without impediment."[74] More important, however, was the impetus he gave to further exploration in search of the Passage through the publication of his book *The Worlde's Hydrographical Description* (1595), which was a theoretical and practical discussion of land and water distribution showing that the Northwest Passage must exist and that its "execution is easie."[75] Davis's treatise was based, as so many other works of theoretical geography had been, on the symmetrical continent theory of Crates. Davis reasoned that since the currents of the ocean seemed to flow in some regularity, they must be caused by the shapes of the continents and the spinning of the earth. Since these continents were arranged in a symmetrical manner, it would be easy to find where the passages between them would be through deduction alone. Davis also reasoned that the circumpolar lands consisted of islands surrounding, at the North Pole itself, a great whirlpool into which the waters of the oceans poured, creating the indrawing sea in Martyr's speculative geography of nearly a century before.

A similar imaginary geography was also shown on Mercator's great map of 1595, the *Septentrionalium Terrarum Descriptio,* the first separate map of the North Polar lands. But Davis also had empirical knowledge of the polar seas. "I have now experience of much of the Northwest part of the world & have brought the passage to that likelihood, as that I am assured it must be in one of foure places."[76] This combination of geographical theory and exploratory experience made a powerful argument for the continuation of efforts to locate the indrawing sea and thereby the passage to Cathay via polar waters. In the years after Davis, the efforts to locate a Northwest Passage increased, partly as a result of Davis's optimistic reports, partly as a corollary of Hakluyt's continued reinforcement of the concept in his epic *Principal Navigations, Voiages, and Discoveries of the English Nation* (1589), and partly as an outgrowth of the continuing commercial demands of Europe for a short route to the Orient.

Between the years 1602 and 1632, English, Danish, and Dutch seamen undertook more than a dozen voyages to seek the indrawing sea and the passage to Cathay. These voyages shared a common pattern and common experiences: they were all determined efforts to prove the existence of a geographical feature conceived in theory and imagination. They also all failed in their primary objective. But in the exploration reports that appeared in such publications as the *Pilgrimage* of Samuel Purchas,[77] it is clear that the repeated failures were not due to the fact that the objective of the search did not exist. Rather, failure resulted from cold and snow and low supplies and mutinies and difficulties with the indigenous peoples; these factors always forced a turnabout just before the goal was reached. The chaplain who accompanied George Weymouth's East India Company expedition in 1602 never got to use the embroidered robe of silk and damask that he had been given to wear for an audience with the Khan.[78]

Perhaps the most significant of this series of voyages and the one that had the greatest impact on both the geographical imagination of Europe and the later course of North American exploration was the voyage by Henry Hudson in 1610. Hudson had already made three previous voyages in search of a shorter sea route "by way of the northern regions, whether across to Cathay or elsewhere."[79] When he returned from the last of these journeys (during which he had unsuccessfully sought a passage near the fortieth parallel but had discovered the Hudson River), the Dutch geographer Peter Plancius gave him the journals and logbooks of Weymouth's 1602 voyage. Weymouth had, it seems, gone a short distance into what was later to be called "Hudson's Straits" and wrote that he was impressed with the strong currents that seemed to betoken the presence of the indrawing sea. Encouraged by this report, Hudson sought and gained English support for a fourth voyage, which departed on the ship *Discovery* for the eastern Canadian Arctic in April 1610. Following, as had so many other navigators, what was probably an old Icelandic sailing course, Hudson sailed south around Greenland, entered the strait that Weymouth had mentioned, and in August, entered the great bay that now bears his name. Hudson sailed south into this bay, convinced that he had entered the "Sea of the South" and had found the sea-level passage to Cathay. The expedition reached James Bay, where they spent the winter; the following spring a mutiny against Hudson ensued. He, some of his officers, and several ill men were cast adrift in a shallop and were never heard from again.[80] The conspirators returned to England, where they were imprisoned for a term specified only as "till their captain [Hudson] was found."[81] But the survivors of the expedition told tales of their discovery of "a great floud which . . . set them aflote," and presumably as a reward for having discovered the indrawing seas of the Northwest Passage, they were released. Two of them, Robert Bylot and Abacuk Prickett, were even hired to accompany a new expedition in search of the abandoned Hudson and the Passage, which the English believed had been discovered. When this expedition, commanded by Thomas Button, did not return within a few months, a contemporary chronicler noted: "We may therefore hope that they have passed beyond that strait, and we do not think that we shall hear anything about them before they return to England from East India or China and Japan, by the same road by which they went out. This we hope and pray, may come to pass."[82]

Hudson's discovery had a tremendous impact on European geographers, particularly after it was memorialized in the works of Hessel Gerritz, whose 1612 map carried an account of the voyage on the reverse side. The English translation of Gerritz's 1612 edition was grandly entitled "An Account of the Discoverie of the Northwest Passage, which is expected to lead to China and Japan by the north of the American continent, found by H. Hudson."[83] For generations the enthusiasm and imagination of European merchants had been fired with the hope of finding a short route to the Orient, and now it had been found. When *Purchas his Pilgrimes* published the news that Hudson had found "a vast sea" that, so far as he knew, "had no bounds toward the west," there did not seem to be room for further doubt as to the existence of the indrawing sea. The great Passage was there; all Europe had to do was to sail through it to the "Sea of the South" and to the pearls, spices, and gold of the East.[84] So great was the enthusiasm that in 1612 a company known as "The Governor and Company for the Merchants of London, Discoverers of the Northwest Passage" was granted a royal charter for further exploration and proceeded to make plans for the exploitation of Hudson's discoveries.[85]

The End of the Early Search

Under the sponsorship of the North West Company, a series of English voyages were undertaken from 1612 to 1632, and the names of Thomas Button, Robert Bylot, William Baffin, William Hawkeridge, Thomas James, and Luke Fox were entered

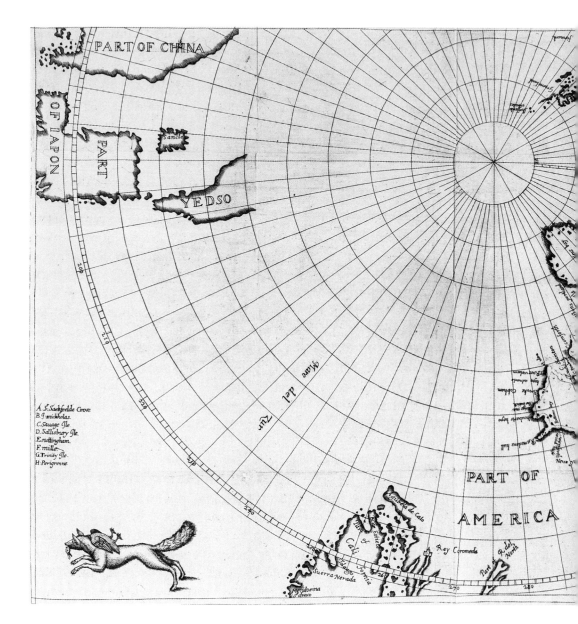

PART OF CHINA

OF IAPON

PART

Sanct.

YEDSO

Mare del Zur

A S.Sackfeelde Crove:
B J. michholas.
C.Sauage Jle.
D.Sallisbury Jle.
E.nottingham.
F. mille.
G.Trinity Jle.
H.Perigrenne.

PART OF

AMERICA

Gribeta de Calo

Straict

Cali

Rey Coromeda

Golfo Flormia

Suerra Nerada

Part R. del North

Mendocina
S.Draco

14. *Polar Map* in Luke
Fox, *North-West Fox*,
1635. Courtesy of John
Carter Brown Library
at Brown University.

on the rolls of those who sought to prove the existence of a geographical feature conceived in logic and imagination and therefore, presumably, demonstrable in fact. These voyages, brought
to the reading public by Samuel Purchas, added immeasurably
to the knowledge of the geography of the Canadian Arctic; they
also confirmed the existence of western Canada as a barrier of still
unknown width between the Atlantic and Cathay, a conclusion
that seems to have been accepted by the North West Company.

By 1632, the quest for the passage "by the northwestward" and through Arctic waters would be virtually concluded for nearly a century (fig. 14). Still, the geographical will-o'-the-wisp of the passage to India and Cathay remained a powerful geographical idea, and even after a generation of failed expeditions, the last of the English explorers who sought the Passage—the self-styled Luke "Northwest" Fox—would blame his failure to find the Passage not on the fact that it was not there but on the fact that he ran short of supplies before reaching it. For Fox, as for all those who had gone before him and had, like him, failed to discover through experience a geographical feature conceived in the imagination, the Passage still existed. "Howsoever it was not my fortune [to find the Passage]," he wrote, "yet I praise GOD for that I have brought home the newes thereof, though I have left it for him whose time God shall be pleased to ripen for the same."[86]

Fox's statement is a perfect demonstration of the durability of imaginary geography, and even though, after 1632, there was a long hiatus in the search for the Passage by sailing northwest from Europe, there was no end to the idea itself. Like so many other illusory geographical features, the Passage simply shifted location, and after Fox, the waterways used to follow the will-o'-the-wisp were not "the broad sea channels of the problematic passage, but the narrow broken waters of the rivers of the west."[87] There is a direct connection between Fox's optimism that a passage did exist, waiting only for "him whose time God shall be pleased to ripen for the same," and the instructions that Thomas Jefferson gave to Meriwether Lewis in 1803. For Jefferson, as for Sebastian Cabot and Luke Fox and all the others who dreamed dreams of the Passage to India, the geography of imagination and hope and desire merged with the geographical experience and empirical knowledge of exploration to produce a concept that, more than three centuries after Columbus, would continue to haunt both maps and minds.

The Early Cartography of Maine in the Setting of Early European Exploration of New England and the Maritimes

David B. Quinn

Many European voyages were made along the northeastern coast of North America as it was gradually revealed from 1497 onward. However, in almost all cases it is impossible to pinpoint the sightings and the landings of the earliest voyagers, since they left no cartographic record that can be clearly associated with a particular stretch of coastline. John Cabot, for example, is now authoritatively said to have reached, at the southward limit of his 1497 voyage, forty-six degrees north, but at the time, and for many years to come, measurement permitted a possible error of as much as two degrees (nearly 140 land miles). In 1502, Miguel Corte-Real, before his death at sea on the same voy-

This paper is dedicated to the late Lawrence and Eleanor Smith, who did so much to preserve the historic sites and shoreline of modern Maine. They were both avid collectors and were also dedicated to assisting scholars who were concerned with the history of New England, especially of Maine. Alison Quinn and David Quinn owe much to their hospitality and their assistance over a long period. It is our great pleasure to know that their extensive map collection on America is now to be a permanent memorial to them in the University of Southern Maine.

age, certainly reached some part of what is now the Maritimes or New England. The voyage of Sebastian Cabot in 1504 probably touched land well down below the parallel of, say, forty-two degrees thirty minutes. Sebastian Cabot sailed the whole coast in 1509, but we do not know where he put in or how close he came to identifying any specific features of the New England-Maritimes area. That is about as much as we can say until we reach firmer ground in the early 1520s. From then on, northern New England and the Maritimes did receive much attention from navigators in the French and Spanish service, which culminated in Jacques Cartier's discovery of the northern entry to the Gulf of St. Lawrence in 1534 and his subsequent entry into the St. Lawrence Valley.

Cartier's success developed from the gradually increasing geographical knowledge acquired by participants of the Newfoundland fishery. If they led Cartier westward at the northern limit of the fishery, they could well have suggested to others that the lands to the south of Cape Breton might also be worth exploring. We must also regard the earliest voyages along the northeastern coast as part of the drive to disclose the general character of the eastern North American continent. It is probable that the apparent concentration on what is now Maine arose from the hope that one of the many inlets that were observed during this process might perhaps open up a passage through a narrow landmass to the Pacific. The Penobscot River was the most obvious entry that presented such a prospect. Its width and its apparent penetration into the interior continued to nourish such hopes, and it gradually appeared most prominently on the maps along with the mythical indigenous "kingdom" and "city" of Norumbega, supposedly on the Penobscot. Norumbega became ingrained in the mythology of early writings on exploration and on successive maps. But much about the development of this myth remains unknown and cannot so far be fully understood. We can work only with such maps, and such descriptions as we have with them, to outline what did happen or what may have happened.

Thus to speak of the earliest cartography of Maine is not easy. We cannot say when and how it began before the Europeans. Did the coastal Wabanakis, who knew Maine's coasts and rivers so well, have any kind of bark guides to help them in their hunting trails? We do not know. The adventurous Micmacs coming down from the Bay of Fundy for corn and plunder might have had something comparable to maps. They are more likely to have needed them than their southern neighbors but may very well not have had them. And what was Maine on the earliest maps we have? Its name first appears in 1622, and it took corporate shape very much later than this.

In the sixteenth century what we call Maine had no meaning as such. Before the English settlement of the 1630s, the lowland coastal area south of Cape Elizabeth was not distinguished from what is now Massachusetts. The Indians of the Saco River were very distinct from those to the north and northeast of them, mainly as a result of their horticultural pursuits. At the other extreme, what is now Washington County with its Passamaquoddy-Maliseet peoples was very much more a part of what we know as the Maritimes and what the French know as Acadia. It is the region from Cape Elizabeth northward and northeastward just beyond Mount Desert that was the essential Maine of the maps that we do have and that was the core of the mysterious Norumbega.

Until the 1520s there is very little that can be assumed about the cartography of what is now New England. But when maps appear, they do so in abundance. The years 1524–29 saw voyages being made and maps deriving from those voyages compiled and circulated. These maps were influential for the rest of the century. The cartographic story starts, indirectly, with Ferdinand Magellan. In 1520 he discovered a route round the southern part of the continental landmasses on the way to Asia. When the *Victoria,* under Sebastián Elcano, finally reached Spain after the first circumnavigation in 1522, both Spain and France made the assumption that there might well be a similar passage through or round the northern part of the continent. In 1512, after his northern voyage of 1508-9, Sebastian Cabot brought Spain the news that there could be a passage round North America only in high and frozen latitudes. Therefore, it seemed worthwhile for the Spanish to try to find a passage through North America in lower latitudes. The same concept influenced the French, or at least Italian merchants and seamen residing in France. Elcano's news that Asia was an incredibly far distance from America by way of the Strait of Magellan provided an impetus to other Europeans to try to find a passage in temperate latitudes, where the distance could be expected to be much shorter and where the passage might be much more tolerable than that survived by Magellan and Elcano.[1] For the Spanish and French, an intensive coastal survey seemed essential.

The Spanish chose Estevan Gomes to lead their expedition. Gomes, an experienced Portuguese pilot in their service, also had some cartographic skills. In 1523 the Spanish began building a ship for him in La Coruña. However, the ship was slow to be finished and equipped, so it was not until early in 1525 that Gomes could set sail. Meanwhile, the silk merchants of Lyon, desperate to obtain supplies of Chinese silk, joined with merchants and seamen of Rouen to equip the *Dauphine* under the command of Giovanni da Verrazzano, a Florentine seaman whose brother Girolamo was a cartographer. Although Verrazzano had initial difficulties, he was able to cross the Atlantic from the Canary Islands early in 1524, nearly a year ahead of Gomes. Between them, however, they began a cartographic record of the shores of the Northeast, particularly of Maine, for the rest of the sixteenth century. Their discoveries, elaborated by the assumptions and guesses of others, dominated virtually all the cartography of Maine and its adjoining shores before the early years of the seventeenth century and influenced even a number of early-seventeenth-century maps.

Neither Verrazzano nor Gomes left us a simple, straightforward cartographic record of his attempt to chart the northeastern North American coast. In both cases we have only indirect access to what they brought back in the way of written "rutters" (sets of sailing directions pointing to features on the coast) or coastal sketches charting what they had seen. Whatever they brought had to be compiled into extended outline charts, with names gathered on the way or given by the explorers, so as to make up a cartographic profile of their American voyages. In this process there was bound to be much misunderstanding of detail and of scale. Latitudes, as already indicated, might be up to or even over two degrees wrong; longitude, which is of less concern to us if we are looking at the broad effect of the discoveries, was not obtainable with current methods of observation. A land-based observation of latitude, however, might be correct to within twenty miles or so; a sea-based observation would be much less accurate. All historians can pay tribute to the value of Verrazzano's letter of July 1524 sent to Francis I and especially the annotated version now in the Beinecke Library of Yale University. They serve as outline guides to the maps.[2]

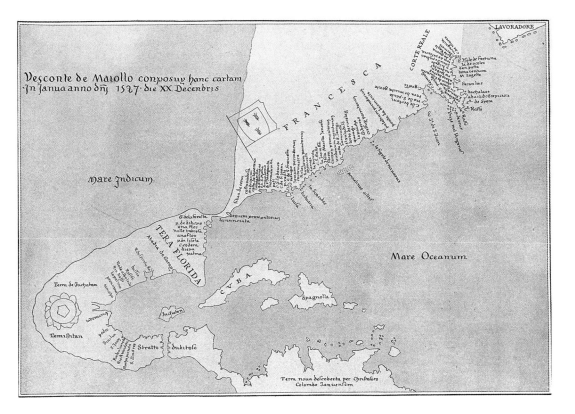

15. Extract from an 1892 redrawing by Konrad Kretschmer of Vesconte de Maggiolo's world map, 1529 (original destroyed in the Ambrosiana Library, Milan, 1943). Courtesy of National Archives of Canada, C-139526.

Girolamo da Verrazzano was the cartographer of the family, but we do not know whether he accompanied his brother on the American voyage — the more general opinion is that he did not. However, he produced the most widely circulated manuscript maps associated with the voyage. He presented a copy of one of the maps to Henry VIII, probably in 1525, and it hung for many years in the Palace of Whitehall. It was not used for a printed version until 1582 (by Richard Hakluyt in his *Divers Voyages*) and is of only marginal value. The map in the National Maritime Museum at Greenwich is based on a map he made before 1528, though it was either recopied or modified after 1536.[3] Vesconte de Maggiolo included much information on Verrazzano's voyage in his world map of 1529,[4] but the map may have been derived from oral sources, since it does not fit the Verrazzano brothers' model (fig. 15). But the crucial depiction of the voyage is on Girolamo's world map of 1529,[5] presented to Pope Clement VII in order to establish that it was not only the Spanish who had explored and had claims to North America (fig. 16).

16. Extract from
Girolamo da Verraz-
zano, world map
presented to Pope
Clement VII in 1529,
showing the New
England coast ex-
plored by Giovanni
da Verrazzano in
1524. Courtesy of
the National Ar-
chives of Canada.
By permission of the
Vatican.

This map, along with Giovanni's letter to Francis I of July 1524, provides us with a good idea of what Giovanni da Verrazzano recorded of his voyage along the shores of northeastern North America. The names that Verrazzano gave to inlets northeastward from Cape Cod have caused much speculation. In most cases they cannot be identified, but the major inlet that is shown is clearly Penobscot Bay. At some point he disembarked, precisely where is not known, north of the Saco River at least, and encountered "terra onde he male gente" (the land where there are bad men), which is usually thought to be the first recorded European contact with the coastal Wabanaki people and hence the earliest name given to what was later to be known as Maine. The name "oranbega" is found near the coastal entry, which is thought to represent Penobscot Bay (on the National Maritime Museum map it is "oranbegha"). Oranbega was to have a long history; however, on these maps it is not especially set out or attached to a recognizable inlet. It was this depiction of the New England shore that appears on many maps and globes in the later

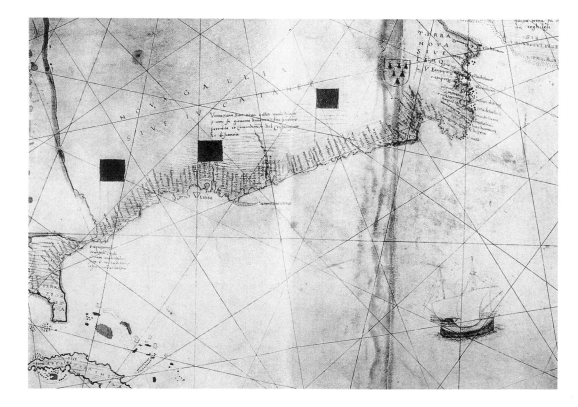

part of the sixteenth century. The Maggiolo map had little influence on other cartographers, even though it has a sharper depiction of what is clearly Penobscot Bay, with the name "Anapis."

Important as Verrazzano's contribution was to the placing of the Maine shoreline on the map, it was overshadowed for many years by his cartographic profile of northeastern North America as a whole. His observation that the Carolina Outer Banks reflected an easy passage to the Pacific was an exciting possibility. The image of America having a narrow waist was to be very persistent in cartography. When this observation was combined with Cartier's discovery of the St. Lawrence in the 1530s, the slim-waisted continent, which could be crossed at about thirty-five degrees north and penetrated also from an entry between forty-six and fifty degrees, appeared very attractive to those who sought access to the Pacific. Consequently, Verrazzano's profile of northeastern North America was either glossed over or replaced by another.

The most important single figure in the cartography of Maine was Estevan Gomes.[6] It was his emphasis on the Penobscot, up which he penetrated for some distance and which was much exaggerated on all subsequent maps derived from his voyage, that made Maine such a prominent feature of the cartography of the East. Diego Ribeiro's world map (the Castiglioni map) was almost certainly made up from Gomes's charts at the time of his return to La Coruña in August 1525, with the aid of the currently received Spanish *padrón real* (royal patent), or standard chart. Ribeiro's world map depicted Cape Cod and the Penobscot in a form that was to persist, with modifications of various sorts, for the rest of the sixteenth century and into the next.[7] Since no firsthand narrative of the voyage is known, there is no way of checking the maps against what the explorer himself said. Consequently, Gomes's discoveries were at the mercy of subsequent cartographic fashions. However, Ribeiro left his imprint more permanently on the famous world map sent to Pope Clement VII to impress on him the Spanish view of the division of the world, outside Europe, between Spain and Portugal, as enshrined in the agreement of 1527 on the limits of their claims in the Far East.[8] If the 1525 and 1529 maps had both remained in manuscript, it scarcely would have mattered that whereas Cape Cod was named "Cabo de Arenas," the Penobscot remained un-

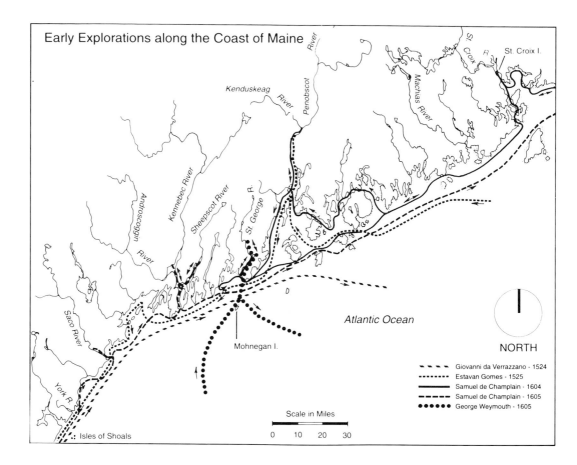

Early Explorations along the Coast of Maine

Kenduskeag River

Penobscot River

St. Croix R.

St. Croix I.

Machias River

Androscoggin River

Kennebec River

Sheepscot River

St. George R.

Saco River

York R.

Mohnegan I.

Atlantic Ocean

NORTH

Isles of Shoals

Scale in Miles

0   10   20   30

- - - - Giovanni da Verrazzano - 1524
········· Estavan Gomes - 1525
———— Samuel de Champlain - 1604
– – – – Samuel de Champlain - 1605
●●●●● George Weymouth - 1605

17. Reconstruction of the routes of early explorers in Norumbega. Based on plate 2 in Gerald E. Morris, ed., *The Maine Bicentennial Atlas: An Historical Survey* (Portland: Maine Historical Society, 1976).

named—in fact the name beside it in 1529 was merely *arecifes* (reefs), though the cape at its southern entry (Owls Head?) was named "Cabo de Muchas Islas."

What brought the northeastern profile a wider audience was its appearance on the Spanish master charts, the *padrón real* of 1527 and, subsequently, that of 1536 (e.g., the 1536 one in the Hague Atlas), and the leaking of these supposedly secret documents in France and Italy, where they could be incorporated into future manuscript or printed maps. The official Spanish charts tended to bring Cape Cod well to the south of its real position between forty-one and forty-two degrees and to draw up the entrance to Chesapeake Bay to a higher latitude than thirty-seven degrees, the coast between the two being unexplored by France or Spain throughout the remainder of the sixteenth century. As a result, some of the maps of the later part of the century conflated Cape Cod, with the cape at the southern entrance to Chesapeake

Bay (Baya de Buena Madre), and so distorted the profile of the Northeast. At the same time the maps tended to exaggerate still further the size and importance of the Penobscot, which had acquired by 1539 at least the name of "Rio de las Gamas" (Deer River). Alonso de Chaves, the Spanish cosmographer, in his rutter of about 1539 (sailing directions based on the *padrón real* of 1536), noted, with some approach to accuracy: "Rio de las Gamas in the coast to the north is 43 degrees and north-east of the Cabo de Muchas Islas eight leagues. This river is the greatest to be found on the whole of this coast. It is ten leagues wide at the mouth: it is full of islets and reefs. It enters by way of the north."[9]

In the 1540s, Alonso de Santa Cruz, head of the cartographic office of the Casa de la Contratación in Seville, compiled his *Islario,* of which four copies—one with texts and no maps, the others with maps—survive.[10] It is this work that brings us closest to Gomes and his discoveries. Santa Cruz would have had in his charge the original sketches that Gomes brought back in 1525, and he is the most important authority on Gomes. But positive identifications of river entries are still conjectural. The late Professor William P. Cumming made a list of likely identifications, in which emphasis is placed on the Massachusetts coast. My opinion is that after Gomes explored Cape Cod Bay, he passed rapidly to what is now the Maine coast, and that the maps foreshorten the shore between, say, Boston Harbor and Casco Bay, which could be the "Rio de Buena Madre" of the map. The "Rio Seco" would then be the Kennebec, and the *archipelago* would be Muscongus Bay, so that "Cabo de Muchas Islas" would be Owls Head and "Rio de las Gamas" would be the Penobscot. There is little controversy about the last two, but the identifications of the names along the coast farther northeastward are open to question. However, Penobscot Bay was so sharply marked that it remained the primary point of reference.

The French were in early possession of a version of the 1536 *padrón real,* and the Penobscot (originating with Gomes) was to appear on almost all the Dieppe school of maps, with some variations in nomenclature. These maps represent the flowering of French cartography between 1540 and 1560. Jean Alfonce de Saintonge (probably a Portuguese who had obtained French nationality) piloted the Sieur de Roberval's colonizing fleet to the St. Lawrence in 1542, and shortly after his return to France he compiled a remarkable *Côsmographie,*[11] unpublished until 1904.

In this work he says that he sailed southward on his return voyage, and he shows a sketch of the Penobscot labeled, for the first
time, "Riviere de Norenbegue," thus beginning the long association of the Penobscot with a variant of Verrazzano's "oranbega."[12] His "Cap de La Franciscane" to the west of the entry
could be Cape Small, but this is only a guess. Alfonce's work
has been disbelieved largely because a printed work, *Les voyages
avantureux*, published in 1559 and purported to be his alone, was
in fact a much altered and distorted brief version of the cosmography. However, it was here that details of his supposed voyage
up "the great river of Norumbega" appeared. The Dieppe maps
all retained the feature (i.e., the great river), but the most important derivative from them, the printed Sebastian Cabot map of
1544, gave the bay no name. There seems little point to referring
in detail to the many maps that follow this particular tradition;
but somehow, at about the middle of the century (or after 1559?),
the myth of a "city" of Norumbega on the Penobscot arose. No
one has yet been able to track down its origin. The semiofficial Spanish map of 1562 has only "Rio de Gamas."[13] Certainly
on the very important and significant printed world maps, those
of Abraham Ortelius in 1564 and Gerardus Mercator in 1569,[14]
Norumbega and its city are present. There is a castle on the left
bank of the Penobscot, indicating a major town; the bay is now
the Rio Grande, which at its head splits into two major rivers,
and across the region behind it appears the name "Norombega."
This depiction was to be the classic layout for central Maine for
the rest of the century.

England had not yet contributed to the cartography of New
England. However, by 1527 a large Verrazzanian map hung on a
wall in the Palace of Whitehall. This map first commanded attention when Sir Humphrey Gilbert began to plan a colony in
Norumbega between 1578 and 1583. Dr. John Dee, Gilbert's principal cartographical adviser, presented a map to Queen Elizabeth
in 1580, in which he was content to use Mercator's depiction of
the Penobscot, with Mercator's name "Norombega" for the region. However, in 1582 Dee made Gilbert a chart of the northern regions on a polar projection that showed the Penobscot not
as a river but as a channel running through from the Atlantic
to the St. Lawrence River—with the name "Noronbega" at its
side.[15] The only English authority who we know had personal
experience of the Penobscot was an English seaman-trader, John

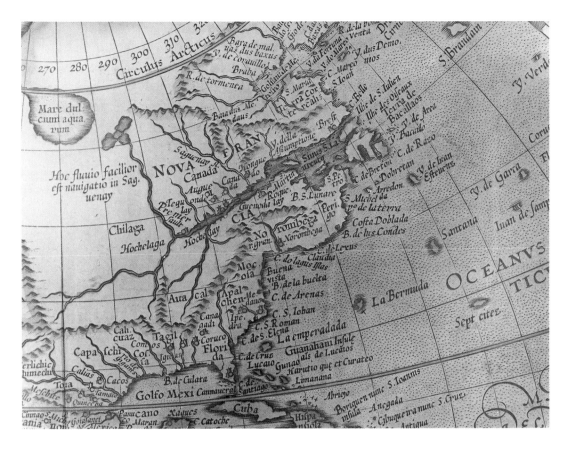

18. Detail showing Norumbega from Michael Mercator, *America Sive India Nova*, 1595. Like Gerardus Mercator's 1569 map, from which this one is derived, the map features the castled city of Norumbega. Courtesy of Osher Cartographic Collection, University of Southern Maine.

Walker,[16] who is said to have penetrated fifty miles up the river and to have found a collection of large skins, almost certainly moose, in an empty Indian house on the bank. The same mistake, or mistaken theory of a channel, is made in the map published in Richard Hakluyt's *Divers Voyages* in 1582, a map identified as having been made by Michael Lok.[17] In this map, North America has a Verrazzanian waist—taken, it is believed, from the map in Whitehall—but a Gomes Penobscot. Since this map was published, this eccentric view of the Maine shore, with the whole area from the Penobscot to Cape Breton labeled as "Norombega," became public property in England. However, Edward Wright's important map contributed to the second volume of Hakluyt's *Principal Navigations* in 1599 (fig. 19). Although the map shows the Penobscot as a wide inlet reaching near the St. Lawrence, it does not take the Penobscot all the way through to the St. Lawrence.

The French come on the scene again in 1583. Etienne Bel-

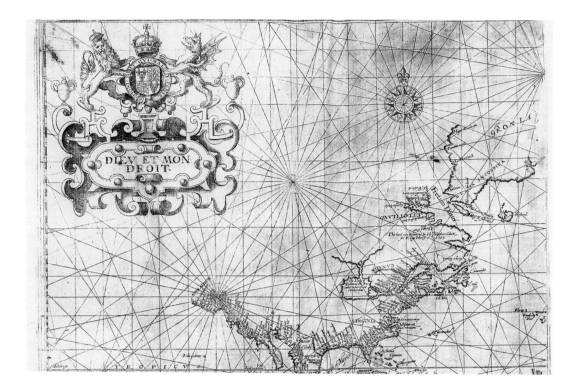

19. Extract from Edward Wright, *Map of the World*, in Richard Hakluyt, *Principal Navigations*, 1599, p. 2. Courtesy of John Carter Brown Library at Brown University.

lenger, of Rouen, took his ship to the Maritimes, explored the Bay of Fundy, then proceeded along the coast southward. We are told, "To the west of that Iland (Nova Scotia) about 20 leagues he found a great River into which he ran up with his smale Pynnasse seaven leagues and thinketh is navigable three or fowrescore leagues."[18] Bellenger communicated his coastal sketches to the cartographer Jacques de Vaulx, who in 1584 prepared a very creditable map of eastern North America, the Caribbean, and part of South America.[19] He accepted Bellenger's definition of Nova Scotia as an island and continued the coast southward, inserting a number of coastal features on the northern coast of Maine derived from Bellenger but depicting his "great River" in Spanish style and with the name "Rivière de Gamas." There can be little doubt that Bellenger made his way up the Penobscot, though whether he obtained many of the furs and skins he brought back from the Wabanakis is not clear.

The great atlases that circulated throughout Europe, the *Theatrum Orbis Terrarum* of Ortelius of 1570 and the Mercator *Atlas* of 1595, both show the Penobscot as Norumbega. Norumbega even merited a separate map in Cornelius Wytfliet's *Atlas* of

1597, elaborating Mercator's 1569 view. So the century ends with Maine as Norumbega and with its principal estuary characterized as a major feature of the North American coast. This information was encapsulated in the English view of Wright's published map of 1599.

It was, however, in the years between 1602 and 1608 that the Maine coast was systematically examined by the English and the French. The contact with Maine that Bartholomew Gosnold made in 1602 was tangential only. On his outward voyage, the English explorer sighted Cape Small at his first landfall, and his "Savage Rock" was Cape Elizabeth, where he encountered Micmac marauder-traders. Martin Pring in 1603 was the first Englishman to make any extensive exploration of the Maine shore, but unfortunately the narrative we have deals only with his initial contact. My view, which is not shared by others, is that his Foxe Island was Mount Desert, but he did enter the Penobscot and, in all, spent three weeks exploring. In the twenty-two lines of narrative that cover this important examination of the coast, we learn only that he found four main inlets—one barred and one so open that he could sail up five miles without difficulty. Since this included the whole coast as far south as Cape Cod Bay, identifications are many and various. What is clear from later records is that Gosnold and Pring did bring home rough charts, which had some influence on later maps.[20]

George Weymouth's expedition in 1605 was a much more serious affair, for he was expected to find a site for an English settlement and explore it in detail. He found and described Monhegan and made his base in the Georges Islands. From there he proceeded up the St. George River. For the detailed description of its exploration, we rely on James Rosier's narrative, published in 1605. According to this document, Weymouth claimed that the river penetrated some forty miles into the interior and that it was followed by ship, by pinnace, and on foot by Weymouth and his men. In fact the total distance covered from the coast was twenty miles at most, and even this would have taken Weymouth well past the estuary to the site of modern Warren. The description that accompanied the voyages is of much value, since it was the first detailed account of any part of Maine by an Englishman. Rosier tells us of Weymouth's careful determination of latitude and variation and of "his perfect Geographicall Map of the countrey, he entendeth hereafter to set forth."[21] Weymouth was perfectly competent to produce such a map, but perhaps the distortions of distance in the narrative rendered it unwise for him to do so, for no map has ever been found.

However, the description that was obtained later from the coastal Wabanaki Indians captured by Weymouth and brought to England, "the description of the Countrey of Mawooshen," is of great cartographical interest, since it tells how well the country, both its coasts and its interior, was known to its people even if it had not yet been defined on a map. The description begins with what is probably the Union River to the east of Mount Desert and moves along the shore by way of Penobscot (in the version we have, it is confused with Pemaquid). It continues westward with the St. George, Sheepscot, and Kennebec (as "Sagadahoc") rivers, with much detail on the region's complex of waterways. From there the description follows the Presumpscot (flowing into Casco Bay) and Saco rivers, providing details of villages and their chiefs and information on the interior basin in the upper reaches of the Kennebec. This version is much compressed, but it could now, with some questions outstanding, be expressed cartographically.

The voyage that brought back accurate knowledge of much of the Maine coastline to England was that of Thomas Hanham and Martin Pring late in 1606. Unfortunately, neither a continuous narrative nor the map made on the voyage survives, only indications of this map in a later one, the Velasco map, which will be discussed later. However, one can say that these explorers (and Pring already knew how and where to look) eliminated the St. George River and selected the Kennebec as the site for the colony that was soon to be sent out from Plymouth, England. However, one cannot tell precisely what cartographical equipment the two ships, the *Gifte of God* and the *Mary and John*, carried when they entered St. George Harbor, Weymouth's old anchorage, on August 6 and 7, 1607, or when the *Gifte of God* entered the Kennebec on August 13. The colonists chose Atkins Point in the north of Sabino Head as the site for their settlement. Between then and October 8 they constructed an elaborate fort, though it was probably not finished in that time period. A remarkably full plan of the fort exists, which can be relied on, with some deduction because of the unfinished character of the work. It is the only direct cartographical evidence we have for the Sagadahoc Colony (or Popham Colony) of 1607-8.

This is not the place to discuss the colony in detail, but it is worth mentioning the limits of the boat reconnaissances made by the colonists during their brief stay. The first exploration appears to have reached the confluence of the Kennebec and the Androscoggin (August 17–18); the second explored some distance up the Androscoggin (August 22–23); and the third made the farthest penetration of the interior. However, the claim to have gone beyond the latitude of forty-five degrees is almost certainly an exaggeration, even if we can be certain that they passed the site of Augusta but did not reach the headwaters of Moosehead Lake (the existence and location of which the Wabanakis were well aware, as shown by the description of the land named Mawooshen). Therefore, the assumed "head of the river" they claimed to have reached remains undefined. Contemporaneously, the *Mary and John* was making an effective reconnaissance of the coastline to the southwest, investigating, in particular, the islands in Casco Bay, sighting Cape Elizabeth, and anchoring off Richmond Island before returning (August 28–30). These creditable explorations were, with little doubt, charted in some detail, but no vestiges of these cartographic records survive in their original form. Further explorations—mainly, it would seem, within the Kennebec River system—were made in 1608 and are entirely undocumented. English knowledge of the Maine coast may have been carried a little further still by fishing and fur trading voyages over the next six years, but it was not until 1614 that Captain John Smith made a careful reconnaissance of a substantial part of the coast and, more important still, put it on permanent record in his printed map of 1616 (fig. 82).

To have gone so far without acknowledging the major part the French played in the exploration and cartography of Maine has been necessitated by the need to retain some coherence in the sequence of events on the English side, thus making it possible to consider the French contribution in isolation. In 1603 Henry IV granted to the Sieur de Monts the French rights to American land north of forty degrees. The grants enabled Samuel de Champlain, the representative of Henry IV with the Sieur de Monts, to carry out, between 1604 and 1607, the most comprehensive examination of the New England coast and some of its rivers that had so far been attempted.[22] They also allowed Champlain to leave the fullest written and cartographic record of any part of eastern North America so far.[23]

On his first reconnaissance from St. Croix to the south in September 1604 he examined and named "L'Isle des Mount Déserts" and was able to establish that it was an island. A mishap to his pinnace brought him and an Indian guide to the entrance of the Penobscot. On his way he left another name that has survived, "Isle Haulte" (Isle de Haut). Champlain sailed up the bay ("Pentagoët") into the Penobscot River, where, near the site of Bangor, he made contact with Bashabes, the chief sagamore of the coastal Wabanakis, from whom he learned much about the interior. However, he found the "city" of Norumbega to be a myth and found the river, as distinct from the bay, a disappointment. Coming downstream, he turned southward outside Muscongus Bay and anchored at Weymouth's old anchorage, St. George Harbor. From there he returned to St. Croix with an accurate chart. In March 1605 he set out again after his hard winter at St. Croix and sailed down to the mouth of the Kennebec. Circumventing the islet of Sequin ("la tortue"), he charted a channel upstream. He has left us a chart of his entry and first anchorage. He was able to get Indian guides who took him through the dangerous Back River into the main channel of the Sheepscot to approximately the site of modern Wiscasset. From there he turned back, this time taking the easier passage by the Sassanoa River to the main channel of the Kennebec, sailing up to the confluence with the Androscoggin at Merrymeeting Bay.

Throughout, Champlain was given information by the coastal Wabanakis about the interior between the Kennebec Basin and the St. Lawrence, and we can assume that this was done largely by Indian maps drawn on sand or on bark, since he had yet no fluency in Wabanaki languages (though he got their names for places uncannily correct). When he left the Kennebec, his passage westward was rapid, and he did not explore further estuaries, although he noted such openings he saw until he had passed Casco Bay and began to work southward. He next explored Saco Bay ("Chouacoit"). There he saw, and recorded on another harbor chart, the first Indian corn-growing settlement. His later discoveries to the south need not concern us. He called in at Saco Bay again in late July on his return voyage and then sailed on, anchoring off Isle de Haut. He next sailed back to move his base from St. Croix to Port Royal. However, on the way he heard that an English ship, Weymouth's, had been seen near the mouth of the Penobscot. The third New England cruise, between September 9 and November 14, 1605, added nothing new on Norumbega, though it perhaps allowed Champlain to make some additions and corrections to his chart. His general chart covering 1604 to 1607 may have been completed by the time the Sieur de Monts's colony left Port Royal in 1607 and arrived in France at the end of September.

This map (*les cotes et grandes Illes de la nouvelle france*), never published in its original form, was revolutionary. It is now in the Library of Congress and has been finely reproduced by that institution (plate 2). The map depicted the coast from southern Massachusetts to Cape Breton in significant and largely correct detail, allowing for compass variation. There are, to our modern eyes, faults of scale and failures to follow some lines of investigation far enough — missing the Sheepscot River after he found out so much about the rest of the Kennebec system, for example. But from the Saco River, Richmond Isle ("Ile de bacus"), Casco Bay ("baye de Merrhen"), Sequin ("Ile tortue"), Kennebec ("Quinibequi"), Isle de Haut ("Ille haut"), Penobscot ("Pentegoët"), "Norumbeque" (still there at the head of the bay but no "city"), Mount Desert ("I. Monts desers"), Great Wass Island? ("C.de courelles"), we have a remarkable conspectus on the Norumbega shore, continued, of course, both south and north (with a much exaggerated Nova Scotia).

The 1612 map of New France as a whole (published in *Les Voyages* [1613])[24] substantially repeats the Maine shore of 1607 but on a smaller scale (fig. 20). The nomenclature is very similar ("chouacoit," "tortue," "quinibeqey," "illes iettes," "pentegoit R," "noronbergque," "ineueane," "illes longues"), with only minor variations but without the freshness and, of course, the color of the 1607 original. The contribution of Champlain to the early cartography of Maine cannot be overestimated.

Marc Lescarbot anticipated the 1612 map by publishing a map of northeastern North America in the first edition of his *Histoire de la Nouvelle France* in 1609,[25] but his map is derivative of Champlain's materials and has little independent value except as the first cartographic record of French activities from 1604 to 1607 (fig. 32).

Toward the end of 1610 an English cartographer, who might have been Samuel Argall, provided material for a remarkable map ranging from the Carolina Outer Banks to Labrador.[26] He gave considerable prominence to Maine. He included in his depic-

20. Samuel de
Champlain, *Carte
geographique de la nou-
velle franse en son vray
meridien,* in his *Les
Voyages,* 1613. Courtesy
of National Library of
Canada, L-3127.

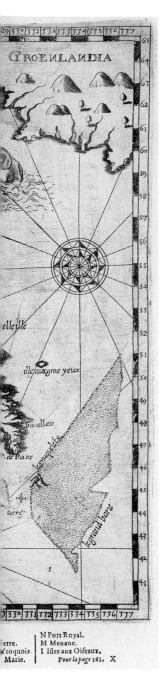

tion material that was derived not only from English charts and maps that have now disappeared, though correlated by Argall in 1610, but also, it seems, from the unpublished Champlain map of 1607 and from later data on the St. Lawrence gathered since Champlain had been there, 1608–10. How this map was finally assembled we do not know, but it appears to represent the result of effective espionage on the part of the English authorities if not by Argall alone. If so, it is ironic that the map, or a replica of it, survived only in the Spanish archives, having been sent to Spain in March 1611 by Alonso de Velasco, the Spanish ambassador in London. This map is known as the Velasco map (fig. 21).

"Ile Lobster" appears to be Richmond Island, and "C. Porpos" is Cape Elizabeth. The Kennebec is "sagadahok," though its upper reaches have the name "Cinebague" (Champlain's 1607 "Quinibague" is at the mouth of the river). "Tahanock" is the name given to what one would conclude to be the Sheepscot. However, it might be Weymouth's St. George River, since it has "I St George" some distance from its mouth, though this might be Monhegan (most probably it is a conflation of the Sheepscot, possibly discovered by Hanham and Pring with the St. George). The mouth of the Penobscot is well covered, with French names "I. Penduit," "Iles Basses," and "I. haute," derived from some version of a Champlain map, with the Penobscot itself called "R. Pentegoët" (Champlain's "Pentegoët"). A strange feature is the appearance, well out to sea from the mouth of the Penobscot, of "S. Georges Banck," with an island to the south of it, which would seem to be a misplaced (or duplicated) Monhegan. The final name along the shore is "Iles de Mont Desert," rather too far north from Penobscot Bay. Even though the Velasco map does not have the original authority of the 1607 Champlain map and appreciably differs from the latter in detail, there is clearly a dependence on Champlain's map or something very similar. With its features for the rest of eastern North America, it is the most expert map yet made of this coast, for it includes what is almost certainly the Hudson, discovered in 1609, as well as an advance version of John Smith's map of Virginia, which appeared in print only in 1612.

There is no cartographical evidence of the 1611 English voyage under Edward Harlow to the islands off the mouth of Penobscot Bay or of the more serious French exploration of the bay and river by Charles de Biencourt, with the Jesuit Father Pierre Biard, in

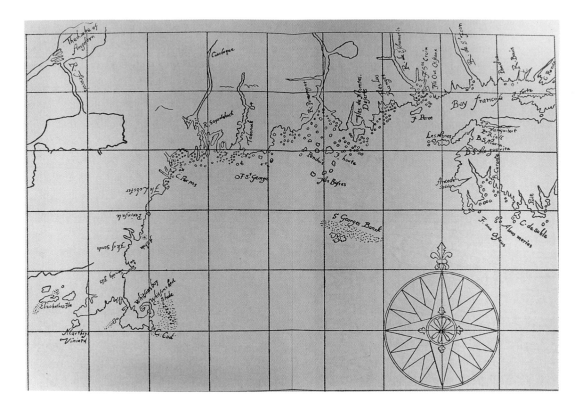

21. Tracing of extract from the Velasco map of 1610, sent to Spain in March 1611. From Henry Burrage, *The Beginnings of Colonial Maine, 1602–1658* (Portland: Marks Printing House, 1914). The original is in the Archivo General, Simancas.

the same year. There is also no record of a more significant French development of 1613. When the ship *Jonas* carried a Jesuit mission up the Penobscot to found a mission near the mouth of the river, the sailors got lost and brought the missionaries and those who were to assist them in founding a new colony up the eastern shore of Mount Desert instead. Certainly, the site of Saint Sauveur has led to controversy. Father Lucien Campeau has learnedly argued that the colony was on the mainland and in Frenchman's Bay, and this is supported by the historian Marcel Trudel. But a day-long search some years ago by a party of archaeologists, myself, and Father Campeau could find no place on Frenchman's Bay that appeared a possible, let alone a likely, location for a settlement. The older suggestion, accepted by the historian Henry Burrage and others, was that Indians guided the expedition back to the south of Mount Desert and settled Saint Sauveur on Somes Sound. But for the present, the accepted orthodoxy is that the site *was* on Frenchman's Bay. Samuel Argall, sent by the Virginia colony to expel the French from all the territory south of forty-five degrees north latitude that the English claimed, was led to Saint Sauveur shortly after its foundation. He removed the French, chasing some away and taking others to Jamestown, and then went north again to destroy all vestiges of Saint Sauveur as well as Port Royal.[27] This was the first clash between the English and the French in Maine, though it was not to be the last. France relied on a 1603 charter, which gave France rights down to forty degrees, whereas the English relied on the Virginia Company charter of 1606, which claimed the whole coast from thirty-eight to forty-five degrees as an English preserve. But the English had the force, if not the colonists, to retain Maine within their sphere of influence for this time and for many years thereafter.

Captain John Smith's exploring zeal had been kept on a leash ever since his return from Virginia in 1609. True, he had published his important *Map of Virginia* in 1612 — description, text, and map — an invaluable document on the Chesapeake venture (fig. 81). But it was not until 1614 that he obtained enough backing to take two ships to Monhegan — used since 1608 as a base for English fishing expeditions — in order to take whales and explore the coast (for gold). One ship soon parted from him, and with the other and a shallop, he explored a substantial part of the New England coast from Mount Desert to Cape Cod. In 1616 he gave an account of his activities, based on the absence of previous reliable maps.

> I have had six or seven plats of those Northern parts, so unlike to each other, and most so differing from any true proportion or resemblance of the country, as they did me no more good than so much waste paper, though they cost me more. It may be it was not my chance to see the best: but lest others may be deceived as I was, or through dangerous ignorance hazard themselves as I did, I have drawn a map from Point to Point, Isle to Isle, and Harbour to Harbour, with the Soundings, Sands, Rocks, and Landmarks as I passed close aboard the Shore in a little Boat; although there are many things to be observed which the haste of other affairs did cause me to omit. For being sent more to get present commodities than knowledge by discoveries for any future good, I had no power to search as I would; yet it will serve to direct any who should go that way up safe Harbours and the Savage habitations.[28]

Smith evidently had an Indian companion, since he gives a reasonably full account of Wabanaki names of natural features and communities. However, the printed map, though superior to anything England had yet seen, was, in its engraved version, considerably less revealing than his text claimed (fig. 22). Also, to get publicity for his map, he induced the Prince of Wales to bestow English names on the features that he had noted in compiling the map. The most important, in its significance for the future, was the naming of the whole area from Cape Cod to the northern opening of Penobscot Bay "New England." This name stuck, inspiring English attempts to settle there during the next few years. The only other name that has survived from this publicity exercise is Cape Elizabeth. However, the parts of New England Smith emphasized in his text were in Massachusetts and, by extension, in southern Maine. On "Norumbega" he was dismissive. "But because it was so mountainous, rocky and full of isles, few

22. Extract of John Smith, *New England,* 1616. Courtesy of University of Southern Maine.

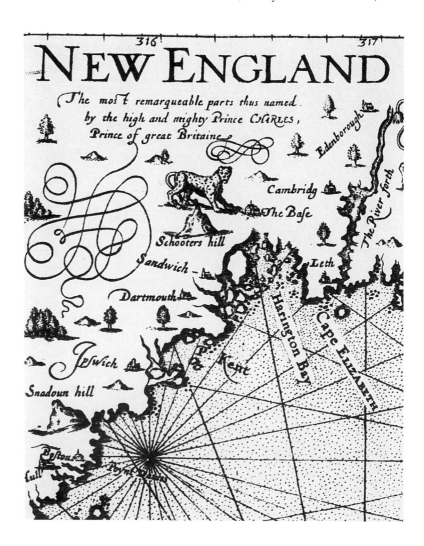

have adventured much to trouble it."[29] This was scarcely true, but it was a verdict that succeeding colonizing efforts would take into account. Maine (or the Maine to which the name "Norumbega" was attached) remained marginal to European penetration and settlement for precisely the reasons Smith had indicated (except for its fishing offshore). However, it was ironic that the part of the North American coast (apart from Florida) that received the most attention from explorers and cartographers in the sixteenth and early seventeenth centuries was the most neglected in the era of settlement and exploitation that followed.

CHAPTER THREE

On the Meaning of a Name
"Norumbega" and the Representation of North America

Richard D'Abate

"Norumbega" is the name of an intriguing puzzle in the history of European exploration. In the relatively brief period between the 1530s and the early 1600s, "Norumbega" was thought to be a New World paradise, a rich, cultivated, civilized spot in the northern wilds of America that had somehow been prepared for the coming of the Europeans. Although no one in the sixteenth century could say for sure where "Norumbega" was, its rumored existence caused explorers, sovereigns, and investors to turn longing eyes to the cold Northeast, as though the name gave back an image of their own desires.

Even though late-nineteenth-century antiquarians thought they had discovered its exact location (a small town not far from Boston), "Norumbega" remains an illusive historical fact. All the evidence for its geography and associations and origins is unstable or contradictory. On maps of the New World, where the name is most often found, "Norumbega" can appear and vanish from year to year, alter its spelling, migrate through many degrees of latitude, and change references—sometimes naming a city, a river, a region, or all three. The name seems to have something to do with Giovanni da Verrazzano, whose 1524 voyage made the unbroken eastern coast of North America a startling new fact of European knowledge. A variant of "Norumbega" appears for the first time on the map prepared by the explorer's brother in 1529, and yet the name is never mentioned in Verrazzano's own account—his famous letter to the king of France. In later years the name became associated with a distinctive geographical feature, probably what is today the Penobscot River along the coast of Maine, and yet this river was neither explored nor recorded by Verrazzano. Period accounts assert that "Norumbega" is an Indian word, a name used by one of the sixteenth-century northeastern tribes to describe its own nation; some even think it may be one of the first borrowings from a native language to appear on a European map. And yet there is no clear corroboration for such an origin, either historically or linguistically.

The question, then, is not only how to solve the puzzle of "Norumbega" and how to make sense of its sixteenth-century significance but also how to decide the sort of puzzle it is. Is there a positive historical and geographical fact hidden beneath the evidence—a real ancient kingdom of "Norumbega," as both the Renaissance and later antiquarians believed? Or is "Norumbega" yet another of the geographical myths so common in the era of exploration? Will its explanation reveal anything interesting about the way people represent the significance of their experience in the world?

Perhaps the first point to make in answering these questions is that "Norumbega" is a word, and like all words, like linguistic signs in general, it does not represent reality so much as human thought about reality. In the normal course of time, the meanings symbolized by words become usefully fixed, so it is possible for us to exchange our thoughts, without much difficulty, about the color "blue," the thing called "table," or the town named "London." And yet these are only customary agreements between those of us who share the language: there is no necessary relationship between an experience or place or physical object in the world and the signs by which those things are understood. There is always, in other words, a potential dislocation between reality and its representations in human thought. This is especially true when knowledge of anything in the world is in its formative stages, when the meanings of the signs used to designate aspects of a new reality are still fluid, or only partially tested, or not completely agreed upon. The history of the early years of European exploration in the New World provides excellent examples.

The simple and often overlooked fact about the first explorers is that they did not live in America. The pattern of early European exploration was almost always the same: brief, intense, scarcely informed, and often hurried experiences in the New World, followed by the making of images of those experiences, images that would be read, understood, and validated in the Old World. In fact, because legal claims, reputations, and further funding often rested on the discoveries, the importance of bringing an image — a map or an account — to the attention of the right people at home often made explorers impatient in the midst of their own explorations, as if they could not make the transfer between the experience and its representation fast enough. Christopher Columbus is perhaps the best example of such an exquisitely contradicted man. His log, written as if the king of Spain were listening to his every word, reveals not only a man attracted equally and seductively to each new and unknown plant, custom, and landscape that showed itself but also a man overwhelmingly aware of wasting time. "I do not really care to know such detail, for I could never see it all in fifty years; . . . I kept moving in order to see all of this so that I can give an account of everything to Your Highness."[1]

A famous moment from Verrazzano's voyage is also instructive. As Verrazzano sailed along the coast of what is today North Carolina, he came to the narrow isthmus of land that nearly encloses Pamlico Sound and separates it from the Atlantic (fig. 23). In looking across this sandy barrier into what seemed to be a very large and unending body of water, Verrazzano thought he saw an inland sea, and in his determination to discover a passage to Asia, he interpreted it as the ocean that carried on to India, China, and Cathay. He mistook the true conformation of the sound because he did not know what any adventurous native might have known: that behind the water of the sound there was land, not more water. In the absence of experience to the contrary, or time to test his hypothesis, or an informant whose language he could understand, he simply interpreted the evidence of his senses in the light of his most powerful preconceptions and then made an image to prove it.

If the knowledge of the first explorers, like that of first tourists everywhere, was based only on confused and overwhelming

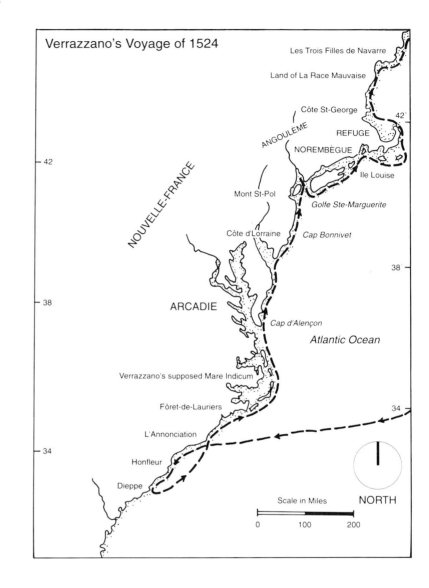

23. Route of Verraz-
zano's voyage. Based
on David B. Quinn,
*North America from
Earliest Discovery to
European Settlements*
(New York: Harper
and Row, 1977), map
no. 157.

impressions and scanty experience, the knowledge of those in
the Old World was even more removed from fact, since their
experience of the New World was derived from the accounts
and images being sent back. Without experience of their own
in the New World, they had no reason to doubt the sources.
The image of Verrazzano's famous inland sea, for instance, appears for the first time on manuscript maps of 1527 and 1529—
the two sources from which the geography of his discoveries became known to Europe. These maps were in turn copied and
modified by many other cartographers, with the result that from
1530 until the early seventeenth century, the characteristic conti-

nental pinch of the Verrazzanian sea became a piece of the iconography of North America—became, that is, an image of what some Europeans believed was geographical reality (fig. 24). The inland sea remained one of the possible truths about the New World—remaining longer in some European countries than in others—until it was generally falsified by new knowledge of the land, knowledge gleaned from yet other explorers' accounts and other maps. As Bernard Hoffman has pointed out, "The European image of North America developed through a process of slow and painful accretion, with many maps representing abortive efforts to synthesize logical configurations out of fragmentary and confusing information."[2] From the time of Verrazzano's voyage, more than one hundred years of exploring and mapping were required to produce an image that corresponds to what we now believe are the geographical facts of the northeastern coast.

This is an especially important point in thinking about the objective status of anything signified by names or latitudes on the early maps. Because the essential fiction of every map is that it represents things that have some sort of positive being in the world, the temptation to coordinate the records of early discovery with "true" positions in today's geography (that is, with our accepted images of reality) is often irresistible. And though it is not impossible, there are good reasons for caution.

William Francis Ganong, perhaps the most thorough student of the subject, makes the point that the place-names of the early explorers had very little sticking power because there was no one interested in applying them "on the ground."[3] Like any linguistic sign, a place-name requires a community of speakers who will agree that a certain name should be attached to a certain piece of the landscape. However, in the early sixteenth century, there was no one on the coast who could be persuaded to keep and use any of the names given by the explorers. Verrazzano was obviously aware of this when he named a group of three islands that may have been near the Maine coast "Le Figle di Navarra" (the daughters of Navarra). This form of conventional compliment to a powerful European nobleman looks back to the Old World for its context, since there was no one in the New World for whom such a name would make sense—no one yet ready to recognize French social distinctions. Certainly the native inhabitants who lived and moved in the region, and who had not yet been forced to take the European experience of their land into account, had

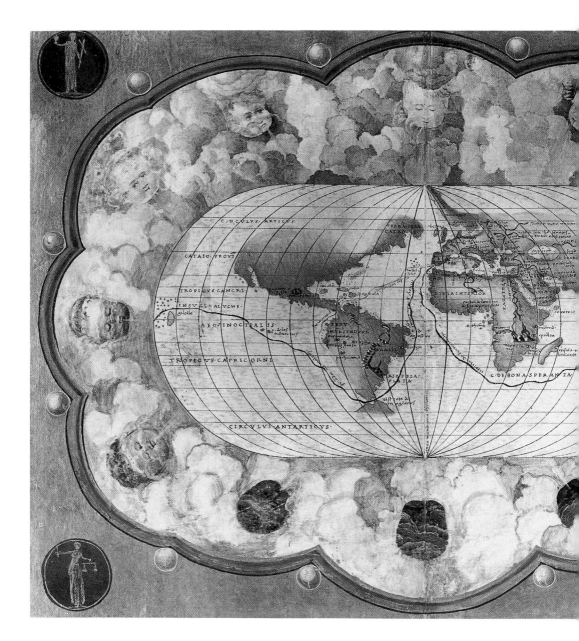

24. Battista Agnese, *World Map*, 1544. Courtesy of John Carter Brown Library at Brown University.

their own indigenous and no doubt finely grained system for differentiating one local place from another. They did not need a new name for the three islands. Whereas the native nomenclature had a living local constituency, European names in the early period belonged, in a sense, only to the maps.

The fixing of European cartographical nomenclature, as well as its crossing with the native system, was a function of settle-

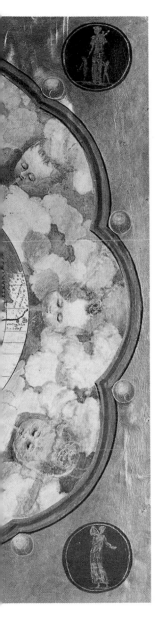

ment: the powerful desire of Europeans to know, live on, and own the land. Although this process began early in the regions held by Spain, it did not begin in earnest in the Northeast until the French and the English began serious attempts at colonization in the seventeenth century. Then the giving of names, in fact the very delineation of space on the maps, became an aspect of a serious ideological and political struggle: whoever had the power to define — to enforce agreement about — the way geographical reality would be represented also had the power to take possession of that reality.[4] But until there were interested parties, names belonging to many maps of the sixteenth century were without anchor, free to wander and appear and disappear. This is why, for instance, an unclaimed name like "Norumbega" can simply arise, mushroom-like, while Verrazzano's own "Refugio," perhaps the most important of his place-names, can vanish entirely, or why his "Arcadia" can have a cartographical migration from roughly Maryland to Canada.

Similar problems beset the interpretation of latitude, which may be surprising, since numerical measurements always seem, at least intuitively, immune to entanglement. And yet, as only one-half of a conceptual system for representing position on the globe (the other half, longitude, could not yet be measured with any accuracy), degrees of latitude had only a marginal advantage over names in sticking to newly perceived and incompletely understood bodies of land. Although explorers in the period were capable of measuring latitude with considerable precision, those numbers could not be carved into the earth for all to see and agree upon. Rather, latitudes had to be interpreted in a symbolic drawing of spatial relationships — a map.

On a map, the position and scale of any feature — its spatial meaning — was created by the feature's relationship to the position and scale of all the other features, most of which, unfortunately, were only dimly known in the sixteenth century. Of necessity, the picture was incomplete. Although some cartographers of the period had superb judgment (and good information) about what went where in the New World, the exact positions of even major geographical features on most maps were simply approximations. The Penobscot River, which empties into an extremely wide, island-studded bay, just above forty-four degrees along the Maine coast, is a good example, especially since it is a feature with which the name "Norumbega" was often associated.

On a few of the maps produced between the 1530s and the 1540s the unmistakable pie-shaped wedge of the river is introduced on the northeast coast at forty-one degrees (New York City), forty-two degrees (south of Boston), forty-four degrees (about right), and forty-five degrees (Nova Scotia). On other maps the name "Norumbega" can be found to cover a region stretching from forty to fifty degrees—from Philadelphia to central Quebec.

If features on the early maps have the equivalent of five hundred to one thousand miles of room to wander, and if these maps were copied and modified by others whose attachment to first-hand information from the New World was increasingly remote, then the chances of identifying exactly where anything is on a sixteenth-century map of North America are not good. In fact, what we find is that points on the map can overlap and displace each other and that whole pieces of coast can be lost or newly formed. And each of these changes creates a tradition of imagery in succeeding maps, with a corresponding influence on European thought. One cannot use names, latitudes, or even entire maps as though they were objective indices to "real" places on earth.

To live in the representations of a New World rather than in the New World itself is to inhabit a fluid region, one where the signs by which experience is understood and communicated are as open to mutation, mirroring, and manipulation as they are to objective testing. This might be called the semiotic problem in the history of early exploration: the fact that in this period, the potential dislocation between the experience of a new reality and its subsequent representation in European thought is at a maximum. From a historical point of view, this means that the traditional narrative of who, what, when, and where—the old short route to positive knowledge—must be augmented or even supplanted by a discussion of the stories, maps, accounts, and images—the signs—in which human action is refracted, multiplied, reshaped, and understood. The importance of the fabulous paradise of "Norumbega" is that it can be discovered only in such a discussion. It is not a real geographical or historical fact, in the old narrative sense, nor is there a simple linear explanation that will help make sense of it. "Norumbega" is the name of an idea that many Europeans shared for a brief period of time. It was founded on a few brief but important experiences in the New World and was then fully formed only in the representations of European thought, where it ultimately remained. To pursue the puzzle of

"Norumbega" is to glimpse how deeply human knowledge may be, at any point, constructed in its own, self-reflecting imagery.

The history of the development of the concept of "Norumbega" encompasses over fifty years. It has a French phase and an English phase, and it is played out most visibly on maps. However, through it all, one document (in which the name "Norumbega" never appears) is always central: the letter Verrazzano wrote to the king of France describing his voyage. In fact, the paradisiacal reputation of "Norumbega" rests entirely on the contents of this letter and its eventual dissemination.

The letter describes Verrazzano's departure in 1524 from Dieppe, France, and makes it clear that his intention, like that of almost every other European explorer before him, was to reach the Indies. "I estimated," he said, speaking of the decision to take a northern route above the recent Spanish discoveries around the Caribbean, "there would be some straight to get through to the Eastern Ocean." However, what he confirmed as he sailed was the disappointing fact that America was a complete continental landmass—"another world with respect to the one [the ancients] knew."[5] His landfall and his progress up the coast in search of a Northwest Passage, which he found tantalizingly close in the inland sea of Pamlico Sound, are described. However, he continued north, doing his explorer's duty: appraising the economic value of plants and minerals, testing the temper of the native inhabitants, locating harbors, and claiming the land for his king. The claims were staked by the stops he made and the names he gave along the way: "Arcadia," "Angoulême," "Refugio," "Le Figle di Navarra," and others. On reaching what he recognized as land already discovered by the English—that is, Newfoundland—he returned to France.

The most extraordinary part of this letter, which is in fact almost one-quarter of the whole, is a beautifully detailed, imaginatively charged description of his stay in "Refugio"—a fifteen-day idyll in a bay that he said was at the same latitude as Rome, a piece of corroborating information that allows us to say with some certainty that he had probably come into the Narragansett Bay of Rhode Island. What is most important about "Refugio," however, is how Verrazzano understood and described his experience there. Three strong impressions came together in Verrazzano's mind to form the warm and visionary recognition that "Refugio" was somehow unlike any other place he had seen: the native inhabitants had an aristocratic bearing, their reception of him and his crew was civil and gentle, and the landscape was beautiful and fertile.

As his ship entered the wide, island-studded bay, a number of natives came on board, among them two kings.

> [They] were as beautiful of stature and build as I can possibly describe. . . . These people are the most beautiful and have the most civil customs that we have found on this voyage. They are taller than we are; they are a bronze color, some tending more toward whiteness, others to a tawny color; the face is clear-cut; the hair is long and black, and they take great pains to decorate it; the eyes are black and alert, and their manner is sweet and gentle, very like the manner of the ancients.[6]

It is tempting to think of this moment of observation as perhaps the most neutral instant in the long dark relationship between the European and the Native American—the moment *before* the machinery of domination was set in motion.[7] And yet, even if we discount the subtle presumption that allowed Verrazzano to gawk with such care and delight—to make the Indian his object—Verrazzano's reference to the ancients shows that the process of ideological assimilation had already begun. When natives seem to act savagely, as they did, according to Verrazzano, both before and after his stay in "Refugio," they are simply Indians, but when they are extraordinary in some way, they become a branch of those anciently civilized races that were also the cultural progenitors of the Europeans. Like the Stoics, the natives at "Refugio" were, according to Verrazzano, courteous, generous, not easily swayed by trifles, attracted to essential matters like the workmanship of arms, and not ignorant of science. "When sowing they observe the influence of the moon, the rising of the Pleiades, and many other customs derived from the ancients."[8]

It is clear from other points in Verrazzano's letter that the ancients were always on his mind, whether in summoning up the landscapes of Arcadian pastoral fiction or in checking his calculations for the measurement of the earth.[9] In this he was a true citizen of the Renaissance, which always looked to the ancient world for the reaffirmation of its thought and culture. This was more than simple intellectual habit. The ancients were considered the point sources from which civilization had first diffused; there were no other ways for an advanced culture to come to be. The ancients were the ancestors in whose works and history Renaissance Europe could always find its own reflection. From the ancient Greeks, Romans, and Trojans, it had received its heroic-secular-intellectual self and from the ancient Hebrews, the seed of its spiritual-Christian self. Europeans, of course, considered themselves direct descendants in this line, but they did leave room, prompted by certain passages in Aristotle and the Bible, for the possibility that other peoples, in prior ages, had also had contact with the ancients. An encounter with the new and the strange thus became a search for similitudes and ancestral likenesses: what was like the ancients was like the Europeans and could therefore be accommodated and understood. For Verrazzano, primed as he was, the magic wand of Western civilization had already touched the natives of "Refugio" and made them *like*.[10]

Verrazzano's eagerness to turn the natives into ancients must then be understood as a kind of deep compliment, a sign of his pleasure, contentment, and intense egotism. After a dangerous journey in an unfamiliar world, he and his crew were finally being treated well. The natives, as he tells us, fed them, joined them politely at their own meals, helped with their chores, and organized games of sport for their entertainment. In good company, Verrazzano accorded his hosts the fullest measure of respect he was capable of, which was to recognize in their ancient civility their likeness to himself. This is perhaps why he did not raise the issue of religion at "Refugio." Later, when he was discourteously received by a different tribe of Indians farther up the Maine coast, he immediately noted their ignorance of religion—that is, their difference from himself. Apparently, manners and gentilesse made all the difference to a gentleman in the field.[11] In perhaps the most extraordinary act of largesse and complimentary accommodation, Verrazzano, while looking at the modest architectural achievements of his hosts, attributed to them the power and means of creating, with a little help, that unique symbol of the civilized world both ancient and modern, the city. "There is no doubt that if they had the skilled workmen that we have, they would erect great buildings, for the whole maritime coast is full of various blue rocks, crystals, and alabaster, and for such a purpose it has an abundance of ports and shelters for ships."[12] Clearly, what Verrazzano began to see in the inhabitants of "Refugio"—in their beauty, skill, and ancient gentility—

was the capacity for a rich, civilized life on the European model. A city could be located there; the way had been prepared.

The same assimilating vision began to transform the region as well as the natives. Whereas Verrazzano noted a profusion of indigenous, self-generating fruits and animals, recalling the labor-saving conditions in the Garden of Eden, the special fertility of "Refugio" was in the land itself, ripe and waiting for familiar crops. "We frequently went five or six leagues into the interior and found it as pleasant as I can possibly describe, and suitable for every kind of cultivation—grain wine or oil. For there the fields extend for 25 to 30 leagues; they are open and free of any obstacles or trees, and so fertile that any kind of seed would produce excellent crops."[13]

Although the economic goal of Verrazzano's voyage was to find a passage to Asia, and although at the end of his letter he expressed disappointment at not having gotten through the "obstacle" of North America, the sight of vast expanses of open meadows must have been an aphrodisiac to an explorer raised among the overfarmed and increasingly divided fields of Europe. Jacques Cartier recorded a similar moment on his first voyage to Canada in 1534, when fields as good as those in Brittany already seemed in a vision plowed and sowed.[14] The emphasis on the land in the early accounts of the Northeast may have been compensation for not finding easily portable assets like gold, but to imagine that the New World, like the Old World, could be a productive agricultural place was to begin to see its value in a new light. It was to anticipate that moment in 1602 when, "ravished at the beautie and delicacie of this sweet soile," John Brereton would stand near Cape Cod and think England but a barren place by comparison.[15]

In Verrazzano's visionary description of "Refugio" is the dawning possibility that Europeans might take, farm, and live in this place. By the time he sailed from "Refugio," Verrazzano was thinking about military security: in the middle of the estuary there was a sort of rock "suitable for building any kind of machine or bulwark for the defense of the harbor."[16] Certainly there would be a fort, since what is worth taking is worth defending. Here, in Verrazzano's story of "Refugio," and in the characteristic European intellectual attitudes that inform it, we have almost the entire content of the concept of "Norumbega." All the physical details of the eventual myth were in place: an approach through a broad bay with islands, the suggestion of extensive interior regions, the gentle and advanced people, the crystal city and the fort. And the essential meaning was also clear: "Norumbega" was that magnetic spot in the northeastern part of the New World —wealthy, civilized, welcoming, and fecund—that had already been prepared to receive Europeans. It was a place like unto their own, an idealization of home, the mirror of their desires.

Unlike the information on a map—unlike the infamous inland sea, for instance—there was no way to falsify or to objectively test the yearning, pleasure, and enthusiasm that Verrazzano suffused into his account of "Refugio." It was a story, an indestructible and continually suggestive image that drew other images and stories to it. Within a month of his return, Verrazzano was having copies of his letter sent to Florence to support his fund-raising for a second voyage, and there is some evidence that his efforts included England and Portugal as well.[17] There is good reason to believe that his letter was fairly well known in Europe even before its first official publication in 1556. What remains to be shown is how Verrazzano's story and "Norumbega" come together.

"Norumbega" appears in writing for the first time in the form "Oranbega," an inconspicuous place-name on the 1529 manuscript map of Girolamo da Verrazzano, the explorer's brother. The name is not used in Verrazzano's famous letter, but there it enigmatically is on the map, in the northeastern corner of the continent, near "Le Figle di Navarra" and quite a bit north of the bay of "Refugio" (fig. 25). Within fifteen years it is obvious that something has happened to "Oranbega." Now spelled in some variant of the form "Anorobegua" or "Anorombega," the name proliferates on maps.[18] It is usually attached to a unique and very recognizable northeastern image that is clearly not on Verrazzano's map: the pie-shaped, internally dotted wedge we now associate with the Penobscot River in Maine.

This association continues on maps and globes as long as the idea of "Norumbega" lasts. In the early period, we find Gerardus Mercator's first essay of this arrangement on Gemma Frisius's globe of 1537, which he engraved, and on his own globe of 1541. The same conjunction is especially noticeable in the mid-1540s on the beautiful manuscript maps of the French Dieppe school, which synthesized information from a number of cartographic traditions, including Cartier's voyages to Canada, which began in 1534 (plate 3). However, at the same time, there was a grow-

25. Tracing of detail of North America from Girolamo da Verrazzano, *World Map*, 1529. From Willam F. Ganong, *Crucial Maps in the Early Cartography of Canada*, 1931. By permission of the Vatican.

ing recognition that all "Norumbegas," regardless of their spelling or what they signified on maps, had something to do with Verrazzano's early voyage, a voyage that as time passed became increasingly identified with its one most brilliant moment: the discovery and description of "Refugio." A prime piece of evidence is an anonymous document, *Discorso d'un Gran Capitano di mare Francese del Luoco di Dieppa* (Discourse of a Great French Sea Captain of Dieppe), which was first published in 1556 but dates itself internally to 1539. Historians usually take the *Discorso* to be an indication of what was commonly understood about "Norumbegan" matters, at least among the French, in the closing years of the 1530s. "This coast was discovered fifteen years ago by Giovanni da Verrazzano in the name of the king of France. . . . The inhabitants of this country are tractable, friendly and peaceful people. The land has a great abundance of fruit; oranges, almonds, wild grapes, and many other kinds of aromatic trees grow there. This land is called Norumbega by its inhabitants."[19] There are a number of interesting suggestions in this passage, but the main point is clear: "Norumbega" and Verrazzano's discovery—the bountiful country of friendly and peaceful natives, clearly the "Refugio" of his letter—are one and the same.

Other key suggestions by Verrazzano about "Refugio" are amplified in the only other significant textual mention of "Norumbega" before 1556, an unpublished work by Jean Alfonce de Saintonge, the pilot who sailed on Cartier and the Sieur de Roberval's

voyage to Canada in 1541. Here "Norumbega" was identified with the great island-studded river it was so often associated with—clearly the Penobscot. But the idealization of the natives found in Verrazzano's letter was also reinforced, and the existence of an actual city—a mere potentiality in the letter, the necessary consequence of attributing to the Indians the capacity for classical civilization—had become a fact. The *riviere de norembergue*, Saintonge said,

> is more than forty leagues at its entrance and retains its width some thirty or forty leagues. It is full of islands, which stretch some ten or twelve leagues into the sea. . . . Fifteen leagues within this river there is a city called Norombegue with clever inhabitants and a mass of peltries of all kinds of beasts. The citizens dress in furs, wearing sable cloaks. . . . The people use many words which sound like Latin and worship the sun, and they are fair people and tall.[20]

Almost sixty years after this was written, Samuel de Champlain sailed up the Penobscot in search of this fabulous city of "Norumbega." He found an unimpressive collection of huts and declared its existence a myth.[21] It is, of course, possible that there had been a native encampment on the Penobscot known to Saintonge, just as there had been one in the 1530s at the site of present-day Montreal, which Cartier called Hochelaga. Like Hochelaga, the encampment could have vanished in the intervening years before Champlain's voyage. However, it is usually thought that Saintonge was not speaking from experience but was trying to interpret general hearsay about the region in the light of Verrazzano's descriptions. That the Indians in his city of "Norumbega" speak a Latin-sounding language is perhaps the giveaway. An image of city-like towers attached to the great river can already be seen on Pierre Desceliers's *Mappemonde* of 1546; this image is a forerunner of the characteristic castle-city that would eventually appear on Mercator's world map of 1569, Abraham Ortelius's beautiful 1570 map of North America, and many others.

Two questions about the explosion of interest in Norumbega and its identification with Verrazzano seem to stand out, particularly in relation to the cartographic evidence. The first is how "Oranbega," the earliest form of "Norumbega," came to appear on Girolamo da Verrazzano's map of 1529. Some notion of its origin, or what geographers and others of the period thought to be its origin, might help explain its later prominence. The second question is how the "Refugio" of Verrazzano's letter could have passed its associations on to a feature—the great river—that is neither shown on his map nor mentioned in his letter, perhaps the most confusing but also the most intriguing synthesis of representations in the "Norumbega" story.

Historians who conjecture about the origin of "Norumbega"— the reason it appeared in the first place—usually look to one line in the passage of the *Discorso* for evidence: "This land is called Norumbega by its inhabitants." In other words, "Norumbega," like "England" or "France," was thought to be a name used by the native inhabitants to describe their own country. If this were true, then the "Oranbega" on Girolamo's map had been picked up in the New World, either by Verrazzano himself, who failed to mention it in his letter, or by Girolamo through some indirect means. "Oranbega" might then very well be, as one scholar suggests, the first native place-name introduced into European cartography.[22] Ganong, who is the most skeptical scholar on the issue of an indigenous origin, finally broke down and proposed it was indeed Verrazzano himself who had heard the word while at "Refugio," making "Norumbega" a name for the country of the Narragansett Bay.[23] Samuel Eliot Morison believed Girolamo got the name from a firsthand Portuguese source and that it came from the region near "Le Figle di Navarra," which would make it a name for the country of the Penobscot in Maine.[24] In either case, a European awareness that the name was of native origin—that a country of that name already existed in the New World—might go some way toward explaining why the name was preserved and why it had such cachet in the sixteenth century, especially as it became associated with Verrazzano's paradisiacal vision of "Refugio."

Unfortunately, there is no sound evidence that the word "Norumbega" was in any way picked up from the New World, that it was the name of a native country there, or that it corresponded to anything in a native language of the period. To make the assertion of a native origin stick, historians usually turn to modern languages of the various Wabanaki tribes (the Native Americans of present-day Maine and the Maritime Provinces) to find surviving cognates. If cognates exist, then there is some reason to believe that the name had been used by the sixteenth-century Algonquian ancestors of the Wabanakis and hence that Europeans could have borrowed it. A number of possible choices do suggest themselves, but a certain wariness is required. The question of what the sounds "nor-um-be-ga" may have meant to an early native speaker, assuming the word was used at all, opens a whole new semantic horizon. If words are the signs of some set of conceptual relations existing in people's minds, then their meaning is a function of the specific contexts — psychological, linguistic, cultural, and historical — in which they are used. The appropriation of a word from one context to another almost guarantees that its meaning will be changed or destroyed. To wonder about the question of the origin of "Norumbega" is really to place oneself at the intersection of two formerly parallel and independent histories of meaning: one of which, the sixteenth-century European one, is familiar and fairly well understood, whereas the other, the sixteenth-century native one, is in many ways unavailable. Inferences about this native history can of course be made, but the possibilities need to be contemplated with some imagination and with an eye for our own ignorance. The native origin of "Norumbega" is an open question, but we will return to it at the close.

The second important question about "Norumbega" is how the discoveries of Verrazzano became cartographically superimposed on the image of a great river he never saw and how they became named with a name he never recorded. In the years between 1529 and 1556, in the minds of many Europeans who thought about North America, the paradise of "Refugio," the image of the Penobscot River, and the name "Norumbega" merged.

The explanation of this merger brings to light the only other experiential event in the New World, besides Verrazzano's stay in "Refugio," that has any bearing on the history of the idea of "Norumbega." This was the voyage of Estevan Gomes, whose few discoveries greatly affected the European cartographical vision of the Northeast. In 1525, only a few months after Verrazzano's voyage, Gomes sailed along the same piece of northern coast that Verrazzano had just visited; however, Gomes was both more and less thorough than Verrazzano. Along the Maine coast he went deeply enough up the Penobscot ("El Rio de Las Gamas") to see how great a river it was and sailed tightly enough into Massachusetts Bay to sense the characteristic outcropping of Cape Cod. After rounding Cape Cod, Gomes sailed

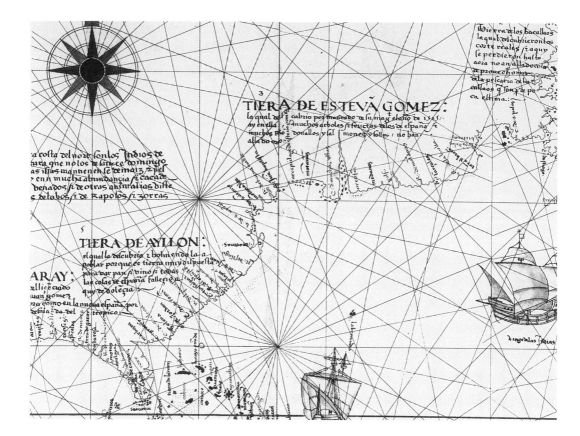

Within the map image the following labels and annotations appear:

TIERA DE ESTEVÃ GOMEZ.

TIERA DE AYLLON.

ARAY

26. Detail of tracing of North America from Diego Ribeiro, *World Map*, 1529. Courtesy of Maine State Archives.

due south and then home. He thus lost the chance to corroborate the existence of Narragansett Bay, Verrazzano's "Refugio," and much else that Verrazzano had seen.[25] Gomes "lost" the coast between Cape Cod and New York and, with it, "Refugio." Perhaps more important, so did Diego Ribeiro, the royal cartographer of Spain. Ribeiro's tremendously influential maps, following Gomes, simply closed over that piece of the North American coast (fig. 26). Just as Verrazzano's preconceptions had been drawn into the image of geographic reality, so Gomes's ignorance had caused a piece of that reality to be erased. However, there were now two traditions for the representation of northeastern geography: a purely cartographical Gomes-Ribeiro tradition, with its preeminent northern "Rio de Las Gamas"; and a Verrazzanian tradition, drawn from both the first manuscript maps of his voyage and his letter, which was usually characterized by the inland sea, a relatively unarticulated northeastern coast, and sometimes those familiar names—"Arcadia," "Angoulême," and "Refugio," among others. The reconciliation of these two traditions presented later cartographers, who had access to both, with a number of dilemmas. Perhaps the most important was where to put the famous "Refugio."

Verrazzano's letter declared unequivocally that the island-studded bay of "Refugio" was on a parallel with Rome, about forty-one and two-thirds degrees (about right for today's Narragansett Bay).[26] Ribeiro had, of course, eliminated the piece of coast on which the actual "Refugio" sat, but he did introduce another major island-studded feature, "Rio de Las Gamas," where "Refugio" could have been, that is, in the middle of a vaguely northeastern region whose latitude ranged between forty-one degrees and forty-five degrees. Thus Verrazzano's letter contained a brilliant written description for forty-one and two-thirds degrees, but no cartographical feature, whereas Ribeiro's maps included an important cartographical feature in roughly the same latitude, but no written description. One can see that the natural inclination—the tendency to opt for meaning-making connections in the absence of any other information—was to put the two together, to assume that the paradise Verrazzano called "Refugio" was in fact the same northeastern "spot" discovered by Gomes and drawn so prominently by Ribeiro. As Ganong has pointed out, Euphrosynus Ulpius's globe of 1542, combining elements of both traditions, provides a kind of fossil evidence that this identification was being made: the name "Refugio," in the form "promont. refugium," is clearly superimposed on the Penobscot River image (fig. 27).[27]

The great river-city-paradise produced by the marrying of Verrazzano's "Refugio" and Ribeiro's "Rio de Las Gamas" was, as we have seen, most often subsumed under some variant of the name "Norumbega." The frequent appearance of this particular synthesis on maps throughout the 1530s and 1540s suggests the dominance of Ribeiro's "river" tradition and, perhaps, a preference for nicely articulated coastal images. This was not the whole story, however. As the *Discorso* suggested, "Norumbega" was also thought a country—that is, a region in the New World, a more generalized geographical concept. Such an idea was usually not made very clear on most of the maps that followed Ribeiro's. Here there was room for the reassertion of more purely Verrazzanian ideas.

In the 1548 Venice edition of Claudius Ptolemy's *La Geografia,* the Italian cartographer Giacomo Gastaldi presented his *Tierra*

Nueva, the first printed map to focus so centrally on an image of the northeastern coast of North America. In this clearly Verraz-zanian map, one can see that the famous piece of coast lost by Gomes but discovered by Verrazzano has been restored—from "Angoulême," roughly New York Harbor, to "Refugio," roughly Narragansett Bay. (With wonderful but unintentional irony, Gastaldi followed an entirely different tradition for the representation of what are today the Canadian Maritimes, compressing the present coasts of Massachusetts and Maine completely out of existence—another lost piece of coast.) There are the variants of the names made famous in Verrazzano's letter, including "Arcadia" and "Refugio." But encompassing them all is a new regional appellation, "Tierra de Nurumberg," which of

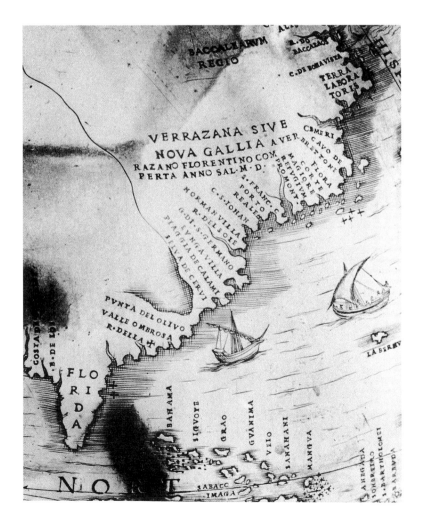

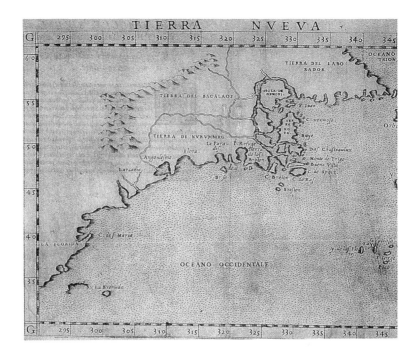

28. Giacomo Gastaldi, *Tierra Nueva*, in Claudius Ptolemy, *Geografia*, 1548. Courtesy of Smith Cartographic Collection, University of Southern Maine.

course did not appear in Verrazzano. This map, in other words, is an attempt to show how the Verrazzano discoveries and the burgeoning concept of a "Norumbega" region could work together geographically. "Norumbega" is the land one heads to in order to reach paradise, the "Port of Refuge" (fig. 28). In later maps, even those following Ribeiro, this regional notion becomes much stronger, until what is perhaps the ultimate cartographic synthesis is reached in Ortelius's elegant map of 1570, which shows a city of "Norumbega," on a great river, in a great region of "Norumbega" (plate 5).

Gastaldi presented similar geography again eight years later in an important woodcut map (fig. 3). "Port de Refuge" is prominent in the "Terre de Nurumbega," and toga-clad figures of Indians strike classical poses — Verrazzano's New World ancients. The fact that the entire region of "La Nuova Francia" seems to be an island suggests that Gastaldi was trying to incorporate, however vaguely, information about the Cartier explorations in the St. Lawrence region of Canada. The notion that there was a major river like the St. Lawrence coming down from the north, as well as the possibility of a major river like the Penobscot pushing inland from the east, led some sixteenth-century cartographers to simply bring the two rivers together, thus isolating a

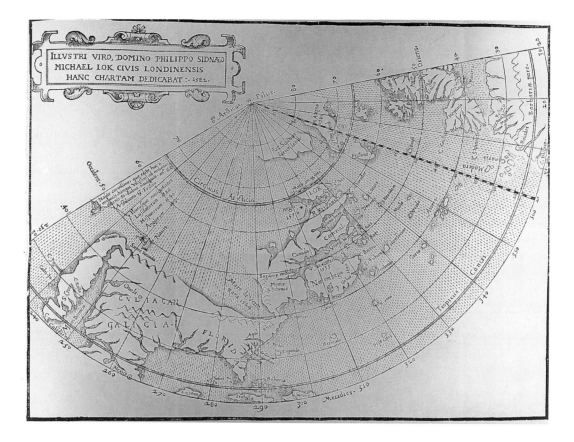

ILLVSTRI VIRO, DOMINO PHILIPPO SIDNÆO
MICHAEL LOK CIVIS LONDINENSIS
HANC CHARTAM DEDICABAT :. 1582.

29. Michael Lok, *Map of America*, in Richard Hakluyt, *Divers Voyages*, 1582. Courtesy of University of Southern Maine.

tempting chunk of the Northeast. This formation would become particularly attractive to the English in later years (fig. 29).

Gastaldi's map was published in Giovanni Battista Ramusio's *Terzo Volume delle Navigationi et Viaggi,* a vast compilation of discovery narratives published in Italian in 1556. This work is, in a sense, the most significant watershed in the history of the meaning of "Norumbega," since it makes available for the first time most of the key written texts related to "Norumbega." In a separate section entitled "Of the Land of Norumbega," Ramusio includes the first publication of the Verrazzano letter, translated into Italian, complete with its glowing record of "Refugio." Included also is the *Discorso d'un Gran Capitano,* complete with the passage that draws the line between Verrazzano's discoveries and the country of "Norumbega"; the Gastaldi map is placed as an illustration to the *Discorso.* Cartier's first two narratives are also found here, suggesting that Canada and Norumbega were shaping up as regional cousins. Ramusio thus compiles a complete brief for the idea of "Norumbega" and hence for the entire geography of northeastern North America. It is probably reasonable to assume that up until Ramusio, "Norumbega" was more or less a French idea. However, with the publication of the *Terzo Volume,* "Norumbega" received a more public, more pan-European exposure, and it was mainly from this source that the English concept of "Norumbega" was drawn. The two brief voyages of Verrazzano and Gomes, the power of the tale of "Refugio," and nearly thirty years of cartographical drawings in which the shapes of the New World were shifted, reformed, and superimposed had made "Norumbega" a species of fact.

In 1582 Richard Hakluyt published *Divers Voyages,* an English translation, in part, of Ramusio's *Terzo Volume.* It is a seminal work, not only in the transmission of the idea of "Norumbega" but also in the creation of England's entire concept of America. Hakluyt's *Divers Voyages* is among the earliest published calls to the English nation to consider colonizing the New World—to throw off England's long lack of interest in America and to reassert, in effect, the proprietary interests in the Northeast that John Cabot had established for the Crown by his voyage to Newfoundland as far back as 1497. Every aspect of the Verrazzano "story" is a significant implement in Hakluyt's persuasive arsenal, including an assertion in the introduction, corroborated nowhere else in the literature, that Verrazzano had been in touch with King Henry VIII immediately after his voyage and had given him a map on which the inland sea—the tantalizing closeness of a Northwest Passage—was apparent. "Master John Verarzanus . . . in an olde excellent map, which he gave to king Henry the eight, and is yet in the custodie of master Locke, doth so lay it out, as is to be seen in the mappe annexed to the end of this boke, beeing made according to Verarzanus plat."[28] Hakluyt's motives here are interestingly mixed. On the one hand, Verrazzano serves as proof of a Northwest Passage, which would certainly make colonization in the North all the more attractive if by a skip and a jump Asia could be reached; on the other hand, the early link between Verrazzano and the king suggests that there might be some political basis for a claim to the lands of New France.

Politics may be one reason the English championed Verrazzanian geography at a time when other, more reliable, European cartographic traditions were becoming accepted, though certainly the idea of a Northwest Passage continued to exert a strong influence throughout Europe. A look at Michael Lok's map mentioned by Hakluyt suggests other reasons (fig. 29). Making unmistakable use of the inland-sea tradition, the map is in fact placed as an illustration for Verrazzano's letter, "The relation of John Verarzanus, A Florentine"—its first translation into English. Both run under the heading "The discovery of Morumbega [*sic*]."[29] The map itself, a kind of cartoon, shows a Verrazzanian sea, placed at a very high forty-degree latitude, pinching off a convenient piece of the Northeast. This landmass is then further subdivided, in the fashion of the Gastaldi map examined earlier, by the joining of something like the St. Lawrence with something like the Penobscot to produce a plump, large, enticing island, between forty and fifty degrees, called "Norombega." The geography of this map is so fluid and creative that a kind of homology between "Norombega" and England seems to have been intended: both are islands, both are contiguous to continental landmasses, and both are quite near each other, like mirror images. Finding similitudes, as we saw in Verrazzano's description of "Refugio," is the sincerest form of appropriation. These reflections may be only subliminal in the map, but the text of *Divers Voyages* makes them explicit: "Norumbega" is in fact the special object of England's colonial intentions, the mirror of its desires.

"Norumbega," as a name and as a cartographical image, was the conceptual focus of England's geopolitics in the New World in the 1580s. It was the place, as Hakluyt wrote to Queen Elizabeth, where England would plant its foot against Spanish world supremacy and bolster its own sagging economic system through the creation of new markets.[30] As David Quinn has shown, Hakluyt's *Divers Voyages* was put together specifically to promote the New World colonial enterprise of Sir Humphrey Gilbert, which would presumably further England's national goals.[31] Gilbert, a Renaissance man of action and business, had received from the queen in 1578 a patent to much of northeastern North America. *Divers Voyages* was meant as an assertion of England's title to that tract and as a piece of real estate advertising to help presell to investors the estates Gilbert had laid out in the land they called "Norumbega." What better way to stimulate the minds of prospective buyers than by having them read the account that had from the very beginning created the idea of a specially prepared, cultivated, and unthreatening paradise for Europeans in the northeastern part of the New World? This account was, of course, Verrazzano's letter. In the margin of the text of the letter as printed in *Divers Voyages,* at precisely the point where the famous description of "Refugio" begins—with its civilized natives, the lush meadows, the potential city of alabaster—we find this notation: "The Country of Sir H [umphrey] G [ilbert's] Voyage."[32] It is "Refugio" alone, and not all the unattractive places that Verrazzano saw on his voyage, that carries the imprimatur of Sir H. G. In other words, if you buy into the English "Norumbega" of Sir Humphrey Gilbert, you will get Verrazzano's paradise.

For the English, "Norumbega" became the sign that most persuasively and efficiently communicated the attractiveness of settlement in the New World. Its imagined geography and its imagined qualities were reflections of or acceptable displacements for England's own idea of itself. In this, the seminal notion implicit in Verrazzano's account of "Refugio" was fulfilled: that some day Europeans might do more than pass through the New World; they might live in it, own it, and prosper. As can be seen from Cornelius Wytfliet's map of 1597, "Norumbega" soon joined Virginia as the northernmost of the two spheres of English colonial interests in North America (fig. 30). By the 1630s, when colonies were in place, when maps were improving, and when the reality of what it meant to inhabit someone else's land was beginning to dawn, Captain John Smith, Indian fighter and instigator of so much of his country's colonial activity, could look back to his first voyage to "Norumbega," a place "now called New England."[33]

Finally, the possible Indian meaning of the word "Norumbega" must also be considered. In the European mind, the name "Norumbega" subdivided the emerging reality of America and, in the simplest sense, marked the northern corner as "desirable." Those who, like the English, had the power to enact their desires in the physical world also had the power to fill the conceptual space held by the name "Norumbega" with their own meanings, just as their people filled the land itself. A new, more delimited political, geographical, and imaginative reality deserved a new name. The displacement of "Norumbega" by "New England" thus closes the European history of its meaning. But this brings us back, finally, to the possibility of a second history of the name, the possibility that even before Europeans began to elaborate their ideas about America, the word "Norumbega" had had an

30. Cornelius Wytfliet,
Norumbega et Virginia,
1597. Courtesy of
Smith Cartographic
Collection, University
of Southern Maine.

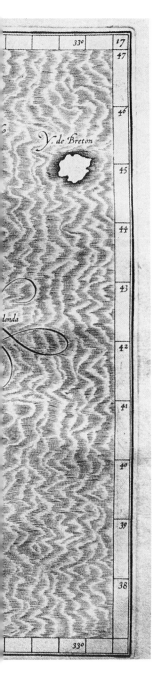

Indian meaning. To ask for this meaning, as suggested earlier, is to pursue a different line of inquiry, not because names function differently in the minds of Indians but because the history of the set of conceptual relations that "norumbega" stood for in the minds of sixteenth-century natives cannot be followed as can that of the Europeans. But a few things are certain: first, a potential history of the native meaning does exist; second, in its most essential features it would have nothing to do with the history of the European meaning; and third, our usually glib attempts to appropriate neat dictionary definitions from the vocabularies of present-day native languages and apply them to the past are either insignificant or just the beginning of a long process of thought about how the world gets known through language.

Let us assume that the few definitions that we have from current Wabanaki sources are useful guides to something permanent in the idea of the name "norumbega." The suggestions include the following: "where there is quiet water between rapids" (vaguely attributed by Morison to the Wabanaki in general);[34] "where the river is wide" (from the Penobscot Indians); and "where the river flows back" (as in a tidal river, from the Maliseets). Clearly, then, it is safe to say that "norumbega" is a piece of Wabanaki nomenclature of rivers, and we might go so far as to assume that something like it was used among one or more tribes of the Algonquian group that probably existed in the Northeast in the sixteenth century. This leads to a probable scenario. When an explorer swung his arm across the terrain somewhere along today's New England coast and asked a native, with whom he could only crudely communicate, for the name—meaning the name of the part of the country the natives called their own—he was given instead local information about the body of water they were near. The European's concept of regional ownership meant nothing to the native, whereas every aspect of the conformation of rivers held significance.

But what set of river conceptions, informed by what differentiating experiences, emotions, traditions, and visions, might have been summarized in the name "norumbega" for an Indian of the sixteenth century? Some subtle web of relations must have existed behind the linguistic sign because that is how language works for everyone. Perhaps "norumbega" signified in everyday use "the wide part of the river," but the reason such a notion as "the wide part of the river" existed would have been because it established a contrast with something else in the minds of those who used it. Did the wide part of the river mean, in contrast to its narrow inland course, the part nearest the sea? And did the word carry some sense of the seasonal and emotional distinctions that may have gone along with thinking about the hard winter life spent inland and the easier summer life spent near the shore, when food stores were infinite and the fellowship was warm and fluid? Or was "the wide part of the river" the place where it was difficult to set fish weirs, as opposed to the narrow runs between rapids farther up? Or was it the place that was dangerous to cross? Or was it the place that was safe, in its breadth and openness, from the fear of the water spirits who guarded access to the deep interior—the same spirits, perhaps, that the Indians of Canada impersonated in the year 1535 in their efforts to scare away, unsuccessfully, a determined band of French explorers?

There is really no way to know, but contemplating the possible uses of "norumbega" leads us to assume that in the minds and languages of the natives who met the first explorers, the world was as complex and nuanced as it was among the Europeans and is among ourselves. And just as there was a Verrazzano, and a Hakluyt, and an Elizabeth, this contemplation leads us to ask about individuals, the most local site of the meaning of any word. Was it a man, or a woman, or a child who spoke the word "norumbega"? And what different meanings did the word hold for each of them? And what were their names?

PART TWO

"Wenooch"; or, Who Are These Strangers? Native Americans and the European Encounter

Introduction

Harald E. L. Prins

Several years ago, a Native elder in Maine asked, "What was America called before the white man?" Perhaps a bit ingenuous, his question indicates that beyond the dozens of registered prehistoric sites and thousands of retrieved archaeological artifacts, we possess precious little cognitive information about the indigenous cultures of New England and the Maritime Provinces in the precontact period. In spite of increasing evidence of prehistoric Wabanaki material culture allowing archaeologists to conjecture traditional subsistence strategies, settlement patterns, burial practices, and exchange networks, we are generally deprived of information telling us about their worldviews. Because they were a script-free people, the ancient Wabanakis (forebears of the Micmacs, Maliseets, Passamaquoddies, Penobscots, and Abenakis) left us without any written records documenting how and what they thought, felt, or did in their lives. Without direct evidence of the ways in which they imagined their world, it is almost impossible for us to reconstruct their symbolic universe. Without understanding their culture's cognitive framework, we have no clues to their mental state or feelings. These problems, of course, also limit our ability to fully comprehend Wabanaki reactions to the waves of Europeans arriving on their shores.

But, as the chapter written by Kenneth M. Morrison suggests, some of the ideological edifice of these ancient Wabanaki cultures has actually been preserved. As remnants of native oral tradition—myths, legends, stories, and songs—these internal "texts" are revealing of ancient spiritual beliefs and moral values, informing us how Wabanaki ancestors regarded their homeland and how they related to their human and animal neighbors.

In "Children of Gluskap: Wabanaki Indians on the Eve of the European Invasion," Harald E. L. Prins sketches the stage on the eve of the European invasion of northeastern North America. Reconstructed from numerous scraps of information winnowed from an array of archaeological, historical (written and oral), linguistic, and anthropological sources, this composite represents an effort to describe Wabanaki culture before its collapse in the course of the seventeenth century. As such, this chapter is an effort to present a historical ethnography of the Wabanakis, rather than a native history of the cultural dynamics involved as a consequence of the European invasion.

Evidence of early Wabanaki adaptation to European presence in the region is offered by Bruce J. Bourque and Ruth H. Whitehead. Using early French and English sources, they trace the unique dynamics of early culture contact and seek to demonstrate that native mariners from the Gulf of St. Lawrence, sailing in European shallops, were initially in control of the fur trade in the Gulf of Maine region. In his essay on native perspectives on the exploration of Norumbega, James Axtell provides us with colorful descriptions of the natives' reactions to the Europeans landing on their shores.

Although the written documents produced by early European explorers, merchants, and missionaries provide us with graphic details and precise chronological dates pertinent to native history, it should be noted that they are "external" sources. As accounts of what happened in the course of the encounter, they are highly selective; as ethnographic records of indigenous cultural traditions, they typically refer only to the most superficial aspects of Wabanaki society.

Notwithstanding these predicaments, each chapter succeeds in shedding some light on remote cultural events. To a degree, they all rely on conjecture or some other theoretical device in order to transcend the limits imposed on them by a general dearth of relevant information. Due to some analytical differences between some of the authors, mainly centering on the use or abuse of oral tradition as a reliable source of historical information, the following texts show some provocative contrasts in interpretation. Together, however, they form a unique interpretive complex that enriches our critical understanding of the cultural dynamics involved during that fateful encounter, which has forever altered the human condition in northeastern North America.

CHAPTER FOUR

Children of Gluskap
Wabanaki Indians on the Eve of the European Invasion

Harald E. L. Prins

The native people of northern New England and the Maritime Provinces originally referred to their homeland as Ketakamigwa (the big land on the seacoast).[1] The area was thought of as the eastern part of a large island. This island was the earth as they knew it.[2] They referred to it as "top land," surrounded by the "great salt water." It was imagined as the center of a horizontally stratified universe, crowned by a sky-world where the spirits of the dead lived on as stars. Below was the netherworld, the realm of hostile spirits appearing in reptile form. A mysterious life force known as Ketchiniweskwe (great spirit) was thought to govern this universe.[3]

As inhabitants of the region where the skies first turn light in the morning, the native people of the northeastern coastal area were traditionally known as Wabanakiak (the people of the dawn).[4] They believed themselves to be the children of Gluskap,

I thank Arthur Spiess and Emerson Baker, for their comments on an earlier draft of this paper, and especially my wife, Bunny McBride, for her skillful editorial hand.

a primordial giant creature who came into being somewhere in the Northeast "when the world contained no other man, in flesh, but himself."[5] The meaning of his name is not certain and is sometimes translated as "good man," "the liar," or as "man out of nothing."[6]

As Gluskap's children, the Wabanakis have been the inhabitants of Ketakamigwa ever since time began. Their descendants today include the people belonging to the Abenaki, Penobscot, Passamaquoddy, Maliseet, and Micmac tribes. Roaming through their homeland, the original Wabanakis became thoroughly familiar with all the natural features of the landscape, knowing the precise location of each river, lake, cape, and mountain. As hunters, fishers, and gatherers, they took regular stock of the available resources in their habitat and knew in great detail "what the supply of each resource was: deer, moose, beaver, fur-bearers, edible birds, berries, roots, trees, wild grasses. They knew the districts where each was to be found when wanted and, roughly, in what quantities."[7]

Of course, such ecological intimacy was possible only on the basis of a thorough geographic understanding of the immediate environment. But to what extent the Wabanakis' knowledge extended to territories beyond their tribal boundaries remains unclear.[8] It appears that they were familiar with territories as far south as the Hudson River, knew the area west until the St. Lawrence River, and could find their way north to Newfoundland, perhaps even beyond.

Historical Ecology of Wabanaki Habitat

Until the end of the Ice Age about twelve thousand years ago, no human occupied the region now known as New England and the Maritime Provinces. However, when the glaciers retreated, small bands of Paleo-Indians moved into the tundras, preying on big game such as the mastodon, mammoth, musk-ox, and, most of all, large herds of grazing caribou. A few material remains, including flint spearpoints, knives, and scrapers, have been found at their ancient camping places and kill sites at locations such as Debert, Munsungun, and Aziscohos lakes.[9] With climatic warming, the tundras of these Paleo-Indian hunting bands transformed gradually into a woodland habitat. The emerging woodlands represented a rich mosaic of tree stands with widely varying compositions. Environmental conditions initially favored white pine, followed by birch, oak, and hemlock. About five thousand years ago, a modern ecological system developed, with warm summers and cold winters marked by up to five months of snow-covered ground. Northern hardwoods such as maple, elm, ash, and beech appeared in the forests, followed later by spruce. Some of these trees, in particular the white pine, were enormous in dimension, measuring up to 5 feet in diameter and reaching more than 150 feet in height.

Broken by swamps, lakes, and ponds, these enormous territories have been drained by several major river systems since the end of the Ice Age. The 240-mile-long Penobscot, for example, collects water of 322 streams and 625 lakes and ponds, draining a total area of 7,760 square miles. The remainder of the territory is drained by the Restigouche, Miramichi, St. John, St. Croix, Kennebec, Androscoggin, Saco, and several other rivers.[10] Typical for this woodlands habitat, which became the homeland of the Wabanakis, is its thriving wildlife, traditionally its abundance of white-tailed deer along with moose and caribou. In addition, black bear, wolves, raccoons, red foxes, lynxes, bobcats, fishers, martens, otters, and skunks have long prospered here, as have rodents like beavers, muskrats, hares, and porcupines. Inland waters, at least seasonally, have formed the natural environment of fish such as salmon, trout, sturgeon, bass, smelt, and alewives; marine life at the coast includes not only an abundance of lobsters and shellfish (in particular, clams and oysters) but also sea mammals such as seals, porpoises, and whales (fig. 31). For thousands of years, multitudes of water birds have flocked to the area, again mostly seasonally—loons, ducks, cormorants, herons, geese, and swans. Pheasants, partridges, pigeons, grouse, and turkeys share in the bounty of the land along with hawks, majestic eagles, and birds of prey.

31. Micmac petroglyph at Kejimkujik Lake, depicting hunters lancing a large fish. In Garrick Mallery, "Picture-Writing of the American Indians," *Tenth Annual Report of the Bureau of Ethnology to the Secretary of the Smithsonian, 1888–1889,* 1893, p. 531. Courtesy of Dyer Library.

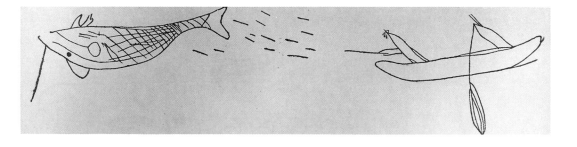

The presence of the Wabanakis in this rich and expansive habitat affected not only the animals they hunted but also the landscape itself. Like many other native groups, the Wabanakis periodically burned the land to improve its natural productivity and aid in hunting. For instance, in the valley of the Penobscot River, "the ground is plaine, without Trees or Bushes, but full of long Grasse, like unto a pleasant meadow, which the Inhabitants doe burne once a yeere to have fresh feed for their Deere."[11]

The Alnanbiaks: The Real People

The following description of the Wabanakis is an ethnohistorical composite, based on information winnowed from an array of archaeological, oral traditional, historical documentary, and ethnographic sources. As an assemblage, it reconstructs their culture as it existed when they first encountered Europeans on their shores. At this time, there may have been some thirty thousand Wabanakis living in northern New England and the Maritime Provinces.[12] They all spoke closely related languages or dialects belonging to the larger Algonquian family. Generally, these people referred to their own kinfolk as the Alnanbiaks, the Ulnooks, or some other term to express the idea of "real people" or "truly humans." These Wabanakis were divided into several major ethnic groups, also known as nations or tribes. Members of each particular ethnic group shared a territorial range and could be distinguished from the members of other groups primarily by a limited set of cultural features, including obvious identifications such as defined styles of dress and speech. The various Wabanaki groups maintained close relations, which allowed them to cope with mutual conflict resulting from intertribal competition for valued resources in their territories.[13]

In the early seventeenth century, French visitors to the region reported that the Wabanakis were divided into three such major groupings from northeast to southwest: the Souriquois, Etchemins, and Armouchiquois. Later these ethnonyms, as first recorded by Samuel de Champlain, were generally replaced by the terms Micmac, Maliseet-Passamaquoddy, Penobscot, and Abenaki (fig. 32). Although they were all linked to each other directly or indirectly by ties of kinship and friendship, they formed distinctive bands ranging in size from as few as fifty members to more than one thousand. These bands were formed primarily

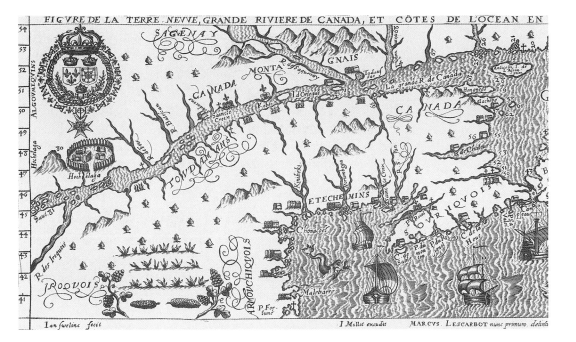

32. Extract from Marc Lescarbot, *Figure de la Terre Neuve, grand riviere de Canada, et cotes de l'ocean en la Nouvelle France,* in his *Histoire de la Nouvelle France,* 1609. Courtesy of National Archives of Canada, NMC 97952.

on the basis of voluntary association between related kin groups. Although individual status differences did exist, the social structure of these tribal communities was fundamentally egalitarian.

Accordingly, their political organization was based on democratic principles, and decisions concerning the commonweal were based on consensus among the members. Their chiefs, known as sagamores, were leaders who were recognized as first among equals. "They have Sagamores, that is, leaders in war; but their authority is most precarious. . . . The Indians follow them through the persuasion of example or of custom, or of ties of kindred and alliance."[14] Responsible for the well-being and general security of their communities, these Wabanaki sagamores presided over the warriors. One such chieftain was Chief Mentaurmet, the sagamore of Nebamocago, the largest of three Wabanaki villages in the Sheepscot River valley. When a party of strangers arrived, Chief Mentaurmet received them, accompanied by "about forty powerful young men stationed around [his wigwam] like a bodyguard, each one with his shield, his bow and arrows upon the ground in front of him."[15]

Under leadership of these sagamores, the bands usually moved seasonally within their own districts, from their particular hunting areas to their favorite fishing, clamming, sealing, and fowling sites. Dispersing in small family groups during the fall, bands re-joined in the spring, usually near rapids or falls where they lived on the basis of an abundance of spawning fish. At these tribal gatherings, sometimes many hundreds of people assembled at one site, exchanging information, making new friendships, find-ing spouses for their children, and engaging in barter.

In charge of the collective pursuit of subsistence, allied saga-mores made formal agreements with each other about territorial divisions within each tribal range. "These sagamies divide up the country and are nearly always arranged according to bays or rivers."[16] The territorial arrangements between the chieftains, each with his own following, enabled the kin groups to opti-mally exploit the ecological diversity of their allocated territory. These were usually situated along tributaries of the various rivers such as the Kennebec or Penobscot or in bays such as Passa-maquoddy. This way, regional bands could carefully adjust their food-collecting strategies to the seasonal rhythms of resident game animals, fish runs, and plant growth cycles without run-ning into conflict with their neighbors.[17]

Material Culture

As a Stone Age people, the Wabanakis tapped into the ever-shifting storehouse of nature for all their immediate supplies. Using primarily raw materials such as stone, bone, wood, and leather, they fabricated most of their own tools and weapons, in-cluding wooden bows and arrows, flint knives and scrapers, stone axes, bone fishhooks, long spears, and wooden clubs, as well as bark baskets, basswood fiber nets, rawhide snares, and traps. For example, bows were made of spruce or rock maple and were then polished with flaked stones or oyster shells and strung with moose sinew. Arrow shafts were made of white ash or young alders fitted with eagle feathers as flight-stabilizers and tipped with bone or flint points. Tribesmen fashioned lances from beech wood, equipping them with a sharply pointed moose bone, and crafted large cedar shields for protection.[18]

For winter travel, the Wabanakis used snowshoes made of white ash or beech, corded with leather thongs. To transport goods over the snow and ice, they used toboggans. As soon as the rivers became ice-free in the spring, they turned to their lightweight birch-bark canoes, which could seat as many as six or seven persons. Sometimes, these boats were made of spruce

33. W. R. Herries, painting of a small Maliseet camp on the banks of a river, 1850s. Courtesy of National Archives of Canada, C115891.

bark or even moose hide.[19] Especially on long-distance journeys, their seaborne craft were occasionally equipped with mast and sail, "which was . . . of bark but oftener of a well-dressed skin of a young Moose."[20]

Tree bark (white birch, as well as spruce) was used not only for the Wabanakis' canoes but also for covering their lodges. In addition to bark, they also used animal skins or woven mats as cover. Well accommodated inside, these wigwams were sometimes lined with "mats made of Rushes painted with several colours."[21] For added warmth, the Wabanakis used deerskins to line their winter quarters. Hemlock twigs or balsam fir needles usually covered the wigwam floor, on top of which were mats, hides, or soft sealskins, all spread around the central fireplace. In addition to the conical wigwam, which typically served as a one-family dwelling, the Wabanakis also built large communal or ceremonial lodges, sometimes measuring over one hundred feet long and thirty feet broad. The great wigwam at Nebamocago in the Sheepscot Valley, for example, could seat "fully eighty people"[22] (fig. 33).

Although the Wabanakis were familiar with pottery (since about three thousand years earlier), more popular were the many different types of birch-bark containers, which were "sowed with threads from Spruce [spruce] or white Cedar-roots, and garnished on the outside with flourisht works, and on the brims with glistering quills taken from the Porcupine, and dyed, some black, others red." They also made "dishes, spoons, trayes wrought very smooth and neatly out of the knots of wood, [and] baskets, bags, and matts woven with Sparke, bark of the Line-Tree [basswood?] and Rushes of several kinds, dyed as before, some black, blew, red, yellow, [as well as] bags of Porcupine quills, woven and dyed also."[23]

Traditional Hunters, Fishers, and Gatherers

Until the period of European contact in the sixteenth and early seventeenth centuries, the traditional Wabanaki mode of subsistence based on hunting, fishing, and gathering persisted in the territories east of the Kennebec River. In aboriginal northeastern North America, this river formed the northern boundary of an indigenous horticulture complex, which had originated in the highlands of Meso America some four thousand years ago.[24]

Beyond this ecological boundary, climatic conditions did not favor an indigenous neolithic revolution. Accordingly, long-standing food-collecting strategies persisted among eastern Wabanaki groups identified as Etchemin (Maliseet-Passamaquoddy) and Souriquois (Micmac).[25] Early Europeans described them as "a nomadic people, living in the forest and scattered over wide spaces, as is natural for those who live by hunting and fishing only."[26] In the pursuit of game, in particular moose, deer, and caribou, Wabanaki tribesmen chased the animals with the help of packs of hunting dogs. Among others, bear, beaver, and otter were also favored targets. Moreover, especially during the summer months, the Wabanakis also hunted water fowl and other birds.

When they were on the coast, they searched for harbor seal and gray seal, which supplied them not only with soft hide but also with meat and oil. This oil was highly valued as grease for their hair and bodies and was also considered "a relish at all the feasts they make among themselves."[27] Sometimes, they also hunted whales or feasted on stranded whales.[28] During their stay on the coast, "when the weather does not permit going on the hunt," they went digging for clams at the muddy flats.[29] Other shellfish were also enjoyed, in particular lobster, "some being 20 pounds in weight." Surplus lobster caught during the summer months was dried and stored for winter food. Lobster meat was also good for bait, "when they goe a fishing for Basse or Codfish."[30]

In addition to traps or weirs, made of wooden stakes and placed in a shallow stream or small tidal bay, Wabanaki fishers used nets, hooks, and lines. Harpoons served to take porpoise and sturgeon, and special three-pronged fish spears enabled the Wabanakis to catch salmon, trout, and bass. Taking their canoes on the water at night, they lured the fish with torches of burning birch bark. This way, a man could spear up to two hundred fish during one trip.[31]

Adding to their diversified diet, the Wabanakis tapped the sweet sap of the maple tree and harvested greens, wild fruits, nuts, seeds, and last but not least, edible roots and tubers. On the basis of such intimate knowledge of nature, some Wabanakis became specialists in herbal medicine. Benefiting from the medicinal qualities inherent in certain roots, leaves, and bark, these Wabanakis brewed select teas or prepared poultices to be used as remedies.[32]

Among these hunters and gatherers, the burden of labor seems to have fallen disproportionally on the shoulders of native women. As one outside observer noted:

> Besides the onerous role of bearing and rearing the children, [women] also transport the game from where it has fallen; they are the hewers of wood and drawwers of water; they make and repair the household utensils; they prepare food; they skin the game and prepare the hides like fullers; they sew garments; they catch fish and gather shellfish for food; often they even hunt; they make the canoes . . . out of bark; they set up the tents wherever and whenever they stop for the night—in short, the men concern themselves with nothing but the more laborious hunting and the waging of war. For this reason almost everyone has several wives.[33]

Those Wabanakis who were migratory hunters, fishers, and gatherers moved every six weeks or so and could set up a village within hours. Among their favorite haunts was a site known to them as Kenduskeag, located on a tributary to the Penobscot (at Bangor). Drawn by the abundance of eel that could be taken here, a regional band of about three hundred members returned to this location each fall, setting up eighteen seasonal lodges and constructing fish weirs. Although there were other seasonal villages as large as Kenduskeag, most of these temporary villages were much smaller. On the shores of the Bay of Fundy, for example, one such Wabanaki encampment consisted of no more than eight wigwams.[34]

Corn Planters in Southern Maine

Generally, the larger tribal communities existed in the region west of the Sheepscot. This area was inhabited by people originally named Armouchiquois (perhaps a derogative, meaning dogs) by their Souriquois neighbors.[35] In contrast to the eastern Wabanaki groups, who maintained a mode of subsistence based exclusively on hunting, fishing, and gathering, these Armouchiquois planted vegetable gardens. Having adopted the horticultural complex of tribes to the south shortly before the arrival of Europeans in the area (probably in the fifteenth century A.D.), these western Wabanaki groups grew hard flint corn, kidney beans, and squash, as well as tobacco, in their village gardens. Although precise estimates for the actual acreage under cultivation are unavailable, an average village with a population of four hundred "would have utilized between 330 and 580 acres of planting fields to insure subsistence maintenance over half a century."[36]

Using a technique called slash-and-burn, the Armouchiquois cleared fertile plains in river valleys. By stoking fires around the bases of standing trees, they burned the bark, thereby killing the trees. Later, they felled the dead trees with stone axes. As one tree toppled, it usually knocked down several others. Later, all this wood was removed by burning. Men cleared the land, and women took charge of the gardens. In May or early June, they planted the fields. With digging sticks, they made long rows of holes, about three feet apart. In each hole they put several corn and bean kernels. Several weeks later, they planted squash seeds in between the growing plants. As a result, the cornstalks became beanpoles, and the leaves of the squash vines smothered weeds. Once harvested, much of the corn was stored for the winter in large holes in the ground. Lined with dwarf-rush mats and covered with earth, each of these "barns" could hold some six to ten bushels. Meanwhile, the Armouchiquois continued to rely on traditional food-collecting strategies as well (fig. 34).[37]

figure des sauvages almouchicois

34. Armouchiquois man and woman. The woman has an ear of corn and a squash; the man carries a quiver on his back and holds an arrow in one hand and a European knife in the other. Detail from Samuel de Champlain, *Carte Geographique de la Nouvelle Franse,* 1612. Courtesy of John Carter Brown Library at Brown University.

In addition to the usual meals of roasted or boiled meat, fowl, fish, and so forth, the corn-growing Armouchiquois feasted on thick corn chowder mixed with clams, fish, meat, or other ingredients. When they traveled, they preferred a simple fare of parched cornmeal mixed with water, known as *nocake,* their equivalent of fast food. Supplementing the corn, they also ate beans and a large variety of edible wild plants. Finally, in the summer, "when their corne [was] spent," squash was "their best bread."[38]

Clearly, horticulture not only permitted higher population densities than in areas inhabited by migratory food collectors but also allowed for more permanent settlement patterns. Reluctant to leave their village gardens unprotected during periods of conflict, these Wabanaki corn growers had little alternative but to defend their settlements against hostile raiders. For instance, one fortified Armouchiquois village, located at the mouth of the Saco River, included "a large cabin surrounded by palisades made of large trees placed by the side of each other, in which they take refuge when their enemies make war upon them."[39]

Regional Trade Networks

Although the Wabanaki bands were mostly self-sufficient communities, their highly mobile way of life enabled them to easily cross territorial boundaries. During periods of peace, for instance, periodic expeditions to neighboring villages took place. However, when intertribal relations turned hostile, the bands could strike against their enemies. Although foot travel was not uncommon, they mostly used their swift canoes, which made travel much faster and easier (fig. 35).[40]

Etchemin and Souriquois hunting groups living east of the Kennebec traded with the Armouchiquois from Saco and elsewhere, who supplied them with surplus produce from their gardens, "to wit, corn, tobacco, beans, and pumpkins [squash]."[41] On their long-distance trading journeys, Wabanaki tribesmen in general bartered such things as beautiful furs, strong moose-hide moccasins, dressed deerskins, and moose hides with the Narragansett and other southern neighbors. These trade goods were exchanged for luxuries such as wampum (blue and white beads made of quahog shell). Wampum was a specialty of the Narragansett of Rhode Island. "From hence they [neighboring tribes] have most of their curious Pendants & Bracelets; from hence they have their great stone-pipes, which will hold a quarter of an ounce of Tobacco . . . they make them of greene, & sometimes of black stone [with Imagerie upon them]. . . . Hence likewise our Indians had their pots wherein they used to seeth their victuals."[42]

35. Detail showing Micmac canoes from Jean-Baptiste Louis Franquelin, *Carte pour servir a l'eclaircissement du Papier Terrier de la Nouvelle-France*, [1678]. Original in Bibliotheque Nationale, 125-1-1. Reproduced from a photograph in the National Archives of Canada, MNC 17393.

Personal Appearances

Described as "of average stature . . . handsome and well-shaped,"[43] the Wabanakis were generally "betweene five or six foote high, straight bodied, strongly composed, smooth skinned [and] merry countenanced."[44] Their robust life-style and ordinarily protein-rich diet made them a healthy people. Moreover, they made regular use of sweat baths, followed by massage, and "afterwards rubbing the whole body with seal oil" or other animal fat in order to "stand heat and cold better." By greasing themselves, they were also protected against "mosquitos, [which then] do not sting so much in the bare parts."[45] According to one early European traveler to the region, "You do not encounter a big-bellied, hunchbacked, or deformed person among them: those who are leprous, gouty, affected with gravel, or insane, are unknown to them."[46]

Their personal fashions, including hairstyle and ornamentation, not only reflected individual taste but also served as cultural markers indicating social divisions based on ethnic affiliation, rank, age, gender, or marital status. Decorative devices, such as headdresses, could involve colorful arrangements with bird feathers, wampum, dyed porcupine quills, or moose hair.[47]

Among eastern Wabanaki groups, in particular the Souriquois and Etchemin, adult men typically tied "a knot of [their hair] upon the crown of their head, some four of five fingers long, with a leather lace, which they let hang down behind."[48] Sometimes, a few bird feathers were woven into these topknots. When a warrior died, his relatives "upon his head stuck many feathers," before his burial.[49] In contrast to the adult men, boys wore their hair "of full length." They tied it "in tufts on the two sides with cords of leather." Some of them had their hair "ornamented with coloured Porcupine quills."[50]

At times, these eastern Wabanakis differed from their corn-growing neighbors west of the Sheepscot, who were clearly recognizable by their distinct hairstyle. Typically, these Armouchiquois shaved "their hair far up on the head," leaving it very long at the back, which they combed and twisted "in various ways very neatly, intertwined with feathers which they attach[ed] to the head."[51] Farther south, in Massachusetts Bay, tribesmen commonly wore their hair "tied up hard and short like a horse taile, bound close with a fillet . . . whereon they prick[ed] feathers of fowls in a fashion of a crownet."[52]

Sagamores were sometimes distinguished by their own particular headgear. Their prerogative was a bird with an aggressive reputation, described as a "black hawk" (probably the eastern kingbird). Viewed as a symbol of their bravery, the dead bird's "dried body" was affixed to the topknot in their hair. Although most Wabanaki men plucked out their scant facial hair, some chieftains distinguished themselves by growing beards.[53]

Among the eastern Wabanakis, in particular the Souriquois, adult women generally wore their hair loose on their shoulders. However, those who were not yet married wore theirs "also full length, but tie[d] it behind with the same cords." They beautified themselves by making "ornamental pieces of the size of a foot or eight inches square, all embroidered with Porcupine quills of all colours." One visitor described the ornament: "It is made on a frame, of which the warp is threads of leather from unborn Moose, a very delicate sort; the quills of Porcupine form the woof which they pass through these threads. . . . All around they make a fringe of the same threads, which are also encircled with these Porcupine quills in a medley of colours. In this fringe they place wampum, white and violet."[54]

In addition to wearing wampum necklaces and bracelets, Wabanaki men as well as women also pierced their ears, often in several places. Special pendants "as formes of birds, beasts, and fishes, carved out of bone, shels, and stone" hung from their pierced ears, in which they sometimes also stuck "long feathers or hares' tails."[55]

As noted earlier, Wabanaki tribesmen also used paint to distinguish themselves. "When they goe to their warres, it is their custome to paint their faces with a diversitie of colours, some being all black as jet, some red, some halfe red and halfe black, some blacke and white, others spotted with diver kinds of colours, being all distinguished to their enemies, to make them more terrible to their foes."[56] For instance, whereas Etchemin tribesmen at Pemaquid painted "their bodies with black; their faces, some with red, some with black, and some with blue,"[57] Souriquois mariners on the southern Maine coast were reported to have had "their eyebrows painted white."[58]

The Wabanakis, as well as their southern neighbors, also marked their skin with red and black tattoos. Among the Souriquois, and probably among the other native groups as well, women tattooed the skin of their husbands or lovers. At the Massachusetts coast, for instance, tribesmen had "certaine round Impressions downe the outside of their armes and brestes, in forme of mullets [stars] or spur-rowels [and] bearing upon their cheekes certaine pourtraitures of beasts, as Beares, Deares, Mooses, Wolves, &c, some of fowls, as of Eagles, Hawkes, &c."[59] These designs probably represented their animal guardian spirits or family totems. The Wabanakis believed that wearing such tattoos endowed them with special spirit power.

Garments were made by the women, who dressed the hides by scraping them and rubbing them with sea-bird oil. Next, the women cut the supple leather and stitched the pieces together as robes, mantles, breechclouts, leggings, or moccasins. Finally, the leather was painted or "ornamented with embroidery," using dyed moose hair or flattened porcupine quills. In addition to making a "lace-like pattern" or "broken chevrons," they also "studded [their clothing] with figures of animals," which were probably symbolic as well.[60] Small, funnel-sized copper objects, made of thin sheets rolled into form, were also used to embellish their clothing. Sometimes, the "leather buskins" of Wabanaki children were also decorated with these "little round pieces of red copper."[61]

During the warmer seasons, Wabanaki men usually donned a mantle made of smoothly dressed white moose hide or tanned deerskin, along with a soft leather breechclout, leggings, and moose-hide or sealskin moccasins. Usually, the moose-hide moccasins were made from old and greasy leather coats, which the women "embellish with dye & an edging of red and white Porcupine quills."[62] Occasionally, the men also wore coats made of wild goose or turkey feathers. When the weather turned cold, they were warmly dressed in thick fur robes made of beaver, otter, raccoon, or even bear skins. Black wolves were also highly valued; these furs were "esteemed a present for a prince" among the native peoples of the region.[63]

Place-Names: Turning the Landscape into a Map

Native place-names in Wabanaki territories generally convey essential geographic information, describing the distinctive features of a locality such as its physical appearance, its specific dangers, or its precious resources. A name might, for instance, note where certain animals could be hunted, fish netted, or plants harvested. Specifically, *Shawokotec* (for Saco) referred to "the outlet of the river," *Pemaquid* signified "it is situated far out," *Machias* described "bad little falls," *Olamon* was the spot where "red ochre" for paint could be found, *Passamaquoddy* was attractive as "the place with plenty of pollock," *Kenduskeag* was the "eel-weir place," and *Cobossecontee* (near Gardiner) was "the place where "sturgeon could be found."[64]

Such place-names show how thoroughly familiar the Wabanakis were with the particular challenges and opportunities of their habitat. Ranging widely throughout northeastern North America, Wabanaki tribespeople depended dearly on such topographic marking points for their physical survival. Accumulating over hundreds, perhaps even thousands, of years, their individual experiences were committed to collective memory not only in the form of place-names but also in the form of tribal lore, tales, legends, songs, and, ultimately, myths. Thus embedded in their cultural fabric, place-names contain vital elements of ecological knowledge. Indeed, the purpose of place-names was "to turn the landscape into a map which, if studied carefully, literally gave a village's inhabitants the information they needed to sustain themselves."[65]

On their journeys, moving swiftly in their lightweight birch-bark canoes, the Wabanakis were guided by this knowledge. Place-names might indicate where to expect such difficulties as swift currents, dangerous rapids, and gravel bars or might suggest which fork to take or where to portage to a connecting travel route. Such information was crucial, especially when traveling for purposes of long-distance trade or raiding parties, but also during regular seasonal migrations. To this day, many place-names in New England and the Maritimes still contain elements of ancient Wabanaki toponyms.

Beyond the previously mentioned ecological toponyms, some place-names may derive from certain political realities in traditional Wabanaki society. For instance, early seventeenth-century European records reveal that Wabanaki tribesmen inhabiting the Maine coast in that period referred to the region from Cape Neddick to Schoodic Point (the end) as *Mawooshen* (also spelled *Moasson*).[66] Under this name, they apparently understood an area "fortie leagues in bredth, and fiftie in length, [comprising] nine rivers, [namely the] Quibiquesson, Pemaquid, Ramassoc, Apanawapeske, Apaumensek, Aponeg, Sagadehoc, Ashamahaga, Shawokotec."[67] Although we may always remain in the dark about the precise meaning of *Mawooshen,* it probably refers not to a stretch of land but to the confederacy of allied villages under a regional grand chief known as the Bashabes.

Other place-names make sense only in the context of native culture — place-names whose meanings are expressed in the context of the Wabanakis' particular worldview as recounted in myth. Traditional native storytellers attributed many topographic features in the landscape to the legendary activities of Gluskap, their culture-hero, who shaped the earth in a particular way so as to make it "a happy land for the people."[68] According to one story, rivers such as the Penobscot were formed when Gluskap killed the monster frog that had caused a world drought. The released waters streamed down the mountainsides toward the sea. Gluskap paddled along the coast in his canoe and entered all the rivers emptying into the ocean. "He inspected them. Wherever there were bad falls he lessened them so they would not be too dangerous for his descendants. He cleared the carrying places. Then he left his canoe upside down where it turned to stone [near Castine]. It may be seen there yet."[69]

In another legend, Gluskap beached his canoe on the eastern shore of Penobscot Bay and chased a moose up into the woods for a great distance.

> On the beach at the point mentioned is a rock about twenty-five feet long, shaped like an overturned canoe. The rocks leading from it bear footprints of Gluskap, which reappear frequently in the interior of the country according to some of the Indians who claim to have seen them. At another place farther down he killed the moose and cast its entrails across the water. There they still appear as a streak of white rock on the bottom of the bay at Cape Rosier. After cooking the moose he left his cooking pot overturned on the shore of Moosehead Lake and it is now to be seen as Kineo mountain on the eastern margin. . . . When the Indians find stones possessing natural shapes, resembling a face or a person, they sometimes keep them [saying]: "It looks like Gluskap, I guess he left his picture on it."[70]

Native Cartography

Although there are no indications that the Wabanakis kept permanent cartographic collections, there is evidence that they made maps for temporary needs. If, for instance, a local scout

36. *Wikhegan* map on birch bark (ca. 1840) by Gabrien Acquin, a Maliseet, describing his hunting trip. The *wikhegan* was left for his friend, who had gone down the river. From Mallery, "Picture-Writing of the American Indians," 336. Courtesy of Dyer Library.

encountered enemy tribesmen secretly roaming in the area, he would illustrate this for his kinsmen by scratching on a piece of bark a picture of the place, indicating the streams, points, and other landmarks. Sometimes, he would leave incisions in the bark of a tree near a stream, where his friends would follow by canoe, or place sticks on a trail, indicating that a message in picture writing, known as a *wikhegan*, was hidden nearby.[71]

Commenting on the use of such *wikhegan* among the Wabanakis inhabiting the Kennebec River area, a French missionary reported: "There [one of the tribesmen] took the bark of a tree, upon which with coal he drew [a picture of] the English around me, and one of them cutting off my head. (This is all the writing the Indians have, and they communicate among themselves by these sorts of drawings as understandingly as we do by our letters). He then put this kind of letter around a stick which he planted on the bank of the river, to give news to those passing by of what had happened to me" (see fig. 36).[72]

Wikhegan also served to depict regional maps. "They have much ingenuity in drawing upon bark a kind of map which marks exactly all the rivers and streams of a country of which they wish to make a representation. They mark all the places thereon exactly and so well that they make use of them successfully, and an Indian who possesses one makes long voyages without going astray" (see figs. 37 and 38).[73]

At certain points on the travel routes of the Wabanakis, tribespeople marked messages on rock ledges, which may have served as information centers. Traditionally, such *wikhegan* could be found on the ledges in Hampden Narrows, which was therefore

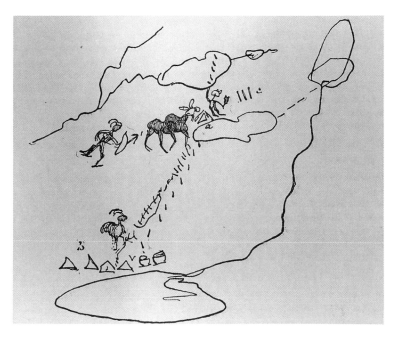

37. *Wikhegan* map on birch bark (ca. 1800) by Chief Selmo Soctomah, a Passamaquoddy Chief from Pleasant Point, describing a moose hunt. From Mallery, "Picture-Writing of the American Indians," 339. Courtesy of Dyer Library.

known as *Edalawikekhadimuk* (place where are markings). These marks probably indicated "the exact number of canoes going up and down the river."[74] Such markings also existed at Fort Point in Stockton Springs, a place the Wabanakis knew as *Aguahassidek* (stepping ashore). One of the traditional Penobscot tribal leaders recounted that "on their annual trip to salt water for the purpose of fishing," his ancestors "gave names to a number of places along the bay and river." Landing on the west bank of the river where it flows into Penobscot Bay, "they only stopped long enough to make the sign of their visit, showing which direction they were going, the number of their party and canoes, etc. On account of its being a marking place no one was ever allowed to mar or deface its outline by using it for a camping ground."[75]

Today, remarkable petroglyphs with canoes, birds, moose, humans, and other designs remain visible on a ledge at the west bank of the upper Kennebec River (Embden). Similar glyphs can still be seen on coastal rocks at Machias Bay (Birch Point). One mark at Machias appears to represent a native woman with seafowl on her head. One local Passamaquoddy hunter interpreted this symbol to mean "that squaw had smashed canoe, saved beaver-skin, walked one-half moon all over alone toward east, just same as heron wading alongshore." The hunter also noted that the three lines hammered out below the figure together resembled a bird track, or a trident, and represented the three rivers —the East, West, and Middle rivers of Machias—that merge not far above Birch Point (fig. 39).[76]

Wenooch: Who Are These Strangers?

Thinking themselves to be the easternmost people on earth, the Wabanakis were unaware of Europeans until they sighted the first sailing ships in the early sixteenth century. Initially amazed to see bearded strangers landing on their shores, they "could not get over their wonder as they gazed at our customs, our clothing, our arms, our equipment," reported one of the early French visitors to the area.[77] Their original surprise is reflected in the Wabanaki name for the alien-looking invaders from across the ocean: *wenooch* (stranger), derived from their word for "who is that?" Other telling names, used by neighboring tribes, include "boatmen" (*mistekoushou*), "coat-men" (*wautaconauog*), and "sword-men" or "knife-men" (*chauquaquock*).[78] New technologies, in particular steel knives, hatchets, copper kettles, glass beads, awls, mirrors, woolen cloth, and eventually firearms, were especially appreciated by the Wabanakis and could be had in exchange for wild animal pelts.

38. *Wikhegan* map on birch bark (ca. 1885) by Nicholas Francis, an old Penobscot hunter (from Old Town), representing a beaver trapping district near Moosehead Lake. From Mallery, "Picture-Writing of the American Indians," 338. Courtesy of Dyer Library.

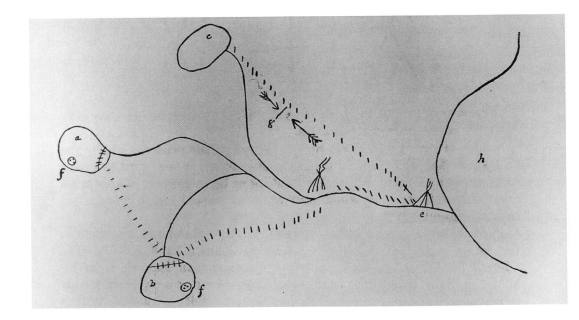

39. Petroglyphs at Birch Point, Machias Bay. From Mallery, "Picture-Writing of the American Indians," 1893, plate 12. Courtesy of Dyer Library.

Despite their sometimes high regard for European innovations, the Wabanakis typically regarded the strangers "as physically inferior" and "found them ugly, especially because of their excessive hairiness."[79] According to one early European who lived among the Wabanakis: "[They] regard themselves as much richer than we are. . . . Also they consider themselves more ingenious, [and] they conclude generally that they are superior to all christians."[80] An eastern Wabanaki (Micmac) tribesman may have revealed the natives' typical attitude toward the Europeans who landed on their shores when he said: "You deceive yourself greatly if you think to persuade us that your country is better than ours. For if France, as you say, is a little terrestrial paradise, are you sensible to leave it?"[81]

Although no early Wabanaki maps on birch bark or other material are believed to have survived, some documentary records indicate native cartographic skills. A wonderful piece of evidence concerning native mapmaking skill is a reference in Captain Bartholomew Gosnold's account of his voyage to the Maine coast in 1602. Referring to a surprise encounter with a party of Souriquois traders at Cape Neddick, he reported, "One that seemed to be their commander . . . with a piece of chalk described the coast thereabouts, and could name Placentia [Plaisance] of the Newfoundland."[82]

Other early European records comment on the guiding skills of Wabanaki tribesmen living in the Pemaquid coastal region. Sir

Ferdinando Gorges, for example, a well-known English entrepreneur who acquired colonial title over parts of Maine as its "Lord Proprietor," wrote that he understood the natives themselves to be "exact pilots for that coast [between Cape Cod and Cape Breton], having been accustomed to frequent the same, both as fishermen, and in passing along the shore to seek their enemies."[83]

During the same period, the French navigator Samuel de Champlain ran into some native mariners off Cape Ann, who offered him an accurate description of the region ahead. "I made them understand, as best as I could, that they should show me how the coast lay. After having depicted for them, with a piece of charcoal, the bay and the Island Cape, where we were, they represented for me, with the same crayon, another [Massachusetts] bay, which they showed as very large. They put six pebbles at equal distances, thus giving me to understand that each of these stood for as many chiefs and tribes. Then they represented within this bay a river [Merrimac] which we had passed, which extends very far."[84]

But, given the strategic potential of geographic intelligence, it is understandable that Wabanaki tribesmen became increasingly reluctant informants when strangers came to their lands requesting vital geographic information, such as the location of lakes, rivers, mountains, and other marking points in the landscape. This resentment became clear when an English surveyor requested their help on an expedition to the upper Penobscot and Moosehead Lake region in the 1760s. "The Indians are so jealous of their countrey being exposed by this survey," he wrote, "as made it impractable for us to perform this work with acqurice."[85] When finally a few tribesmen were induced to serve as guides, they did so on condition that the foreigners take no notes and make no maps.[86]

Their request was not heeded. Soon, an abstract grid of meridians and parallels clamped the wilderness. Forced to yield to analytical cartographic representation, Ketakamigwa was no longer terra incognita to the strangers. Powerless to shield their homeland from European intruders, the Wabanakis may have recalled what their divine hero Gluskap told them as he climbed on the back of a giant whale to travel to an unknown island in the western seas: "I shall leave you and shall hearken no more to your calling, but shall wait the calling of the Great Spirit. Strange things shall happen, but those who bring about the changes will tell you all about them so you may understand them."[87] Indeed, the Wabanakis have come to understand the changes, and all too well. Yet, as Gluskap's children, they endure and "look for the end of their oppressions and troubles when he comes back."[88]

CHAPTER FIVE

Mapping Otherness
Myth and the Study of Cultural Encounter

Kenneth M. Morrison

The historic encounter of northeastern Algonquians and Europeans derived from mythic antecedents. A large literature has explored the intellectual heritage Europeans brought to discovery, but little has been done to reveal Native American thinking on the other side of the frontier.[1] Native American reactions have been overlooked because scholars have commonly rejected mythology as merely imaginative stories and have favored written history as an objective and therefore truer form of memory. In fact, continuing to reject oral tradition as a primary historical source ignores much interdisciplinary work about the nature of myth and so distorts our understanding of history.[2] Northeastern Algonquian myth actually makes it possible to reconstruct the reality assumptions that shaped Native American assessment of European humanity.[3] These stories show that from the beginning of contact, Algonquians had an informed and realistic view of the challenges of cultural encounter.

To begin with, it must be recognized that the difficulty of mapping an Indian view of contact stems not from a poverty of written sources but from a failure to explore in innovative ways the alternative records that do exist. Jonathan Z. Smith, historian of religion, reminds us that even with written records, the historical enterprise is always secondary, derivative. Smith's now famous dictum, "map is not territory," suggests that stories ought to be studied for the cultural evidence that they do embody.[4] Myth and folklore document the vital mentality and adaptive imagination used by northeastern Algonquians to shape their side of the discovery process.

To map the sources of the Algonquians' encounter with new, European forms of cultural otherness therefore requires several levels of inquiry. Initially, the tension between myth and history must be resolved. Here students of folklore, sociolinguistics, religious studies, and anthropology offer methods of reevaluating the manner in which all humans orient themselves in time and space.[5] Second, once we appreciate that the encounter between Europeans and Algonquians entailed a clash of religious meanings about the nature of past, present, and future, then the mythic orientations of northeastern cultures can be studied with considerable precision to reveal the Algonquians' sense that the historical contact with Europeans was tumultuous. Finally, the lessons of mythology—explored in story and applied in historical action—can lead to a reevaluation of contact: there was more to that story than Europeans, as historians have since realized. In fact, the study of mythology makes it possible to reverse an ethnohistorical dependence on European documents. Recorded Algonquian stories allow us to read European documents with an eye to distinctive Native American perspectives toward the era of discovery.

The study of mythology reveals the ways in which particular cultures come to be created and the ways in which such primary stories influence historical change. Creation myths ponder the beginning in order to weigh the ethical dilemmas people face in the present.[6] It is crucial to recognize that myth is not fixed in a canonical text true for all times and places. To the contrary, spoken myth is lived—uttered, sung, danced, and applied in the countless ethical decisions in which people make sense of their lives.[7]

Myth is central to the study of cultural encounter precisely because it provides the template shaping a people's ongoing production of ethnic identity. Mythic stories require a dynamic re-

lationship between storyteller and audience. In this way, myth
produces meaning dialogically in the give-and-take of agreement and disagreement. The thrust of myth—this is important,
valuable, this isn't—derives directly from the cosmogonic fact of
violence and disagreement since the beginning of time. If ethnic
identity provides some security in a world of hostile others, then
it derives from a people's agreement on common values. In this
sense, intercultural contact ought to be studied as a potentially
decentering situation in which people come to question their
values, resulting in their identity being sustained or threatened.
Of course, the opposite might be simultaneously true: myth de-
clares that for northeastern Algonquians, cultural survival consisted of finding stories that explained the reason for conflict and
that mapped out the remaining constructive possibilities.

Myth and the Religious Nature of Otherness

Algonquian cultures all shared the same symbolic social orientation in understanding and working with the religious problem
and challenge of otherness. Given their northeastern ecological
setting, particular forms of otherness were given in their creation mythology. Algonquians opposed the positive person Summer against the threatening person Winter. They also juxtaposed
nurturing relatives with dangerous strangers. They recognized
a frightening tension between center and periphery, between
the hunting camp—the particular domain of women, shaped by
the domestic values of sharing—and the forest—the domain of
men, where danger and violence prevailed. These culturally per-
vasive symbolic tensions can best be seen in the way in which
Algonquian myth ascribes positive, sharing power to the culture
hero Gluskap and threatening, antisocial power to the forest-
and winter-dwelling cannibal giants variously called windigo,
kiwakwe, and chenoo.[8]

Gluskap the hero embodies the creativity through which the
world can be transformed for human well-being, but he is not
a godlike being. His stories convey the central mores of Algonquian religious practice. Religious responsibility, he taught, begins with a compassion tempered by necessity. For example,
Gluskap confronted selfish evil from the start. One story relates
that he killed his twin brother, Malsum the Wolf. Malsum, like

40. Bentwood box, probably Penobscot, mid-nineteenth century, displaying the double-curve motif characteristic of the Indians of Maine and the Canadian Maritime Provinces. Courtesy of Maine State Museum.

the cannibal giants, cared only for himself. He killed his and Gluskap's mother by slicing through her flesh rather than endure the normal pain of being born.[9]

Like the world itself in that beginning time, Gluskap was still unformed, and so adversity shaped his character. He made mistakes, and his stories show that in itself error is not evil. Rather, Gluskap dignifies human struggle by learning the hard way. One myth says that for the best of motives, Gluskap trapped and penned up all the world's animals and netted all the fish. Touched by the gesture, Gluskap's grandmother, Woodchuck, nonetheless chided him for his excess. Gluskap released the captives so that his descendants might live.[10] Another story reveals Gluskap in the process of taking revenge. Evil entities had kidnapped his grandfather, and Gluskap pursued. When he caught up with the malefactors, he discovered their fear of retribution. Having already learned the compassionate key lesson of caring for others, Gluskap stayed his hand.[11]

In Gluskap's mythic cycle, the development of personal maturity through sensitive concern for others goes hand in hand with world transformation. In a series of actions, Gluskap countered the baleful impact of hostile entities who had shrugged off other people's well-being. Enlisting the cooperation of others, Gluskap abated callous Winter, moderated Wind, who threatened to destroy the world, and slew a giant frog who had hoarded all the world's water.

Although everything Gluskap did transformed the world for the better, slaying the frog has special significance for understanding the intimacy of Algonquian relations with animals. After being deprived of water by the frog and dying of thirst, many of the people rushed into the waters now flowing freely over the Northeast and were transformed into fish and animals. Algonquians denote the nature of this new kind of otherness with the term *ntu'tem,* a form of the more familiar anthropological term *totem. Ntu'tem* means both "my relative of a strange race" and "my spouse's parents." Both senses of the word indicate how Algonquians conceptualized the religious ideal of solidarity between what Europeans and Euramericans separate as humans and animals. Treating animal others as kin also suggests that Algonquians were willing to extend themselves positively to European others as well.

When Gluskap left the Algonquians (an event that some stories place at the coming of Europeans), he left a religious heritage of ritual acts empowering people with responsibility for the ongoing job of maintaining and transforming the world. Gluskap's power, *ktaha'ndo,* continued to provide what the anthropologist Frank G. Speck calls the "social dynamics" of Algonquian life. Translated as the highest power, *ktaha'ndo* should be understood as the primal origin of all world-affecting abilities, the category of power that Algonquians call *manitou.* Gluskap's life shows that power could be used and abused and, thus, that correct living consisted of compassionate confronting of antisocial adversity. If threatening otherness was a fact of life, then Gluskap showed the possibility of cooperation.[12]

It follows that Algonquian religion stressed that the struggle against the dangers of otherness had high value and that people (human and otherwise) faced responsibility. For example, when No-chi-gar-neh, the great person Air, empowered the first shamans, he warned them not to use power against their fellows. In these ways, then, Gluskap and No-chi-gar-neh established the ethical premises by which Algonquian peoples faced the challenge of history. Theirs were not defeatist religions. To the contrary, Algonquians knew by definition that present trouble needs to be faced constructively. For them, religion concerns the myriad ways in which they confronted hostile others and mediated their dangers.[13]

If Gluskap modeled positive power, the cannibal giants embodied antisocial divisiveness, a disordered violence that existed both in the cosmos and in history. Categorically, entities of the cannibal giant class shared a vicious, envious, and selfish nature. Cannibal giants expressed the antithesis of the cosmic ideal of cooperation. They were responsible for their own degradation because they not only refused to share but also actively betrayed other people's trust. Having the power of metamorphosis, the ability to shift form, cannibal giants were insidious, pretending to be long-lost relatives only to bide their time before indulging their perverse appetite for human flesh. In this way, cannibals also revealed the effects of violating the kinship ideals that Gluskap had established as the order-generating norm.

Cannibals were creatures of winter and of the forest outside the domestic world of safety, which derived from Gluskap's world transformation. As such, cannibals threatened positive social relations. The cannibal giants defined the social adversity that Algonquians faced in everyday life, both inside and outside the kinship group. Since Algonquians understood that power could be used for good or ill, uncertainty about alien others (and even about relatives) defined the religious challenge and so shaped the religious task. Algonquians knew that human beings could become cannibals, just as they themselves could follow Gluskap's benevolent lead. Supportive and threatening others defined their cosmos and thus exposed the tensions people always face in their relations with each other.

Using power to harm others became the hallmark of cannibal perfidy, but Algonquians also understood that there were ways to deal with even the most intransigent cannibals. Gluskap held out hope. Shamans with impeccable concern for others' well-being could effectively counter the cannibal threat. More, since humans became cannibals because they hardened their hearts to their kin, humane care also held out the potential of a transformative cure. A number of stories from all over the Algonquian Northeast indicate that considerate social relations could begin the process of healing. The stories show that when addressed as father or grandfather, the cannibal reacted invariably with astonishment. In addition, when Algonquians persisted in expressing real personal concern against cannibal estrangement, they conveyed to even the most antisocial monsters the possibility of constructive change. Such stories are vitally important because they demonstrate that although Algonquians appreciated that life and danger were synonymous, they also knew that Gluskap had given them effective power. When the stranger threatened, kindness offered the hope of a more constructive alliance.[14]

Before examining how these polarized mythic principles shaped Algonquian reaction to European others, we should note a final mythological lesson: myth encapsulates the fluctuating tensions that shaped Algonquian history. Myth remembers history as moral challenge and so records Algonquians' general conviction that Gluskap gave them a religious system that worked. The advent of Europeans, of course, posed the possibility that there were other ways of doing things, and myth recalls that Algonquians considered that possibility.

Encountering Otherness: Applying Gluskap's Lessons

There is no doubt that Native Americans scrutinized European newcomers from the vantage point of traditional concepts of power and that they perceived Europeans' technological advantage. But technological muscle did not produce a sense of cultural inferiority in the Indians. It has become a scholarly commonplace that Native Americans enthusiastically adopted selected aspects of European material culture.[15] It is also certain that technological prowess alone mattered little to Algonquian assessments of European character. Mythological thinking in terms of Gluskap and cannibal giants concerned itself with the social implications of technology. As a culture creator, Gluskap showed that technology ought to be bent to human welfare. Gluskap's teachings effectively rejected European-style materialism. Europeans, of course, used materialistic thinking as the main rationale for judging Indians as savage, but Algonquians recognized and rejected that way of assessing cultural otherness. Algonquian evaluations of European others were far more cogent. Whereas Europeans dismissed Native American humanity in negative terms—they did not have technology, law, or religion—Algonquians used precise behavioral criteria. Just as Gluskap taught, Algonquians valued people who used power for socially constructive purposes. Since Europeans often acted in grasping, profit-seeking ways, their behavior declared, albeit nonverbally, that they were not to be trusted. Cannibal fears, rather than supernaturalistic awe, shaped the Algonquian reaction to European strangers.[16]

The difference between historians' common assumption that

41. This seventeenth-century brass kettle was typical of those traded to the Wabanakis. It was excavated at a Native American site on the Penobscot River near Winterport, Maine. Courtesy of Maine State Museum.

Native Americans were in awe of European discoverers and the Algonquians' actual response can be glimpsed in a 1605 encounter between the Wabanakis and an English party led by George Weymouth. The Weymouth expedition not only reveals factors that escape an awe theory but also illustrates the English treachery that told the Wabanakis that these newcomers threatened their traditional moral universe.

Although he certainly thought of himself as having the upper hand, Weymouth met the Wabanakis at a disadvantage. Europeans were late in forging a direct trading relationship with the Indians of Maine, but by 1605 the Wabanakis had had the better part of a hundred years to plumb European morality. In the years before Weymouth's reconnoiter, the Wabanakis had met many other explorers and, more important, had forged trading relationships with the neighboring Micmacs and Montagnais, who had more regular contact with European fishermen.

Weymouth's account of his encounter shows that the Wabanakis had come to appreciate both the opportunities and the dangers of commercial contact. Weymouth did not realize that two other English voyages in 1602 and 1603 had left a bad impression.[17] Probably for this reason, the Wabanakis were none too eager to board Weymouth's ship. Instead, the Wabanaki spokesman declaimed so "very lowd and very boldly" that the English "conjectured that [they] should be gone." Weymouth was inclined to caution when he found the Wabanakis "a people of exceeding good invention, quicke understanding and redie capacity." This assessment certainly contradicts Weymouth's suggestion that he wielded the upper hand. To convey his supposed superiority, Weymouth magnetized a sword so that the Indians would "imagine some great power" and "for that to love and feare" the English.[18] Weymouth achieved nothing of the sort.

The Wabanakis thought that they had good reason to stand their ground: the English noted that they were "very jealous" of their women. Nor did the Wabanakis capitulate to English wiles. When Weymouth invited two of them to sleep aboard his ship, their companions refused unless some of the English slept ashore. Rather than awe, therefore, the Wabanakis acted out of a sense of studied distrust and, further, countered English guile effectively. Despite their caution, Weymouth returned to England carrying six captives, thus confirming the bad impression.[19]

The Weymouth voyage marks a watershed in what would be a long history of violence in Wabanaki-English relations. Two of the captives made it back to Maine, where they showed that they had had ample opportunity to come to despise English character. Nahanada sailed with Martin Pring in 1606, and Skidwarres returned with the Popham colonists in 1607. Forcing Skidwarres to lead him to a village, Captain Raleigh Gilbert met people determined to resist but willing to communicate. The conversation conveyed nothing to ease Wabanaki doubts. Two days later, the entire village suddenly withdrew "them Selves from us into the woods and Left us." Sill wanting to make a good impression, Gilbert released Skidwarres, and the Popham colonists sailed west to settle on the lower Kennebec River.[20]

The brief history of the Popham Colony reveals that the Wabanakis remained confident in their relations with the newcomers. However, the colony's existence led to factional tensions among the Wabanaki people. Skidwarres and Nahanada urged their fellows to withhold vital support, and after the death of George Popham, the settlers' resentment led to open violence. Retaliating, the Wabanakis killed eleven colonists and brought the colony to an end. A French Jesuit, Pierre Biard, provides direct evidence that the Wabanakis were assured by tradition that they had the means to cauterize wounds inflicted by inconsiderate strangers.

42. Samuel de
Champlain visited
the mouth of the
Kennebec in 1605,
two years before the
Popham Colony estab-
lished itself there.
Samuel de Champlain,
Quinibequay, from
his *Les Voyages,* 1613.
Taken from the 1878
reprint, courtesy of
Dyer Library.

"These people make a practice of killing by magic," the priest observed.[21]

Wabanaki oral tradition indicates, however, that even the use of power in defensive war had ominous, long-range implications. The story remembers that European contact created tribal divisiveness and recounts that in choosing shamans to watch the colonists, the Wabanakis triggered resentment among shamans who were overlooked. Shamanistic rivalries were the direct result. More seriously, some shamans went so far as to threaten to use their power against any of their fellows who aided the English enemy. In this way, the shamans brazenly flouted Gluskap's injunction that power ought to be used positively. Coercion violated the religious norm. Thus, although the Wabanakis successfully eliminated the Popham Colony, the shamans' threats suggested that they too were dangerous. If the Algonquians came to experience a crisis of faith, that too derived from tradition.[22]

The study of mythology is essential to understanding the course of Indian-white relations because the stories reveal the motives that lay behind the Algonquian behavior that European documents describe. Almost to the man, English chroniclers thought Algonquians beneath regard. Henry Hudson expressed the typical contempt when, in a single afternoon's frenzy, he ransacked a Penobscot village and reported the event without justification or apology.[23] In the face of such violence, the fact that some Algonquians continued to strive for workable relations suggests the power of Gluskap's constructive ideal of alliance even with monsters. The mythical ideal of cooperation explains why Algonquians considered themselves morally superior to European others, giving them the confidence to meet violence with righteous contempt. A Micmac put the indictment succinctly to the French Jesuit Pierre Biard: "We are not thieves like you."[24] This statement was no isolated condemnation.[25]

Given the events of the seventeenth century, it is all too easy to think of northeastern Algonquian peoples as unwitting victims of European invaders. Events were monumental—wave upon wave of devastating epidemics pummeled the Algonquian peoples, liquor took its toll, political factionalism reflected an ongoing religious crisis as individual communities struggled with the ideal of solidarity, and war with the English became a way of life. Europeans loomed large in Algonquian existence, and in defining the Algonquian understanding of an enemy, Dr. Peter Paul pinpoints what was fundamentally at contest. The word *enemy*, said Dr. Paul, "means he hates you as much as you hate him."[26] The stories themselves remember the central dilemma of that animosity.

Myth texts reveal that Algonquians rethought the character of the beginning of time in order to account for the great others of European religion. Gluskap remained at the center of Algonquian history, sometimes as Christ's first created person and sometimes as his partner. In either case, a telling historical lesson emerged: Gluskap's power for creating solidarity continued to define the religious goal both in internal relations with relatives and in external relations with dangerous outsiders. Moreover, in identifying Adam both as the father of Europeans and as the source of antisocial evil in the world, Algonquian myth continued to identify cosmic and cultural otherness (now understood in terms of an earthly geography of differing forms of ethnicity) as both challenge and opportunity.[27] In postcontact history, Gluskap's teachings became all the more urgent.

CHAPTER SIX

Trade and Alliances in the Contact Period

Bruce J. Bourque and
Ruth H. Whitehead

Europeans who voyaged to the Gulf of Maine between 1602 and 1610 found that European manufactured goods were abundant among the native people. These goods have been widely assumed to have come from European traders or fishermen who were expanding from their bases in the Gulf of St. Lawrence. On the contrary, European visits to the Gulf of Maine before 1610 were infrequent and were intent on exploration, not trade.

This issue is important to understanding the ethnohistory of this region. Attributing the early fur trade in the Gulf of Maine to the European presence there has obscured the fact that the commerce was actually initiated by groups of acculturated native middlemen from the eastern Gulf of Maine and Nova Scotia. Thus, the extent of native adaptation to, even active exploitation of, the European presence has not been recognized. Indeed, these

"Trade and Alliances in the Contact Period" is a revised version of "Tarrentines and the Introduction of European Trade Goods in the Gulf of Maine," Bruce Bourque and Ruth Whitehead, *Ethnohistory* 32:4, copyright 1985, Duke University Press. Reprinted with permission of the publisher.

middlemen interacted with and emulated Europeans so extensively that the very cultural dichotomy between native and European, a dichotomy that is axiomatic to most historical studies of the fur trade, becomes blurred.

Europeans in the Gulf of Maine in the Sixteenth Century

When Bartholomew Gosnold led the first major English expedition to explore the New England coast in 1602, one member of the company, John Brereton, observed that the natives there possessed "a great store of copper, some very redde, and some of a paler colour."[1] The following year, Martin Pring, another Englishman, reported that some of the natives residing at what is now Saco, Maine, had "plates of Brasse a foot long, and half a foote broad before their breasts."[2]

Elsewhere in his narrative, Brereton provides a brief but intriguing account of a meeting with natives off what is now Cape Neddick, Maine. The party included "six Indians in a baske shallop with a mast and saile, an iron grapple, a waistcoat and breeches of black serge, made after our sea fashion, hose and shoes on his feet." Brereton concluded from their appearance and "from some words and signs they made, that some baske or [other vessel] of St. John de Luz [a French port in the Bay of Biscay]" had "fished or traded in this place."[3]

According to Samuel Eliot Morison, "Many English and other fishing vessels must have caught codfish on the Maine banks during the last decade of the sixteenth century."[4] Others suggest earlier dates. David Quinn estimates that in the period 1527–80, "ranging the shores of Nova Scotia and possibly Maine was not unusual for Basque and Breton summer traders and fishermen."[5]

But there is support in the historic record for only a handful of brief voyages along the Gulf of Maine coast before 1600 and few, if any, before the 1520s. During this period, Europeans made only brief contact with the natives of the area. Some, like Giovanni da Verrazzano and possibly Simão Fernandes, did barter a few articles with them, but the purpose of these voyages was exploration, not trade.[6]

Perhaps the most interesting account of trading activities in this era was made by the Englishman John Walker. In 1580 he landed at Penobscot Bay and took from an unattended building "III[c] [probably three hundred] dry hides, whereof the most part

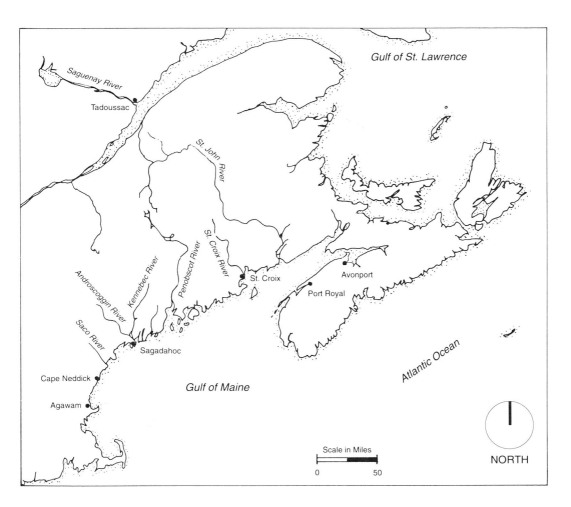

43. Norumbega and the "Tarrentine" trade. Based on Bruce Bourque and Ruth Whitehead, "Tarrentines and the Introduction of European Trade Goods in the Gulf of Maine," *Ethnohistory* 32 (1985), p. 329.

of them were eighteen foot by the square."[7] Judged by their size, these must have been moose hides. It may be inferred that such a large concentration in a single structure meant that the hides were intended not for the local population but for export, ultimately to Europeans; but Walker provided no further clues as to their intended destination.

It is possible that the anonymous fishermen invoked by Frank T. Siebert, Morison, Dean R. Snow, and others brought European goods to the Gulf of Maine during the sixteenth century. But it is not probable, because the proposition unrealistically assumes that the Gulf of Maine lay within convenient range of sixteenth-century Newfoundland fishing fleets. In fact, the distance from Placentia, Newfoundland, to Penobscot Bay was thirteen hundred kilometers. It was not until after Jacques Cartier's voyages between 1534 and 1542 that the Gulf of St. Lawrence fishery reached even as far out as the Grand Banks, and there is little to suggest that either the French or the English used the Newfoundland fishery as a staging area for early voyages to the Gulf of Maine.[8]

Furthermore, as Edwin Churchill has stated, "Considering the multitude of records of provisioning, voyages, accounts, sales, etc., from the Newfoundland fisheries it is impossible to believe that numerous vessels could be sent to New England with not one record surviving."[9] He argues further that early-seventeenth-century explorers in the Gulf of Maine were genuinely surprised by the abundance of fish there. For example, James Rosier, who chronicled George Weymouth's voyage to Maine in 1605, described a good day of fishing near the St. George River estuary. "In a short voyage [a] few good fishers [could] . . . make

44. The Basque whalers of Newfoundland are depicted in *On the Taking of Whales,* from Andre Thevet, *Cosmographie Universelle,* 1575. Courtesy of Osher Cartographic Collection, University of Southern Maine.

a more profitable return from hence than from Newfoundland: the fish being so much greater, better fed, and abundant with traine [traine-oil]; of which some they desired, and did bring into England to bestow among their friends, and to testify the true report."[10] Significantly, as impressive as this and other early accounts of the New England fishery were, not one of their authors was yet aware that the peak fishing season was from January through March.[11]

A final possible source of sixteenth-century European visitors to the Gulf of Maine was voyages that may have stopped along the coast for reasons incidental to their main purposes. The most likely prospects were French pirates or privateers who preyed on Spanish shipping off the coasts of Florida and farther north. Quinn claims that by 1560, French marauders had been visiting the Atlantic coast as far north as Virginia for many years and that they traded with Indians. However, their vessels probably would not have ranged as far north as the Gulf of Maine. Indeed, Quinn is able to cite only a single 1546 voyage as far north as Chesapeake Bay.[12]

Churchill has pointed out that even the explorers who came after 1600 encountered no other Europeans.[13] During his 1605 visit, Samuel de Champlain learned that Weymouth had been in the area, but the two did not meet, and neither of them saw evidence of previous European visitors.[14] Rosier is explicit on this point. "We diligently observed, that in no place, about either the Islands, or up in the Maine, or alongst the river, we could not discerne any token or signe, that *ever any Christian had been before*" (italics added).[15] Furthermore, Champlain had earlier met a large group of Etchemins from the Penobscot Bay area, including the great sagamore Bashabes, who "were much pleased to see us, inasmuch as *it was the first time they had ever beheld Christians*" (italics added).[16]

Thus, all data indicate that sixteenth- and early-seventeenth-century European visitors to the Gulf of Maine were few and far between and were certainly insufficient in number to explain the quantity of trade goods seen by Brereton and Pring among the natives. Given below are two possible alternative sources for these goods as well as a probable intended destination for the three hundred hides seen by Walker in 1580. Neither alternative depends on the direct presence of Europeans.

Etchemins in the St. Lawrence Valley

Early French sources label the native inhabitants between the Kennebec and St. John rivers as Etchemins.[17] But when Champlain and François Grave du Pont first visited the St. Lawrence in 1603, they met some Etchemins in the Montagnais village of headman Anadabijou at Tadoussac, an important trading center at the mouth of the Saguenay River on the north shore of the St. Lawrence. On May 27 these Etchemins, in company with some Algonquians and Montagnais, had just returned from a raid on the Iroquois.[18]

Though it was not until 1605 — two years after this raid — that the Etchemins at Penobscot first saw a Christian, those involved in warfare on the St. Lawrence may already have met some Europeans in this northern region. Perhaps the late-sixteenth-century displacement of the "St. Lawrence Iroquoians" from the stretch of the St. Lawrence that is across the divide from the St. John and Penobscot rivers allowed these Etchemins direct access to the St. Lawrence fur trade. The precise date of this displacement or depopulation is not known, but the available data suggest it took place in the last decade of the sixteenth century.[19]

The Etchemins remained at Tadoussac until at least July 11 and apparently had furs to trade with native middlemen there.[20] They might have returned to the Gulf of Maine with European trade goods. This was certainly the case by about 1606-10, when natives from the area between Pemaquid and the Penobscot River were traveling to the north for more than fifty days "to another River where they [had] a trade with Anadabis or Anadabiion with whom the Frenchmen [had] had commerce for a long time."[21] *Anadabiion* seems clearly to be a mistranscription of Champlain's Montagnais headman Anadabijou. Natives living west of the Kennebec, whom Champlain and his contemporaries labeled Armouchiquois and who included those with the European-made metal goods seen by Brereton and Pring, were more remote from Tadoussac and less likely to have been trading there.[22]

Souriquois in the Gulf of Maine

A second account of Gosnold's encounter in 1602 with Indians sailing a Basque shallop was written by Gabriel Archer, another member of Gosnold's company. It augments Brereton's

The Cataract of NIAGARA, some make this Water-Fall to be half a League while others reckon it no more than a hundred Fathom.

A View of y̆ Industry of y̆ Beavers of Canada in making Dams to stop y̆ Course of ă R rivulet, in order to form a great Lake, about wᶜʰ they build their Habitations. To Effect this; they fell large Trees with their Teeth, in such a manner as to make them come Crofs y̆ Rivulet, to lay y̆ foundation of y̆ Dam; they make Mortar, work up, and finish y̆ whole with great order and wonderfull Dexterity. The Beavers have two Doors to their Lodges, one to the Water and the other to the Land side. According to y̆ French Accounts.

45. *View of Working Beaver.* Detail from Herman Moll, *A New and Exact Map of the Dominions of the King of Great Britain,* 1715. Courtesy of Osher Cartographic Collection, University of Southern Maine.

report and provides important information regarding a source of European goods in the Gulf of Maine before 1600. "There came towards us a Biscay shallop, with sail and oars, having eight persons in it. . . . They came boldly aboard us. . . . One that seemed to be their commander wore a waistcoat of black work, a pair of breeches, cloth stockings, shoes, hat and band. . . . These with a piece of chalk described the coast thereabouts, *and could name Placentia of the New Foundland; they spoke divers Christian words*" (italics added).[23]

Here, then, we have Indians encountered on the central Maine coast, Indians who were familiar with Placentia and spoke the lingua franca that developed in the Gulf of St. Lawrence during the fifteenth and sixteenth centuries.[24] The prevalence of this St. Lawrence trade language has not been widely recognized. Yet according to the lawyer and explorer Marc Lescarbot, the natives along the Gaspe shore spoke "half Baske" during the first decade of the seventeenth century.[25]

Quinn correctly identifies the native mariners as Micmacs (Souriquois). During the next decade, more contacts occurred between Europeans and shallop-sailing Indians, and there is little doubt that these too were mostly Souriquois, who occupied the area east of the St. John River.[26]

The first encounter was recorded by Lescarbot, a passenger aboard Jean Poutrincourt's ship *Jonas* when it was approached by two "chaloupes," one sailed by two Souriquois who had painted a moose on their sail.[27] A month later two other shallop-sailing natives, Messamouet and Secoudon, accompanied Champlain and Poutrincourt on a voyage from St. Croix Island to Saco on the western Maine coast.[28] Champlain implies they visited Saco to improve relations with the Armouchiquois sagamore Onemechin, but Lescarbot's account casts a different light on the visit. "They had much merchandise, gained by barter with the French, *which they come hither to sell*" (italics added). Furthermore, during the negotiations, Messamouet pointed out "how of past time they had often had friendly intercourse together and that they could easily overcome their enemies if they would come to terms and make use of the friendship of the French . . . in order in future to bring merchandise to them and to aid them with their resources, whereof he knew and could the better tell them, because *he, the orator, had once upon a time been in France and had stayed at the house of M. de Grandmont, Mayor of Bayonne*" (italics added).[29] Onemechin, however, was unimpressed, and his rebuff of Messamouet's offer was one of the factors that led to a major Souriquois and eastern Etchemin raid on Onemechin's village in 1607.[30]

The third recorded encounter between Europeans and Indians sailing shallops was in 1606 at Port Royal. Panonias, a Souriquois, had been killed in Penobscot Bay by some Armouchiquois. His body had been delivered by Bashabes to another Etchemin, Ouigamont, sagamore of St. Croix. Ouigamont, in turn, carried it in his own shallop to Port Royal.[31] The killing of Panonias was the second and immediate cause of the Souriquois-led raid on Saco. Lescarbot tells us that Membertou, the sagamore who organized the multiethnic raiding party, traveled with "chaloupes & canots."[32] In addition, they had to their advantage some muskets lent by the French.[33] This is the first mention of firearms in the hands of natives in the Gulf of Maine.

A fourth encounter occurred off La Have on August 1, 1607, when Englishmen bound for the Kennebec to establish a colony met two shallops sailed by members of Messamouet's band, who were "prophering skins to trook with us." Furthermore, "ytt seem that the french hath trad w them for they use many french words . . . we take these peopell to be terentyns."[34] The term *terentyns*, variously spelled, has confused historians of the region, but Siebert convincingly argues that it applied primarily to the Souriquois, later called Micmac.[35] Our data suggest that it probably includes some eastern Etchemins as well.

A fifth encounter began on July 17, 1609, when Henry Hudson met with natives at a harbor in Penobscot Bay or just east of it. They told Hudson that the Frenchmen "do trade with them; which is very likely, for one of them *spake some words of French*" (italics added).[36] Then, on July 20, "two French Shallops full of the country people came into the Harbour. . . . They brought many Beaver skinnes and other fine Furres, which they would have changed for redde Gownes. For the French trade with them, for red Cassockes, Knives, Hatchets, Copper, Kettles, Trevits, Beades, and other trifles." Hudson was apparently not equipped for trade, but he wanted the furs, and on July 25 he resorted to force. "In the morning we manned our Scute with foure Muskets, and six men, and Tooke one of their Shallops and brought it aboord. Then we manned our Boat & Scute with twelve men and Muskets, and two stone Pieces or Murderers, and drave the Salvages from their Houses, and took spoyle of them, as they would have done of us."[37] Thus, the shallop-sailing traders were probably local residents (Etchemins) rather than itinerant Souriquois from the east.

That the Montagnais and Souriquois used European vessels during the early seventeenth century has been briefly noted by Bruce Trigger, Quinn, and L. Turgeon.[38] The previously cited encounters indicate, however, that even the Etchemins of Penobscot Bay were employing shallops in the fur trade by 1609.

Native adoption of European shallops meant far more than the mere replacement of one small craft by another. In fact, shallops were generally large. Some ranged up to twelve tons and twelve meters (forty feet) in length and had more than one mast.[39] Furthermore, according to a seventeenth-century Jesuit missionary, the Souriquois handled them "as skillfully as our most courageous and active sailors in France."[40]

Although the primary motivation for coastal trading voyages must have been the barter of European goods for furs, the traders sought other commodities as well. Lescarbot, for example, said that they imported shell beads from Armouchiquois country, and this has been confirmed by the discovery of Busycon beads in association with an early historic native burial at Avonport, Nova Scotia.[41]

Trigger and Neal Salisbury suggest that Messamouet and Secoudon traveled to Saco in 1606 to trade for Armouchiquois agricultural surplus. Both argue that because the Souriquois were deeply involved in fur trapping, they tended to run short of food and made up the shortfall through barter with the French and with the agricultural Armouchiquois.[42]

At first glance, this seems a logical hypothesis, but it is at odds with two early accounts detailing the items being offered by traders. In 1603, Champlain encountered a party of probable Souriquois on their way to Tadoussac to "barter arrows and moose flesh for . . . beaver and marten" from the Etchemins, Algonquians, and Montagnais in Anadabijou's village.[43] The commodities offered seem particularly well suited for trade to a group recently returned from a war and presumably short of stored food and ammunition. The willingness of the Souriquois to trade moose meat for furs suggests that in this case, at least, they were not worried about their food supply.

The second account refers to the very meeting at Saco to which Trigger and Salisbury refer. Both imply that Messamouet and Secoudon sought agricultural surplus from Onemechin in return for European goods. Although Onemechin did, indeed, provide Messamouet with "corn, tobacco, beans and pumpkins" when the latter departed, this gift followed Messamouet's earlier presentation of "kettles, large, medium, and small, hatchets, knives, dresses, capes, red jackets, *peas, beans, biscuits, and other such things . . . merchandise which in those parts was worth more than three hundered crowns*" (italics added).[44] Again, foodstuffs, this time of European origin in forms specifically designed for long-term storage, were being offered by the traders. Further-

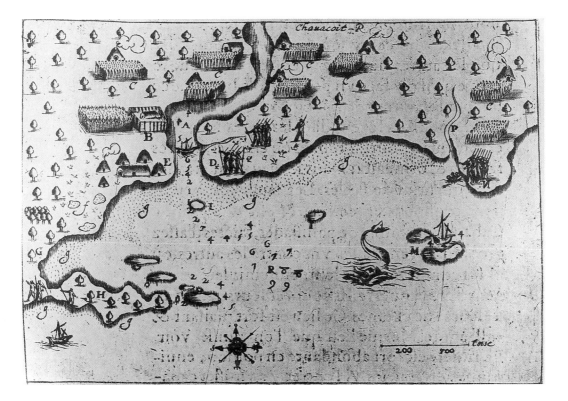

46. In 1605 Samuel de Champlain visited Chouacoit, the agricultural village at the mouth of the present-day Saco River. Samuel de Champlain, *Chouacoit River*, from his *Les Voyages*, 1613. Taken from the 1878 reprint, courtesy of Dyer Library.

more, Messamouet was clearly not content with Onemechin's insulting response to his largess and vowed revenge on him.[45] Thus, although the shallop-sailing traders may occasionally have sought food, their primary goal was more probably the acquisition of furs for resale to Europeans in the Gulf of St. Lawrence.[46]

The scope of Souriquois and Etchemin middlemen appears to have been considerable. They probably never rounded Cape Cod to trade in southern New England, but several sources suggest that by the beginning of the seventeenth century they ranged as far west as Massachusetts Bay. Champlain's comment regarding his 1606 visit there is most explicit:

Those who live here have canoes built out of a single piece. . . . This is how they build them. After taking great trouble and spending much time in felling with *hatchets of stone (for except a few who get them from the Indians of the Acadian coast, with whom they are bartered for furs, they posses no others)* the thickest and tallest tree they can find, they remove the bark and round off the trunk except on one side where they gradually apply fire throughout its whole length. . . . When it is hollow enough for their fancy, they

scrape it all over with *stones, which they use in place of knives*. The
stones from which they make their cutting tools are like our musket flints. (italics added)[47]

This passage clearly identifies Souriquois or Etchemin middlemen as the source of the Massachusetts trade goods, and it also
points out a dramatic contrast in the degrees of acculturation at
the opposite ends of the Gulf of Maine, a distance of less than
480 kilometers. One can easily imagine Souriquois traders like
Messamouet, the former houseguest of the mayor of Bayonne,
profitably exploiting the stone-tool-using natives of Massachusetts Bay.

We suspect that by 1600, the pattern we have described had
been in place for some time. First, we believe that the three hundred hides appropriated by Walker in 1580 had been gathered
from the Penobscot hinterland for the European market. If
Europeans had not yet begun to trade in the Gulf of Maine,
natives themselves must already have begun to transport wholesale fur lots to the Gulf of St. Lawrence. Second, invitations
to visit France, like that offered Messamouet, suggest early re-
cruitment of native entrepreneurs into the fur trade. Third, and
perhaps most important, the theft of Etienne Bellenger's pinnace in 1583 suggests that the Souriquois of southern Nova Scotia
already knew how to handle European vessels. Perhaps they even
regarded Bellenger as an interloper on their fur-trading territory.
In any case, during the next three decades, shallop-sailing traders
emerged among Souriquois and eastern Etchemins as far west as
the Penobscot. Finally, there are numerous indications that by
1604, political unrest was widespread in the Gulf of Maine, at
least in part because of Tarrentine attempts to control their fur-
producing clients there. For example, the sagamores Bashabes
and Cabahis warmly received Champlain at the Penobscot River
in 1604 because they wished to trade directly with the French and
obtain protection from "their enemies, the Souriquois and Canadians."[48] Onemechin's motives in rejecting Souriquois overtures
in 1607 were probably similar to those of Bashabes and Cabahis
in that he too perceived a means of bypassing the middlemen
to deal directly with the French. However, the French could not
save Onemechin, nor could they prevent the Souriquois from
later killing Bashabes and ravaging his people in about 1615.[49]

During the first half of the seventeenth century, native middle-

TERRA DE LABORADOR

ISOLA DE
DE MONI

47. Detail showing a fishing shallop from Giacomo Gastaldi, *La Nuova Francia*, in Giovanni Battista Ramusio, *Terzo Volume delle Navigationi et Viaggi*, 1556. Courtesy of Smith Cartographic Collection, University of Southern Maine.

men in the lower St. Lawrence lost ground to European traders who bypassed them to establish direct contact with the primary fur producers.[50] In the Gulf of Maine this process seems to have occurred much more rapidly. As early as 1610, aside from trading based at Port Royal, two French ships were trading at the mouth of the St. John, and a Frenchman named Platrier had established a trading and fishing station at St. Croix that may have persisted until 1613.[51]

In 1614, Captain John Smith noted that in addition to his own considerable activity in the fur trade, the French were dominating trade in the eastern Gulf of Maine, "two French ships . . . had made . . . a great voyage by trade" near Boston, and Sir Francis Popham's ship was on a routine trading voyage to the Kennebec.[52] It is clear from his remarks that by 1614, Europeans were in direct competition for furs in the Gulf of Maine. This must have placed native middlemen at a distinct disadvantage vis-à-vis their European competition.

The increased European presence in the region brought another even greater disadvantage for native middlemen: disease. Smallpox, measles, and other European diseases rapidly reduced

48. Artifacts from Maine Indian sites of the seventeenth and early eighteenth centuries. The jaw's harp and glass and ceramic beads were traded directly to the Indians; the brass arrowheads, copper beads, and tinkling cones were probably made by the Indians from worn-out kettles; and the two beads in the upper right were made out of shell. Courtesy of Maine State Museum.

native populations as well as, no doubt, the volume of middleman trade. The infamous 1617–18 epidemic in the Gulf of Maine was catastrophic.[53] However, this was not the first epidemic, for the Jesuit Pierre Biard commented of the Souriquois and the Etchemins of 1611–13, "[They] are astonished and often complain that since the French mingle with and carry on trade with them, they are dying fast and the population is thinning out . . . one by one the different coasts according as they have begun to traffic with use, have been more reduced by disease."[54]

These early epidemics appear to have resulted from Souriquois contact with European traders in the Gulf of St. Lawrence, for

Biard states that west of the Androscoggin, the Armouchiquois did not "diminish in population," [55] probably because, as Lescarbot said, they had "yet no commerce with us." [56] Among the Souriquois, however, the toll was severe. In 1610 alone, the Souriquois at La Have lost sixty persons, "the greater part of those who lived there." [57] This epidemic may have claimed Messamouet himself, for he is not mentioned after 1607; Secoudon, his trading partner, was dead by 1613. [58]

When their role as middlemen in the fur trade declined, the Tarrentines increasingly resorted to raiding voyages along the New England coast, probably attempting to maintain control over fur producers or simply to steal what they could no longer obtain by trade. As late as 1632, for example, thirty Tarrentines attacked natives at Agawam (now Ipswich, Massachusetts), killing seven. They also stole some fishnets and supplies from nearby English settlers. Massachusetts Governor John Winthrop stated in his original manuscript that they arrived in "two fishing shallops." [59]

Conclusion

The earliest detailed ethnographic data from the Gulf of Maine, from the first decade of the seventeenth century, clearly indicates that European trade goods had penetrated the region. By 1602, sheet copper and brass were common in western Maine. By 1605, iron axes were present among the Massachusetts. Even earlier, in 1580, large numbers of what were probably trade hides were stockpiled at Penobscot Bay. Few European voyages are on record before these accounts; the few that are made minimal contact with native people in the region.

Many authors have suggested that anonymous European voyages were the source of trade goods in this area. The analysis of the historical record of European activity in the New World during the sixteenth and early seventeenth centuries indicates, however, that even though such voyages cannot be ruled out altogether, there is no evidence of them. Most probably, European fishing and trading activities in the Gulf of Maine remained insignificant until the first decade of the seventeenth century.

The presence of trade goods in the Gulf of Maine before 1604, then, is explained not by direct European trading in the area but by two other, more plausible factors. First, by 1603 Maine natives were directly involved in the St. Lawrence fur trade and even in the warfare that arose over competition for access to European traders. These natives carried at least some furs and hides up the St. John and Penobscot and down the Riviere du Loup and Chaudiere in return for trade goods from those areas.

Second, and more important to the movement of trade goods west of the Kennebec, were the activities of shallop-sailing native middlemen, whose significance in the Gulf of Maine has been overlooked. By the early 1600s, Tarrentine-Souriquois middlemen, joined by some eastern Etchemins, had mastered the art of coastal navigation in sailing vessels known as shallops. Apparently they ranged the entire Gulf coast, bartering European goods they brought from the St. Lawrence for furs. By the time this pattern was first observed in 1602, it may have been in place for decades.

The Tarrentine entrepreneurs' fortunes declined rapidly after Europeans penetrated the Gulf of Maine to trade directly with local fur producers. Almost simultaneously, unfamiliar European diseases decimated their bands. After a major epidemic in the western gulf in 1617–18, the trade volume probably dropped even further. Despite these setbacks—indeed perhaps because of them—Tarrentines continued to make coastal voyages, more often to raid than to trade, until at least 1632.

The Tarrentines were not the only middlemen to arise on the North American fur trade frontier. By 1603 the Montagnais at Tadoussac had also transcended the role of mere fur producers to become middlemen, profitably supplying European traders with furs from the interior in exchange for manufactured goods. Other groups later did the same on the St. Maurice and Ottawa rivers to the west, and Eric Wolf has argued that as the fur trade spread beyond the St. Lawrence, it continued to create short-lived groups of native middlemen who serviced European traders via "natural lines of penetration from the east coast up the rivers, along chains of lakes and over inland areas." After brief prosperity, most middlemen were overtaken by disease and warfare or were bypassed when Europeans made direct contact with their fur suppliers.[60]

As Alfred Bailey and Trigger have pointed out, the Montagnais at Tadoussac became middlemen primarily because they could control traffic on the Saguenay River, the crucial outlet from a very large and fur-rich hinterland.[61] They and probably later middlemen to the northwest operated by blocking the access of fur producers to European traders, a practice that incidentally triggered much of the warfare that characterized the fur trade frontier. The profitability of such operations was directly linked to the volume of furs funneled through their territories.

The Tarrentine case is somewhat different. Like the Tadoussac Montagnais, local groups in the Gulf of Maine might have controlled the flow of furs from their own hinterlands, but these groups must have been too small to generate much profit, especially when the distance to market was great. However, by adopting European-style navigation, the Tarrentines were able to amass the yields of several small catchments along the Gulf of Maine and efficiently transport the aggregate to markets in the Gulf of St. Lawrence.

The coastal nature of the Gulf of Maine fur supply doomed the Tarrentines to a precipitous decline once European traders arrived there. Whereas middlemen in the St. Lawrence drainage could maintain their market position so long as they could hold their territories, those in the Gulf of Maine could not hope to stem, even temporarily, direct European penetration to native fur producers after the Europeans entered the region. The Tarrentines survived as middlemen only so long as they could outstrip the Europeans themselves in expanding the fur trade.

CHAPTER SEVEN

The Exploration of Norumbega
Native Perspectives

James Axtell

In re-creating the story of Norumbega before the fateful advent of the Pilgrims in 1620, we should listen to—and really try to *hear*—some voices that are seldom even thought to have existed. These are the voices of the native Norumbegans who met and usually welcomed the seaborne strangers from Europe. Although the natives spoke tongues and dialects very different from those of Elizabethan England and Henrician France, we are able in a few instances to eavesdrop on some of their interior and external dialogues, to catch glimpses of what they were thinking and how they were feeling about the novel visitors to their shores.

But why should we bother? Since the Indians could not write and therefore left us no collectible publications of their own, why should we go to the trouble of discovering their views on these Norumbegan events? Two reasons—better than affirmative action and historical fashion—suggest themselves. The first and more philosophical is that "society is an interweaving and interworking of mental selves. . . . The imaginations which people have of one another are the solid facts of society."[1] If we wish to recapture the historical essence of the meeting of past cultures on the rocky margins of Maine or anywhere else, we have to imagine the imaginations of all the participants, not just an easy or select few. For—and this is our second reason—people act on the basis of what they *think* is true, not necessarily on what *is* true. Indeed, in some sense, reality itself is socially constructed or imagined. When the Europeans and the Indians reacted to each other, they did so because of their respective ideas and feelings about each other, attitudes that drew their meaning and symbolic force from acquired and largely unconscious cultural contexts.[2] If it is granted that we must seek the native perspective, or more accurately, native perspectives, is it actually possible, particularly when thoughts and feelings are not always best captured in words and when spoken words, by their very nature, vanish the instant they are voiced? Clearly, a great many ethnohistorians would be out of work if it were *not* possible. Our sources are several, although each kind carries its own limitations. For pre-1620 Norumbega, there are only three types of major importance.

The first and most familiar sources are the written and cartographic records literally manuscripted by the European explorers. Although these seamen were interested more in Norumbega's natural and mineral resources than in its natives, they usually had to interact with the latter to learn about or gain access to the former. This entailed considerable "conversation" with the Indians, through ambiguous sign language, elementary trade pidgins, native interpreters who had spent time on European ships or in European ports, or, less frequently, sailors who had picked up some native phrases from Indian shipmates or trading partners. Even when the natives remained silent, their actions were often eloquent expressions of their attitudes toward the newcomers, if we but read them in cultural context.

Our second source category consists not of evanescent and easily misinterpreted words but of subterranean sherds, middens, and postmolds found in native sites. Because the members of a culture tend to pattern their behavior in similar ways, the artifacts they make and the ways they use and dispose of them tell us much about some of the values and ideals they cherish and about some of the events in their lives, events that may not be documented in any other way.

Finally, a type of source with which traditionally bookish historians are distinctly uneasy is the recollection of native peoples who pass down, through the generations, oral accounts of "events" long in the past. Whether these events were "historical" or "mythical" (in a Western sense), oral traditions about them often give us unique insights into the emotional ambiance and normative resonance of those occurrences from a native perspective. Oral accounts may not tell us just *when* a particular event occurred, but they almost always convey how the native participants *felt* about it at the time and often what kind of moral natives drew from it.

If we bend our ears southwestward, toward Puritan Massachusetts, we might be able to catch a few faithful echoes of native responses to the earliest European men and ships in Norumbega's waters. This is the best resort we have because the lethal plague of 1616–18 and subsequent European irruptions seem to have left an unhappy silence in the native oral record of coastal Maine. Fortunately, two early settlers of the bay colony listened carefully to Indian survivors of the plague in the area and recorded their tribal memories of the first Europeans. Since the conceptual worlds of the eastern Algonquians were essentially similar, we should be able to hear something of the Wabanakis' responses to the first "Igrismannak" in their waters.[3]

During his four-year stay in Massachusetts, William Wood learned that the Indians had been "ravished with admiration" at the first European ship they saw. Like many of their brethren up and down the Atlantic coast, they took it for "a walking island, the mast to be a tree, the sail white clouds, and the discharging of ordnance for lightning and thunder, which did much trouble them." When the thunder stopped and the island dropped anchor, the natives hopped in their canoes to go pick strawberries there, which may place the incident in late May or early June. However, when the ship gave them a friendly salvo in salute, they cried out (in the English pidgin common by the early 1630s), "What much hoggery [anger], so big walk, and so big speak, and by and by kill." Whereupon they beat a hasty retreat to shore, not daring to approach the ship again "till they were sent for" by the bearded "coat-men" or "sword-men" (as their Narragansett neighbors called them) (fig. 49).[4]

The version of this symbolic event heard by Edward Johnson, perhaps in 1630–31 when he traded on the Merrimack but probably after 1636 when he settled near the bay, was richer in emotional and historical detail than Wood's. As Johnson understood it, the whole Massachusetts tribe was "affrighted" by the first ship in their bay. "Wondering what Creature it should be," they paddled from place to place "stiring up all their Country-men to come forth, and behold this monstrous thing." Johnson noted, "At this sudden news, the shores for many miles were filled with this naked Nation, gazing at this wonder, till some of the stoutest among them" decided to approach the creature by canoe. When they got within range, they "let fly" a shower of arrows at the becalmed ship. Some of their bone-tipped shafts bounced harmlessly off the hull, but others "stuck fast," causing the warriors to wonder why "it did not cry."

49. Title page of William Wood, *New England's Prospect*, 1634. Taken from the 1898 reprint, courtesy of Dyer Library.

NEVV
ENGLANDS
PROSPECT.

A true, lively, and experimen-
tall defcription of that part of *America*,
commonly called NEVV ENGLAND:
difcovering the ftate of that Coun-
trie, both as it ftands to our new-come
Englifh Planters; and to the old
Native Inhabitants.

Laying downe that which may both enrich the knowledge of the mind-travelling Reader, or benefit the future Voyager.

By WILLIAM WOOD.

Printed at *London* by *Tho. Cotes,* for *Iohn Bellamie,* and are to be fold
at his fhop, at the three Golden Lyons in *Corne-hill,* neere the
Royall Exchange. 1634.

Their curiosity suddenly turned to terror when the captain ordered a cannon fired, "which stroke such feare into the poore Indians, that they hasted to shore, having their wonders exceedingly increased." Wrapped in amazement, the tribe huddled anxiously as the ship's crew furled the sails, manned the longboat, and rowed to meet them. The natives fled into the woods, "although now they saw they were men" who signaled them to "stay their flight" in order to trade. When the sailors held out shiny copper kettles, the Indians gradually regained their composure and approached, "much delighted with the sound" of the kettles when struck and "much more astonished to see they would not breake, being so thin."

This encounter was fraught with more than ordinary significance for these southern Norumbegans because "not long" after —Johannes Kepler and Pierre Gassendi saw it in November 1618 —a "bright blazing Comet" hung in the southwestern sky three hours every night for "thirty sleepes." Like most Europeans, educated and credulous alike, the natives beheld that "uncouth sight" in "great wonderment" and fully "expected some strange things to follow." The Massachusetts phase of the horrifying plague— which Johnson misdates in the summer of 1619—was the first. Then came the last straw: a large "Army of Christ" bent on supplanting native "paganism" and making southern New England a kinder, gentler place.[5]

J. Franklin Jameson, the editor of Johnson's *Wonder-Working Providence,* thought that the Massachusetts might have been remembering the well- (if self-) publicized visit of Captain John Smith in 1614. This is virtually impossible and underlines the fallacy of resorting to native folklore for historical specifics. Smith did sail into Massachusetts Bay early in the summer (around strawberry time), but his ship was attacked by only four bowmen from some rocks near a narrow passage. Moreover, he had been preceded that year by at least two French ships, which, to his annoyance, had garnered the best furs in six weeks of active trading.[6] But the French had also traded in Massachusetts waters for several years, perhaps decades, before Smith made his first and only voyage to New England. As both archaeological and written records make clear, copper kettles were a standard item in the French, not the English, trade kit in the late sixteenth and early seventeenth centuries. Smith touted the vendibility of

50. Theodore deBry, *The Harbor of Lisbon,* in *Admiranda Narratio Fida Tamen . . . Virginia . . . Americae,* 1528–92. Courtesy of Smith Cartographic Collection, University of Southern Maine.

coarse cloth, hatchets, beads, mirrors, and other "trash," but not relatively expensive kettles.[7]

Editor Jameson probably would not have made his venial mistake if he had read the extant literature of Norumbegan exploration. For no matter how early a European ship is known to have touched on New England's shores, Indian reactions or possessions suggest that it had been preceded by others. When Gaspar Corte-Real kidnapped fifty-some Indians in 1501 from what sounds like Maine, one man possessed "a piece of broken gilt sword," which to the Venetian ambassador in Lisbon "certainly seem[ed] to have been made in Italy." A native boy was wearing in his ears "two silver rings" made just as certainly in Venice.[8]

Twenty-three years later, Estevan Gomes filled his galleon with fifty-eight Indians "of both sexes," perhaps from islands at the mouth of the Penobscot River, where the natives had come for summer fishing.[9] We have to ask how both of these Portuguese entrepreneurs managed to entice on board so many agile and normally suspicious natives. The likeliest answer (given the scattered and secondhand sources we have) is that many Norumbegans, as early as 1501 and certainly no later than 1524, were familiar enough with seagoing Europeans to swap "rare and valuable furs" for merchandise that pleased them.[10] Only by luring trade-minded and probably unarmed natives away from the wooded security of their encampments could the Iberians have shanghaied so many in such large batches. Indeed, in light of the Indians' later reticence to expose their women to European ogling, we have to wonder how Corte-Real and Gomes were able to snatch any females at all. Perhaps these early captures explain the subsequent caution, rather than being rendered problematical by it.

The more pertinent question we must ask is, can we tell anything about how the native victims felt toward their kidnappers? Since Gomes had violated his sovereign's explicit instructions not to use violence against any natives, his Indians were "set at liberty" but were still in Toledo the following year. Whether they ever saw home again is unknown but not likely.[11] Corte-Real's human booty was "seen, touched and examined" by an Italian diplomat as soon as the natives disembarked at Lisbon in October 1501. After a four-week trip, these tall, tattooed, long-haired strangers, clothed in otter skins, seemed to have adjusted to their enslavement reasonably well (we have no idea how they were treated on shipboard in port). Even while the curious Italian was discovering the "small breasts and most beautiful bodies" of the women and (consequently?) the "terribly harsh look of the men," the natives behaved "gentl[y]," "laugh[ed] considerably and manifest[ed] the greatest pleasure." Whether this was genuine emotion or the best face they could put on a frightening and desperate situation we will never know, but common sense points to the latter. The hopelessness of their predicament must have hit them with extra force when not one of their captors could understand their speech and when they had been "spoken to in every possible language" known in that cosmopolitan port-city. Without communication, their very humanity was put in jeopardy, even as the Europeans acknowledged the humanness of their "form and image" and of their "not harsh" if indecipherable language.[12]

Giovanni da Verrazzano's leisurely and more peaceful visit to New England in 1524 discovered more about Norumbegan reactions to the bearded visitors than any other voyage until the seventeenth century. When he tacked into Narragansett Bay in April, he was met by twenty canoes of painted locals "uttering various cries of wonderment" at the structure of the *Dauphine*, the French crew, and their manufactured clothes. But they kept their distance until the Frenchmen imitated their gestures and shouts of joy and threw them a few "trinkets." Then the natives, including two chiefs, showed them where to anchor, brought them food, and "confidently came on board ship." Pointedly missing were their women, who, although they were invited, waited in the canoes or, in the case of a curious "queen" and her attendants, withdrew to a nearby island to escape the "irksome clamor of the crowd of sailors." All of this behavior sounds like that of people who had had some experience in dealing with European ships and randy seamen. So does their courteous but not overly deferential treatment of the French, who were quick to recognize when they were being regarded as minor or major divinities. That one chief asked about the ship's equipment, "imitated [French] manners," and "tasted [their] food" carried no such connotation.[13]

Yet other behavior seemed to belie any previous experience or perhaps to suggest that the natives' previous encounters had been unusually benign. The first anomaly was their response to European trade goods and technology. If they were familiar with maritime traders, they certainly acted peculiarly toward known best-sellers. We can understand their preference for their own reddish copper to pale and gold objects, but what do we make of their apparent disinterest in cloth of any kind, even their favorite reds and blues, and in "metals like steel and iron"? "For many times when we showed them some of our arms," wrote the astonished captain, "they did not admire them, nor ask for them, but merely examined the workmanship. They did the same with mirrors; they would look at them quickly, and then refuse them, laughing." The only items they really prized were decorative: "little bells, blue crystals, and other trinkets to put in the ear or around the neck." Furthermore, Verrazzano makes no mention of any furs being offered in trade; April would have been the right time for trade-minded hunters to dispose of their winter catch.[14]

Another piece of anomalous behavior (judged by later events in

Norumbega) is that the Narragansetts allowed French excursions to penetrate inland five or six leagues to visit their largest fields and villages. The natives' "sweet and gentle" conduct throughout the explorers' two-week stay suggests either that previous European visitors had not bitten the hands that fed them or that the natives regarded the newcomers as traditional "spirits" or manitous, the extent of whose powers was still unknown and who therefore deserved respect and circumspection.[15]

Much less ambiguous were the behavior and the attitudes of the Norumbegans whom Verrazzano found on the coast of Maine. These natives had undoubtedly had considerable experience with Europeans and had not found it particularly salutary. Since Gomes arrived in Maine after Verrazzano, other voyages must have given the Indians their first taste of Christian "civility." In stark contrast to the courteous denizens of "Refugio" (his name for Narragansett Bay), Verrazzano found the Mainers "full of crudity and vices," devoid of manners, of "humanity," and of agriculture, and "so barbarous that we could never make any communication with them, however many signs we made to them." The Indians also made it clear that they did not want the sailors to land, even for trading. When twenty-five armed Frenchmen brazened their way inland and made several unwelcome visits to their houses, the natives "shot at [them] with their bows and uttered loud cries before fleeing into the woods."[16]

If the French were in any doubt about the natives' attitudes toward them, it was quickly dispelled by the Indians' trading etiquette. "If *we* wanted to trade with them for some of *their* things," Verrazzano complained, "they would come to the seashore on some rocks where the breakers were most violent, while we remained in the little boat, and they sent us what they wanted to give on a rope . . . ; that gave us the barter quickly, and would take in exchange only knives, hooks for fishing, and sharp metal" (italics added). Then, in a priceless gesture of farewell, these reluctant, persnickety customers "made all the signs of scorn and shame that any brute creature would make, such as showing their buttocks and laughing."[17]

For half a century after Verrazzano's reconnaissance of the Atlantic coast, we hear virtually nothing of European activities in Norumbega. After Jacques Cartier's tactless kidnapping of Chief Donnacona and several Stadaconans from Quebec, the St. Lawrence was closed for more than forty years to French traders, the likeliest sailors to make side trips around Cape Breton and Nova Scotia to Maine's promising shores. When Europeans did return, they witnessed a new force in down-eastern economics: Micmac (and later Etchemin) middlemen who facilitated trade between French ships in the Gulf of St. Lawrence and the fur hunters of Norumbega, as far south as Massachusetts. These were the enterprising folks who met English explorers in the first decade of the seventeenth century, sailing French and Basque shallops (apparently stolen) of no mean size, sporting harlequin combinations of European clothes and native skins, and speaking trade pidgins of recognizable French and Basque elements.[18]

The first English ship of record to encounter one of these nativized craft was captained by Bartholomew Gosnold, who was headed for Verrazzano's "Refugio" to plant a winter trading post. As soon as he sighted the Maine or Massachusetts coast in May 1602, eight Micmacs in a "Biscay" shallop sailed out to greet him with "signes of peace, and a long speech." After "boldly" climbing board the English ship, they drew a chalk map of the local coasts and tried to talk the crew into staying to palaver and trade. But Gosnold had other fish to fry and sailed off to Cape Cod to catch them.[19]

Unable to find Narragansett Bay, Gosnold settled for wooded and well-watered Elisabeth's Isle on Buzzard's Bay, which was "unpeopled" save by summer crabbers from the mainland. There and in trips to the mainland, the English had largely peaceful engagements with the trade-savvy natives, who "offered themselves . . . in great familiaritie" and plied their guests with food and anything they happened to be wearing or carrying. The usual exception, of course, was the women, whose menfolk paid "heedfull attendance" on any who sidled too near the sailors and who themselves "would not admit of any immodest touch." A handful of natives helped the English dig sassafras, and a large group traded furs after due deference was paid to their chief. He received as gifts a straw hat, which he wore, and two knives, whose shiny sharpness he "beheld with great marvelling." The same party was feasted with ship's beer and dried cod, but the mustard condiment "nipp[ed]" their noses, "whereat they made many a sowre face."[20]

We would like to know how the proud natives responded to the Englishmen's obvious "sport" at their discomfort and perhaps anxiety (not knowing whether they had been poisoned). For re-

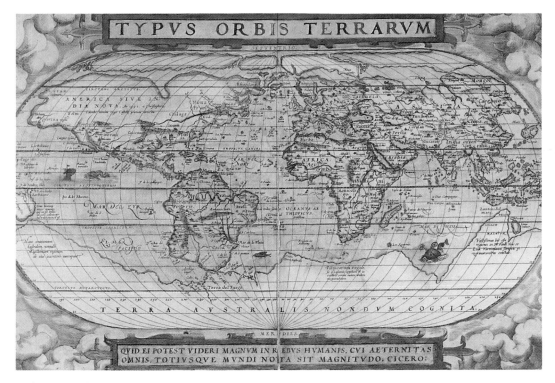

1. Abraham Ortelius, *Typus Orbis Terrarum,* in his *Theatrum,* 1570.
Courtesy of Smith Cartographic Collection, University of
Southern Maine.

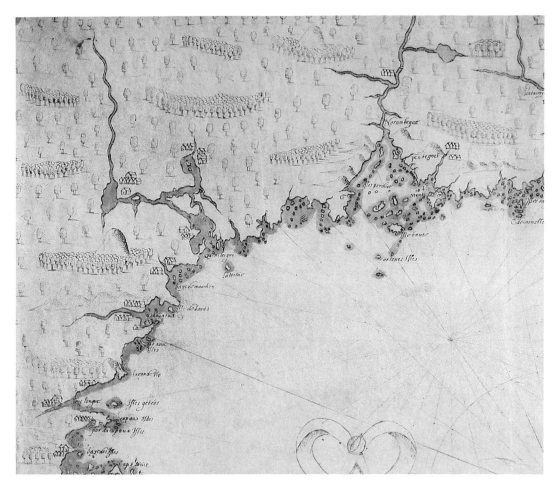

2. Extract from Samuel de Champlain, manuscript map of New
France, 1607. Courtesy of Library of Congress, Geography and Map
Division, Vellum Chart Collection #15.

3. Pierre Desceliers, *Mappemonde,* 1546. Inset: detail showing
Norumbega. From a ca. 1854 redrawing courtesy of the National
Archives of Canada, NMC 40461.

4. Gerardus Mercator, 1512–94, and Jodocus Hondius, 1563–1612,
from Henricus Hondius, *Atlas ou Representation du Monde . . . en Deux
Tomes, Edition Nouvelle,* 1633. Courtesy of Smith Cartographic
Collection, University of Southern Maine.

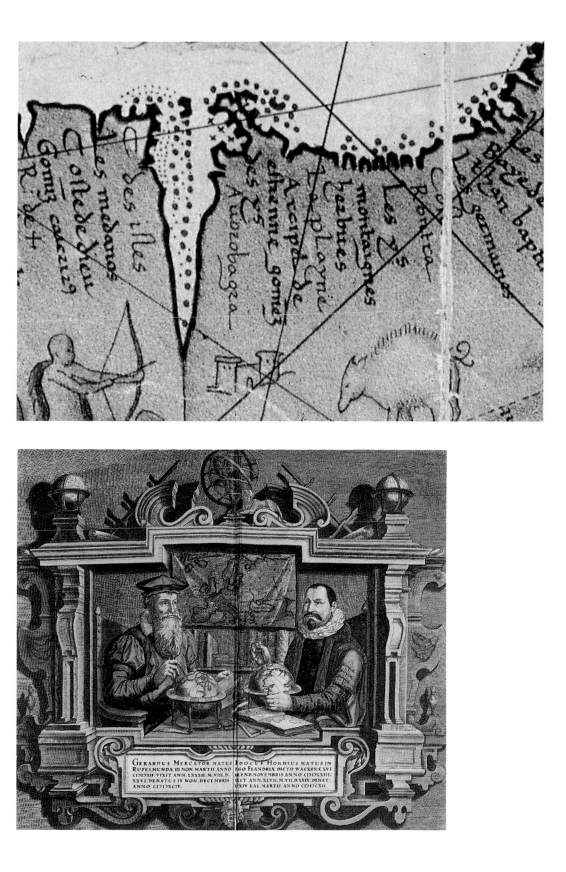

5. Abraham Ortelius, *Americae Sive Novi Orbis, Nova Descriptio,* 1570.
Courtesy of Smith Cartographic Collection, University of
Southern Maine.

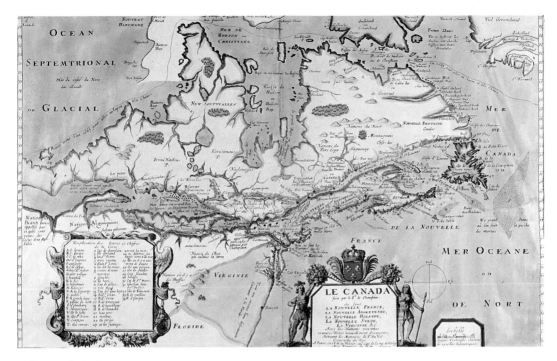

6. Pierre du Val, *Le Canada faict par Le Sr de Champlain,* 1677.
Courtesy of Smith Cartographic Collection, University of
Southern Maine.

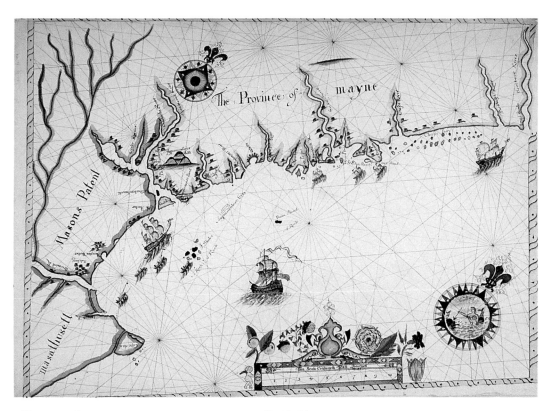

7. Tracing of *Piscataway River in New England* (by I. S.), ca. 1665. Courtesy of the Baxter Rare Maps Collection, Maine State Archives. Original in the British Library.

8. Early fishing stations throughout the North Atlantic would have looked similar to this one in Newfoundland. Gerard van Edema, *A Fish Station in Placentia Bay, Newfoundland,* ca. 1690. Courtesy of the Royal Ontario Museum.

9. Tracing of *Map of the Province of Mayne,* ca. 1653. Courtesy of the Baxter Rare Maps Collection, Maine State Archives. Original in the British Library.

10. William Godsoe, *A Plott of Mr. Humphrey Chadburns Farm
at Sturgen Creek Taken October 6–7, 1701.* Courtesy of Maine State
Archives.

51. Considered a cure for syphilis, sassafras was sought by Bartholomew Gosnold and other early explorers. *Tweede Boek: Beschreiving van 't Norder-America,* in Arnold Montanus, *America,* 1671. Courtesy of Smith Cartographic Collection, University of Southern Maine.

lations soured before the food-short English pulled out after one month. Two or three incidents may have contributed to the Indians' change of heart. The first was Gosnold's stealing a canoe that four men had temporarily abandoned in fear. Another was his disingenuous handling of the theft of an English shield, a theft that he had connived at "onely to trie whether they were in subjection" to their chief. The English got their jollies when, "with feare and great trembling," the natives restored it, thinking (no doubt correctly) that the well-armed intruders "would have beene revenged for it." Perhaps even a humorous incident carried darker meaning for the Indians. When one man offered to swap an artificial beard of animal hair for the apparently unnatural red beard of a sailor, he was of course rejected and probably laughed at in the bargain. Whatever stuck in their craw, less than two weeks into the strangers' stay, four natives attacked two crewmen who had been sent to collect seafood. One took an arrow in the side, and the other escaped injury or death only by leaping after his assailants and cutting their bowstrings.[21]

The following year (1603) an English voyage under Martin Pring spent seven weeks digging sassafras at a barricaded post on the tip of Cape Cod. They too began on a jolly note with the Indians but had clearly outstayed their welcome by the end. Like Gosnold's group, Pring's party played host to large sorties of curious natives, whom they entertained with small gifts, food, and the homely melodies of a young guitarist. But they also purloined a large birch-bark canoe, a rarity in southern New England. Worse yet, when they tired of the natives' eager company, they let loose their two great mastiffs, Fool and Gallant, one of whom carried a half-pike in his mouth to show that he meant business. Understandably, the Nausets were more afraid of the huge-jawed dogs than of twenty Englishmen and must have resented mightily such "savage" treatment. Accordingly, on the eve of the Englishmen's departure, they set fire to the woods where the English were working, after 140 warriors had been foiled in an earlier attempt to surprise the lightly guarded post and the napping workmen.[22]

For the next five years, English investors turned their attention toward the cold heart of Norumbega, what was now called "North Virginia." Because of the active French and Micmac presence in Maine's waters, English relations with the Indians there were trickier and more complex than they had been around Cape Cod and were made more so by English actions. Captain George Weymouth's trading expedition in the summer of 1605 provided the inspiration for the more ambitious Sagadahoc colony two years later but may inadvertently also have contributed to its premature demise.

Weymouth's crew encountered their first Wabanakis in St. George Harbor when three canoes made for a neighboring island. Responding to a hat-waving invitation from the English, one canoe approached, and a sagamore began to speak "very lowd and very boldly . . . as though he would know why we were there." He pointed with his paddle toward the sea, and the Englishmen "conjectured he meant we should be gone." But a brave show of trade goods and how they were used seemed to change the natives' tune, even though most of the items—except peacock feathers and clay pipes—must have been familiar fare. To new eyes, the natives "seemed all very civil and merrie: shewing tokens of much thankefulnesse, for those things we gave them."[23]

During the next few days Weymouth consolidated his good fortune with more openhandedness and a little technological wizardry. He feasted visitors below deck, where they "marvelled much" at the construction of the cook's kettle and metal can (which may indicate this particular group's lack of direct experience with European ships). When the crew set their seine net, they gave most of the catch to the "marvell[ing]" and no doubt grateful spectators, who in turned impressed the English by their careful sharing of all food with their absent women and mates and by their prompt return of pewter dishes lent to carry the food. To entice the locals to trade, Weymouth left trade goods in a conspicuous path and bestowed on their sagamore a shirt (apparently a true novelty), a large knife, a necklace, a comb, and a mirror, "whereat they laughed and," unlike Verrazzano's Narragansetts, "tooke gladly." The Indians were also offered aqua vitae, but they would not drink it after having a taste; they much preferred small beer or cider, sugar candy, and raisins.[24]

English technology also played a role in securing the natives' attention and initial respect if not long-term affection. They were "most fearefull" of firearms and "would fall flat downe at the report of them," a tactic that suggests some acquaintance with Europeans.[25] When James Rosier, the *Archangel*'s scribe and cape merchant, began to collect Wabanaki vocabulary, the natives brought him natural specimens just to see him make his magical black marks on the thinner-than-birchbark paper, marks the silent import of which other Englishmen could fathom more easily than their own shamans could read native minds at a distance.[26] The finale was Weymouth's plucking up a knife and needle with his magnetized sword, all "to cause [the Indians] to imagine some great power in us," Rosier admitted, "and for that to love and feare us."[27]

During this moment of good feelings, the natives and the English swapped guests for the night. The English emissary was Owen Griffin, one of the two crewmen the voyage's sponsors planned to leave with the Indians over the winter; he happily stood hostage for three natives who slept on deck in an old sail. (Avoiding Pring's gaff in etiquette, Weymouth tied his dogs up whenever any Indians visited the ship.) The natives ashore treated Griffin to a two-hour religious dance, in which he par-

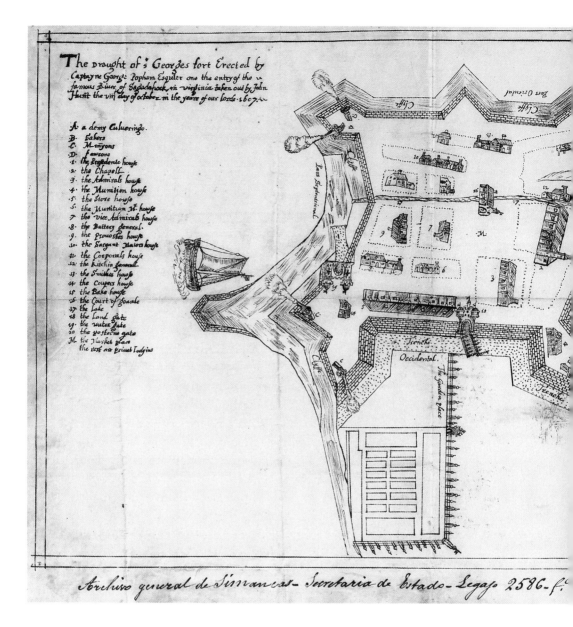

52. Tracing of *Draught of St. George's Fort*, 1607, better known as the Popham Colony. Clearly the short-lived colony never achieved such an ambitious plan. Courtesy of the Maine Historic Preservation Commission. Original in the Spanish Archives, Simancas.

ticipated by singing and "looking and lifting up his hands to heaven." As we might expect, the Indians were as unsuccessful in interpreting his gestures as he was theirs. By turn, they pointed to the moon, the rising sun, and the stars to ask what he worshipped, but each time he signaled his denial, and they ended up "laughing one to another."[28]

Other aspects of English behavior must have been equally puzzling. One morning, after two days of brisk trade, the ship sud-

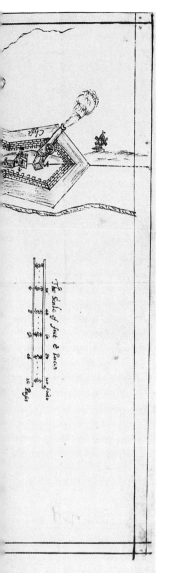

denly closed shop and sent all canoes home because "it was the Sabbath day," although that evening, after the official end of the day, half a dozen crewmen went ashore to see if they could raise any truck with the ship's biscuits, which the natives inexplicably fancied. There the cape merchant refused certain local foods in trade and drove a hard bargain for four goslings because, he said, he wanted "always [to] make the greatest esteeme [he] could of [English] commodities whatsoever." Such close-fisted conduct, contrasted with Weymouth's liberality aboard ship, cannot have pleased the natives, to whom generosity was the prime social virtue.[29]

But relations took a nosedive on the fifth day when the English seized five Wabanaki warriors by the hair (the only option given their near-nudity) as future interpreters and informants for their sponsors. Two of the men were below deck at the cook's fire; the other three had to be lured away from their numerous companions (Griffin counted 283 during the dance). All were inhabitants of the nearby Pemaquid village; one was Nahanada, its sagamore. The English added insult to injury during the next few days by planting a cross up the St. George River, marching around the interior on a "parching hot" day in armor, refusing to meet with Bashabes, the supreme sagamore of the region, and pestering a sagamore who had come to redeem his neighbors to sell his official red roach coronet. Although the captives were treated kindly and were ready students (and teachers) of language, they may have exacted small but keen revenge when, after seeing English cattle, they told their captors of native dairy production. "They make butter and cheese of the milke they have of the Rain-Deere and Fallo-Deere, which they have tame as we have Cowes."[30]

After a year's immersion in things English, Nahanada and his "brother" Amooret were returned to native life at Pemaquid. In 1607 a third captive, Skidwarres, shipped out with Raleigh Gilbert's colony headed for Sagadahoc. After two years abroad, he was intended to serve as a trusted interpreter-liaison with his tribesmen. But as soon as he introduced the colonists to Nahanada's armed and wary people at Pemaquid, he slipped into the native crowd and never again cast his lot with the newcomers.

During the Popham Colony's brief existence, Skidwarres and Nahanada made only two documented appearances, but they clearly played a key role in defeating its economic ends. Early in

October they and three others showed up at the heavily armed fort to join the one hundred colonists at table and, as it turned out, church services. For their timing they had to endure public prayers both morning and evening; one witness thought they attended with "great reverence & sylence," and another thought they "seemed affected with our mens devotions." Having learned the art of flattery from English adepts, the Indians told their hosts, "King James is a good King, his God a good God, and Tanto [their own evil deity] naught." Yet they also let slip, not without purpose, that Tanto had "commanded them not to dwell neere, or come among the English, threatening to kill some and inflict sicknesse on others, beginning with two of [Nahanada's] children, saying he had power, and would doe the like to the English the next Moone." This potent prophecy did not stop one native visitor from staying behind, trading the beaver coat off his back and expressing a wish to visit England.[31]

A month earlier, Skidwarres and Nahanada had also promised to take the English to Bashabes on the Penobscot to open a profitable trade, which in September was highly improbable. More likely the Indians knew that Bashabes, the overlord of Mawooshen, a nine-river region of some ten thousand people, expected that "all strangers should have their addresse to him, not he to them." At the appointed time the guides vamoosed into the interior; the English could not find their way alone and so returned empty-handed. To judge from the report of a ship captain who returned from Sagadahoc in mid-December with a number of frozen settlers, the colony's anticipated fur trade was likely never to materialize. One reason was the ubiquitous French; four ships that year had combed the coast as far south as Massachusetts. Another was the fractured leadership of the colony: the president and people "devid[ed] themselves into factions, each disgracing the other, even to the Savages, the on[e] emulatinge the others reputation amongst those brutish people." The chief obstacle, however, seemed to be the former captives. Not only were the local natives "exceeding[ly] subtill and conninge" in concealing the source of all the commodities the English wanted, but if by chance any Indians appeared ready to reveal those sources, the turncoats were hustled off by Nahanada and Skidwarres and prohibited—probably on pain of death or of offending Tanto—from showing their faces near the fort.[32]

A key player in this tug-of-war was Sabenoa, the local sagamore of the lower and middle Kennebec. After the colonists began construction of Fort St. George without his permission, he and four men canoed down to inform them—in "broken English"—that he was "Lord of the River of Sachadehoc." He then invited a delegation to visit his village upriver. After an exchange of hostages, a delegation went to Sabenoa's village. When they arrived, they were met by "50 able menn very strong and tall . . . all new[ly] paynted & armed with their bowes and arrowes." Apparently without any gift-giving to dissolve the tension, and only a teasing show of trade goods for the future, the English headed home in their shallop. Predictably, they were soon intercepted by three canoes carrying sixteen warriors, who said they wanted to trade. When the English disdained their tobacco and small skins, the pursuers' true motive became clear: one Indian stepped into the shallop and, pretending to light his pipe, seized the firebrand used to ignite the English matchlocks and threw it into the river. His comrades then grabbed the boat rope and prevented a soldier from landing to secure another fire. Fortunately, the combatants came to a Mexican standoff and departed with no casualties except their trust. The Wabanakis cannot have lamented the departure of the last settlers the following summer, particularly when the French supplied their needs better and did not stay long enough to spoil the neighborhood.[33]

But the Norumbegans would get no peace. Maine's coastal waters and then its rivers soon became a wild international frontier of cutthroat competition and cultural domination. And the plague-weakened natives bore the brunt of the damage, as they did everywhere in North America—the victims of a geopolitical reality they could not foresee and could only partially fashion.

PART THREE

"Planting, Ruling, Ordering and Governing"

European Colonization and Settlement

Introduction

Edwin A. Churchill
and Emerson W. Baker

Throughout the seventeenth century, Norumbega was a land largely controlled by its native population. However, during this period the presence of the Europeans would gradually grow as they settled along the coast and made conflicting territorial claims against each other. These French and English settlements were lightly populated and sometimes tenuous, but people were drawn to a land whose wealth of natural resources implied a promising future. Despite the native presence on the land, only a few settlers acknowledged the Wabanaki claim to territory. The 1620 charter forming the Council for New England typified this thinking when it stated that the aim of the company was "the planting, ruling, ordering and governing" of the region. The charter completely ignored the existence of a native population that already occupied the land. It was this sort of cultural indifference by the English as well as by the Wabanakis that would cause the prolonged series of frontier wars that would virtually destroy the way of life familiar to both groups.

John G. Reid follows the complex and largely ineffective English and French efforts to colonize the region. Various proprietors, representatives of the English Crown, and Massachusetts officials vied for control of the English region, from the eastern-most settlement of Pemaquid to the colony's western boundary at the Piscataqua River. Meanwhile, to the east at Pentagoet, the modest French efforts at settlement were disrupted by a civil war followed by sixteen years of English occupation.

The various political squabbles began not long after the arrival of English fishermen, the first widespread presence along the Norumbega coast. Faith Harrington traces their story, starting with the discovery of the superb New England fishing grounds in the early seventeenth century. First exploited by Virginians for sustenance, the fishing areas were increasingly taken over by the commercial efforts of English West Countrymen. Still in its infancy in the 1620s, the fishing industry rapidly matured with the establishment of year-round stations between Monhegan Island and Cape Ann. These operations served as the launchpad for the growth of both the fisheries and the permanent settlements in northern New England.

Meanwhile French entrepreneurs at Pentagoet and points northeast established the colony of Acadia, which was economically based on the fur trade with the Wabanakis. During the 1980s Alaric Faulkner and Gretchen F. Faulkner excavated the French fort at Pentagoet (1635–74) and began ongoing work at the nearby habitation Saint-Castin (ca. 1677–ca. 1690). The Pentagoet soldiers and colonists principally sought to separate themselves from their surroundings, huddling in forts, importing European durable goods via French channels, and consuming European types of food. Saint-Castin altered this pattern, settling with 160 Etchemins and marrying a native woman.

With the possible exception of Saint-Castin, most early settlers in Norumbega looked to their mother lands for support as they began their settlements. The Anglo inhabitants especially strove to re-create the rural English landscape that they had left. Edwin A. Churchill examines the governmental, economic, and social frameworks developed for the achievement of those goals, as well as comparable aspects of French counterparts in Acadia. These Europeans faced many elements in the New World that hampered their success, including harsh climate, poor soil, voracious predators, political wrangling, and disadvantageous trade relations. As a result, these communities were highly vulnerable during economic and military crises.

During his brief stay in the province of Maine, Deputy Governor Thomas Gorges would witness both the potential of the region and the weaknesses of his colony. The future looked bright when he arrived in 1640, but by 1643 the colony floundered as the English Civil Wars cut off emigration to Maine and signaled the rise of the Puritans, a change that would soon lead Massachusetts Bay to an economic and political hegemony over the region. Examining Gorges's letterbook and the archaeological remains of his manor house in present-day York, Emerson W. Baker provides a close-up look at Deputy Governor Gorges and his Maine. It was a Maine where diverse English cultural backgrounds were coming together into what the colony's proprietor, Sir Ferdinando Gorges, hoped would be a great and thriving endeavor from which he could govern all of New England.

Sir Ferdinando's dream would never come to pass. Instead, his colony slipped under the control of Massachusetts. Control by the bay colony brought a degree of stability to Maine, but it did not last for long. In 1674 the French abandoned Pentagoet after it was destroyed by raiding Dutch pirates. The next year saw the outbreak of King Philip's War. Within a few months this conflict in southern New England triggered a separate but clearly related war in Maine. King Philip's War in Maine lasted three years, but it was just the first phase in over eighty years of intermittent warfare among the English, Native American, and French populations of Maine. By the end of the seventeenth century, Maine —the heart of Norumbega—had become a poor embattled territory buffeted by many contenders, a far cry from earlier, more promising times.

CHAPTER EIGHT

Political Definitions
Creating Maine and Acadia

John G. Reid

At the opening of the seventeenth century, Norumbega, or the territory later known as the state of Maine, was essentially unaffected by European colonial claims. A few contacts between native and nonnative people had already occurred in the fur trade; however, no European nation had attempted colonization. Even a century later, the European grip on the area was loose. The native inhabitants, the Wabanakis, proved fully capable of mounting a strong defense against unwelcome intrusions, although European claims had been asserted and in some places consolidated. A French presence survived on the Penobscot River, with Wabanaki protection. English assertions of jurisdiction over the entire area as far northeast as "the River St. Croix and a right Lyne from the head of that River to the River Canada [St. Lawrence]" were substantiated only by occasional military expeditions and by colonial communities in Wells, York, and Kittery.[1] The retreat, rather than the expansion, of European settlement characterized political history in the last decades of the seventeenth century. Even the name "Maine," originally applied by the English in 1622 to the territory between the Merrimack and Kennebec rivers, had fallen into disuse with the northeastward expansion of the authority of the colony of Massachusetts. Nevertheless, by the turn of the eighteenth century, many of the elements had been created that would eventually work to define the state of Maine.

The early seventeenth century saw an upsurge of interest in North American colonization among the nations of northern Europe. It was based in part on a desire to emulate the long-standing Iberian colonial conquests in the Americas and to exploit whatever precious metals might be found. The possibility of finding the elusive Northwest Passage was also influential. The immediate reasons for the awakening of English, French, and Dutch interest, however, were more prosaic. They reflected increasing commercial exploitation of North American resources. By 1600, European fisheries had expanded from Newfoundland waters to the coasts of the northeastern mainland. Commercial fur trading in the Gulf of St. Lawrence and on the Atlantic coast had become profitable as the price of beaver in Europe rose substantially from the 1580s onwards.[2] There were also political factors. The end of the French wars of religion in the 1590s, the establishment of peace between England and Spain in 1604, and the inauguration in 1609 of a truce in the conflict between Spain and the Netherlands combined to create circumstances in which northern European governments could look beyond immediate crises and toward the possibilities of imperial expansion to North America. Three major territorial claims affected Norumbega. In 1603, the Crown of France granted to Pierre du Gua, Sieur de Monts, the power to settle and govern the lands between the fortieth and the forty-sixth degrees of latitude—from present-day New Jersey to Cape Breton Island—as the colony of Acadia. The English colony of North Virginia, contradictorily, was defined in 1606 as lying between the latitudes of thirty-eight and forty-five degrees. Further complication was added by the Dutch grant of 1614 to the New Netherland Company for the territory from the fortieth to the forty-fifth lines of latitude.

To translate vast territorial claims into actual colonial settlement was no easy task. The French initiated efforts to do so in 1604. The de Monts expedition, which settled St. Croix Island (later Dochet's Island), had a disastrous winter and departed for the more promising site of Port Royal (near the present Annapo-

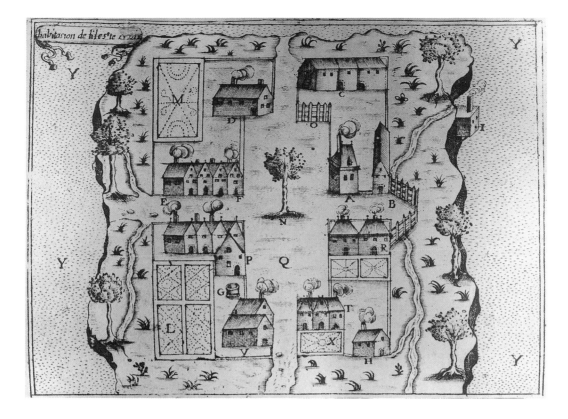

53. Like the English at the Popham Colony, the French had grand designs for the St. Croix Colony, plans that were never realized. This idyllic map was probably drawn to attract colonists. Samuel de Champlain, *Habitasion de L'Isle Ste. Croix,* from his *Les Voyages,* 1613. Taken from the 1878 reprint, courtesy of Dyer Library.

lis Royal, Nova Scotia) in 1605 (fig. 53). Effectively confined on their small island by harsh weather, the colonists had run short of firewood and had subsisted largely on salt meat and melted snow. Not surprisingly, the death rate from scurvy had been high. The first English colonists arriving at Sagadahoc, at the mouth of the Kennebec River, in 1607, fared even worse. As well as encountering problems of climate and disease, the English quickly alienated the Wabanakis on whose lands they sought to establish themselves. The settlers' retreat back across the Atlantic in 1608 represented the abandonment, for the time being, of any attempt by the English to colonize North Virginia. According to Sir Ferdinando Gorges, one of the colony's chief promoters in England, the episode was a "wonderful discouragement, . . . in so much as there was no more speech of settling any other plantation in those parts for a long time after."[3] A further attempt by the French, near Mount Desert Island in 1613, was also short-lived. Established as a mission settlement by four Jesuits, the colony of Saint-Sauveur was destroyed within weeks by an English expedition from Virginia, which also went on to burn the French habitation at Port Royal.[4]

Thus, during the first two decades of the seventeenth century, there was essentially no nonnative political history of Norumbega. None of the attempts to bring about settlement had survived more than a few months. Neither the St. Croix nor the Sagadahoc ventures had moved beyond the quasi-military organization that was characteristic of North American colonial efforts of this era. The immediate intention of the Jesuits at Saint-Sauveur had been to develop a native rather than a nonnative community. The failure of each — and the accompanying reality that the remaining nonnative presence was confined to fishing harbors, where population was either purely seasonal or represented "overwintering" rather than permanent settlement — meant that the political culture in the area continued to be that of native people. The Wabanakis had leadership structures that were decentralized and based on persuasion rather than force. Their migration cycles were often misunderstood by Europeans as implying an aimless nomadism rather than their true purpose: the harvesting of diverse resources. The native peoples, by 1620, had experienced serious losses as a result of European epidemic disease, and population density was accordingly less than in aboriginal times. As a result of all these considerations, colonists frequently underestimated the native ability to respond coherently to the challenge presented by European settlement; later experience in Maine would demonstrate that this was a serious error.

From the beginning, the French were more often successful in establishing harmonious relationships with native inhabitants than were the English. Kennebec Wabanakis complained to a visiting Jesuit in 1611 of the behavior of the Sagadahoc colonists three years before. "[They] recounted the outrages that they had experienced from these English; and they flattered us [the French], saying that they loved us very much."[5] In the later years of the century, the relationship between French and native people would emerge as the crucial support of any continuing French presence in the area and would be embodied by 1690 in an outright military alliance.[6] For all that, harmony was not an invariable rule. In 1636, Abraham Shurt — an English trader at Pemaquid who traded successfully with native people on both the Penobscot and the Kennebec — reported on French-native con-

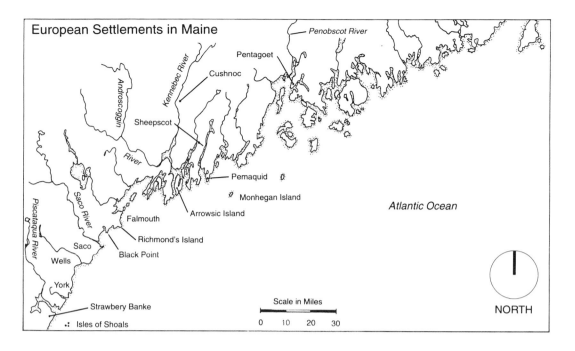

European Settlements in Maine

Penobscot River

Pentagoet

Cushnoc

Kennebec River

Androscoggin

Sheepscot

River

Pemaquid

Monhegan Island

Arrowsic Island

Falmouth

Atlantic Ocean

Saco River

Piscataqua River

Saco

Richmond's Island

Black Point

Wells

York

Strawbery Banke

Isles of Shoals

Scale in Miles

0   10   20   30

NORTH

54. Seventeenth-century French and English settlements of Maine and Acadia.

flict at Pentagoet, a French post at the present location of Castine. "Here comes natives from thence," Shurt commented, "and sayes that they will remove to some other parts, they are so abused by them [the French]."[7] Yet the persistence of French trade on the Penobscot River, based at Pentagoet, showed that this episode was an incident in a more general pattern of French-native cooperation, just as the role of Shurt and other English traders in the Kennebec-Penobscot region was atypical of the pattern of tension and hostility that English settlement caused elsewhere.

Pentagoet, as well as being an important site of French-native interaction, was crucial to the French-English dispute over the conflicting claims of the two nationalities. Soon after the formation of the Pilgrim colony at New Plymouth, merchants from that settlement began to trade furs with the Wabanakis. By the end of the 1620s, they had established trading posts on the Kennebec River and at Pentagoet. One of the merchants involved, Isaac Allerton, who was estranged by this time from the Plymouth colony as a result of disputes over the allocation of profits, moved even farther east in 1631 to establish a post at Machias. All these establishments were in territory claimed by the French, and their importance as lucrative centers of the fur trade made them desirable for economic as well as political reasons. A French

55. Charles de Menou
d'Aulnay, Sieur de
Charnisay, ca. 1644.
Courtesy of New
Brunswick Museum.

attack expelled Allerton from Machias in 1633. Two years later
Pentagoet was seized by Charles de Menou d'Aulnay, Sieur de
Charnisay, at the time chief lieutenant to the French governor
of Acadia, Isaac de Razilly. From Razilly's death in 1636 until his
own death in 1650, d'Aulnay would emerge as the most powerful
figure in Acadia (fig. 55). That Pentagoet was his personal conquest emphasized its strategic importance, and by the summer of
1636 d'Aulnay was seeking an understanding with New England
—specifically with the colony of Massachusetts Bay, now clearly
the most powerful of the New England colonies—to place the
effective French-English boundary between the Penobscot and
Kennebec rivers. D'Aulnay, according to Governor John Winthrop of Massachusetts, "professed that they claimed no further
than to Pemaquid, nor would unless he had further order."[8] The
equilibrium that now effectively prevailed would be shaken in

the 1640s by Massachusetts support of d'Aulnay's political rival in Acadia, Charles de Sainte-Étienne de La Tour, and would be interrupted in 1654 when an English naval expedition under Robert Sedgwick captured Pentagoet and other Acadian centers. Nevertheless, the events of the 1630s had conclusively ended the frictions implied by the vast territorial claims originally made by the French and the English and had established that the real border between their spheres of influence lay in the Kennebec-Penobscot region.[9]

Already by that time, the English presence was well established farther southwest on the Maine coast. Gorges and others had combined in 1620 to form the Council for New England, chartered by the English Crown for "the planting, ruling, ordering and governing" of all America between the latitudes of forty and forty-eight degrees.[10] The council never exercised its theoretical powers of government, and its chief function from 1620 until its demise in 1635 was to make land grants to its members and others. In 1622 the council granted to Gorges and his partner, John Mason, all the coastal land from the Merrimack River to the Kennebec, and westward from the head of each river to sixty miles from its entrance, as the province of Maine. In practice, Gorges was interested primarily in the territory from the Piscataqua to the Kennebec, and Mason's responsibility for the remaining area was made formal in late 1629 with his acquisition of the first New Hampshire patent. Gorges's authority was strengthened in 1635, when one of the final acts of the council was to make a sole personal grant to him of the Piscataqua-Kennebec area, to be known as "New Somersetshire." At the time, the English Crown was considering how to assert itself in the government of New England, in view of the conspicuous failure of the council and in view of the equally evident success of the colony of Massachusetts Bay in establishing its own institutions independently of the council's jurisdiction. In 1637 a royal manifesto named Gorges as prospective governor of all New England, but by 1639 that plan had been abandoned in the face of political resistance from Massachusetts. Instead, Gorges received a full proprietary grant to an area including the same coastline as New Somersetshire but extending farther inland. It was to be designated "the Province of Maine."[11]

The confusing succession of grants of Maine territory in the 1620s and 1630s was symptomatic of a series of economic and political problems that had emerged from English colonization efforts in this part of North America. First of all, none of the land grants of the Council for New England had succeeded in attracting significant bodies of settlers. The only settlements that had done so were the unconventional ones at Plymouth and Massachusetts Bay, where the commercial and political motivations that had previously represented the norm of European colonization in North America were overshadowed — at least initially — by religious purposes. The Massachusetts colony, though based on a royal charter, had asserted a degree of political autonomy that was deemed dangerous by the English government. Second, in northern New England, the relatively few colonists who had settled had done so not as organized groups but rather as individuals and families who had arrived with English-based commercial ventures in the fishery and the fur trade — normally with land grants from the Council for New England — and had elected to stay, frequently after the demise of the enterprise that had employed them. One major example was the Laconia Company, formed in 1629 with the involvement of Gorges and Mason to exploit the inland fur trade but eventually concentrating on the fishery in the Piscataqua area until its bankruptcy in 1635. Another was the fishing center at Richmond's Island owned by English West Country merchants from 1631 until the early 1640s. These and other ventures employed chiefly males, although they also brought smaller numbers of women, either as employees or in fulfillment of land-grant stipulations that they must settle families in New England.[12] Settlement by scattered clusters of such colonists gave no guarantee of either political or social coherence, and the brief sojourn of Gorges's nephew William Gorges as governor of New Somersetshire from 1636 to 1637 was too short to bring about lasting change. An English traveler, John Josselyn, in 1638 described the coastline of northern New England as "a meer Wilderness, here and there by the Seaside a few scattered plantations."[13] Neither in societal nor in governmental matters had the efforts of Gorges and the Council for New England attained their desired end of establishing a populous and structured colonial presence.

The chartering of the province of Maine was intended to correct these problems. As well as being a counterweight to the continuing growth and the autonomous tendencies of Massachusetts, it was designed as a framework within which the political culture of Maine would be shaped according to the principles of proprietary colonization. Landholding would be based on a variant of the conventional European practices of *féodalité*, with the proprietor at the apex of a structure based on leases granted in return for rents and services. Government would also proceed from the proprietor, and Sir Ferdinando Gorges announced his intention to govern through a council made up of his own appointed officials and elected representatives of the landholders. In 1640 he dispatched another kinsman, Thomas Gorges, as governor. Thomas, who quickly convened a general court at Saco, was optimistic for both the economic and the political future of the province. "I like the country well," he wrote to Sir Ferdinando in September. "The air is health[y], the feilds are fruitfull." To another correspondent, Thomas confided, "Longe have these poor people groaned for want of government." But he added that he looked forward to rapid improvement.[14] He was too sanguine. The province of Maine never fulfilled its intended objectives. Thomas Gorges, no matter how ceremonious his court proceedings, could do little to enforce his jurisdiction over any recalcitrant land patentee who chose to reject his authority. Even the support of Sir Ferdinando was uncertain in view of his increasing involvement, on the royalist side, in the crisis in England, which led in 1642 to civil war.

When Thomas Gorges departed in 1643, probably to fight in the English Civil Wars, the province of Maine disintegrated. One faction, headed by the Casco resident George Cleeve, arranged to purchase a dormant land grant of the Council for New England, which predated the Maine charter, and proclaimed the "Province of Lygonia," extending from Cape Porpoise—just northeast of Wells—to the Kennebec. The town of Wells had been settled in 1641 by John Wheelwright and his followers, who had been expelled from Massachusetts as adherents of Anne Hutchinson during the Antinomian controversy of 1637 and had moved northeastward by way of New Hampshire. Wells was granted extensive powers by Thomas Gorges to regulate its own land allocations, and it increasingly acted autonomously. A Maine court record of 1651 referred to "the inhabitants of Wells, who formerly deserted this government."[15] Thus, the power of the province of Maine was restricted to the two small settlements of Agamenticus (later renamed York) and Kittery, and even there its standing was tenuous. Cut off from any effective links with

England by the death of Sir Ferdinando Gorges in 1647, the province of Maine was nominally controlled by a self-proclaimed "boddy politick and Combination" of leading land patentees headed by the Agamenticus resident Edward Godfrey.[16]

In 1652 the colony of Massachusetts intervened. Acting on a new interpretation of the boundaries specified in the colony's charter, which purported to bring all the territories southwest from Casco Bay within its jurisdiction, the Massachusetts general court sent commissioners to accept the submission of Kittery and then Agamenticus, now designated as the county town of the newly created county of Yorkshire corresponding to the claimed portion of Maine. Despite opposition from Godfrey and other major landowners, both communities accepted the new regime. The process was repeated at Wells, Cape Porpoise, and Saco in 1653, and by 1658, even George Cleeve had agreed to the inclusion of the remaining Lygonia settlements. For Massachusetts, there were good reasons for extending the colony's bounds in this way. Between 1641 and 1643, it had similarly expanded to encompass the settlements of New Hampshire. Rumors of efforts by Portsmouth residents to throw off Massachusetts jurisdiction provided one reason for expanding further to secure control of the entire Piscataqua area. The strategic value of the Piscataqua River itself was also important, given the tensions that were shortly to result in the Anglo-Dutch war of 1652–54. English-Wabanaki tensions in Maine provided a further reason for Massachusetts to intervene in an area where political fragmentation inevitably implied English military weakness, and the abundant natural resources of Maine—fish, furs, timber, and land—gave an additional incentive. For many residents of the Maine communities, there were equally good reasons for supporting the Massachusetts initiative. One implication of the change was the entrenchment of the New England town system as the basis of landholding. Land grants would henceforth be made by the town, rather than depending on the proprietary structure, and would be free of proprietary rents and services. In this respect, the significance of the annexation by Massachusetts varied from town to town. At Kittery, for example, it merely reinforced a practice that had quietly originated in 1648, whereas at York, there was an extended conflict between Godfrey and the town over allocations of land considered by Godfrey to be within his property. Increasingly, the existing population of all the settlements was now augmented by migrants

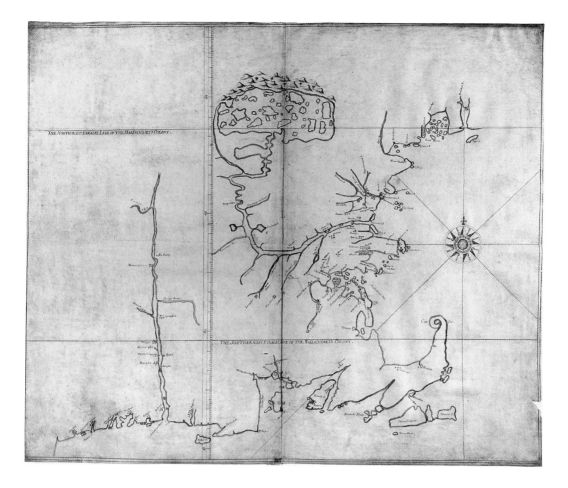

56. Map of Massachu-
setts boundary claims
by William Stoughton
and Peter Bulkeley,
1678. Courtesy of John
Carter Brown Library
at Brown University.

from Massachusetts, so that support for Massachusetts jurisdiction was likely to grow. By 1658, with the submission of the towns renamed Scarborough (formerly Black Point and Blue Point) and Falmouth (Spurwink and Casco), there was every reason to expect that the county of Yorkshire would be a lasting creation.[17]

The restoration of Charles II to the throne of England in 1660, however, introduced new complications. The changes of the 1650s, although carried out with minimal reference to England, had occurred during the Commonwealth period and the Protectorate of Oliver Cromwell. Soon after the monarchy was restored, the new government was approached both by Edward Godfrey and by Ferdinando Gorges, grandson of Sir Ferdinando and claimant to his North American interests. Attempting to taint the actions of Massachusetts with disloyalty to the Crown, Godfrey and Gorges pressed for redress of their personal losses of property through reversal of the annexation of Maine. The result was a complex series of disputes in which the English government attempted to assert its authority in New England while Massachusetts set about defending its autonomous practices and its jurisdiction over northern New England. In Maine itself—or Yorkshire, depending on which side one was on—factional conflicts reemerged, and the attempt by an English royal commission to establish an impartial regime in 1665 was short-lived. Three years later, Massachusetts control was successfully renewed; in 1678, the colony succeeded in purchasing the patent of the province of Maine from a frustrated Ferdinando Gorges. The royal Committee for Trade and Plantations regarded the purchase as being "of evil . . . consequence" and called for its abrogation, but for the time being it would stand.[18]

In the meantime, the Restoration era had also bequeathed other questions regarding the status of the territory northeast of the Kennebec, which had never been part of the province of Maine. In 1635, the Council for New England had designated the area from the Kennebec to the St. Croix River as "the county of Canada." Originally awarded to the son of Sir William Alexander, Earl of Stirling, the grant passed to Stirling himself after his son's death in 1638. Virtually bankrupted by his earlier, unsuccessful efforts to colonize New Scotland—a Scottish colony claiming boundaries equivalent to Canada's Maritime Provinces and the Gaspé Peninsula, and thus in direct conflict with the French colony of Acadia—Stirling was in no position to attempt settlement of the area.[19] Furthermore, the French presence at Pentagoet would have prevented him from doing so. During the sixteen-year occupation of Acadia that followed the Sedgwick conquest in 1654, Sir Thomas Temple briefly asserted powers of government over what the English had designated Nova Scotia, including the entire area northeastward from Muscongus (southwest of Penobscot Bay). Temple originally governed, from 1657, on behalf of Cromwell, although—unlike his associate William Crowne, who pursued the fur trade on the Penobscot—he never resided in Nova Scotia.[20] He obtained a new patent as governor from the Crown in 1662, but two years later the territory of Nova Scotia was curtailed when the duke of York acquired a large grant of land. It included not only the existing Dutch colony of New Netherland, renamed New York after its military conquest by the English later in the year, but also the territory between the St. Croix River and the Kennebec and extending back to the St. Lawrence.[21]

On the Kennebec, northeastward at Pemaquid and Sheepscot, and as far as Penobscot Bay, there were English settlements by mid-century. Although evidence is sparse, travelers' accounts indicate a substantial population. Samuel Maverick wrote in 1660 of "many families," and John Josselyn described "Cattle and Cornlands" after a visit later in the 1660s.[22] For the time being, little was done to assert the duke of York's authority, and in 1667 the treaty of Breda committed England to restore to France the colony of Acadia. That this agreement conflicted with the duke of York's 1664 patent was made explicit in Charles II's order that Pentagoet was to be included among the "forts and habitations" specifically handed over.[23] By the summer of 1670, Pentagoet had become the military headquarters of Acadia and the seat of its governor, Hector d'Andigné de Grandfontaine. Among Grandfontaine's goals was to assert the French claim as far as the Kennebec, and in 1671 both he and Simon-François Daumont de Saint-Lusson, an envoy of the governor of New France, reported to France that the English inhabitants of "Kennebequy and Paincouit [Pemaquid]" could readily be won over to the French allegiance.[24] However, in 1672, ninety-six of the residents signed petitions requesting the Massachusetts general court to extend its jurisdiction farther northeast. Massachusetts hesitated, then complied. A court that convened in Pemaquid in July 1674 proclaimed the establishment of the county of Devon. It lasted only three years, until the New York council resolved that "it would be advisable to send to take Possession and assert the Dukes Interest at Pemaquid, and parts adjacent Eastward."[25] The construction of a new fort at Pemaquid followed later in 1677, and until the end of the 1680s it continued as an outpost of the English in the Northeast.

The 1680s proved to be a turbulent decade in the political history of the province of Maine and all New England. From 1680 to 1684, Maine—that is, the province bounded by the Piscataqua and Kennebec rivers—was governed by Massachusetts in its new capacity as the holder of proprietary rights to the area. A council headed by the Massachusetts magistrate Thomas Danforth now administered the province and—by contrast with the previous arrangements for the county of Yorkshire—did so in a way that made Maine politically distinct from the parent colony. Instead of sending delegates to the Massachusetts general court, the Maine towns were represented at annual general assemblies of the province. Maine was also distinguished by the partial restoration of proprietary forms in the reintroduction of quit-rents for land. This, along with tax impositions and what one hostile observer described as "those Allotments of Land which Mr. Danforth and others of the [Massachusetts] magistracy have made to themselves out of the Province of Maine," provided fuel for grievances that soon reached the English government, although the willingness of the new government to protect the essential integrity of the landholding structures of the towns earned it an adequate level of popular support.[26] For all that, the grievances contributed to the more general process by which disputes between the Crown and Massachusetts led to the cancellation of that colony's charter on October 13, 1684. After a period of uncertainty, during which the Danforth council continued to govern Maine, both Maine and Massachusetts were incorporated in 1686 in a new "Dominion of New England." Governed for the Crown by Sir Edmund Andros, a military officer who also carried the title of captain-general, the dominion included by 1688 not only New England but also New York and the Jerseys. It continued until the spring of 1689, when Andros was overthrown in the wake of the English Revolution of 1688–89. Provisional regimes were established in the several colonies, with Massachusetts resuming its administration of Maine pending a permanent settlement.[27]

Throughout the period from 1670 to 1689, however, the political history of the English in the territory later defined as the state of Maine was profoundly affected by non-English peoples: the French and, most powerful of all, the native inhabitants. The new French regime at Pentagoet quickly encountered difficulties. Despite ambitious plans in France for a triangular trade that would join Acadia and other French colonies in North America with the French West Indies and France itself, Acadia's main trading links continued to be with New England. Necessary as this trade was for the Acadian communities, it was illegal from the viewpoint of the parent country, and in 1673 Grandfontaine was dismissed on suspicion of personal involvement in the trade he had been instructed to discourage. Pentagoet continued briefly to function as a military and fur-trading post until its capture and destruction by a small Dutch sea force in 1674. The raid was hardly a serious reassertion of the Dutch territorial claim, since it was not sustained by any continuing presence. Left in nominal charge was John Rhoades, a New England merchant who was soon arrested and convicted in Boston of piracy on the basis of his association with the Dutch raiders. This episode, fleeting as it was, marked the end of the formal French occupation of Pentagoet—Port Royal would henceforth be the headquarters of Acadia—though not of the French presence there.[28] At the time of the raid, one of the fort's officers was Jean-Vincent d'Abbadie de Saint-Castin, who escaped and took refuge with the native inhabitants. Later marrying Pidianske, the daughter of a Penobscot chief, Saint-Castin continued to reside at Pentagoet. Through this marriage alliance, both Saint-Castin and the Penobscots strengthened their ability to resist any English incursions. With the Boston merchant John Nelson, they had a close trading relationship. With the New York authorities at Pemaquid, relations were not as cordial. One Pemaquid official, Anthony Brockholst, declared in 1682 that Saint-Castin's interests were "of no Importe . . . knowing the Extent of his Royal Highnesses [the Duke of York's] Limitts which must be Maintained."[29] Later in the decade, Sir Edmund Andros actively harassed Saint-Castin in efforts to induce him to recognize the English claim to rule as far as the St. Croix River. Andros himself led a raid on Saint-Castin's house in 1688, rifled it in his absence, and gave word that Saint-Castin "should have all goods restored if he would demand them at Pemmaquid and come under obedience to the King [of England]."[30] Far from complying, Saint-Castin and the Penobscots, in cooperation with the French forces at Port Royal, prepared for war.

When war came, however, it did not proceed directly from this episode. It was the result of long-standing tension between the English and the Wabanakis farther southwest. English settlement of the province of Maine, destructive as it was to the environmental balances on which native societies depended, and carried out—some specific purchases of native land notwithstanding—without any general agreement or understanding between native and nonnative peoples, could be seen by the Wabanakis only as an act of aggression. Although native responses were remarkably moderate, given the importance of what was at stake, conflict inevitably developed at times. "The country is in great fear of the Indians," reported Thomas Gorges in 1642. In 1660, the towns of Scarborough and Falmouth described themselves to the Massachusetts general court as "the fronteire townes" in the face of "Som late Indian tended and intended motions."[31] Matters came to a head in September 1675, following English attempts to disarm the Wabanakis in view of the earlier outbreak of King Philip's War in southern New England and following the drowning, by English seamen, of the infant son of a Saco chief. War thereupon began. Although not all the branches of the Wabanakis took part, it was a costly conflict on both the native and the nonnative sides. English lives were lost in all the Maine communities. For the Wabanakis, losses in battle were aggravated by food shortages arising from the protracted disruption of agriculture, hunting, and trade. Peace was finally agreed to in April 1678, with terms that included the future payment by the English to the Wabanakis of an annual tribute of corn.[32]

The peace agreement of 1678 symbolized the reality that colonization depended ultimately on the sufferance of native inhabitants, who retained considerable military power, and their strength deserved to be seriously pondered by the English in Maine. From the perspective of political history, the treaty indicated that all the English governmental arrangements had an underlying provisional quality, no matter how confidently they might be proclaimed. Native inhabitants retained the ability to intervene, if provoked to do so. The lesson was not well learned by the colonists. The annual tribute soon fell into arrears while disputes continued to arise over land, river fishing rights, and damage done to Wabanaki crops by English-owned cattle. Again, a crucial incident occurred on the Saco River, when English militia seized twenty Wabanakis and sent them to Boston as hostages in the fall of 1688. A reciprocal seizure and a misunderstanding over arrangements for an exchange launched another full-scale conflict.[33]

The crisis was further complicated by the results of the English Revolution of 1688–89. The revolution replaced the Catholic and pro-French James II with his Protestant daughter Mary and her husband, William of Orange. William, as captain-general of the Netherlands, was already a military rival of France. War between England and France began in the spring of 1689. Because the revolution also led to successful revolts by political opponents of the dominion of New England, there followed a period of military and political disorganization in the English colonies.[34] At the same time, the outbreak of war prompted formal military cooperation between the French and the Wabanakis. French observers were impressed by the effectiveness of the native forces that captured the English fort at Pemaquid in August 1689, and in 1690 French officers fought side by side with the Wabanakis.[35] The results for the English were predictable. Of the Maine settlements, only Wells, York, and Kittery remained by the end of the summer of 1690, and even they were vulnerable to the raiding warfare that would persist intermittently for the next twenty years.

The 1690s, though a decade of war, did witness political developments significant for Maine. In 1691 the English Crown replaced the provisional government of Massachusetts, which had existed since the revolution, by a new charter that included not only all of Maine but also Plymouth and even—though it was not in English hands—Nova Scotia. Thenceforth, the remaining Maine settlements were governed as a part of Massachusetts, though under the title "District of Maine" from 1778 until the creation of the state of Maine in 1820. In 1693, some Wabanaki leaders signed a peace treaty with the new governor of Massachusetts, Sir William Phips. Other Wabanaki groups, however, suspected English intentions and preferred the French alliance, and the treaty did not stand.[36] War continued, and in 1696 Pemaquid—reoccupied and its fort reconstructed by the English in 1692—fell once again to French and native forces. War between France and England ended for the time being in the next year but resumed shortly after the turn of the century. War between the English and the Wabanakis was interrupted in 1699 by a temporary revival of the treaty of 1693, but conflict quickly flared up again in the new century.

The political history of Norumbega in the seventeenth century began with the assertion of European claims to native territory and continued with efforts to consolidate these claims through colonization, including—for the English—complex disputes regarding the political status of the settlements made. By the end of the century, native power had been reasserted, and much of the English political posturing of earlier years had come to seem arcane and superficial in the face of the more general question as to whether English settlement could or should be sustained. Some developments would later prove to have begun the process by which the state of Maine would ultimately be defined:

the introduction of the name "Maine" to designate territory; an English colonial presence that would gradually assert numerical and geographical primacy over native people in the eighteenth century; and the increasing significance of the Piscataqua and St. Croix rivers as political boundaries. In themselves, however, the seventeenth-century endeavors of European powers and Eur-american colonists to assert control over native territory had led mainly to conflict and confusion. By 1700, European political control of Norumbega was far from guaranteed.

CHAPTER NINE

"Wee Tooke Great Store of Cod-fish"

Fishing Ships and First Settlements on the Coast of New England, 1600–1630

Faith Harrington

Fishing played a critical role in the English colonization of coastal New England. The dry cod fishery required an expansion not only into previously uncharted waters but also onto unfamiliar and ungranted lands. The fishermen needed to establish fishing stations where the cod could be hauled in, processed, and then dried for several weeks in the open air — an effective yet rudimentary technology that required the fishermen to occupy and claim new lands.

Although fishing activities in early-seventeenth-century New England, and specifically the dry cod industry, played a crucial role in the English colonization process, the delineation of these activities has remained a superficial exercise for most historians. However, there have been some exceptions to this rule. For example, Harold Innis's *The Cod Fisheries* cannot be overlooked; although written in 1940, it remains today a classic on the formation and structure of the European cod fisheries from the sixteenth through the early twentieth centuries. Considerably less scholarly yet quoted even more often are Charles L. Woodbury's *The Relation of the Fisheries to the Discovery and Settlement of*

North America (1880) and Raymond McFarland's *History of the New England Fisheries* (1911). Neither of these works are based on the careful, scholarly, archival research found in Innis's book. Fortunately, in recent years, there has been a refocusing of attention on the early fisheries of northern New England. Edwin Churchill has described the social and material conditions of the difficult existence these fishermen faced in the first four decades of the seventeenth century, and Alaric Faulkner has detailed the archaeological research on Damariscove Island, concentrating on the technical aspects of the fishery. Meanwhile Canadian researchers have provided excellent comparative information for the Canadian Maritimes and Newfoundland.[1]

This chapter focuses on the importance of early fishing activities to the first phase of settlement in Norumbega, beginning with the initial exploratory voyages to the area and the promotional accounts that encouraged investors to become involved in the profitable fisheries of New England. The chapter also investigates the connection between the early Jamestown settlement in Virginia and New England during the first decade of the seventeenth century, as well as the expansion of the New England fishery in the next two decades.

Encouragement for Fishing in New England, 1600–1620

In the first two decades of the seventeenth century, many expeditions were dispatched from England to survey the coast of New England, describe the landscape and inhabitants, and determine the potential of the region in terms of natural resources. Most early visitors to New England encouraged the development of the fisheries there, particularly the cod fishery with its well-established market throughout England, Europe, and the West Indies. Early accounts often compared the potential of the New England fishery with that of the successful Newfoundland fishery, finding New England far superior for a legion of reasons.

Captain John Smith publicized the bountiful fishing of New England in his writings and recognized that the best time of the year for fishing in New England was earlier than in Newfoundland (February instead of mid-May), allowing an earlier return to markets. William Wood noted that the fishermen could make a larger profit in New England, receiving shares of about fourteen pounds rather than the six- or seven-pound shares from Newfoundland; furthermore, furs could be obtained from the Indians and sold in Europe for a good price. Another advantage to fishing in New England recognized by some early explorers was the favorable climate for drying the codfish. In Newfoundland, ice conditions shortened the length of the fishing season, and fog was prevalent throughout the entire season, hindering the taking of cod and also complicating the process of curing it. However, in New England, the warmer, sunnier weather permitted fishermen to catch and cure fish almost anytime during the year. According to the promoters, not only was the fishing season earlier, the weather warmer, the waters friendlier, the fish closer to shore, and the expenditures less in New England than in Newfoundland, but also the fish were bigger and it took less fishing to make a quintal, the standard hundredweight sold at market.[2]

Bartholomew Gosnold was one of the first Englishmen to return home with detailed descriptions of the geography, climate, inhabitants, and fishing potential of New England. In 1602 Gosnold commanded two ships, the *Concord* and the *Dartmouth*, chartered by Sir Walter Raleigh. Rather than just explore or fish, Gosnold attempted to begin a colony—England's first effort at starting a colony since the failure of Roanoke fifteen years before. He sailed with a crew of thirty-two people, twenty of whom were expected to remain as settlers. Two crew members—John Brereton, an Anglican priest, and Gabriel Archer, a "Gentleman"—recorded firsthand accounts of the venture. As they sailed the coast of southern Maine, they were approached by a Basque shallop manned by eight Micmacs (Souriquois) led by one who was dressed in the European garb. The natives demonstrated their knowledge of the coast by drawing it and could even "name Placentia of the New-found-land."[3]

The Indians' awareness of Placentia in southeastern Newfoundland, where the Spanish and the English had been taking cod since the 1580s, indicates that the southern Maine Indians were well aware of European fishing and trading activities at the cod fisheries in Newfoundland by the first few years of the seventeenth century. By the second decade of the seventeenth century, the initial, sporadic interactions between New England Indians and European explorers grew into regular trading opportunities.[4]

After Gosnold's intriguing encounter with the Indians dressed in European clothing, he and his crew sailed south from Maine to Cape Cod and Martha's Vineyard. Although they were not taking fish for profit, the crew did explore some of the possible fishing grounds, with considerable success. Of their experience on Cape Cod in 1602, Brereton writes, "We had pestered our ship so with Cod fish, that we threw numbers of them over-boord againe; and surely, I am persuaded that in the moneths of March, April, and May, there is upon this coast, better fishing, and is as great plentie, as in Newfound-land."[5] Brereton was convinced that the fishing would be extremely productive if the ships arrived a little earlier than they had. Only later, by the 1610s and 1620s, was it confirmed that the best fishing for cod was actually during the cold months of late December, January, February, and March.[6]

During their voyage along the New England coast from Maine to the islands off Wood's Hole, Gosnold's crew saw plenty of mackerel, herring, and other fish but knew it was cod, with its marketability in European ports, that would make the long fishing trips worthwhile. The gentleman Gabriel Archer recorded the crew's experiences in southeastern Massachusetts and went on to explain how Cape Cod became so named. "Neere this Cape we came to anchor in fifteene fadome, where wee tooke great store of Cod-fish, for which we altered the name, and called it Cape Cod."[7] New England would be a marvelous place for a fishery, Brereton wrote, not only because of the abundance of cod but also because the fishing was close to shore in water only seven fathoms deep, compared with depths of forty to fifty fathoms in the offshore Newfoundland fishing grounds. Besides, these promotors wrote, Newfoundland was cold, difficult to fortify, imperiled by pirates, and an expensive place to send ships because they had to be laden with men and stores enough for voyages both there and back and also had to carry the salt necessary for the fish processing.

But Brereton's interests stretched further than fishing. He envisioned New England as an English entrepôt, where the commodities of fish, whale, and seal — and the oils from each of these — along with naval supplies (pitch, tar, turpentine, and rosin), timber, hemp, flax, grapes, furs, metals, and minerals could all be shipped to England, France, Spain, and Portugal in return for wine, oil, fruit, spices, sugar, silk, gold, and silver. His promotional account concluded that this trade would create a world market in England and provide buyers for English woolens.

These enthusiastic accounts of Gosnold's voyage prompted

the merchants of Bristol (a group headed by the mayor, Richard Hakluyt, and including an alderman and a geographer) to outfit the fifty-ton *Speedwell* and the twenty-six-ton bark *Discoverer.* In 1603 Martin Pring sailed these vessels down the coast of what is today Maine and New Hampshire and headed south to Cape Cod, entering Massachusetts Bay, which Gosnold had overshot the year before. On his way south, Pring stopped in Penobscot Bay and recorded that he had found "an excellent fishing for Cod, . . . better then those of New-found-land." He added, "Withall we saw good and Rockie ground fit to drie them upon."[8] Pring and his crew were encouraged further by their observation that salt could probably be made here. At the end of this voyage, Pring sent home the *Discoverer* laden with sassafras, a plant that grew wild in New England and that was highly valued throughout Europe at this time as a cure for syphilis. Although both he and Gosnold experienced disturbing exchanges with the Indians in southern New England, these were not disturbing enough to discourage the more determined and entrepreneurial colonizers.[9]

At this time, the English decided to organize an expedition to meet the challenge of French exploration in North America and to establish an English presence there. To that end, George Weymouth set sail for New England in 1605 in command of the *Archangel.* In James Rosier's 1605 narrative of the Weymouth expedition, he described the good fishing and a new discovery made by the crew in Pemaquid Harbor. "Our men tooke Cod and Hadocke with hooks by our ship side, and Lobsters very great; which before we had not tried."[10] Even Weymouth tried his luck at fishing, and with good results, causing Rosier to remark, "It sheweth how great a profit the fishing would be, they [the fish] being so plentifull, so great and so good, with such convenint drying as can be wished, neere at hand upon the Rocks." His observation of the convenient drying rocks echoes Pring's statement two years earlier. Their luck was also good near St. George Harbor, where they discovered a fishing bank and where Rosier was "delighted to see them catch so great fish, so fast as the hooke came down." Rosier had an eye for other maritime advantages New England could offer the sailor-fisherman besides the excellent stores of fish, and he approvingly described the vast size of the St. George River and harbors and their sandy bottoms, which had "a tough clay under for anker hold."[11]

The adventures of the Frenchman Samuel de Champlain, who

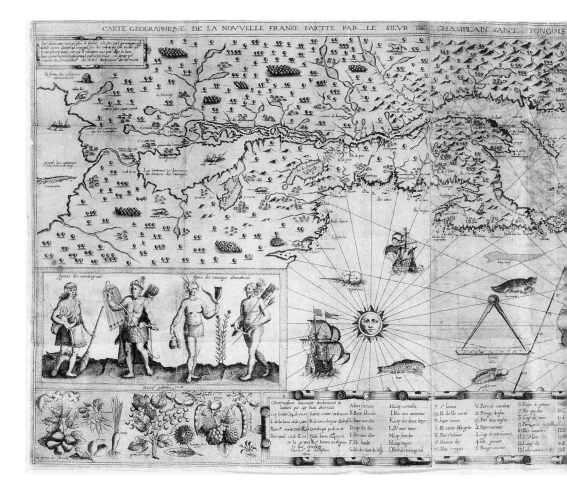

57. Samuel de
Champlain, *Carte
Geographique de la
Nouvelle Franse*, 1612.
Courtesy of John
Carter Brown Library
at Brown University.

explored the coast of New England in 1605–6, resulted in an
excellent series of maps, which provided details on the native
inhabitants, marine and plant life, and topography of the area.
His maps could also be used as coastal navigational charts, since
they depict water depths, characteristics of harbors, and fishing banks, including the Grand Banks, as shown on Champlain's
1612 *Carte Geographique de la Nouvelle Franse* (fig. 57).[12]

Lord Chief Justice John Popham, who was at the zenith of his
power and influence in England at this time, backed several expeditions with Sir Ferdinando Gorges for the purpose of setting
up stations for cod fishing and for trading with the New England
Indians. In 1606 they backed a repeat voyage by Pring, who sailed
the coast of Maine until he reached Sagadahoc at the mouth of
the Kennebec River. From Sagadahoc, he headed home to report
that he had finally found a seemingly ideal site for settlement.[13]

Pring's news prompted Popham and Gorges to send out another expedition in June 1607, with Raleigh Gilbert and George Popham commanding the *Mary and John* and the *Gift of God,* respectively. James Davies, a member of the expedition, reported in his narrative of the voyage that the crew caught larger codfish off Small Point and near the islands of Damariscove, Wood, and Outer Heron in Maine than any caught off Newfoundland.[14] Davies expressed his delight at the size of the fish during these summer months of late July and August several times in his account. "We found fyshe aboundance so large and great as I never Saw the Lyke Cods beffor nether any man in our shipe."[15]

The Popham expedition was the first attempt after Gosnold to establish a year-round settlement in New England. Gilbert and Popham proceeded to the mouth of the Sagadahoc River, where their 120 passengers disembarked and hurriedly built a small village with fifty cabins, a storehouse, a chapel, and a blockhouse. They conducted a short but successful trading session with the local Indians that winter, but they were unprepared for the severity of the weather, and they suffered scurvy and respiratory ailments. Many died, including Governor George Popham, and the rest decided to leave by the fall of 1608. Although this expedition failed to establish a permanent colony, it helped to familiarize the English with this geographical area and to stimulate efforts at establishing fishing and trading posts in New England.

In 1611 the ruins of the Popham Colony were visited by the French Jesuit priest Father Pierre Biard, who was accompanied by Charles de Biencourt, both having traveled from present-day Annapolis, Nova Scotia. In the Kennebec River area, Biard and Biencourt met the local Indians. Biard wrote in *The Jesuit Relations:* "These people do not seem to be bad, although they drove away the English who wished to settle among them in 1608 and 1609. They made excuses to us for this act, and recounted the outrages that they had experienced from these English."[16] Evidently, one major reason for the downfall of the Popham Colony was severe behavioral problems resulting from the fact that the English colonists were totally unprepared to experience a northern New England winter without any of the amenities to which they were accustomed. They also refused to trade with the local Indians, who told Father Biard that the English had closed their doors and sent out their dogs when the Indians had come to trade.

The Virginia Connection, 1607–1625

Father Biard's account of the Popham Colony reveals the cultural conflict between Native Americans and the first English colonists in Maine. But even more important for our purposes, it contains information that is critical to an understanding of how, when, and where New England's earliest communities (many of which began as seasonal fishing stations) were established. Biard noted that the Virginians made "a voyage every summer to the fishing grounds of the Peucoit [apparently the nearby Matinicus] Islands, to obtain fish for food during the coming winter."[17] Thus by 1611 and possibly several years earlier, the Virginians had a habit of coming to the islands around Pemaquid to catch a supply of fish for the winter.

The New England fishery does not seem to have been established before the first mention of Virginians plying the coastal waters of New England for the purpose of subsistence fishing. Between 1607 and 1608, starvation, sickness, and death were plaguing the new Jamestown colony, prompting action on food procurement as well as political reorganization. William Strachey, the first historian of Virginia, remarked in 1607 that there was better fishing in New England than on the banks of Newfoundland—an observation that may have signaled the beginning of regular trips there, although it is likely that there was already a general knowledge, at least among seamen, of the excellent New England fishing grounds. Interestingly, then, many of the early fishing ships working the waters of northern New England in the first decade of the seventeenth century came from the fledgling southern colony of Virginia and not from English ports. Furthermore, it is important to note that the ships sent from Virginia not only were dispatched earlier than those from English ports but also were involved in subsistence fishing, with the aim of feeding their starving population, and not "commercial" fishing, with the aim of making the largest possible profit.

At Jamestown, the Virginians were provided with abundant marine resources and excellent native fishermen who could teach them how to utilize these resources; however, they found themselves unable to turn the situation to their advantage. One reason for this was that the original goal of the Jamestown settlers did not include fishing; supposedly, they were interested instead in promoting a legitimate barter with the inhabitants (although they were abusing and plundering these local residents). Neither the settlers nor the Virginia Company in London, which arranged and financed the endeavor, realized that for a colony to be successful and permanent, it had to be self-supporting by raising its own crops and carrying out its own fishing and hunting. The men who were sent knew very little about either planting or fishing, so that out of the 105 colonists who disembarked at Jamestown in May 1607, only 38 men were alive at the end of the year.[18] Another reason for their failure was the colonists' inability to form a mutually satisfying relationship with the local Indians. Although the first impressions were of hospitality, English adventurers and native leaders soon found themselves deadlocked in struggles over land and power.[19]

Hunger, disease, and death continued to plague the new colony, causing the promoters in England to effect a political reorganization in 1610, which empowered Lord De la Warr as governor and fortified the colonists with both new supplies and new hope. Captain Samuel Argall was specially commissioned by the authorities in England to deep-sea fish for the benefit of the Virginia colony. Accompanied by Sir George Somers, he sailed to Bermuda for hogs and fish, but their two pinnaces, or small sailing vessels, were blown off course on the way, positioning them near Cape Cod, where they fished instead for a couple of days. After catching many codfish and some halibut, they returned to Jamestown around the middle of August when the fishing began to fail.[20] Hence, one of the first Virginian fishing vessels recorded in New England happened to arrive inadvertently. This serendipitous twist of fate apparently was responsible for the beginning of the trend noticed a year later in 1611 by Father Biard when he mentioned that the Virginians already had a habit of coming to the islands off the central coast of Maine to fish.

Problems increased for the Virginia colonists after about 1615, when complaints began to be published in London stating that they were interfering with free ocean fishing. Sometime before February 22, 1615, a tract entitled *The Trades Increase* was published anonymously. This tract stated, "The Virginia Company pretend almost all that main twixt it and Newfoundland to be their fee-simple, whereby many honest and able minds, disposed to adventure, are hindered and stopped from repairing to those places that they either know or would discover, *even for fishing*" (italics added).[21] The tract was clearly sympathetic to the efforts of those in England trying to explore, settle, and fish in New England during the 1610s and attempted to exclude the fishermen of the southern colony from the entire coast administered by the Virginia Company at this time.

The minutes of the Virginia Company from late 1619 to June 1621 portray the northern colony's attempt to exclude the Virginians from fishing in northern waters, although the original patent stated that the seas were free and that therefore each colony could fish in the other's territory. Sir Ferdinando Gorges and several other members of the Northern Virginia Company petitioned Parliament in March 1620 for a new charter that contained a fishing monopoly. By November 1620, a corporation called the Council for New England was created, with Gorges, who recognized the profitability of the New England fisheries, playing a key role.

Finally, in June 1621, an agreement was reached—actually a reestablishment and reconfirmation of two earlier orders—declaring that each colony had reciprocal rights to fish at sea within the bounds of the other, provided that the seas were used only for "sustenation of the people of the Colonies there and for the transportation of people into either Colony." Rights to the shore for drying nets and curing fish and to the available woods for building and repairing fishing houses, flakes, stages, and boats would be assigned by the appropriate governor at "reasonable rates."[22]

However, settling the dispute over free fishing did not bring prosperity to the Virginian fisheries. By 1625, supplies of salt for preserving the fish were low, and accounts from the mid-1620s note that vessels with fish from New England were arriving in Virginia, suggesting that Virginian fishing enterprises were still disorganized and that most of the salt fish were coming from the northern fishing grounds.[23]

The Virginians, then, were the first fishermen to exploit, albeit on a small scale, the abundant stock of codfish in New England's waters. Shortly after their arrival, they came to depend on this resource for subsistence, not for profit or trade. Strachey's praises, sung in 1607, for the potential of a New England fishery may mark the beginning of Virginian efforts to take fish here, but certainly by 1611, when Father Biard recorded his forays along the central coast of Maine, the Virginians were recognized as seasonal visitors exploiting the winter fishery. Between 1608 and 1614, the southern colonists appear to have dominated the New

England fishery, since the only ships that have been recorded as fishing there were those sent from Virginia to secure food supplies for the southern colony. At this time, there was a growing knowledge, at least among seamen, of the excellent New England fishing grounds.

Unfortunately, the actual number of ships sent by either Virginians or West Countrymen during the first two decades of the seventeenth century is unknown, but one can add the number of fishing vessels recorded in various accounts to arrive at a set of minimum numbers. Unfortunate also is the fact that the only figures for several years (1614, 1615, and 1618) are derived from the writings of Captain John Smith, a man sometimes inclined toward exaggeration and perhaps especially so when writing about his favorite cause: the promotion of the New England fishery. Yet this skepticism may be unfounded because for the years 1622, 1623, and 1624, when we have independent counts, Smith's numbers are corroborated quite closely.[24]

Smith breaks the near complete silence of the first decade and a half of the seventeenth century with his descriptions of the fishing expeditions from 1614 to about 1620. In 1614, some information on the scale and nature of fishing activities comes into focus with Smith's account of his voyage to Monhegan Island with four merchants from London. Their intent was to hunt whales and search for gold and copper, but failing in these endeavors, they took furs, codfish, and train oil. Smith mentioned that at this time, along with Popham's ship, there were two French ships, all in nearby waters. Of Smith's forty-five-member crew, thirty-seven fished in seven boats (or about five to a boat), which they had assembled on Monhegan Island, catching enough fish to reap a good profit on shiploads of dry fish that they sent to Spain and England. Evidently, the six-month voyage cleared fifteen hundred pounds, which was a sizable amount considering the fairly low costs incurred in outfitting and manning the voyage.[25]

Fishing ships continued to sail from Virginia to New England throughout the second decade of the seventeenth century. In 1615, again according to John Smith, a group of fishermen arrived in March and found enough fish to stay through mid-June. At that time, they freighted a three-hundred-ton ship with fish for Spain, and another ship sailed to Virginia "to relieve that Colonie."[26] Whether or not this ship was the same one sent by the Plymouth Company and sailed by Sir Richard Hawkins, the

58. This English cod-fishing station in Newfoundland would have been quite similar to stations in Maine. Detail from Herman Moll, *A New and Exact Map of the Dominions of the King of Great Britain*, 1715. Courtesy of Osher Cartographic Collection, University of Southern Maine.

ship that had been previously fishing and trading on the coast near Pemaquid in 1615 is unclear.[27] In 1619 Captain Thomas Dermer, an associate of Smith's, sailed to the island of Monhegan from Plymouth, England, in a vessel fishing for Virginia.[28] During that same year, John Rolfe, the tobacco experimenter, wrote about the fishing activities of the Virginians to Sir Edwin Sandys, a Londoner active in the Virginia Company's affairs. Rolfe noted that a Captain Warde had sailed to Monhegan Island in May and returned in July, having caught only a small quantity of fish there because he was so low on salt that he could not preserve many. Rolfe also wrote, "There were some Plymouth ships where he [Warde] harbored, who made great store of fish which is far larger than Newland [Newfoundland] fish."[29] One of the ships

A View of a Stage & also of ỹ manner of Fishing for, Curing & Drying Cod at NEW FOUND LAND.
A. The Habit of ỹ Fishermen. B. The Line. C. The manner of Fishing. D. The Dressers of ỹ Fish. E. The Trough into which they throw ỹ Cod when Dressed. F. Salt Boxes. G. The manner of Carrying ỹ Cod. H. The Cleansing ỹ Cod. I. A Press to extract ỹ Oyl from ỹ Cods Livers. R. Casks to receive ỹ Water & Blood that comes from ỹ Livers. L. Another Cask to receive the Oyl. M. The manner of Drying ỹ Cod.

mentioned by Rolfe was probably Dermer's. The important point in this detailed chronology is that by 1615 at least, the Virginians were being joined by West Country fishermen in their quest for New England codfish, particularly around the islands and peninsulas of the central coast of Maine.

Expansion of the New England Fishery, 1620–1630

The West Countrymen were plying the waters of New England in search of cod not for purposes of subsistence, as were the Virginian fishermen, but to obtain profit in the large-scale international cod market. Compared with earlier years, 1615 appears to have been a bumper year for sending fishing ships to New England waters. For the first time, a total was recorded—four ships, which seem to represent a considerable increase in activities, probably as a direct result of the profit gained by Smith's trip during the previous year of 1614.

The number of ships sent from England doubled again the next year. If the accounts are true, this level of activity represents twice the investment in ships, gear, and labor of the preceding year.[30] Smith reported four or five ships sailing from Plymouth to fish and trade, with the same number sailing from London during 1616. Of those that sailed from London, Smith wrote that a two-hundred-ton ship arrived in New England after six weeks and returned to England within five months with forty-four men and boys "full fraught [freight]" with furs, train oil, and greenfish. Another sailed to the Canary Islands with dry fish, "which they sold at a great reate."[31]

Smith was candid about the problems that beset him while trying to promote the New England fishery. Some of these problems were caused by the weather, others by the crew and those preparing the ships, and still others by the investors and merchants financing the voyage. In 1617, for instance, he tried to arrange more fishing expeditions, but the three ships and fifteen men provided him were wind-bound for three months in England and missed the fishing season, sailing instead for Newfoundland.[32] More difficulties beset Smith in 1618 when he had four ships prepared at Plymouth, but "by reason of their disagreement" (possibly an allusion to dissension among those preparing the ship or among the crew), the season was wasted and only two of the four actually left. One vessel of two hundred tons did manage to return, "well freighted," to Plymouth within five months; the other sailed to Bilbao with dry fish and made a good return there.[33] Then again in 1619, disagreement prevented all the other ships (total number unknown) except one from leaving Plymouth. This two-hundred-ton vessel sailed with thirty-eight men and boys, and when it returned six weeks later, its freight was sold for twenty-one hundred pounds, not counting the furs, "so that every poore Sayler, that had but a single share, had his charges, and sixteene pound ten shillings, for his seven moneths worke."[34]

This excerpt is also enlightening for the insight it provides into the share system. This system required that one-third of the profit from the fish and train oil be given to the ship's owner for the use of the vessel; another third was given to the owner of the operation for the cost of the men's victuals and the salt, nets, hooks, lines, and other implements for catching and processing the fish; the final third went toward payment of wages for the crew. Importantly, this excerpt suggests that even the poorest sailors, or those with the least experience and skills, could earn a decent wage if the fish were biting. In 1619 this payment of one share valued at about sixteen pounds for seven months' work represented a substantial wage for a young fisherman.

The third decade of the seventeenth century saw an expansion of the New England fishery, although it still remained on a small scale when compared with the Newfoundland fishery. Smith recorded a peak number of six or seven vessels in New England waters in 1620, with three ships reporting good earnings.[35] In Smith's words, the three vessels had made such a good voyage that "some Sailers that had but a single share, had twenty pounds, and at home again in seven moneths, which was more than such a one should have got in twenty moneths, had he gone for wages any where [else]."[36] This payment of twenty pounds per share was higher than the payment of sixteen pounds and ten shillings considered high the year before and was more than a sailor could make fishing in Newfoundland or anywhere else for that matter. The other ships made less-successful voyages, according to Smith because they sent "opinionated unskilfull men."[37]

The small number of fishing vessels working in New England waters at this time contrasts sharply with the number working in Newfoundland waters. In 1621 a customs officer at Plymouth recorded that 250 ships were sent from western England to Newfoundland, whereas only eleven ships returned from New

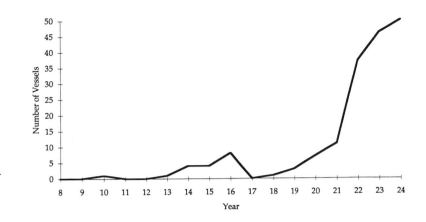

59. Chart of the number of vessels fishing in New England, 1608–24.

England. He reported that these eleven ships had discovered "nice fishing places," and he expected that others would depart for the following season. At that time, fourteen ships were preparing to sail—a larger figure than in any previous year but still considerably less than the hundreds preparing to sail to Newfoundland.[38]

By 1620 the total number of fishing vessels recorded as sailing to New England was probably less than the average number going annually to Newfoundland for a hundred years. The New England fishery was still of less actual value than the well-established industry of Newfoundland. This fact is important because it implies that any discussion among members of Parliament, for example, about the "American" fisheries probably evoked the Newfoundland and not the New England fishery and that, correspondingly, legislation would be considered and adopted as it affected the better-known and more important fishery in Newfoundland.

After 1620 the number of ships fishing in New England grew (fig. 59). Thirty-seven English vessels made good voyages in 1622, and of them, thirty-five came from the West Country, with about two joining them from London in late April.[39] These two ships, one weighing 220 and the other 100 tons, belonged to Ambrose and Abraham Jennens (or Jennings), the owners of Monhegan Island. One of these ships carried sixty new passengers to Plymouth Plantation. Smith wrote, "It is a wonder [how the Plymouth colonists] could subsist, fortifie themselves, resist their enemies, and plant their plants." The Pilgrims were "wanting most necessaries for fishing and fowling."[40] As we will see, the Pilgrims' lack of preparedness did force them to seek provisions from fishermen occupying settlements like the one on Damariscove Island off the coast of central Maine. In the following year of 1623, a record number of fishing vessels—forty-five—sailed from England, and "all made a better voyage than ever."[41]

Although Smith was known to embroider on the facts, his figures on numbers of fishing vessels are corroborated several times by other writers. For example, his figure of thirty-seven vessels in 1622 is close to the number sighted by Edward Winslow when he sailed to Damariscove in May of that year and en route sighted Thomas Weston's ship, the *Sparrow,* and about "thirty sail of ships."[42] Smith's figure of forty-five vessels for 1623 corresponds closely with Sir William Alexander's statement that forty to fifty vessels were then fishing in New England waters.

The widely available account of Christopher Levett provides another important source on numbers of fishing vessels for the year 1623 and a check on Smith's figure of forty-five. In his description of a voyage he took along the Maine coast that year, Levett recorded six ships at the Isles of Shoals, nine at Cape Newagen, and two at Sagadahoc and mentioned other "divers ships" at certain places along the coast without specifying numbers. In general, these figures match up fairly well with the other reports. The only figure that is grossly out of line is a mention by Emmanuel Altham of "400 sails" (or ships) along the Maine coast in 1623. Writing a letter in 1623 to his brother Sir Edward Altham of Essex, Emmanuel noted, "Voyages of fishing hath been found and made this year, here hath been at Monhengan, Damerill's Cove, Anquam, Pemaquid, Sagadahoc and the Isles of Shoals—all principal places for fishing—about 400 sail."[43] According to Altham, the majority of New England fish was being sold in Spain at this time for "ready gold," since the fish were in great demand and commanded a high price at market. As noted by Churchill, there are two possible explanations for the discrepancy between the number of ships Levett counted and Altham's four hundred ships: either Altham was exaggerating wildly (a habit not uncommon for him) or he was counting every small shallop as well as every large fishing ship.[44]

By the end of the first quarter of the seventeenth century, then, fishing ships with burdens of fifty to two hundred tons were sailing yearly to the New England fishing grounds sometime between January and March, depending on the weather. Financed by a consortium of merchants and manned by a crew of about fifty men, the ships left from Plymouth, Falmouth, or one of the other western ports, carrying fishing equipment, provisions, salt, nails, lumber for building boats, and a variety of work tools. The men's first task was to find a suitable harbor close to the fishing grounds with a good supply of timber and a gently sloping shoreline where they could dry the codfish.

By the 1620s there were at least ten temporary fishing stations set up along the coast between Monhegan Island in Maine, which was one of the major stations, and the south shore of Massachusetts, along with several other harbors that were probably in common use at this time. The fishing crews would settle down temporarily at one of these stations or harbors and prepare for fishing by constructing or repairing the necessary fishery apparatus, assembling the fishing shallops, and readying their equipment. Fishing would begin by late February or March, and with luck, the crew would be sailing for home with a full hold in early summer to arrive home before September. By this time the locations of the many large fishing banks off the coast of New England and Canada were well known. Sir William Alexander's map published in 1624 designates all the major banks from Cape Cod to Newfoundland, and when this map is compared with a contemporary map of the fishing areas of the northwestern Atlantic, there is very little discrepancy between the two (figs. 60 and 89).

Early Fishing Stations in New England, 1620–1630

By the early 1620s, several fishing and trading stations were flourishing along the coastline from Maine to Massachusetts. This section of the chapter defines the sphere of fishing activity in New England from about 1620 (even earlier in some cases) until about 1630. The geographic focus is the coast and islands of New England beginning with Monhegan Island, which is the farthest north or, more correctly, farthest "Downeast," and ending with the Cape Ann fishing station near present-day Salem. Only those stations that were operating as fisheries are discussed here, thereby omitting other early sites of the region.[45] The dates for establishment are conservative; there is some evidence

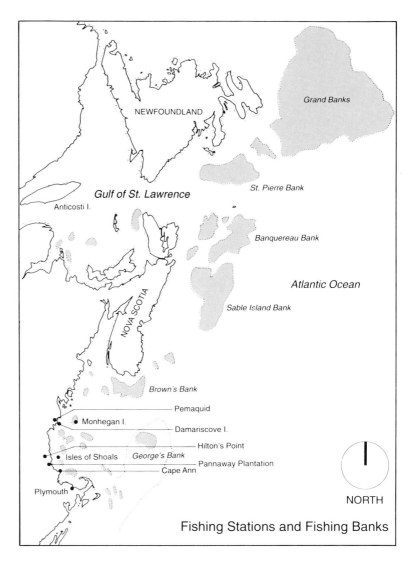

NEWFOUNDLAND

Grand Banks

Gulf of St. Lawrence

St. Pierre Bank

Anticosti I.

Banquereau Bank

Atlantic Ocean

NOVA SCOTIA

Sable Island Bank

Brown's Bank

Pemaquid

Monhegan I.

Damariscove I.

Hilton's Point

Isles of Shoals   *George's Bank*

Pannaway Plantation

Cape Ann

Plymouth

NORTH

Fishing Stations and Fishing Banks

60. Fishing stations along the New England coast, 1600–1630, also showing the principal fishing grounds of the region. Based on Douglas R. McManis, *Colonial New England: A Historical Geography* (New York: Oxford University Press, 1975), map no. 104.

that several of the stations were operating earlier than the dates listed. The documentary evidence for these first-period fisheries is supplemented whenever possible by the archaeological record.

Like most of coastal Maine, Monhegan Island was probably first sighted by Europeans visiting this coast in the 1520s or so. But it was not until the early 1600s that explorers began to persistently and actively investigate the coast of New England. In May 1605, George Weymouth anchored his ship on the north side of Monhegan Island and "with a few hooks got above thirty great Cods and Hadocks."[46] In 1614, John Smith also had a positive experience fishing near Monhegan. Smith's crew of thirty-seven men caught and processed about forty thousand fish between the last of April and July 8.[47]

By 1619 a winter fishery existed on Monhegan, for in that year Captain Edward Rocroft's mutinous crew deliberately sailed for the island in order to spend the winter there. Although Monhegan may not have been a permanent settlement by 1619, the mutineers' behavior suggests that a small group of fishermen were staying there year-round and living in what must have been fairly substantial buildings, necessary for protection against the high winds and freezing weather of New England winters.[48] By 1625 Abraham Jennens (or Jennings), an active merchant from Plymouth, England, had started a fishing settlement at Monhegan. However, it did not prosper, and in 1626 Jennens decided to break up the plantation and sell its contents at an auction.[49] Never well situated for trade with the local Etchemin Indians because of its distance from the mainland, Monhegan experienced further difficulties after the Council for New England lost its fishing monopoly in about 1625 and the fishery there went into a state of decline. Evidently, there was a lull in activity at Monhegan from about 1626, when it was sold by Jennens, until about 1635.

The decline at Monhegan must have benefited nearby Pemaquid. Abraham Shurt was probably managing a fortified trading post and fishing operation there by 1628 or 1629. He was the agent for the two Bristol merchants who were proprietors of Pemaquid, Robert Alsworth (or Aldworth) and Gyles Elbridge. Pemaquid continued as a fishery at least into the late seventeenth century, at which time the economy had diversified to include several farmers and some soldiers who were stationed at the fort there.[50]

Extensive archaeological excavations have uncovered many stone-lined cellar holes from the early settlers' homes, along with clay tobacco pipes, ceramic sherds, nails, bricks, and fishing equipment. The archaeological remains of fishing gear are varied, indicating the different fishing strategies employed by the Pemaquid settlers to obtain this readily available, high-protein food that promptly formed a staple in their diet. Several fishhooks, a fish spear probably used for killing larger fish during the seventeenth century, a hook or gaff for hauling in large fish, sinkers made of folded lead and pierced with holes to attach to the line, and compasses (or dividers) used for navigation were unearthed during the excavations.[51]

Damariscove Island is located offshore from Pemaquid, about

three miles southeast of Boothbay Harbor and near the cod-fishing banks off today's Maine coast. During the seventeenth century, Damariscove Island possessed all of the natural resources for a successful dry cod fishery: a deep and protected harbor where vessels could maneuver and where there was room for staging areas; a fairly flat shoreline for drying flakes; a wood supply for heat and building materials; a freshwater supply; and most important, proximity to the fishing grounds. Although "Damerils Iles" was noted by Smith, John Pory's account of 1622 provides us with the first documentation of fishing activities on Damariscove Island. Pory, an official of the Virginia Company who made an extensive tour of the New England coast, wrote that "Damerills's Cove" was then owned by Gorges and occupied by thirteen men who were "to provide fish all the year with a couple of shallops for the timely loading of a ship and to keep that island to be farmed out in Sir Ferdinando's name to such as shall there fish."[52] These fishermen took precautions against French and Indian incursions by constructing "a strong palisado of spruce trees some ten foot high, having besides their small shot one piece of ordinance and some ten good dogs."[53] This permanent palisaded fort, evidently armed with a cannon and mastiffs, provided protection and a base of support for their year-round operations. Under the patent issued to Gorges by the Council for New England, his agents there were to collect fees for the use of land where various fishermen carried out their operations. From scattered documentary references, it appears that Damariscove was used mainly by ships belonging to West Country merchants and by others from Plymouth Plantation, the Virginia Company, and Thomas Weston's group at Wessagusset.[54]

In 1632 Damariscove was included in the Pemaquid patent granted to Alsworth and Elbridge by the Council for New England. Ownership of the island and licensing of the cod fishery was held by these two Bristol merchants through the 1630s, during which time the island remained a fishery.[55] The beginning of the English Civil Wars ended this period of proprietary control over the fishing industry, and by about 1640, trade had virtually ceased between New England and England. Massachusetts-based vessels began to take the place of British ships, requiring more handling of goods and causing prices of manufactured English goods to escalate. By the late 1640s, English proprietary control had ended completely, and the Massachusetts domination of the Damariscove fishery had begun.[56]

During archaeological survey work in 1979 and 1980, thousands of artifacts were uncovered, including several finds dating to the earliest period of fishing activity around the cove: pipe fragments, trade beads, fragments of bellarmine bottles, delftware, Rhenish stoneware, North Devon gravel tempered ware, and sgraffito ware.[57] The stone footings for at least two early fishing stages were revealed during extremely low tides, and archaeological evidence of postholes in the flat area adjacent to the island's deep harbor may be the remains of footings for wooden flakes.

The Isles of Shoals, located eight miles offshore from Kittery Point, Maine, were the site of another early fishing station. In 1605 Samuel de Champlain noticed them off to the east, and Captain Smith also praised the potential of these islands, although there is some question as to whether he actually landed on them. Smith favored the islands enough to name them after himself on his 1616 map of New England. Christopher Levett touched first at the Isles of Shoals after completing his ocean crossing from England. Here he must have known that he and his crew could find shelter, food, fresh water, and even company. Levett wrote: "The place is found to be a good fishing place for six ships, but more cannot well be there, for want of convenient stage room, as this year's experience hath proved. The harbor is but indifferent good."[58]

Levett's description suggests that the harbor at the Shoals was not large enough to accommodate the staging required for more than six ships. Furthermore, if each of these ships carried their average number of fifty men, the islands would have been inhabited by about three hundred fishermen in 1623. (Most of the time, however, only about one-quarter to one-third of the men would be onshore, processing the fish; the rest would be out fishing.) In this case, there must have been numerous stages, flakes, cabins, huts, and work sheds here at this time, although Levett did not mention them.

During the seventeenth century, most members of the fishing community at the Shoals located their dwelling houses on the southwest end of Appledore, approximately a half-mile removed from the noise and smell of the western coves where the codfish were processed. Numerous dwelling houses, some with attached ells or free-standing outbuildings, are described in property records dating from as early as the 1640s. In some cases, fairly detailed descriptions of the types of wooden structures at the Shoals have been recorded. For example, when Miles Pyles of Devon, England, sold his property and buildings for eighty quintals of "merchandable [cod]fish" in 1665, he described his property, beginning with his "dwelling house, with the leantwo adjoyneing to it, and the Eastward halfe of [his] garden, as It is now fenced In, and the small stage on the Easterne side of the great stage, as It is now fitted, with a little house adjoyneing to ye Eastward end of the Storre house, also a moreing place with ye Cable now there unto belonging, alsoe all the flakes or fishing Rowmes on the Earsterne side from the Brew house to John Odihornes rowme."[59]

The record of this property transaction affords a detailed look at architecture at an early cod fishery, as well as a glimpse at subsistence practices vis-à-vis the reference to an enclosed garden and a brewhouse. Wood supplies must have been in steady demand at the treeless Shoals and were probably shipped from the nearby mainland as soon as timber mills were erected. During the initial seasonal occupation of the fishery, sections of the fishery apparatus—stages, flakes, and storerooms—as well as the ships and shallops may have been sent from England. Smith carried nested, ready-for-assembly halves of shallop hulls onboard his larger vessel in 1614.[60] By the 1630s, however, sawn boards would have been readily available from the many tidal sawmills constructed along the nearby Piscataqua River and its tributaries.

To date, archaeological testing has focused on three stone foundation sites on the southwest end of Appledore Island (fig. 61). One of the sites is alleged to have been William Pepperrell's dwelling house, which was erected in about 1676 and occupied by Pepperrell until he moved to the mainland in about 1680. The archaeological evidence at the alleged Pepperrell house points to timber-framed construction techniques employing handwrought rosehead nails and leaded casement windows, probably with interior plaster wall treatment.[61] The other two sites probably represent foundations for one-story, or one-and-a-halfstory, center-chimney structures following the prevalent building tradition on the islands, as evidenced from archival research and the one or two surviving buildings believed to date to the eighteenth century at the Shoals.

61. Archaeological sites on Appledore Island. Courtesy of Faith Harrington.

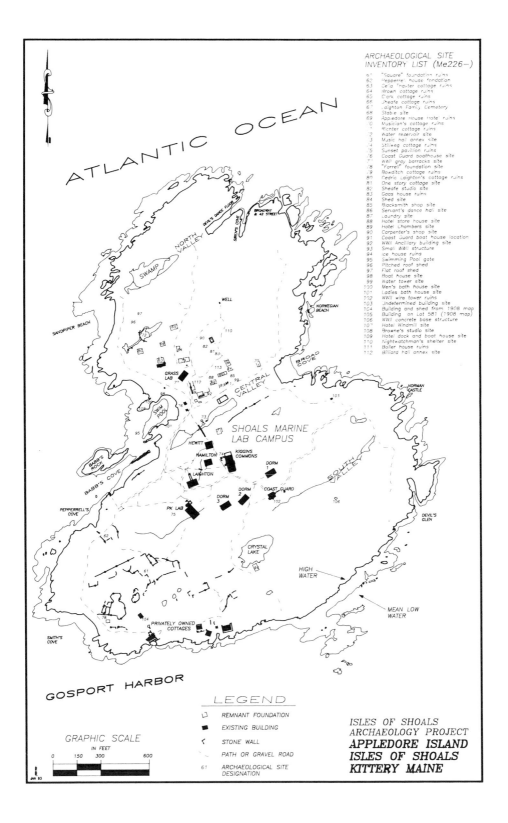

ARCHAEOLOGICAL SITE
INVENTORY LIST (Me226-)

61 "Square" foundation ruins
62 Pepperrel house fondation
63 Celia Thaxter cottage ruins
64 Brown cottage ruins
65 Clark cottage ruins
66 Sheafe cottage ruins
67 Laighton Family Cemetery
68 Stable site
69 Appledore house hotel ruins
70 Musician's cottage ruins
71 Richter cottage ruins
72 Water reservoir site
73 Music hall annex site
74 Stillwell cottage ruins
75 Sunset pavillion ruins
76 Coast Guard boathouse site
77 WWII gray barracks site
78 "Farrell" foundation site
79 Bowditch cottage ruins
80 Cedric Laighton's cottage ruins
81 One story cottage site
82 Sheafe studio site
83 Gass house ruins
84 Shed site
85 Blacksmith shop site
86 Servant's dance hall site
87 Laundry site
88 Hotel store house site
89 Hotel Chambers site
90 Carpenter's shop site
91 Coast Guard boat house location
92 WWII Ancillary building site
93 Small WWII structure
94 Ice house ruins
95 Swimming Pool gate
96 Pitched roof shed
97 Flat roof shed
98 Boat house site
99 Water tower site
100 Men's bath house site
101 Ladies bath house site
102 WWII wire tower ruins
103 Undetermined building site
104 Building and shed from 1908 map
105 Building on Lot 581 (1908 map)
106 WWII concrete base structure
107 Hotel Windmill site
108 Browne's studio site
109 Hotel dock and boat house site
110 Nightwatchman's shelter site
111 Boiler house ruins
112 Billiard hall annex site

ATLANTIC OCEAN

NORTH VALLEY
DEVIL'S DANCE FLOOR
SIREN'S COVE
BROADWAY & 42 STREET
SWAMP
WELL
NORWEGIAN BEACH
SANDPIPER BEACH
BROAD COVE
CENTRAL VALLEY
NORMAN CASTLE
GRASS LAB
SWIM POOL
SHOALS MARINE LAB CAMPUS
HEWITT
BABB'S ROCK
BABB'S COVE
HAMILTON
KIGGINS COMMONS
LAIGHTON
DORM 1
SOUTH VALLEY
DORM 2
COAST GUARD
PEPPERRELL'S COVE
PK LAB
DORM 3
DEVIL'S GLEN
CRYSTAL LAKE
HIGH WATER
MEAN LOW WATER
SMITH'S COVE
PRIVATELY OWNED COTTAGES

GOSPORT HARBOR

LEGEND

⌐┘ REMNANT FOUNDATION
■   EXISTING BUILDING
⟨   STONE WALL
      PATH OR GRAVEL ROAD
61 ARCHAEOLOGICAL SITE
      DESIGNATION

GRAPHIC SCALE
IN FEET
0   150   300   600

JAN 93

ISLES OF SHOALS
ARCHAEOLOGY PROJECT
**APPLEDORE ISLAND
ISLES OF SHOALS
KITTERY MAINE**

Although initially largely a male community, by the late 1640s, women were present at the Shoals in very small numbers. In 1647, a complaint was made against John Reynolds for bringing his wife to Appledore, since her presence was contrary to an unwritten law excluding women, but the court decided that Reynolds's wife could remain because the law was considered obsolete and because a precedent had been set earlier when another woman had been allowed to stay with her husband.[62] The presence of women may indicate that the Shoals station was moving away from a seasonal occupation and toward permanency in the 1640s. The dearth of women in both the archival and the archaeological records at stations during the first couple of decades of the seventeenth century suggests that their presence was probably the exception rather than the rule.

Crossing today's border from Maine into New Hampshire, we enter the Piscataqua River region, where David Thomson's settlement at "Pannaway" was established in 1623. Known today as Odiorne's Point, New Hampshire, it was an excellent choice for a settlement, since it had a good supply of fresh water, an easily defendable location, and extensive salt marshes, which provided salt hay for cattle fodder and thatch for roofing material. It was also located within ten miles of the Isles of Shoals, where a prosperous fishing industry was rapidly getting under way.

The Thomson group consisted of about eight to ten men who were fishermen, traders, and subsistence farmers, although no records survive to indicate the extent of their activities, and the exact location of the original Thomson settlement is unknown. The settlers used local stone in the construction of a large communal dwelling house—the "Great House," named for its large room or "great hall" where many group activities could take place. These large multipurpose buildings were common in the architecture of the first period of settlement in northern New England, and other "Great Houses" were built in the early 1630s at Strawbery Banke, Richmond's Island, and Newitchawanick.[63]

For unknown reasons, Thomson and his family moved south to live on an island in Boston Harbor only three years later. Perhaps the fishery was not as successful as he had hoped, or perhaps he decided to try farming in the Massachusetts Bay area in the company of other English planters.[64] In 1630, Gorges and John Mason assigned Captain Walter Neale the original Thomson plantation at Pannaway as his headquarters. Neale expanded the settlement to include Great Island (now the island of New Castle), the main shores of the Piscataqua, and even the fishery at the Isles of Shoals. Although the expanded settlement did not prove to be a large financial success, there were enough people settled in the Piscataqua region by 1633, when Neale departed for England, to ensure the continuation of the colony. During the 1630s, Strawbery Banke emerged as the political center of coastal New Hampshire, and occupants of the Pannaway plantation continued to farm and fish.[65]

Several individuals can be traced as moving from one fishing settlement to another at this early date. For example, the Hilton brothers first settled with Thomson at Odiorne's Point, but shortly afterward, in 1623 or 1624, Edward and William Hilton split from the Thomson group to move a few miles upriver to set up fishing stages near today's New Castle, New Hampshire. They then moved up the Piscataqua River again, about seven miles, to finally set up fishing operations at a location that soon became known as Hilton's Point. Together with several planters from Pannaway, the Hilton brothers constructed buildings, planted cornfields, and traded with the local Pennacooks.

Farther south at the Cape Ann peninsula, Robert Cushman and Edward Winslow from Plymouth Plantation obtained a large tract of land in 1624. The two men were granted five hundred acres for each planter to "lie upon the said Bay in one place, and not straggling"; their patent from the Council for New England included the nearby islands and all inclusive fishing and hunting privileges.[66] In short, the council was trying to encourage the formation of a cohesive community, not just a dispersed collection of households.

Yet from the outset, the fishery at Cape Ann had plenty of setbacks, suffering from an incompetent fishing master and an inept salt maker who misled Governor William Bradford and others to believe that he was capable of installing a good system of saltworks.[67] Fortunately, the Cape Ann fishery had at least one honest and industrious tradesman—a ship carpenter who worked hard and required the same of his employees. Although the profits from the fur trade helped somewhat to offset the money lost in the fishery that season, the colony faced severe difficulties within the next three years. First, the Plymouth Colony claimed that it held the rights to fish and hunt in the area; second, the location was too distant from the fishing grounds to be practical;

and third, the settlers refused to produce some of life's absolute necessities. Not surprisingly, then, the attempt to establish a year-round fishery failed. Some of the residents were sent back to England while others relocated in Salem, Massachusetts.[68]

Conclusions

This chapter has attempted to delineate the sphere of fishing activity in New England during the period from approximately 1600 to 1630. Interest in the New England fishery began in the early seventeenth century mainly as a result of increased international competition in Newfoundland, both on land for fish processing and drying areas and at sea for prime fishing grounds. The importance of fishing activities in early-seventeenth-century New England has been overlooked by scholars—a bias that is probably due to the greater number of texts written by the Pilgrims and Puritans than those written by, or about, the first fishermen and their families. Indeed, the families of these fishermen were probably not even brought to New England until sometime in the third or fourth decade of the seventeenth century. Important too is the fact that the first fishermen exploiting the grounds off New England's coast did not sail directly from English ports but rather from the fledgling (and starving) settlements of Virginia. These fishermen were plying New England's waters in search of cod to satisfy their own needs, not to obtain profits in the large-scale international cod market. Finally, most of the people who lived along the coast and on the islands during the 1620s and 1630s were located in small fishing communities (many of which would develop into permanent, year-round settlements) and were involved in a nexus of goods, information, and people in early New England.

Fine-grained case studies and comparative interdisciplinary historical archaeological research on fisheries, such as demonstrated here, can provide a microanalysis of the larger process of early European settlement. By noticing the details, we deepen our understanding of a past society at a time when many of its members relocated themselves across the Atlantic Ocean and consequently experienced profound shifts in the ways they viewed their world.

CHAPTER TEN

Fort Pentagoet and Castin's Habitation
French Ventures in Acadian Maine

*Alaric Faulkner
and Gretchen F. Faulkner*

The remarkably varied seventeenth-century beginnings of
Acadia are represented in a number of archaeological sites along
the coasts of Nova Scotia, New Brunswick, and Maine. Most
familiar are two sites that were excavated in the 1960s: St. Croix,
on the Maine–New Brunswick border; and Fort La Tour, in Saint
John, New Brunswick.[1] St. Croix was the site of an unsuccessful
attempt by Sieur de Monts and Samuel de Champlain to settle at
Dochet's Island in the St. Croix River, and it lasted only through
the winter of 1604–5, when the starving company removed to
Port Royal, Nova Scotia. Fort La Tour was a fortified settlement established by Charles de Sainte-Étienne de La Tour on a
point of land at the mouth of the St. John River; it lasted from
1631 until its destruction in 1645. To these pioneering efforts in
Acadian archaeology can be added considerable new information

Previously published as "Acadian Maine in Archaeological Perspective," by
Alaric Faulkner and Gretchen Faulkner, in *Northeast Historical Archaeology* 14,
copyright 1985, Council for Northeast Historical Archaeology. Reprinted with
permission of the publisher.

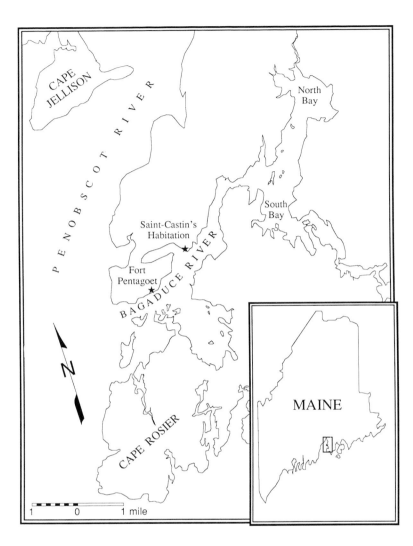

62. Map of Castine Harbor.

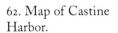

from related sites recently excavated along the coast of Maine—information that reveals the variety of settlement strategies employed by the French in attempting to settle Acadia.

Since 1981, a team of archaeologists from the University of Maine has been studying two major seventeenth-century settlements on the Anglo-Acadian frontier: Fort Pentagoet and Saint-Castin's Habitation. These sites represent three distinct French occupations, established by leaders with very different backgrounds, goals, and strategies. The earlier two occupations occur at Fort Pentagoet at the junction of the Bagaduce River and Penobscot Bay; the third is Saint-Castin's Habitation, situated about a mile and a half farther up the Bagaduce River (fig. 62).

From 1635 to 1654, the French entrepreneur Charles d'Aulnay and an unknown successor defended their private commercial interests in Maine from the relative safety of Fort Pentagoet. In 1654 Acadia was taken under orders from Oliver Cromwell, and the fort remained nominally under English control for the next sixteen years, although there is no clear evidence of an English occupation during this period. From 1670, when Acadia was returned to the French, until the destruction of the fort by a Dutch privateer in 1674, Pentagoet served as the military headquarters for the administration of all Acadia under governors Hector d'Andigné de Grandfontaine and Jacques Chambly. From about 1677 to 1700, Jean Vincent de Saint-Castin, a former ensign at Fort Pentagoet, reestablished French authority nearby at a small trading post that formed a nucleus of a new French and Indian habitation.

Pentagoet I

Pentagoet I, 1635-54, was the first major period of French settlement at the mouth of the Bagaduce. Fort Pentagoet was one of many French investments that blossomed after Acadia was formally ceded to France by the English in 1632, as a condition of the Treaty of St. Germain-en-Laye. It was built on the site of a trading post operated for the Plymouth colonists from 1629 to 1635. Charles de Menou d'Aulnay, Sieur de Charnisay, a French nobleman and entrepreneur, appropriated this outpost in 1635 and began construction of Pentagoet to defend his local commercial interests. D'Aulnay managed several other ventures in Acadia, ranging from a mill near Fort Pentagoet and a homestead on the St. George River to the settlements of Port Royal and La Hève on the other side of the Gulf of Maine.[2] However, Fort Pentagoet was his major outpost on the frontier with New England. From these southwestern headquarters, d'Aulnay controlled the fur trade along the Penobscot and fishing around Penobscot Bay. These operations were financed and supplied through Emmanuel Leborgne, a La Rochelle banker-merchant, who eventually came to Acadia in 1648 to repossess d'Aulnay's holdings and who succeeded d'Aulnay at his death in 1650.

Fort Pentagoet, small only by later standards, represented a tremendous investment on this remote frontier. The compound, half of which has been excavated, was about twenty-four meters

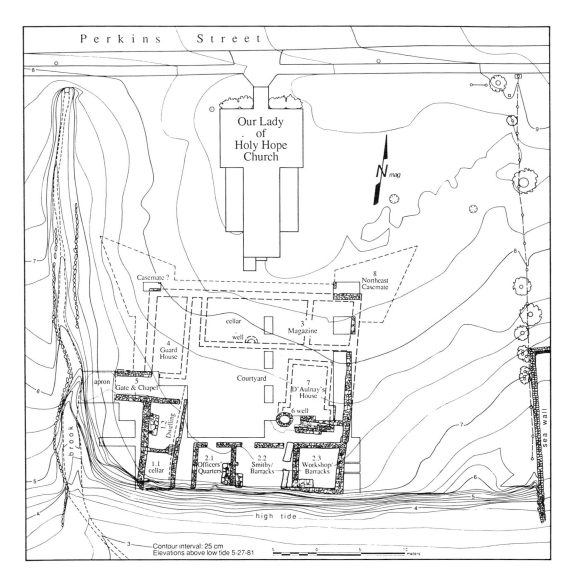

63. University of
Maine excavations
at Fort Pentagoet,
1981–84.

square. Within the curtain walls were six buildings (fig. 63). The oldest structure (7) stood alone on the eastern side of the fort opposite the entrance. Apparently of "charpente," or timber-frame, construction and placed on a stone foundation, it seems to have been the only structure at Pentagoet with glass windows, and it is thought to be d'Aulnay's own residence. A small wattle-and-daub chapel and belfry (5) spanned the entranceway. The rest of the buildings, however, were made of coursed-slate masonry laid up in a clay loam and were incorporated into the curtain wall. These included the dwelling (1), the workshop/officers' quarters complex (2), the magazine (3), and the guardhouse

(4). Of these the magazine (3) and possibly the officers' quarters (2.1) were two stories in height; the dwelling was a split-level, two-story design. When seized by the English in 1654, Pentagoet was manned by a contingent of eighteen men.[3]

D'Aulnay was just one of a half-dozen or so ambitious noblemen and merchants in Acadia who engaged in such ventures. One of these entrepreneurs was d'Aulnay's chief competitor and ultimately his archenemy, Charles de La Tour.[4] La Tour's headquarters at this time were at Fort Sainte Marie, popularly known as Fort La Tour, at Portland Point in Saint John, New Brunswick—a site excavated in 1963 by Norman Barka. The fort was built by La Tour in 1631 and was destroyed by d'Aulnay in 1645. It was comparable to Pentagoet in size, although the structures and defenses were all made of wood, and the site is not as well preserved. The Fort La Tour artifact assemblage, therefore, comes from a context that closely parallels Pentagoet I and therefore invites comparison.

Both d'Aulnay and La Tour were supplied through the port of La Rochelle, d'Aulnay by his creditor Leborgne and La Tour through various merchants including David Lomeron, Samuel Georges, and Guillaume Desjardins.[5] These backers supplied both manpower—usually indentured artisans such as stonemasons, joiners, and armorers as well as common laborers—and merchandise to the Acadian frontier.[6] Consequently, the imported materials at Fort La Tour and Pentagoet are distinct not only from nearby sites in New England but also from certain early French sites such as Champlain's Habitation in Quebec and the St. Croix colony, which were originally supplied through the Norman port of Honfleur.

The ceramics recovered at Fort La Tour and Pentagoet I are remarkably similar to each other. With few exceptions, the collections either are made up of products from the Saintonge region of southwestern France, which is the hinterland of the port of La Rochelle, or are products derived indirectly from the wine trade between La Rochelle and the Low Countries. Both collections are dominated by buff-bodied, green-glazed, earthen storage vessels from Saintonge. These include strap-handled storage jars and pots glazed on the interior or the rim only, as well as apothecary jars and sundry tableware (fig. 64). The two sites also contain comparable amounts of stoneware derived from the Rhine Valley and vicinity. Some are bottles from Frechen, which are adorned

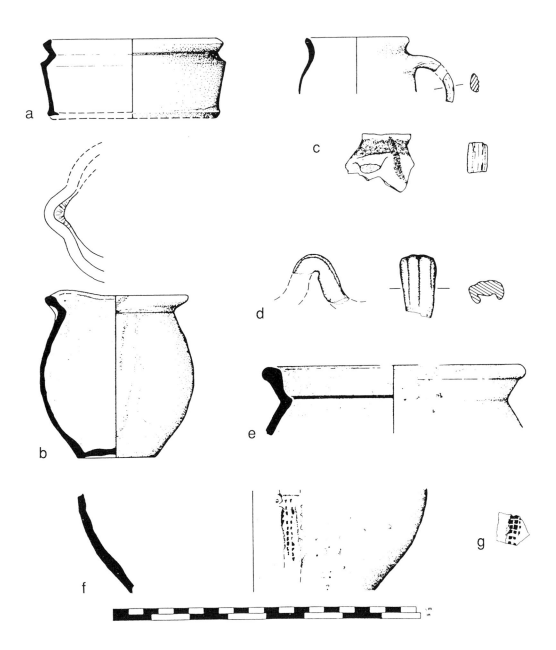

with the mask of a bearded man in appliqué on their necks and medallions or coats of arms about their middles—"bartmann" or "bellarmine" jugs. Others are gray or beige-bodied jugs decorated with sprig-molded rosettes applied to the exterior—either German or Walloon products. Similar tin-enameled plates painted blue on white have been found that are possibly of Portuguese origin, as well as several plain serving vessels of French faience.

64. Green-glazed and polychrome ceramics from Pentagoet I (1635–54). All pieces have similar counterparts at Fort LaTour: *a*, Saintonge apothecary jar, green-glazed inside; *b*, small pot with pinched spout, having a brownish-green glaze on the interior only; *c*, Saintonge polychrome cup or mug painted green, blue, and brown on a clear, yellowish background; *d*, green-glazed rim loop from a bowl or chafing dish; *e*, jar rim, green-glazed on the interior only; *f–g*, applied banding in relief, rouletted in imitation of rope carrying straps, an occasional decoration on green-glazed storage jars.

A few unusual pieces are duplicated at the two locations, including a handle formed like the head of a serpent or dragon, apparently belonging to a faience sauceboat. Significantly, both French assemblages lack specialized milkpans, butter crocks, and other dairy wares, notably the lead-glazed redwares and slipwares universally associated with contemporary English sites.

Many artifacts from Pentagoet I and Fort La Tour were derived from the Low Countries. Those ceramics not from the Saintonge appear to have come through Dutch channels, as might be expected considering the trading pattern at La Rochelle. Leborgne, who supplied d'Aulnay, invested heavily in the wine trade with Flanders and the Baltic, among other locations.[7] The three bartmann medallions found at Pentagoet bear certain coats of arms that are rare on English sites but that frequently circulated in the Dutch trading sphere: the House of Nassau, the city of Cologne, and the city of Amsterdam. All these medallions have been recovered from the cargoes of Dutch merchantmen's vessels that sank during the early decades of the seventeenth century.[8] Likewise, the standard gray-bodied German "Westerwald" tankards and jugs, which are the forms commonly found in English contexts, have a beige-bodied counterpart at Pentagoet, possibly a competing Walloon product. This trade connection with the Low Countries extends to firearms at Pentagoet, all of which appear to have been of Dutch design.[9] At Fort La Tour, moreover, there is an unusually high proportion of ornate, molded tobacco pipestems characteristic of the Netherlands, a few of which are duplicated at Pentagoet.[10]

These archaeological records indicate that the French at Pentagoet I and Fort La Tour did not depend on New England for the supply of most durable goods. However, contemporary documents frequently record trade between the English and the French in Maine, suggesting that the economies of the frontier were ruled by expedience rather than by political allegiance. D'Aulnay, for example, is known to have been in debt to Abraham Shurt, a merchant at Pemaquid, and to have commissioned English ships to supply him with merchandise for trade.[11] This illicit trade certainly included food, powder, and shot[12] and perhaps other nondurable items such as textiles and leather goods.

Some supplies imported by d'Aulnay and La Tour bespeak a life-style that, when viewed from a modern perspective, seems extravagant and incongruous in a frontier setting but that was

65. Relief-molded polychrome chafing dish made in the Saintonge region of southwestern France, from Pentagoet. The vessel is green-glazed on the interior and on the supporting knobs; the exterior is coated with a clear yellowish glaze, and the masks are accented with blue and brown. A strap handle, believed to attach between the base and the body of this specimen, is illustrated separately.

taken for granted as prerequisite for maintaining social position in the seventeenth century. For example, relief-molded polychrome pottery serving vessels were imitative of products of the renowned sixteenth-century potter-artist Bernard Palissy, whose products were themselves imitative of those of goldsmiths and silversmiths. These gaudy ceramics, with their molded masks and relief ornamentation, painted in blue, green, and brown on a pale yellow background, were manufactured up the Charente River from La Rochelle in villages near Saintes. Following the wine trade, such products were successfully marketed throughout northwestern Europe in the sixteenth and mid-seventeenth centuries.[13] Their significance here lies not so much in their elegance or cost as in their functions. Both d'Aulnay and La Tour had chafing dishes to keep their platters of food warm (fig. 65) and miniature barrel costrels to serve liquor at the table. Blue-on-white tin-enameled plates, probably of Portuguese origin, were also found on both sites. These may have been kept only for display, since the glaze on the Pentagoet specimens shows no signs of knife scratches from use. All this formality seems out of place in frontier circumstances, which demanded little more than a barrel top as an eating surface—a scene familiar in contemporary genre paintings.

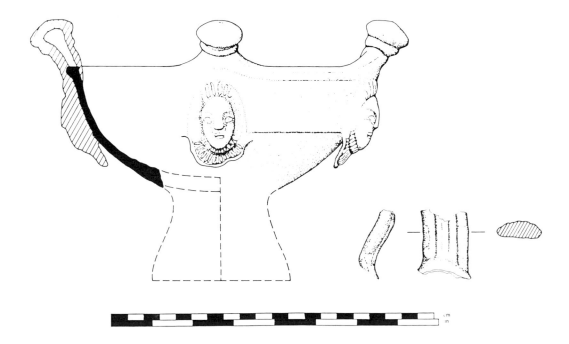

The apparent incongruity of high fashion on the frontier is illustrated further at Pentagoet by items of dress found in refuse immediately surrounding structure 7. This was the supposed d'Aulnay residence, identified, in part, by devices common to the d'Aulnay crest represented on a brass badge found in the refuse: a cross surrounded by an oak leaf cluster.[14] A clip and buckles represent a sling and belt that held the French sword or épée. However, there is little evidence from the repairs represented in the armorer's refuse that swords saw regular use as weapons. They were, rather, hallmarks of noble dress, civilian or military, and were not to be worn by commoners.[15] The same could be said of a broken spur buckle, unmistakable in form, that was recovered just outside d'Aulnay's doorway. The absence of horse trappings such as horseshoes and harness fittings in the smithy remains assures us that there were no horses at Pentagoet; traffic along the intricate coastline was much more practical by boat. A fancy brass clasp hook, embossed with a tulip design, probably connected a man's doublet to his breeches.[16] Gold braid, which in Virginia was reserved by law for the governor, his council, and heads of hundreds, appeared in this midden, as did ornamental braid belting, braided buttons, and a fragment of a satin ribbon.[17] Surely, therefore, the clothing worn regularly on the frontier included some surprisingly formal attire.

The luxury items associated with these early settlements apparently reflect the obligations of the *gens d'épée* (wearers of the sword), serving as status symbols to uphold their noble lifestyle.[18] This applied equally in civilian life as in the military, where the commissioned ranks were reserved for nobility. One of their key duties was to avoid derogation at all costs, and these trappings were among the many prerequisites of acting one's social station during the ancien régime, that is, before the French Revolution. The uncanny resemblance of the two collections, moreover, illustrates the common background, tastes, and supply sources shared by d'Aulnay and La Tour; this background, coupled with their common ambitions, fueled their great rivalry.

The evidence of the day-to-day operation of Pentagoet shows more practical adaptations to frontier living. The extraordinary measures required to maintain the outpost in the face of infrequent supplies are clearly reflected in the refuse from the smithy/workshop.[19] Copper and brass kettles were extensively recycled, producing rivets and patches for repairing everything from other

66. Firearms mainte-
nance and ax repair:
a–c, horizontally
acting "sears," key
wearing parts of a
gunlock's trigger
mechanism, in various
stages of manufacture;
d, unfinished gun
cock, with finished
upper jaw fitted in
place for illustration; *e*,
iron slug coated with
brass; *f*, pistol barrel
repaired by brazing
three separate iron
slugs across a crack;
g, complete ax with
steel bit insert; *h–i*,
sprung and broken
ax eyes; *j*, broken ax
bit; *k*, salvaged ax
blade with steel bit.
All ax fragments have
been cut off by the
smith using the anvil
"handy," a stationary
chisel-like attachment
that fits into a socket
in the anvil.

kettles to boats and furnishing material for the brass welding,
or "brazing," of broken gun parts. New items were also manufactured from copper kettle scrap, such as candle holders, awls,
hinges, saw patterns, musket parts, and even lace tips and tinkling cones used to decorate the fringes of the clothing of the
Europeans and their aboriginal clientele, according to their respective fashions.

Firearms saw heavy use at Pentagoet and frequently exploded.
To minimize these occurrences, and to keep the guns in working
order, the armorer was obliged to repair a wide variety of gunlock
mechanisms. At one extreme were primitive flintlocks, such as
the Dutch-designed "snaphaunce," literally "pecking hen," which
fired when a flint held in the jaws of the "cock" struck a "steel"
or "battery." At the other extreme were more intricate French-
style "wheellocks," which produced a spark using iron pyrites in
a mechanism similar to a modern cigarette lighter. The armorer
maintained these firearms, which not only lacked interchange-
able parts but also worked on entirely different mechanical principles, by scavenging parts and refitting them as best he could.
Certain heavily wearing parts he could not recycle, particularly
gun cocks that held the flint and struck the steel, breech plugs
that sealed gases at the back end of the barrel when the powder
charge was ignited, and parts of the trigger mechanism. These
he made from scratch at the forge and finished with files (fig. 66,
a–d). Gun barrels, which were beyond his capability to make at
the forge, he frequently bandaged by filing grooves across the
nascent cracks, brazing iron slugs in the slots thus formed, and
finally filing the slugs to the contour of the barrel (fig. 66, *e–f*).
Shot was cast from lead as needed, and more surprisingly, simple
"spall-type" gunflints were manufactured on site.

Conservation of materials also extended to hand tools, particularly axes (fig. 66, *g–k*). As steel bits were broken, the dam-
aged area was removed, and new bits or blades were welded to
the salvaged portion of the ax. Conversely, if the eye was sprung
or broken, it was cut off and discarded, and the blade was saved
to be fitted to a new eye.

This Pentagoet I subsistence pattern, which emphasized self-
sufficiency and making do with available resources, was reflected
in diet as well. Of the faunal remains recovered, at least 40
percent represent domesticated animals, predominantly swine,
sheep, and cattle. However, the majority of animal remains repre-

sent wild species: bear, seal, moose, beaver, goose, duck, cod, and striped bass, showing that the garrison relied heavily on native foodstuffs. Many of these ingredients are mentioned as part of a feast provided for Isaac de Rasilly, governor-general of Acadia, by Nicolas Denys, another of d'Aulnay's competitors. The meat of the acorn-fed bear of Pentagoet was specifically praised by Denys, who pronounced it "very delicate and white as that of veal."[20] Two bear heads recovered from the site were neatly cleaved in half along the length of the skull. Although this butchering practice was a convenient method for extracting the brains, it surely also represents an elegant presentation of the bear at the table, served in profile on a platter, as was the fashion for serving veal in France at the time.

Pentagoet III

The second period of French occupation at Pentagoet began with the return of the site to the French in 1670 after sixteen years of English control (Pentagoet II), during which time the

67. Plan of Fort Pentagoet, November 12, 1670. Courtesy of Archives Nationales, Centre des Archives d'Outre-mer, France. Original lettering identifications, for which no key survives: *A,* parade ground; *B,* two-story magazine with cellar; *C,* guardhouse; *D,* a chapel over the fort's entrance; *F,* dwelling; *G,* house for workmen and soldiers (formerly a smithy and a workshop); *H,* small redoubt in front of the fort; *X,* shed for livestock.

fort apparently saw little use. Acadia, now administered through Quebec, was reopened for colonization. However, falling on the heels of major investment in New France in the 1660s, the resettlement plans for Acadia were backed with little royal funding. The region was placed successively under the governorship of two members of the recently disbanded regiment of Carignan Salières: Grandfontaine (1670–73) and Chambly (1673–74). To defend against English incursions, Louis XIV selected Pentagoet as the seat of this military government.[21] Pentagoet III lasted just four years, until the fort was "levelled with the ground" by Dutch pirates in 1674.[22]

The new era saw extensive repairs, renovations, and rearming of the obsolescent fort, but in order not to provoke the English, the French did little expansion of the defenses, as can be seen by comparing successive plans of the fort (figs. 67 and 68). D'Aulnay's residence was now long gone, perhaps destroyed in the English takeover of 1654. Behind it, the east curtain wall, apparently a sod earthworks in Pentagoet I, was now completed in masonry. The former two-room workshop was fully enclosed and remodeled and served as a one-room barracks. Here, above the smithy refuse of earlier times, the excavation team recovered a

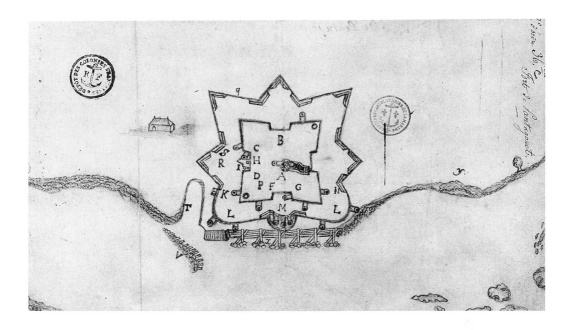

68. Pencil sketch done by Governor Hector d'Andigné de Grand-fontaine of Pentagoet, ca. 1671. Courtesy of Archives Nationales, Centre des Archives d'Outre-mar, France. Grandfontaine's sense of proportion and his artistic ability were somewhat limited, but the efforts of his refurbishing of the fort are reflected in the key that accompanied the original sketch. (Transcribed and translated from the original French by Alaric Faulkner.)

A The fort's plaza [parade ground], which is about twenty-five paces square

B The magazine, which is about thirty paces long and fifteen broad

C The guardhouse, which is about fifteen paces long and ten broad

D A living quarters on the other side of the guardhouse of comparable length and breadth, above which two struc-tures are a small chapel and a bell, which make a roof for the entrance to the gate

F A barracks for the officers, fifteen paces long and ten broad

G Another barracks of similar length and breadth for the workmen and soldiers

H The entrance to the fort

I The entrance to a small redoubt, which is in front of the gate

K The gate of the envelope

L Two platforms, each having two pieces that take eight-pound balls

M Another platform with sod fraises [retaining walls] and embrasures, where there are three pieces, two of eight [pounds] and one of three

N Some small parapets at the re-entrant angles and at the flank-ing angles of the envelope

O Two lookouts standing on the two angles of the bastions

P The steps for climbing onto the rampart

Q The palisades around the envelope

R An oven [forge?] and a shed in front of the gate

S A deep channel to keep water during hot weather

T A cove for keeping small boats

U Pilings to im-pede the flow of seawater

X A seawall to impede the demo-lition of the earth supporting the envelope and platforms

Y An eminence that commands the fort

Z The spring, which is the best and most useful on the island sparse collection of personal items—combs, pins, and needles—found associated with hasp locks and eye-and-staple hinges from wooden chests.

The refuse in the cellar kitchen of structure 1, apparently the new governor's residence, shows a shift in diet, nearly excluding wild mammals and replacing them with cattle and pig and, to a lesser extent, sheep and, incredibly, domestic cats.[23] Geese and ducks were common, and small birds were present in abundance, perhaps serving as pigeon soup as featured in Denys's menu.[24] Fish, principally cod, striped bass, and sturgeon, remained an important part of the fare.[25] Overall, however, this is more the diet to be expected of displaced and periodically starving Frenchmen than of Acadian pioneers.

The material culture of Pentagoet III exhibited little extravagance. Glassware included some fine matching pieces made in the Venetian style, with hollow stems ornamented with spiral ribs and inflated knops, but since such pieces are seen in genre paintings and have been found in recent excavations outside the Louvre in Paris, they appear to have been commonplace items.[26] In general, domestic items were plain and utilitarian. Vessels from southwestern France continued to dominate the ceramics and consisted principally of jars and pots for storage and food preparation, glazed only about the rim to keep covers from sticking. The green-glazed jars were joined by a new round-bottomed, double-handled cooking pot, or "marmite," buff in paste with a clear lead glaze about the rim (fig. 69). Gone were the Saintonge polychrome chafing dishes and miniature barrels, victims of changing fashions and the decline of the Saintonge export market in northern Europe. They were replaced by simpler forms of Saintonge tableware, products made for local French markets rather than for export, which were glazed bright green on the inside and outside surfaces. No ceramic plates or chargers were present, but sherds of decorative blue-on-white tin-enameled plates, apparently from Pentagoet I, were recycled to make colorful disk-shaped gaming tokens.

The supply of manufactured goods remained restricted principally to France, and included items derived from the Low Countries through indirect trade. After 1650, direct commerce between England and France was banned as the result of mutual trade restrictions. Nevertheless, English goods form a note-

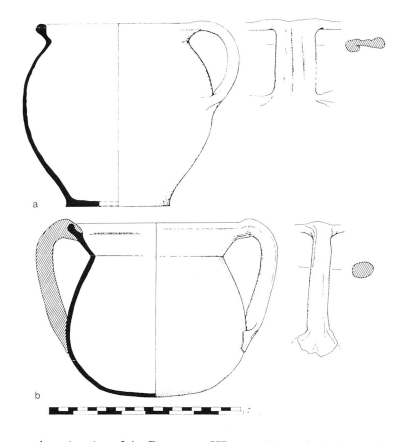

69. Dominant food storage and preparation forms from Pentagoet III (1670–74). Both are buff-bodied and glazed on the interior rim only, except for spatters and excess glaze puddled in the interior: *a*, green-glazed jar; *b*, yellow-glazed, round-bottomed, double-handled cooking pot or "marmite."

worthy minority of the Pentagoet III assemblage. A few isolated redware sherds are probably of English origin, as is a single, large, gravel-tempered jar derived from North Devon. Ten tobacco pipes from Pentagoet III contexts bear the well-known mark "PE," of Philip Edwards I, a Bristol pipe maker at work about 1650–69, giving further evidence for illicit trade, undoubtedly between Pentagoet and its New England neighbors.[27] However, there are nearly five times as many embossed "crusader-and-huntress" pipes of Dutch manufacture in the collection, reflecting typical French supply lines.[28] Lead seals, which certified the quantity and quality of cloth yard goods, include one specimen from the county of Essex, which presumably marked an English woolen fabric, and another from Haarlem, originally attached to nineteen and one-half ells of Dutch linen. Gunflints are all later French "blade" types and were apparently imported. Coinage, in addition to a brass Louis XIV "double tournois," includes a copper "falus" minted in Surat, India, during the reign of Aurangzeb

(1658–1707), last of the Mogul shahs. This latter coin demonstrates Pentagoet's participation, however indirect, in a worldwide network that included the French East India trade.

The Habitation of Saint-Castin

After Pentagoet was destroyed, a former ensign at the fort, who had already established himself as a trader, started a new type of settlement.[29] Jean Vincent de Saint-Castin, later Baron de Saint-Castin, returned to the area sometime after 1677 and set up a trading post within a village of 160 Etchemin Indians — two European buildings within a settlement of thirty-two wigwams.[30] This settlement appears on three maps drafted independently in the 1680s and 1690s, the recent reassessment of which led to the archaeological identification of the site.

Three brief test excavations conducted in 1983, 1984, and 1990 have located the remains of at least four structures and features that can be directly associated with the Saint-Castin occupation (fig. 70). These structures reflect a mix of construction techniques that are as yet not fully understood. However, it is clear, even at this early stage of investigation, that the architecture

70. Excavation plan, 1983–90, at Saint-Castin's Habitation: Structure 1, a storehouse and workshop; Feature 2, a circular stone oven, probably for baking bread; and Structure 2, a dwelling, possibly Saint-Castin's house.

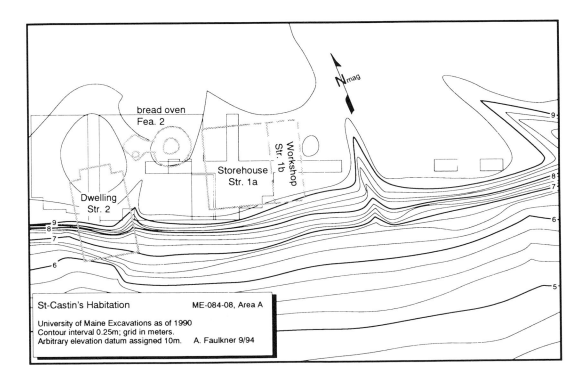

St-Castin's Habitation   ME-084-08, Area A

University of Maine Excavations as of 1990
Contour interval 0.25m; grid in meters.
Arbitrary elevation datum assigned 10m.   A. Faulkner 9/94

consisted of relatively impermanent frame buildings without cellars or substantial foundations. These are represented by shallow stone footings, piles of burned daub from mud-plastered walls, patterns of postholes, rubble from stone chimneys, or some combination of these traits.

A storehouse (Structure 1) was identified in 1983 as scattered fieldstone footings associated with large quantities of lead shot as well as lead ingots, gunflints, and other supplies related to the service of firearms. Nearby, in 1984, half of a circular stone oven (Feature 2) was examined by sectioning it in half. This feature was built largely of slate, probably salvaged from the ruins of Pentagoet, and was at first thought to be a free-standing structure of a general type still in use in Quebec.[31] However, subsequent excavations in 1990 have identified the corner and stone chimney rubble of a small, post-in-ground dwelling with wattle-and-daub walls, Structure 2, which may have been directly attached to the bread oven. A similar house has recently been excavated at an early-eighteenth-century Acadian site in Belleisle, Nova Scotia. Whereas at Belleisle the oven was incorporated into an exterior chimney at the rear of the house, the oven at Saint-Castin's Habitation is situated alongside the structure.[32] This dwelling seems too small to have been Saint-Castin's personal residence, but whether it represents another European structure or one of the cabins or "wigwams" of the Etchemins remains to be determined by further excavation. A third structure, represented only by fired daub and hand-forged nails found embedded in the riverbank, appears to have been almost completely lost to erosion.

The remains of several additional subsurface structures have been identified by ground-penetrating radar scanning but have not yet been tested. These surely include some of the remaining wigwams, outbuildings, and features and possibly a well. No defensive works have been discovered as yet, although some sort of palisade is anticipated near the storehouse. The University of Maine has recently begun major excavations at the site to clarify the settlement plan.

Coming principally from within and around the storehouse, more than 80 percent of the artifacts are tobacco pipes, musketballs, and shot. The marked tobacco pipes were exclusively English, the products of William Evans, Lluellin Evans, and Robert

Tippett, Bristol pipe makers who completed their apprentice-ships in 1660, 1661, and 1660, respectively.[33] Many musketballs and cast shot were found in linear arrangements, where kegs had apparently been spilled, their contents falling between the floor-boards of the storehouse. Cast ingots of raw lead, some of them chopped into smaller pieces, together with casting scraps and pincers, testify to the manufacture of the shot at the site. Gun-flints, however, were apparently imported and were fabricated of a blonde flint usually associated with French manufacture.

Unfortunately, the faunal refuse at Saint-Castin's Habitation is at this point too sparse to make meaningful statements about diet. The collection of domestic refuse is also small, consist-ing of sixty-six ceramic sherds and fifty bottle-glass fragments, but it appears to differ significantly from that of Pentagoet and suggests both different foodways and sources of supply. The ves-sels represented are nearly all associated with food consumption rather than preparation or storage. Although the case is not com-pelling, this suggests that aboriginal practices may have been preferred at the habitation, such as storage of food in bark bas-kets. Fragments of bark believed to represent one such basket were found just outside the dwelling (structure 2), together with other domestic refuse.

The character of the few ceramic and glass fragments that were recovered seems to be more representative of typical English trade routes than of direct trade through French or Dutch sources. A mere three sherds of the utilitarian green-glazed Sain-tonge earthenware, which dominates the Pentagoet collection, were found, and these are of later types, commonly found on early-eighteenth-century sites in Acadia, New France. Several sherds of a lead-glazed redware jar of English manufacture were also recovered. Most of the ceramics represented are Dutch or English delftwares and bartmann jugs from the Rhineland. A sprig-molded jug is of gray stoneware (unlike the beige, Walloon variant from Pentagoet I) and is clearly an early Rhenish product from the Westerwald, a favorite English import. The bottle glass included principally small fragments of dark-green wine bottles and case bottles, typical of wine bottle glass found on English sites, and just one sherd of the light-blue bottle glass commonly found in French assemblages of the period. Indeed, a cargo of wine and other merchandise was confiscated from Saint-Castin's Habitation by the English in 1686 as "contraband," because it had been provided by an English merchant.[34] Saint-Castin was repeatedly charged with trading with the New Englanders by certain of his fellow countrymen, who considered his actions ignoble and even treasonous.[35] The presence of these domestic materials, together with the large number of English tobacco pipes, testifies not only that he was guilty but also that New England may have become his principal source for durable goods.

Although evidence of the Indian presence at the habitation is modest in the areas examined so far, it is significantly greater than at Pentagoet. Some sixty small, round, drawn, glass beads have been found, occurring in aqua-blue, white, and black. The size of this collection is impressive only when compared with the full-scale excavation of Fort Pentagoet, which produced just twelve beads from seventeenth-century occupations, most of which were larger blue beads.[36] The greater density of beads at Saint-Castin's Habitation probably reflects not only the immediate presence of the Indians but also a change from large beads, which were principally kept in strands, to smaller beads, which were used for weaving and embroidery. The beads from Saint-Castin's Habitation, moreover, were found in association with at least seven tobacco pipestem fragments three to four centimeters long, which have been carefully chamfered at the ends. These pipe fragments have clearly been strung as wampum-like beads, for the thin line on which they were threaded has cut deep grooves into the walls of the bore holes. A single piece of lead shot was also found that may have been intentionally perforated for stringing. Beads found in this context do not merely represent trading stock, as was surely the case within the walls of Pentagoet, but were direct evidence of an aboriginal population.

French-English Contrasts

Like most seventeenth-century ventures in Maine, French and English alike, Pentagoet and Saint-Castin's Habitation both show evidence of rapid, and usually catastrophic, abandonment. The holes in the stems of clay tobacco pipes decreased regularly in size throughout the colonial period and are extremely useful for dating these sites because smoking was popular and pipestem fragments were as common as cigarette butts are today. Typically, on Maine sites the pipes become more numerous and their bores became smaller with the growth of settlement over time, stopping abruptly at the hole size most popular at the site's demise. For most early sites in Maine this occurs when the bore has decreased to about 7/64ths of an inch in diameter. This pattern corresponds to the various disasters of the 1670s, particularly the destruction of Pentagoet and other French sites by the Dutch in 1674 and the Wabanaki uprising of 1676, commonly termed "King Philip's War," which all but eliminated English settlement in Maine for several decades. However, Saint-Castin's Habitation is unusual in that its pipestem holes became smaller still, stabilizing at 6/64ths of an inch in diameter. This clearly demonstrates the perpetuation of French settlement in Maine through the last quarter of the seventeenth century, precisely the period of "Indian" wars during which New England was struggling to regain a foothold in the East.

A miscellany of additional threads of negative and positive evidence links the French settlements and often distinguishes them from their English counterparts in Maine. Their significance, however, is not always clear.

Although knives are fairly common utensils, there is a curious absence of spoons in all French occupations. Yet the metal spoon is the predominant eating utensil on contemporary English sites in Maine.[37] This may signify a distinction in the eating habits of the French, who might have sopped up their soups and potages with bread, and those of their aboriginal clientele, who may not have adopted the European spoon. Alternatively, it may merely indicate that the French, who were not known for their metal products, used wooden spoons, which have not survived in the archaeological record.

Also, none of the occupations seem to have been furnished with armor, pole arms, or similar surplus medieval weaponry, suggesting that the provision of such ineffective armament was a quirk of the financial backers of English settlements in Virginia and New England and did not extend to Acadia. Firearms, as might be expected, saw especially heavy service, were repaired often, and were well supplied with flints and shot. But what is remarkable is the predominance at Pentagoet of concealable pistols. Surely these latter weapons were not intended for hunting, but to what purpose were they used—offensive, defensive, or simply amusement?

Another surprise is that although the French are rightfully credited with a missionary role in spreading Catholicism, religious artifacts were virtually absent in all three occupations. Surface collections indicate, however, that by 1648 a Capuchin mission was in operation a few hundred meters west of Fort Pentagoet. A copper sheet commemorating the laying of a foundation for the mission was recovered in 1863, and in 1984, a seal bearing the inscription "IHS" (Jesus savior, of mankind) was found.[38] Unfortunately, no documentation has been discovered that would clarify the relationship of this mission to d'Aulnay's fort or indicate its duration. The later occupation of Pentagoet was served only briefly by a priest.[39] Various priests are known to have settled with Saint-Castin and later with his sons, but their effectiveness remains in question. Here, in southwestern Acadia, French entrepreneurs may have relied more heavily on economics—the supply of firearms, powder, and shot and the extension of credit—than on the fear of God to mediate with the native population.

Conclusions

The three French occupations described here are not strictly comparable, since none of the assemblages are complete. The domestic refuse expected at Saint-Castin's Habitation is under-represented, for example, whereas the contents of the warehouse or magazine at Fort Pentagoet are presumed to have been lost to nineteenth-century pothunting. Evidence for maintenance and repair is abundant in Pentagoet I, but the corresponding work areas for Pentagoet III and Saint-Castin's Habitation have been defined only partially. Furthermore, the fifty-five years or so spanned by these occupations saw many changes in fashion and custom as chafing dishes went out of style and the Saintonge potters ceased the production of polychrome export products. Still, a pattern emerges of three distinct strategies for exploiting this "cosmopolitan" frontier—a frontier still very much dependent on its European sources and a frontier settled to extract fish, fur, and timber for European markets.[40]

The construction and operation of Fort Pentagoet under the private entrepreneurship of d'Aulnay represents capital investment in a central stronghold quite unlike anything built by the Puritans of Massachusetts. Governor William Bradford of Plymouth summed up the situation well when he noted, "To the Great danger of the English, who lye open and unfortified, living upon husbandrie. [the French are] closed up in their forts, well fortified, and live upon trade, in good security."[41] Such small, compact forts kept overhead low, and at Pentagoet, this strategy permitted a handful of employees to monopolize fishing and trading along the Penobscot. Control was sufficiently effective to allow d'Aulnay to engage in shipbuilding and to operate a farmstead and a mill several miles beyond the limits of the fort.

The Pentagoet I compound was a European stronghold that was strictly insulated from the surrounding aboriginal population and that catered to d'Aulnay's personal comforts. D'Aulnay, unlike the later Baron de Saint-Castin, did not fit the stereotype of a French frontiersman: a figure who is absorbed by his new surroundings, adopting the habits and accoutrements of the native population. The ceramics, clothing, and other trappings of French nobility seem as incongruous as the ritual in later centuries of the tea ceremony popularly identified with British officers and gentlemen on the frontier. Maintenance of social position was as important to d'Aulnay as the physical maintenance of the settlement. Nevertheless, both the diet of native foodstuffs and the competence demonstrated in repairing and recycling equipment show a concentrated effort toward self-sufficiency, a thoroughly practical commitment to permanent settlement.

The second French occupation, under the military governorships of Grandfontaine and Chambly, was brief. Pentagoet III was cut short at an early developmental stage, when the French had just regained control of the trading houses along the Penobscot. Under direction from French Minister Jean-Baptiste Colbert, the governors emphasized rebuilding and rearming the fort; the ultimate objective of settling the area with soldier-farmers was never realized. By comparison, the adaptation to frontier living during this second occupation appears to have been less flexible than during the first, with less emphasis placed on self-sufficiency. Foodstuffs were overwhelmingly European domesticates, and the garrison of prospective soldier-settlers demanded European grains for their nascent farmsteads around Pentagoet.[42] Whether it was because they were ill prepared or simply inflexible, the garrison was beset by famine in 1672, and their starvation diet appears to be reflected by the presence of hawk and domestic cat in the food remains. That winter several of the company were sent to Port Royal until additional provisions could be procured from Quebec.[43]

Saint-Castin's approach, settling within an Indian village and taking a native wife, was unconventional, if not innovative. Although he was actually commissioned with the task of winning over the allegiance of the Indians, his strategy was scandalous to most of his contemporaries and superiors, particularly since it involved frequent movement between temporary settlements and trading directly with the English, with no establishment of a permanent European community. Yet as *capitaine des sauvages*, he achieved a most effective relationship with the native population, and as a businessman, Saint-Castin was the most successful. His example was followed by his sons and many others and was perpetuated to good effect through the first decades of the eighteenth century. Archaeologically, the impermanence of structures, the reliance on English supply sources, and the integration of French and Indian settlement have already been demonstrated, setting Saint-Castin's Habitation apart from Pentagoet. What remains of key interest for future work is the study of the organization of the Indian community of which the habitation was a central component.

It is apparent that none of these three settlement strategies parallel the contemporary agricultural settlement of southern New England, which was characterized by the transplantation of the Stuart yeoman's way of life onto New England soil and its subsequent regional differentiation.[44] Although a similar transplantation of French culture may have occurred in northeastern Acadian farming communities such as Port Royal, life at Pentagoet and Saint-Castin's Habitation was no mirror of the overwhelmingly rural peasant society of France during the ancien régime.[45] Farming tools found here were few, and specialized dairy utensils were absent, as would be predicted from Governor Bradford's assessment of the minor role played by agriculture in this region of Acadia. Lifeways represented here differed fundamentally from those in rural France. Whatever the difficulties of the frontier, the diet of the transplanted peasant or craftsman in southwestern Acadia clearly was not limited to grain products, as has been generally portrayed for France. The iron and steel products that came from the forge, as well as the very coal that fueled it, show access to a wider set of raw materials than the "wood and wicker" fabric of French peasant society.[46]

This departure from the Old World prototype is due largely to the specialization of these outposts in commerce rather than in farming. As potentially profitable enterprises, these establishments offered their progenitors relief from some of the strictures of French society, which was deeply rooted in rural life. With few exceptions, aristocrats were prohibited from engaging in manufacturing, manual activity, or retail (and in some areas wholesale) business, which severely limited their ability to maintain and augment an estate.[47] However, on the Acadian frontier, the noble entrepreneur had ample opportunity to engage in the respectable, and potentially profitable, commerce offered by fishing and the fur trade.

In the end, all three strategies employed by the French to settle southwestern Acadia failed. Throughout the seventeenth century, Fort Pentagoet, the most remote of the Acadian outposts, remained underpopulated and became increasingly vulnerable to attack. As France's interest in its Acadian possessions waned during the last quarter of the century, Saint-Castin found himself an isolated representative of French authority, berated for conducting necessary trade with the English. All but abandoned by the French government, he remained allied with the native population. To many English, Saint-Castin appeared to be the chief instigator and perpetrator of Indian hostilities against their settlements, and he bore the brunt of their retaliation. The situation did not improve in the following generation as Saint-Castin's half-Indian sons carried on as *capitaines des sauvages*. After years of intermittent conflict, unable to defend and maintain the colony, France ceded Acadia to the English in 1713.

CHAPTER ELEVEN

Mid-Seventeenth-Century Maine
A World on the Edge

Edwin A. Churchill

By the mid-seventeenth century, nearly a dozen European settlements were perched along the Maine coast. Between Kittery and Pemaquid, small English communities had set their roots; by 1671 nine hundred inhabitants lived in the Kittery-York area, four hundred in Wells and Cape Porpoise, five hundred in Saco and Winter Harbor, five hundred in the Scarborough region, four hundred in Casco Bay, and four hundred more in the Sagadahoc area, a total of slightly more than three thousand people.[1]

Farther east at Pentagoet (present-day Castine), the French had built a fortified trading station and, apart from a period of English occupation from 1654 to 1670 and a brief Dutch disruption (1674–1677), managed to maintain a strong French presence there. Because activities at Pentagoet focused on trade rather than agriculture, the settlement did not expand into a larger community like the English plantations to the west.[2]

In western Maine, English sponsors sent agents and laborers to small fishing and trading posts along the coast in the early and mid 1620s. These individuals, the first year-round settlers, expected to work a few years at the station and then return to

England. Settlers, planning to make this New World their permanent home, began arriving in the late 1620s and early 1630s.[3] These colonists frequently brought their entire families. They came from widely diverse backgrounds. The early settlers often arrived directly from England; some came from the English West Country, others from the southeast, and a few from interior villages. A small number of colonists came from London and other cities, but most brought rural heritages and skills. Later in the century, most of the settlers who moved into the region came from Massachusetts, and most of these came from rural communities rather than from Boston and its environs.[4]

English colonists usually found themselves dealing with local proprietors who had acquired large land grants, most frequently from Sir Ferdinando Gorges's Council for New England. Between the 1630s and 1650s, settlers generally obtained land from the proprietors or other townsmen on a first-come, first-choice basis, and they quickly snapped up the best coastal and riverbank tracts. Later arrivals selected the next-best properties, always making certain that their holdings fronted shorelines, which resulted in long strung-out "ribbon settlements" straggling along the coast and riverbanks. This settlement pattern contrasted with the more compact Bay Colony practices and prompted several mid-seventeenth-century observers to comment on the scattered nature of Maine's settlements. William Hubbard described Kittery as "a long scattering Plantation made up of several Hamlets." John Josselyn stated that the "Town of *Black Point* consist[ed] of about fifty dwelling houses . . . scatteringly built." And Samuel Maverick found that in Casco Bay and along the Kennebec River were "many scattering Families settled." The Frenchman Chevalier de Grandfontaine also noted that the settlement of Pemaquid was made up of "twelve or fifteen very isolated houses" and that the habitations on the Kennebec consisted "of 25 or 30 houses also very far apart from each other."[5]

Relation of Settlers to the Environment

Throughout the seventeenth century the immediate known world for all these communities was exceedingly small. At their backs, at best but a few miles and often much less, stood great forests. The settlers perceived these forests as a wilderness that, in the words of Captain John Smith, would "rather affright than de-

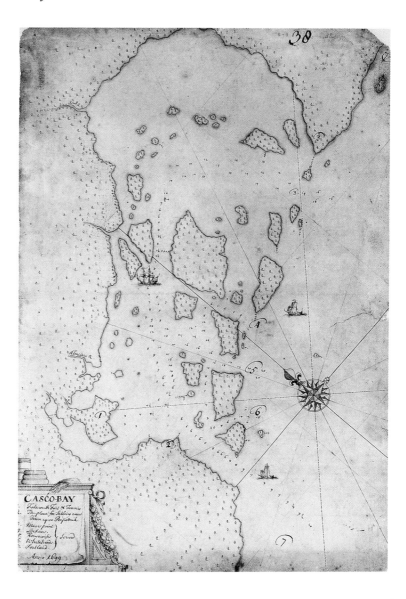

71. Wolfgang Romer, *Casco Bay*, 1699. British Public Record Office, CO 700/North American Colonies, Maine/3. Photograph courtesy of Maine Historic Preservation Commission.

light one."[6] On the other side stood the ocean, at times as hostile and uninviting as the forests. To these colonists, the only familiar world was the series of strung-out homesteads in small settlements hugging the coast and separated by forests, swamps, thickets, and numerous streams, many not fordable. Only beaches, poorly maintained trails, and undependable ferry services provided the minimal points of contact between settlements. Constant prodding from the General Court failed to persuade the inhabitants to improve the vestigial roads, some of which were so bad that they were not even fit for a horse. Instead, colonists usually turned to the sea for extended and even short-distance travel.[7]

The French, isolated at Pentagoet, traveled by boat to other settlements on the St. John River and at Port Royal and often sailed to visit Anglo communities in the west as well.[8] For all of the Maine coastal communities, isolation was an ever-present reality; for the French, at times it must have seemed overwhelming. They rarely traveled overland because, in contrast with the English, they had no horses at their establishment.

European preconceptions brought from the Old World further intensified settlers' anxieties. In their folk traditions, the wilderness was "a great Chaos, the lair of wild beasts and wilder men." The gigantic trees, the nearly impenetrable swamps and thickets, the wolves and bears, and even the native inhabitants all too easily fit into colonists' imaginings that reinforced biblical illusions to the wilderness. Soon, the Anglo populations began to view neighboring Indians as agents of Satan hovering on the fringes of civilization. In the words of the Reverend Michael Wigglesworth, the New World was "a waste and howling wilderness, where none inhabited But hellish fiends, and brutish men That Devils worshiped."[9]

Frequent everyday contacts between the English and the Wabanakis might have moderated some of these Old World preconceptions. Unfortunately, by the 1640s, disease and native warfare had drastically decimated Wabanaki populations. Only a few small groups remained, generally upriver, relatively distant from Maine's Anglo settlements, and well into the dreaded "wilderness." In some eastern English communities, such as at Pemaquid, trade contacts ameliorated tensions to a degree, but even there an arm's-length wariness continued.[10] The French at Pentagoet also showed a distinct uneasiness about local Wabanakis through most of the century. It was not until the arrival of Jean Vincent de Saint-Castin in 1670 that the French began to intermingle with nearby Wabanaki populations.[11]

The English settlers' anxieties turned to terror in the fall of 1642 when rumors circulated of large bodies of belligerent Wabanakis congregating in the interior. Even more frightening to the settlers were specific acts of hostility, including a raid on the post of the Pejepscot trader Thomas Purchase. The catalysts for these hostile acts are not yet wholly understood; still, they lent credence to stories of gathering native tribes. It does appear that some Wabanaki military forces may actually have been forming; ironically, however, this militarization seems to have been in response to Mohawk aggressions from the west, where the New York nation struck out at eastern Algonquians in what was the beginning of a twenty-five-year intertribal contest for control of the fur trade in the interior Northeast.[12]

The idea of wilderness threatened settlers in another way. They viewed the wilderness as a place where a person might lapse into disordered, confused, or "wild conditions" and then succumb to the animal appetites latent in all men and restrained only by society.[13] Massachusetts officials viewed presettlement Maine as a refuge for vicious men. The settlements that sprang up in the 1620s and 1630s established more or less regular government and, within a couple of decades, brought stability to a region that previously had been populated only by more transient inhabitants. Even so, fears about the destabilizing effects of the wilderness on civilization worried the local inhabitants. On islands and less accessible shores, brutality was attributed, with some justice, to lack of government. This is epitomized in the case of the fisherman Gregory Cassell, who in 1654 mortally wounded his boat master, Matthew Cammidge, with a hammer on Monhegan Island. Before dying, Cammidge said he wished he had Cassell "where ther . . . was government" so he could "have the law against him."[14]

The foreboding potentiality for chaos and upheaval in this conceptual wilderness was underscored by the real and unexpectedly frigid winters that greeted the colonists. The first colonists had expected more temperate winters because they knew Maine lay farther south than England, and they were unaware of the arctic current that moved south along the coast or of the polar air masses that glided southeast across the Canadian Shield into northern New England. Indeed, the winters of the 1600s were significantly colder than those of present-day Maine. The earliest colonists arrived in the depths of the "Little Ice Age," a period lasting from the thirteenth to the nineteenth centuries, when the whole northern Atlantic region suffered a definite drop in temperatures.[15]

The French had tried to establish a colony on Dochet Island in the St. Croix River in 1604–5, as had the English at Sagadahoc (at the mouth of the Kennebec River) in 1607–8. Both attempts failed, and the cold was a major factor. As Sir Ferdinando Gorges summed up the Popham venture, "All our former hopes were frozen to death . . . [as] the country . . . was branded . . . as being over cold, and in respect of that not habitable by our nation." Despite those and other equally unpleasant reports, settlers continued to come to Maine in the 1620s and 1630s and, not surprisingly, found the frigid winters "tedious." Unprepared for these conditions, the settlers found their houses drafty and their clothing insufficient to protect them from the bitter cold. They were particularly unaware of how quickly severe cold can freeze exposed flesh. As a result, "men frequently loose theyr Joyntes, sometimes theyr lives." It was no wonder that in the fall of 1642 Governor Thomas Gorges remarked, "Winter now drawes on more feared than ever."

The arrival of summer only minimally dispelled the gloom of winter as life became a preparation for the next cold season. Wood had to be cut and hauled, clothing and cloth had to be made or purchased, and staples had to be stockpiled. More important, fields and gardens had to be planted, tilled, and harvested in an extremely short growing season. Undeniably, the harsh climate had an effect on colonial life. Preparing for and living through winter utilized time, energy, and resources that could have been diverted to other uses had the climate been warmer.[16]

For the English, the Maine environment held a couple of other unpleasant surprises. First of all, the soil proved inferior to that found throughout much of southern England. Low in natural fertility, Maine soil was easily exhausted. It was also acidic, a condition that ties up those nutrients that are in the soil. These limitations were not immediately identified, since the first crops prospered on the available nutrients. When yields fell after only a few short years, however, the soil deficiencies became apparent. The short growing season, drought, wetness, plant diseases, and insects made getting a crop a substantial challenge.[17]

Second, the livestock so carefully transported from England and raised locally were viewed as delectable fare by the local predator population, especially wolves. They loved swine, goats, and red calves (apparently mistaking them for deer) and were fearless, making "no more bones to runne away with a Pigge, than a Dogg to runne away with a Marrow bone." The settlers tried everything they could think of to eliminate the hated marauders, including bounties and traps. The wolves hardly noticed.[18]

So, if the situation was so despicable, why did people continue to arrive and settle in Maine? One can only speculate. The Maine coast was the first land sighted by many English immigrants to America. Perhaps for some, any land was better than more time on board the accursed ship. Others came because of ties with local proprietors and families, and certainly some came because they found that they had differences with Puritan Massachusetts. Later in the seventeenth century, new inhabitants arrived from the south, as land became increasingly scarce and expensive in the established bay communities. Also, most potential settlers arrived in summer, when newly established farms were flanked by green fields and herds of livestock wandered nearby. The sight of numerous fishermen working offshore would have heightened the sense of economic vitality to prospective settlers. The cold season would have seemed remote and perhaps even exaggerated.[19]

Coping with the Environment: Life-styles

Although shockingly harsh, in the long run conditions were not quite as bad as they first appeared. Apart from occasional years of shortages, settlers had adequate food and clothing. Early inventories and archaeological findings reveal that most settlers were able to attain a life-style clearly above subsistence level. Extant inventories of eleven Maine farmers show that all had pewter dishes, and several had stocks of linen, cotton and woolen cloth, napkins, lighting devices, and brass utensils. Four reported books (two to five volumes—Bibles in three instances). Artifacts excavated from Pemaquid, Maine, also include a number of better-quality items, such as fine ceramics, glassware, pewter and brass buttons, silver-plated brass shoe buckles, silver thimbles, brass and pewter spoons, brass and iron Jew's harps, silver cuff links, a brass snuff lid, and an ornamental brass finial (fig. 72). Found in context with such artifacts of daily living as clay pipes, cooking equipment, fishhooks, and farming equipment, these objects suggest a society with a fair quantity of the better things of life.[20]

In contrast, life at Pentagoet may have been more austere than in the Anglo settlements. During the early years when Charles de Menou d'Aulnay, Sieur de Charnisay, first commander of Pentagoet, was in charge, there were some amenities, but most were located at his house site and probably signaled his status rather

72. This group of artifacts, dating from the second half of the seventeenth century, was excavated at Colonial Pemaquid State Park: a trifid-end spoon, a silver seal, a silver thimble, a pine-tree shilling, a silver-plated buckle, and two ornate buckle fragments. These objects attest to life-styles clearly above the subsistence level. Courtesy of Maine Bureau of Parks and Recreation. Photo-graph courtesy of Maine State Museum.

than overall conditions. Other materials including clay pots and repeatedly repaired, refitted, and reused metal objects suggest much more rudimentary life-styles for most inhabitants.[21]

Even as they strove, with some success, to cope with the rugged Maine environment, the French and English saw another threat to their well-being—one another. Earlier in the century each side had accosted the other, and the fear of further incidents always remained. One summer night in 1645, paranoia turned to sheer panic in Falmouth. A group of riotous drunken fishermen fired guns on an island in Casco Bay, and the local inhabitants were convinced they were under French attack.[22] Not surprisingly, each nationality moved to defend itself. In this area, the French appeared to have had a clear advantage—when they were in control of Pentagoet, that is. In 1654 the fort was described as small, "yet a very strong and very well composed peece with eight peece of ordinance and brass, three murtherers, about eighteen Barrels of powder, and eighteen men in the garrison." In 1670 the fort housed twelve cannon and six mortars. This facility, so greatly feared by Maine's English population, proved less formidable when facing an organized military assault, falling in 1654 to an Anglo fleet of four vessels and again in 1674 to a determined Dutch force.[23]

The English colonists sought to establish local militias for military security, but the attempt to set up community forces was not particularly impressive. In 1656, Massachusetts officials groused that several towns were not furnishing "sufficient armes, powder, etc. as the laws requries." The problem continued, and in 1672 Kittery, York, Cape Porpoise, Saco, Scarborough, and Falmouth were cited "for not providing a stock of powder and bulletts according to law." [24]

Even so, by the 1660s, Maine's militia forces consisted of over seven hundred men.[25] The towns tried to maintain a semblance of preparedness, buying at least some powder and shot, holding periodic trainings, and establishing fortified garrison houses.[26] Unfortunately, the scattered nature of the communities created a major problem for gathering forces, and even when the forces assembled, their readiness was probably far less than desirable. For example, estate inventories suggest that many, if not most, inhabitants owned guns, but the quality varied dramatically. Values of "guns" ranged from ten to forty shillings and of "muskets" from eight to twenty-eight shillings, and a number of weapons were classified as "ould." It is most likely that many weapons were of questionable reliability at best, as undoubtedly were some of their owners.[27]

Even as they sought to protect their new settlements from perceived threats, the Maine colonists strove to mold their communities into replicas of the Old World towns from which they came. English settlers named their hamlets after English towns, and even though Kittery, York, Wells, Scarborough, and Falmouth did not much resemble their namesakes, they signaled a crucial tie with the homeland. As Hubbard put it, "That it might not be forgotten whence they had their origin, [New Englanders] imprint some remembrance of their former habitations in England upon their new dwellings in America." [28]

Land management also mirrored the English settlers' heritage. Property was carefully parceled out with deeds (the earliest were long-term proprietorial leases) that delineated the terms and boundaries following English legal usage. The distribution of land also reflected English social-economic hierarchies, and individuals holding more wealth, status, and education were systematically granted more, better, and more advantageously located properties.

English settlers followed familiar Old World patterns in establishing local governments. As one of Maine's earliest governors, Thomas Gorges, pointed out in 1640, "We steared as neere as we could to the course of England." [29] Town government, the court system, and even a still-born legislative structure were all modeled directly on Anglo patterns. Interpretations of court actions more than once pivoted on the colonists' best readings and recollections of English common law. A set of colonial laws was enacted in the young province of Maine in 1642 and sent back to England for approval.[30] Political office holding and preferential marriages further delineated and buttressed traditional status structures in government and society. New World democrats these settlers were not.[31]

The clearest evidence of the vital tie to the English homeland is reflected in the home furnishings the colonists used. Inventories and period objects (many recovered archaeologically) demonstrate an overwhelming reliance on English and European products, which served as well for inspirations for locally produced wares. Even clay pipes, used for that most American pastime of tobacco smoking, were imported from the Old World.[32]

Like the English, French colonists at Pentagoet re-created to the best of their ability, and in the confines of a military post, the rural French life they had known before coming to Acadia. Archaeological recoveries and historical records indicate that clothing, textiles, firearms, and other durable goods used at Pentagoet were overwhelmingly of French manufacture. Other objects arrived via French channels. D'Aulnay strove to maintain not only the physical world but also the social structure of the homeland, outfitting himself in the garb of a cavalier, with elaborate dress including spurs, a clear marker of gentlemanly status in this fort without steeds.[33]

Along with the establishment of governmental bodies and practices to provide local order and the creation of military forces to protect against outsiders, the English communities attempted to secure their spiritual well-being. It was not a simple problem. The small English settlements were often too poor to attract pastors for their churches. Furthermore, several towns contained competing factions, often Anglican and Congregationalist, and occasionally Antinomian and Quaker as well.[34]

By the 1670s, most communities had acquired ministers, the majority of whom were Congregationalists who espoused Bay Colony views. Still, non-Puritan bodies remained strong enough that Maine settlements never assumed the same level of orthodox conformity maintained in Massachusetts. Instead, a sense of tolerance, probably as much a product of necessity as desire, characterized early Maine's religious ethos.

Little documentary or physical evidence remains regarding religious practices at Pentagoet. A Catholic chapel and bell tower surmounted the gate into the fort, and in 1673 and 1674 a Jesuit priest, Father Pierron, lived with the garrison. Several hundred yards from the structure was a Capuchin mission, which had been established between 1648 and 1654. The level of religious participation is not recorded, although it has been suggested that the scarcity of archaeological religious artifacts indicates minimal activity. However, archaeological investigations of Maine Anglo settlement have not revealed many religious objects either, so this verdict seems premature.[35]

Much as the ideology of a threatening wilderness confined the imaginations of early colonists, the need to sustain themselves in this environment required them to redefine their relationship to the unknown. In the process of extracting the resources of their new world, they began to alter that world in ways that would be irreversible. At the same time, the settlers would be altered themselves.

Coping with the Environment: Harnessing Resources

The introduction of European-style agriculture most visibly changed the land. Most newcomers farmed, a fact noted by numerous contemporaries. Josselyn observed, "All these Towns have stores of salt and fresh marsh with arable land, and are well stockt with Cattle." Hubbard noted, "Upon the banks [of Sheepscot] were many scattered Planters, . . . a thousand Head of Neat Cattel . . . besides the Fields and Barns full of Corn."[36] That farming predominated in the English settlements is not surprising. Once settlers arrived, they had to raise crops and live-stock because there was no other reliable source of food. Many of the newcomers had farmed before coming to America, and quite a number of Anglo artisans dropped their crafts to become yeomen on arrival. Livestock, as frequently noted in contemporary descriptions, had descended from small numbers brought from England. Once in the New World, most livestock prospered; some, such as hogs, propagated phenomenally.[37]

Creating farms required tremendous time and energy. The

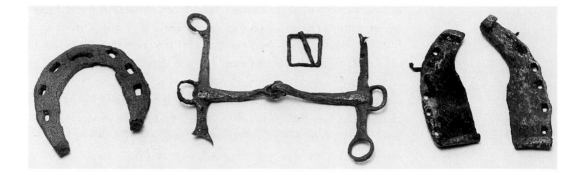

73. A horseshoe, a horse bit, a harness buckle, and an ox-shoe attest to the substantial number of livestock found in early Maine. These artifacts were excavated at Colonial Pemaquid State Park. Courtesy of Maine Bureau of Parks and Recreation. Photograph courtesy of the Maine State Museum.

earliest settlers were able to select sites with coastal and inland marshes for hay and with upland clearings or abandoned Indian planting fields for cultivated crops. However, farmers who wished to expand or settlers arriving later faced the task of clearing new ground. This required felling one hundred to two hundred trees per acre, grubbing out the stumps (a task abandoned later in the century), and clearing off the omnipresent rocks. Only then could crops be planted.[38]

Fishing, the occupation that had first attracted large numbers of Europeans to New England in the 1610s and 1620s, still occupied many inhabitants in mid-century Maine communities. Hubbard indicated that Cape Porpus was "a convenient Seat for Fisherman." Josselyn found Winter Harbor to be "a noted place for Fishers, here they have many stages," and Maverick found "the Islands of Monhegan and Damerells Cove, and other small ones adjacent [to be] Commodius for fishing."[39] In most early settlements, a mix of both farming and fishing organized life. Maverick noted that some settlers in the Sagadahoc region "attend[ed] wholly the trade with the Indians, others planting and raising a stock of cattle and Some at the mouth of the River . . . fishing." Similarly, Josselyn observed that Pemaquid, Matinicus, Cape Newagen, and Muscongus were "all filled with dwelling houses and stages for fishermen, and [had] . . . plenty of Cattle, arable land and marshes."[40]

The developing lumber trade also had much to do with opening coastal Maine land. According to Hubbard, "All or most of [the] . . . Towns and Plantations are seated upon, and near some River greater or lesser, whose Streams are principally improved for the driving of Saw-mills: Those late Inventions, so useful for the Destruction of Wood and Timber . . . that there is scare a

River or Creek in those Parts that hath not some of those Engines erected upon them."[41] In the Berwick-Kittery area, the timber business prospered because of the Piscataqua River system, and at least eleven different sawmills in the region were founded between 1634 and 1659. By the 1670s numerous other mills had been built along the rivers, including ten at York, three at Wells, three at Saco, and several others scattered from Falmouth to the Sagadahoc, where in 1676 the Clarke and Lake establishment had one hundred thousand feet of boards ready for shipment.[42]

Sawmilling depended on outside capital, which meant that little of the profit was reinvested locally. When local entrepreneurs tried to set up sawmills on their own, they frequently found themselves in financial trouble and were forced to look to Boston or Portsmouth businessmen for needed funds. Often these outside entrepreneurs established local mills and, in most instances, collected most of the profits. These same businessmen usually served the commercial needs of the small Maine towns as well, but at terms highly disadvantageous to the inhabitants. This practice contributed to the relative underdevelopment of Maine communities in contrast to the growth of Massachusetts colonies.

The 1660s and 1670s saw increasing occupational diversity among arriving colonists. By the 1670s, blacksmiths, carpenters, and millwrights were joined by coopers, wheelwrights, shoemakers, tailors, and other basic craftsmen essential to an agrarian society. Missing were such artisans as goldsmiths and pewterers. More dependent on an urban setting for supplies, communication, and markets, these more sophisticated craftsmen did not make their way to early Maine.[43]

A vital domestic economy supported economic growth in early Maine settlements. Though nearly invisible in the records, and seldom noted within traditional colonial economic studies, domestic activities carried out by women were, in fact, essential to any settled economy. Men were unable to carry out their respective occupations and trades without the basic necessities of food, clothing, or even a domestic setting for nonwork, all provided by women's work. Women, almost always wives (with daughters and servants), fulfilled essential needs, economic and social. In mid-seventeenth-century Maine, a bilateral economic system was well established, and it was fundamental to the success of the community. The early community of Falmouth was probably typical of Maine settlements. A population profile of Falmouth developed from mid-seventeenth-century census data shows that the community was composed overwhelmingly of family units, with few independent single men.[44]

The Pulitzer prize–winning historian Laurel Ulrich demonstrated that "a woman's environment was the family dwelling and the yard or yards surrounding it," which "would extend from the kitchen and its appendages, the cellars, pantries, brewhouses, milkhouses, washhouses, and butteries . . . to . . . the garden, the milkyard, the well, the henhouse, and perhaps the orchard itself" and would, in terms of gathering and trade, extend into nearby woods or marshes and "into the houses of neighbors and into the cartways of a village or town."[45] The wives' economic contributions were fundamental to their husbands' and families' well-being. They had to obtain foodstuffs (by growing, gathering, trading, purchasing, and so on) and then prepare them for the table, activities that could range from butchering a small pig to baking biscuits in a skillet over an open fire. (In fact, women were experts in starting and regulating fires.) Furthermore, they had to preserve a wide variety of foods, employing a diversity of techniques handed down orally and by demonstration from generation to generation, the fundamental education process for a multitude of domestic skills. Women also had to clothe their families (and often servants) and were expected to be dexterous at knitting, needlework, and sewing. Often the yarns and sometimes the cloth used were home products, although cloth was probably more often acquired through trade or purchase. Numerous other household tasks also had to be dealt with, including repairing and cleaning clothing, feeding livestock, gathering kindling for the fires, and, the most time-consuming, raising children. Women took especially seriously their obligation to teach their daughters and servants the skills needed to run a household.

Women also played a fundamental role in local markets, establishing terms of trade through astute awareness of good value and of what they needed, where to get it, and its barter value. They completed these transactions either through credit on their husbands' accounts or in barter in home products or specific domestic labors. A wife often found herself directly supporting her husband's occupation. She might help plant field crops, manufacture craft items, or handle business transactions in his absence. As Ulrich noted, "Almost any task was suitable for a woman as long as it furthered the good of her family and was acceptable to her husband."[46]

The dual economic structure was essential for the integrity of overall societal viability, a fact underscored by the rapidity with which widows and widowers soon replaced a lost mate.[47] Early inheritance patterns further solidified the structure. In an overwhelming number of recorded cases, male heirs received real estate that could then be used to continue their various economic affairs with the outside world. Women, however, would most often receive household goods, the properties most useful for the establishment and maintenance of the domestic unit, that is, a home. All recognized the importance of this system.[48] Without it, early Maine could never have developed beyond the world of transient fishermen and fur traders.

As stable agriculturally based settlements anchored English colonial society in Maine, the fur trade, one of the earliest economic attractions of the region and the least dependent on settlement economics, receded ever eastward. By the mid 1630s, the region had been roughly divided, with the English controlling the territory west of Pemaquid, the French in charge from the Penobscot River east, and the mid-coast area more or less up for grabs. The smaller river drainages of western Maine were largely hunted out by the 1640s. The Kennebec watershed, originally brought under control by the Plymouth Colony in the late 1620s, was beginning to suffer from declining harvests by the 1660s as Pilgrim interests, the Clarke and Lake Company at Arrowsic, and interlopers all vied for the same fur bearers. Meanwhile, Pemaquid, the easternmost English settlement, maintained a brisk trade with local Etchemins and with French traders at Pentagoet.[49]

By the 1660s, Pentagoet towered over the other trading centers as the key fur mart on the northeastern coast. Through Pentagoet, great bounties of fur were sent to European ports throughout the seventeenth century. Established at the mouth of the Penobscot River, Pentagoet served as the juncture between the colonial world and the great river with its tributaries that penetrated deep into forests unexplored by French or English.[50]

It was that juncture between the known and unknown that left colonials highly nervous. The "wilderness" and its inhabitants, so discomforting to European imaginations, also served as a source for significant economic benefits. To the colonists, the trick was

*An Explanation on the Prospect Draft of Fort William & Mary on Piscataqua River in y*ᵉ *Province of...*

74. Tracing of
Wolfgang Romer,
*The Prospect of Fort
William and Mary on
Piscataqua River*, 1705.
Courtesy of the Baxter
Rare Maps Collection,
Maine State Archives.
Original in the British
Library.

to extract the wealth but not be drawn away from civilization as they defined it. When individuals like the English fur trader Thomas Morton and, later, his French counterpart Saint-Castin chose to adopt native ways of living, they were viewed by their countrymen as having fallen from civilization into savagery. To both English and French, even dealing with or supporting Indians could leave one's reputation in question, especially in times of strife. In general, although colonists carried on trade with the Wabanakis, it was always with deep unease.[51]

Despite the increasingly diverse and complex economic matrix that was evolving in the region by the 1660s and 1670s, Maine's inhabitants found it difficult to accumulate any substantial quantity of wealth. One of the most obvious impediments was obtaining needed supplies. Both English and French settlers in Maine were on the frontier or periphery of the New World colonies. Far from the centers of commerce and offering only limited markets, they had problems attracting outside merchants and, when they did, found they had to pay extremely high prices for what they got. Josselyn, who visited Maine in the late 1660s, noted of Boston merchants bringing supplies to the region, "If they do not gain *cent per cent,* they cry out that they are losers."[52]

English settlers in Maine soon discovered that finding the cash

the Continent of America
y through the Islands for the Tenour shore of uigth
of New Castle in the Great Island D the Church

or goods with which to acquire needed imports was a continuing challenge. Agriculture provided basic needs but rarely produced much surplus. Fishing seemed even less promising for personal gain because, apart from the fishing masters, the fishermen made up the poorest segment of the society. The lumber trade, the region's most lucrative business, brought minimal benefits to the inhabitants, for sawmill construction and operations generally depended on outside capital and most of the profits ended up in the hands of entrepreneurs from Boston or Portsmouth. Settlers earned some cash through day labor, and they had ready access to milled lumber and also received favorable terms in getting their own lumber sawn. However, workers in the lumber industry represented only a small fraction of the settlers.

All of these economic disadvantages eliminated the possibility of locally raising substantial capital to allow the accumulation of wealth. These problems resulted in major burdens on the settlers as they attempted to carry out such public services as building roads, supporting a militia, and maintaining a church and pastor.[53] Under these conditions, a frontier society could survive, and perhaps grow slowly over time, but it had almost nothing to fall back on in time of crisis. A bad season quickly depleted limited surpluses and left the inhabitants critically short of food. An extended military crisis had precisely the same effect. The crises arrived for both the French and the English in the 1670s.

In 1675, long-standing animosities between Indians and settlers in central and southern New England exploded in bloody warfare as a result of an acrimonious dispute between "King Philip" (Metacomet, sachem of the Wampanoags) and the Plymouth Colony. The Wabanakis in Maine at first did not join in. However, that year, a series of seemingly isolated incidents occurred that contributed to escalating hostilities. Maine colonial leaders demanded that the Kennebec Indians turn in their guns, which they badly needed for hunting. In Saco, fishermen accidentally drowned a child of Squando, a major sachem, by throwing the baby in the water to see if it could swim. At about the same time, emissaries from lower New England Indian groups arrived to cajole their Maine counterparts to take retribution for these and other injustices. Finally, the natives of western Maine went to war, and in September, their raids decimated isolated homesteads in several communities, creating panic and causing English inhabitants to move to garrison houses or simply to flee

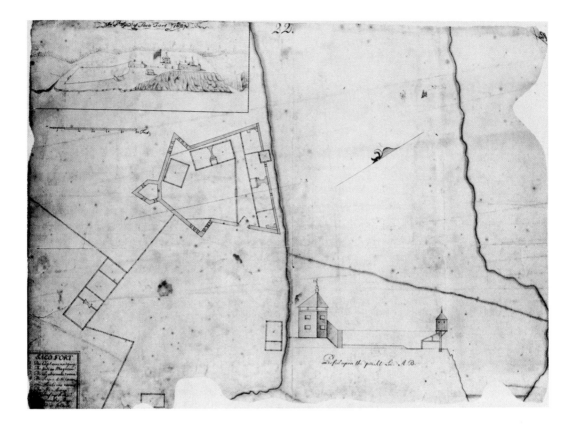

75. Wolfgang Romer, *The Prospect of Saco Fort*, 1699. British Public Record Office, CO 700/North American Colonies, Maine/2. Photograph courtesy of Maine Historic Preservation Commission.

to Massachusetts. The men who remained behind spent much of their time and energies guarding and scouting. Normal field work came to a halt because of the lack of available workers and the fear of ambush, and food supplies soon dwindled alarmingly. At the same time, powder, shot, reliable weapons, and resolve often proved to be in short supply.

After a desperate winter, the colonists found themselves under a far broader attack as Etchemins from the Kennebec eastward joined their counterparts to the west in numerous raids. Although the number of casualties and captives was relatively small, for the English, desperate for basic supplies and vulnerably scattered in isolated garrisons along the coast, the risk of staying in Maine seemed too high. During the late summer and fall, settlers deserted community after community, leaving only the settlements south of the Saco River to maintain an Anglo presence in the region.[54]

For the French, trouble came from an unexpected quarter. In

1674 the Dutch corsair Captain Jurriaen Aernoutsz and his Boston partner John Rhodes set up an expedition that captured, looted, and destroyed Fort Pentagoet. Several members of the victorious party set up a pirate operation, which Massachusetts closed down the following year. In about 1677 Saint-Castin reestablished French control of the area but in a wholly new manner. Having taken a native wife, he lived with the Etchemin Indians and traded with whomever he felt necessary, including the English, which was a prudent stance considering the military strength of his Anglo neighbors and the uncertainty of any support from his homeland. Even so, his trading with the English colonists troubled the French leadership in both Quebec and Paris as France and England intensified competition in the development of worldwide empires. French efforts in the 1670s and 1680s to encircle the English settlements with a string of forts along the Great Lakes and down the Mississippi resulted in conflict between friendly Algonquians and pro-English Iroquois. The pro-French leaning of Maine's Indians and Anglo fears of French aggressions created serious problems for Saint-Castin's carefully nurtured operations. In 1688 his post was rifled by a force from Massachusetts, a move that ensured his enmity toward the English. When Saint-Castin returned to France in the early 1700s, his sons carried on trade with the Etchemins, but their tenure proved short. A struggle between the French and the English was being fought on many fronts between 1703 and 1713. Conflict in Europe, the Far East, and America (where it was called Queen Anne's War) finally was settled at the Treaty of Utrecht in 1713, primarily to England's benefit. As one of the treaty provisions, France relinquished Acadia, including the post at Pentagoet, to the English. Although the French later disputed whether the terms had included centers such as Pentagoet, and although Saint-Castin's sons remained in the area for some time, the post never again came under official French control.[55]

Only after two decades and two more vicious wars would English settlers return to permanently settle the lands east of Wells. By that time, disease, hardship, and warfare had reduced the Native American population to a shadow of what it had been. Another war in the 1720s eliminated the possibility of a Wabanaki threat on any scale larger than small raiding parties, and the fall of Quebec in 1759 finally ended French political and military influence in the region. After 1713, English settlers moved more purposefully into this transformed wilderness, setting up forts, sending military forces after the natives, and beginning inland settlement. It was a world far different from that which they had encountered a half-century earlier, and one in which their very ideas of savagery and wilderness generally precluded incorporating or even acknowledging contributions from the local native people.

CHAPTER TWELVE

The World of Thomas Gorges
Life in the Province of Maine in the 1640s

Emerson W. Baker

In the summer of 1640 Thomas Gorges of Batcombe Farm, Somersetshire, England, arrived in the province of Maine as its new deputy governor. The proprietor and governor of Maine, Sir Ferdinando Gorges, had too many important enterprises in England to travel to his colony, so instead he left the daily governance of the province in the hands of his kinsman Thomas. Although the deputy governor's stay was brief (in 1643 he returned to England to fight in the English Civil Wars), he left two lasting reminders of his visit to Maine. First, several of his copybooks survive, which contain drafts of over eighty letters that he wrote while in Maine. Many of these missives to family and friends back in England describe his home and activities in the young colony. Second, remains of his Maine home survive as an archaeological site; it underwent limited excavation in 1985 and 1986. The copybooks and the excavations, combined with other contemporary documents and comparative data from other early Maine archaeology sites, provide detailed insights into the world of Thomas Gorges and his neighbors in seventeenth-century Maine.

The Maine of Thomas Gorges revealed in these sources differs from the traditional image of colonial Maine. Popular history tells us that Maine was a rural backwater, an economic hinterland of Puritan Massachusetts. Maine was a frontier war zone, a buffer between New England and its enemies, the native people of northern New England and their French allies. This perception is true for the second half of the seventeenth century and the early eighteenth century. However, in the 1630s and 1640s, settlement had only begun in Maine, and Massachusetts had not yet gained political and economic dominance of the region. Stable relations with the Wabanaki Indians created a lucrative fur trade, and the warfare that was to devastate Wabanaki and European society alike was still decades away.[1]

If someone had told Thomas Gorges in 1640 that by the end of the seventeenth century Maine would be a depopulated borderland, ruled from Boston and largely owned by Puritan merchants, he would probably not have believed them. Like any new colony, Maine had suffered its share of problems, but the future looked bright. Indeed, Thomas would have been justified in imagining the reverse, that Massachusetts would develop into a burned-over frontier, ruled by the governor of Maine from his wealthy cathedral city of Agamenticus. Just recently, in the Pequot War of 1637, the southern New Englanders had proved incapable of peacefully dealing with the natives. In that same year, Sir Ferdinando Gorges was named the governor of New England by King Charles I. This was seen as part of a plan by the king to bring the Puritans of southern New England under close control, and Sir Ferdinando, a champion of Charles, the Church of England, and the province of Maine, was eager to take on the task.

Politics, religion, and native relations aside, the economy of Maine also held more promise than that of Massachusetts. In 1640 it seemed clear that Maine possessed a superiority over southern New England in most natural resources. Maine had larger fishing grounds, more fur pelts, and better stands of timber than Massachusetts, all crucial elements for the growth of a colony's prosperity. Even Cotton Mather, the tireless promoter of Massachusetts, later described prewar Maine as "spacious country" and "on many accounts, the most charming part of New England."[2]

Despite these factors, Massachusetts would soon come to dominate Maine. Sir Ferdinando's governorship of New England would never take effect, since the knight and his monarch were soon caught up in the English Civil Wars. The wars would result in the defeat of the Royalists and lead to the rule of the English Puritans, providing support to the growing power of Puritan Massachusetts and its rapid takeover of New Hampshire and Maine. One prime reason for the usurpation of Maine was its small population. While Massachusetts grew rapidly, the Gorges family was never able to attract enough immigrants to their colony. Only after Massachusetts began to take control of Maine in 1652 did the population begin to increase markedly. This growth was largely due to immigrants from Massachusetts and New Hampshire. Maine continued to grow rapidly but only until 1676, when events in King Philip's War in Maine resulted in the exodus of all English colonists from the region north of Saco. Warfare continued for a generation throughout Maine, ensuring that the region would remain a lightly populated frontier region rather than the prospering colony envisioned by the Gorges family. Even so, it is illustrative to examine the world of Thomas Gorges and his neighbors not only to see what might have been but also to view, in its own terms, a colony that enjoyed just as much promise as its neighbors. This approach reveals a view of the past that contrasts markedly with the popular image of colonial Maine as a borderland of Massachusetts.

In the world of Thomas Gorges in 1640, settlers of diverse backgrounds, beliefs, and traditions were coming together to harvest the bounty of a land rich in natural resources, attempting in many ways to re-create the world they had left behind. This sense of continuity with England is perhaps the strongest theme of early settlement in Maine. Although Maine may have been a frontier, full of opportunity, the English residents did their best to mold the land into something familiar. Sir Ferdinando Gorges actually wanted more than mere continuity with the motherland; he envisioned in Maine a chance to build medieval England anew, to bring back the past. In 1639 King Charles I provided him with a new charter for the province of Maine, which gave Sir Ferdinando sweeping powers and privileges to build his kingdom. Sir Ferdinando and his heirs were made absolute lords of an extensive tract. As the historian Charles Banks pointed out: "This memorable charter was more comprehensive than ever before granted by the crown to an individual. By its terms Gorges became an uncrowned monarch in a little kingdom of his own."[3]

Such a kingdom needed a suitable capital, and the settlement of Agamenticus (renamed Gorgeana in 1641 in honor of the proprietor) was to be the capital of this feudal empire. The city (present-day York) received a charter, with enlarged boundaries taking in twenty-one square miles of land. According to the charter, a mayor, aldermen, and forty appointed officials were to run the city. Only in Sir Ferdinando's vision would Agamenticus be a shining capital city with thousands of residents. Agamenticus, first settled in 1630, had fewer than one hundred residents when it was chartered a city in 1641. These early settlers included fishermen, farmers, merchants, and even lumberjacks and millers who worked the Gorges sawmills. Whereas John Winthrop en-

76. York, Maine, as seen in a detail of a tracing of *Map of the Piscataway River,* ca. 1665. Courtesy of the Baxter Rare Maps Collection, Maine State Archives. Original in the British Library.

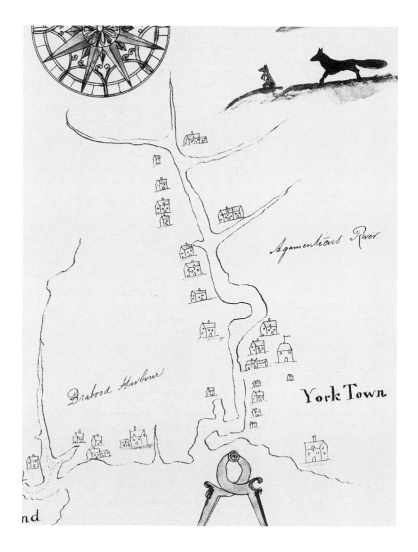

visioned Boston as a city upon a hill, an example of Puritan perfection, Sir Ferdinando planned to make the fishing village of Agamenticus a stronghold of the Church of England, apparently with a bishop in residence.[4]

Thomas Gorges stopped first in Massachusetts, arriving in Boston in June 1640, and soon proceeded north to Maine. At this time English settlement throughout New England was still quite limited. Two years earlier John Josselyn, the son of one of Sir Ferdinando's agents, had sailed the same route from England to Boston and then north to Black Point, Maine, and he had described the entire stretch of coast from Boston to Maine as "being no other than a mere wilderness, here and there by the seaside a few scattered plantations." Boston itself was rather a "village than a town, there being not above twenty or thirty houses."[5] In traveling this route, Thomas Gorges chose to stress the potential of the land. "The country here is plentiful yielding all sorts of English grains and fruits, the rivers pleasant, well stored with variety of fish, the woods well treed with stately cedar, lofty pines, sturdy oaks and walnut trees, with raspberry and gooseberry trees and vines in abundance."[6] Rather than seeing a frightening wildland, Thomas almost seems to describe pastoral arcadia, a land of opportunity. If Maine was a wilderness, as Josselyn described it, so too was all of New England. Indeed, when Thomas arrived, Maine was no more isolated than most other New England settlements, which were all in their infancy.

Thomas immediately took up residence in Agamenticus at the Manor House of Point Christian, the "residence" of the proprietor and governor of Maine, Sir Ferdinando Gorges. Sir Ferdinando never actually visited his colony. In his place he had sent a series of deputies to act as governor and lord of the manor. His young cousin Thomas would be the last in a series of agents sent to oversee the colony. Only twenty-two years old at the time, Thomas was fresh from two years of study at the Inns of Court in London, which little prepared him for the task at hand. Many difficult duties confronted this young man as he took responsibility for strengthening the colony. Sir Ferdinando's manor and his sawmill and gristmill needed attention if they were to become profitable investments. John Winter, the agent of the Trelawney Station on Richmond's Island, insultingly called Thomas "the boy, Gorges." As it turned out, Thomas would prove to be a capable and hardworking administrator.[7]

Although Gorges immediately set about to reorganize the colony and improve Sir Ferdinando's property, like most immigrants he still had time to miss his family and friends back in England. Whenever he encountered a ship bound for England, he hurriedly wrote letters, at times cutting them short to avoid missing the ship's departure. He often worried that his notes might not arrive at their destination, for he knew that they usually passed through several hands on their long journey to England. Even when letters arrived promptly, it took a long time to get an answer from England. Thomas wrote to his father, Henry, and explained, "The time that I expect letters from you is from December till August, and the time you are to expect them from me is from August to till December, for so the voyages of the ships lie."[8]

Thomas was not alone in this plight. Most early settlers in New England suffered the same homesickness. But Thomas may have felt more anxiety than his neighbors, since many of them immigrated in family units, rather than as individuals. Some unattached men such as Thomas did migrate; however, ships' passenger lists indicate that it was rare to find a single woman who ventured to New England. When one did, she was almost always in the company of some family members. Of the women who did come to Maine little is known. In surviving seventeenth-century court records, women rarely show up, for men dominated the legal world of the day. In 1652, forty-eight inhabitants of Agamenticus signed the document under which the town submitted to become part of Massachusetts, and only one of those, Mary Tapp, was a woman. Likewise, Mary Bachelor was the only female to sign the submission in Kittery. In his letters, Thomas Gorges frequently mentions women relatives and friends back in England; however, he almost never mentions the women of Maine, just their husbands. Although women were largely ignored in the documents, the presence of women and families in New England from earliest days gave the colonies a sense of stability and permanence. It is clear from his letters that Thomas Gorges missed family life very much. In his many letters to his parents, brothers and sisters, and other relatives, he eagerly asked for family news, and he grew excited at the possibility of family members joining him in Maine. In the absence of kinsmen, Thomas drew strength and companionship from his family of servants, especially his beloved "Cheddar men," who emigrated with him from his parents' parish of Cheddar, Somerset.[9]

The absence of relatives must have underscored for Thomas the difficulty that New England settlers had keeping in touch with England. In this regard, Gorges was probably lucky that he lived in Maine, a place with good internal travel routes and in relatively close contact with England via transatlantic shipping. Most early Maine residents lived in a narrow band of settlements close to the sea, with the exception of those who occupied several inland trading posts, like Cushnoc. These settlers owned land fronting on the Atlantic or along one of Maine's broad rivers. Point Christian lay about two hundred feet from the Agamenticus River (present-day York River), and archaeological evidence indicates that contemporary Maine homesteads often lay even closer to water. Many are found within one hundred feet of navigable water. The ribbon-like pattern of settlement, reminiscent of the French on the St. Lawrence, provided Maine settlers with a convenient and rapid means of transportation and with access to the latest news and trade goods.

Boats and canoes were very common in early Maine, showing up in the inventories of farmers as well as fishermen. Canoes were the "all purpose vehicles" of the day, being used for everything from fishing to carrying loads of salt hay or manure. Many of these canoes were apparently dugouts, carved out of a single tree trunk (fig. 77). Few roads existed in early Maine, but few were needed because most settlers lived on the water. With a sizable network of rivers and with canoes and other craft available for transport, early Mainers were probably less isolated than settlers of interior Massachusetts towns. Their proximity to water also gave Mainers ready access to the extensive trade network of the North Atlantic. In the 1630s many ships sailing from England used a northern passage and made their landfall in Maine. As a result, Maine residents often received first choice of merchandise and the first news of events in England, even from ships bound for Boston.[10]

Many ships proceeded down the coast to Massachusetts, but others made Maine their final destination. Fishing vessels came seasonally to harvest the bounty of the Gulf of Maine. Thomas Gorges observed that two or three fishing vessels from Barnstable, Devon, fished off the coast near Agamenticus all winter,

77. Dugout canoe
excavated at Biddeford
Pool, 1986. The canoe
was probably made
by English settlers
in the seventeenth
century. Courtesy of
Emerson W. Baker.

taking advantage of the time of year when the cod came close to shore to spawn. Explorations from 1602 to 1605, which culminated with the 1607 Popham Colony, introduced the English to the incredibly rich fishing grounds off the coast of Maine. Within a few years, Maine's bounty attracted increasing numbers of English vessels, fishing for cod and other fish.[11]

However, by 1640 the number of ships sailing for Maine was declining as Boston began to establish itself as the focal point of New England shipping and trade. The seasonal fishing industry also declined as it became difficult for visitors to compete with the growing number of year-round fishing stations on the coast of Maine. Still, some vessels came not as fishing ships but as merchant ships, purchasing the catch of local fishermen. Thomas Gorges noted that in January several Bristol ships would arrive specifically to buy fish caught by the residents. Other merchant craft carried settlers as well as goods, contributing to what is now known as the Great Migration.[12]

Many of these ships came from the West Country of England, the region that was home to Thomas and the rest of the Gorges family. In his letters, Thomas noted ships from Bristol, the major West Country port and the home of Sir Ferdinando Gorges. He also was in contact with fishing ships from Barnstable, Devon, located not far west of Bristol. West Country ships were frequent visitors at Richmond's Island and Pemaquid, continuing a pattern that had begun even before English colonization. In 1623 Christopher Levett had discovered a Barnstable ship in Pemaquid Harbor trading with the local Wabanakis, several years before the English would attempt a settlement there. A physical link between these West Country ships and Maine settlers is particularly apparent at Point Christian, where 30 percent of excavated ceramic sherds are made of North Devon earthenwares, manufactured principally in Barnstable and Biddeford, Devon. Although this is a high percentage, virtually all other seventeenth-century Maine sites include substantial numbers of North Devon wares. Most also contain clay tobacco pipes manufactured in Bristol.[13]

Many ships from the West Country and the rest of England were attracted to Maine because it was a center of the fur trade. As early as the sixteenth century some trade goods found their way to the coast of Maine, either brought directly by the very occasional European explorer or indirectly by a complex Indian trade network, which gained goods from Europeans fishing at Newfoundland.[14]

This trade grew rapidly in the first decades of the seventeenth century as European explorers, fishermen, and settlers moved into the region. Initially the exchange proved beneficial to both sides. The English received beaver pelts used to make fancy felt hats, moose hides for leather clothing, and other rare furs that commanded high prices in Europe. In return the Indians acquired the products of European industrial technology. Virtually any and all English items were traded to the natives, so it is difficult to define a "trade good." For example, excavations at Burr's Hill, a seventeenth-century Wampanoag burial ground in Rhode Island, uncovered traditional trade goods such as metal tools, as well as more unexpected European-made products such as ceramics, wine bottles, horseshoes, and door hinges. Most English merchants traded with both Indians and colonists, so even merchants' inventories of goods do not completely solve the issue of the nature of trade goods. Still, descriptions of the fur trade suggest that most trade goods fell into one of six categories: weapons (firearms, ammunition, and swords); hardware (hatchets, knives, kettles); cloth and clothes (shirts, coats, and blankets); small items (beads, "trinkets," and the like); foodstuffs (corn, peas, and bread); and narcotics (tobacco, pipes, brandy, and rum).[15]

Thomas Gorges apparently did not trade with the Wabanakis, probably because there were no natives left on the Agamenticus River when he arrived there. In 1623 Levett had explored the Agamenticus River and found "a good harbor for ships, good ground, and much already cleared, fit for planting of corn and other fruits, having heretofore been planted by the savages who are all dead."[16] Virgin soil epidemics of various European diseases had swept through southern Maine from 1616 to 1619, and again in 1634, killing thousands of Native Americans who had no immune resistance to these diseases. Even minor European diseases such as chicken pox proved lethal to the natives. Intertribal warfare involving Wabanakis from southern Maine to Nova Scotia during the first two decades of the seventeenth century also reduced the population. The effect of these demographic disasters was so great that in 1634 John Winter observed that aside from a group at the mouth of the Saco River, there were no natives within forty to fifty miles of his post at Richmond's Island. As a result, new settlers in the province of Maine could occupy almost any land they wanted without native interference. Many newcomers took the opportunity to occupy the recently abandoned fields along the Agamenticus and other rivers. Soon English crops grew where native corn, beans, and squash had previously prospered, and English homes sat on sites occupied by the natives for hundreds or even thousands of years. Even the manor house at Point Christian occupied a native site. Prehistoric ceramic sherds found at Point Christian indicate that the

78. North Devon gravel-tempered cooking pot, excavated at Colonial Pemaquid State Park. This vessel is typical of the wares produced in North Devon and exported to York and other Maine settlements. Courtesy of Maine Bureau of Parks and Recreation. Photograph courtesy of Maine State Museum.

site may have been initially occupied one thousand years before Gorges's arrival and may have been inhabited as recently as the late sixteenth or early seventeenth century.[17]

Even if many Wabanakis had been in Agamenticus, Thomas noted that by the 1640s, the fur trade, which had once been a more than profitable enterprise, was "utterly lost, the Indians understanding the value of things as well as the English."[18] Thomas clearly exaggerated the decline of the fur trade, for it would remain somewhat profitable for at least another thirty years. However, the rate of return was certainly not as great as it had once been. In addition to facing astute native traders, fur traders trying to profit from the local fur trade were increasing in number, meaning increased competition and narrower profit margins. Compounding the problem was a gradual decline in the value of beaver and moose pelts in the English market in the middle decades of the seventeenth century as supplies increased and as the demand for fur, hats, and clothing decreased. Finally, added to a declining profitability was a certain amount of economic risk. Thomas Gorges wrote to Sir Ferdinando that Richard Vines, the proprietor of the west side of the Saco River (present-day Biddeford), suffered a great financial loss in 1641 when a bark loaded mostly with his trade goods sank in a violent hurricane.[19]

Although Thomas did not actively participate in the fur trade, he did become acquainted with the native people. The "Great Sagamore" of the local Wabanakis had been one of the early visitors to Point Christian, welcoming Thomas to the country. It is quite possible that this Great Sagamore was the same "Sadamoyt, the great sagamore of the East Country" who visited Levett's Casco Bay habitation in 1624. Although some Englishmen had little respect for the Wabanakis and tried to take advantage of them in trade, Thomas Gorges does not appear to have completely shared this attitude. He wrote his father: "I find them very ingenious men. . . . I take great delight to discourse with them." Much of that discourse was an attempt on Gorges's part to convert the natives to Christianity. However, his attempts fell on deaf ears, for the Great Sagamore was pleased with his own "great God Tanto."[20]

Thomas's attitudes toward the Wabanakis seem to closely parallel the views of Levett, who spent 1623 on the coast of Maine. Both Levett and Gorges were fascinated by the natives and seem to have genuinely gotten along with them. Neither, however, would go so far as to truly trust their new friends. Levett encouraged planters to win the affections of the natives, "which may be made use of without trusting them."[21] Gorges felt that it was safe to cooperate with the Wabanakis principally because the tribes had been greatly weakened by the lethal epidemics that had "swept the most part away."[22]

Unfortunately, Thomas, Levett, and other sources provide only a few details on the native people of southern Maine. Contact between the English and the Wabanakis in southern Maine must have been irregular, owing to the reduced native population levels. Still, Gorges and his contemporaries must have known the answers to many questions pursued by today's scholars. So little is known about the Indians of southern Maine that they must be referred to generically as "Wabanakis," since the names of their bands are not even known. Who was the Great Sagamore who visited Gorges? Where did his people live? What did they call themselves? Were they a relict population, all that was left after the warfare and disease? Or were they newcomers who had moved into the region from the interior, replacing the decimated coastal populace? Or is it possible that they were a combination of the remaining old population merged with people from the interior? Neither Thomas Gorges nor any other observer provided useful clues, and today's scholars must work to resolve this puzzle.

The confusion becomes apparent when trying to unravel the specific identity of the Wabanakis on Saco River observed by John Winter. In 1605, when Samuel de Champlain visited the large native village at the mouth of the Saco River, his Etchemin guides called the people "Armouchiquois," and the village "Chouacoit." It was a large, permanent, palisaded settlement, and according to Champlain's map of the Saco, the surrounding area was filled with small native hamlets, all cultivating their corn, bean, and squash fields. In 1607 Chouacoit was hit hard in a raid by the Souriquois and their allies. Thus began a war that lasted until about 1615, apparently ending with disastrous losses for the Armouchiquois. Then, in 1616 the first epidemic hit Saco. Richard Vines, an English explorer and physician, watched with horror as the villagers of Chouacoit rapidly took sick and died.[23]

Vines returned in 1631 to begin a settlement on the west bank of the Saco River. Others came with him or soon followed, yet these English settlers rarely mentioned the native people of the area. Gone was the large village at Chouacoit. Instead English farmers, fishermen, and lumberjacks occupied the land. The Wabanakis appear to have been somewhat of a presence, but it was a limited and poorly documented presence. Instead of residing in a large sedentary village at Chouacoit, the "Sacos" (as the English called them) seemed to migrate seasonally, up and down the river, often living far in the interior. Were the populous sedentary agriculturalist Armouchiquois the same as the fleeting and migratory Sacos? Or were the Sacos a different people who extended their territory from upriver to the coast as the weakened Armouchiquois were forced to abandon the region or merge with more powerful neighbors? The documentary record provides few clues to the answers to these questions.

Meeting with local native leaders, regardless of their tribal affiliation, was but one of many tasks facing Thomas Gorges. He also was responsible for running Sir Ferdinando's mills, located close to Point Christian. In 1634 agents of Sir Ferdinando had built a tide-powered sawmill and gristmill on a tributary of the Agamenticus River (present-day York River). Unfortunately, when Thomas Gorges arrived he found the mills in need of much repair. Keeping the poorly built mills running would be a constant problem and source of frustration for him.[24]

The sawmill on the Agamenticus was built in an initial attempt to manufacture the harvest from the Maine woods. Thomas observed that the abundance of fish and forests in Maine gave the colony a natural advantage over Massachusetts, which did not share this richness of resources. He often advised Sir Ferdinando to invest more money in making barrel staves and pipe staves, for there was a good market for these wood products, which were mainstays of New England's trade with the Caribbean.[25]

The gristmill was also much in demand to grind wheat flour for the husbandmen tilling the rich soil along the Agamenticus River. When it was operating, the mill ground approximately twenty bushels of wheat a tide. The gristmill was so fundamental to daily life that when Thomas wanted to close it to make much-needed repairs in the fall of 1642, he found that the work would have to wait until the spring because the mill was in constant use. These mills, along with a contemporary sawmill on the nearby Great Works River, were among the first built in the English colonies. Others would soon follow, as lumbermen and merchants profited from the rich stands of timber in Maine and the numerous good locations for both gravity- and tide-powered mills.

Gristmills were a necessary part of growing wheat. However, many farmers focused their efforts on raising livestock. When Thomas Gorges arrived at Point Christian, he found a depleted herd of eleven heifers and a bull. Gradually he built the herd up, fenced in their grazing land, and hired a woman and her daughter to run his dairy. Beef, dairy products, and other traditional English foods were the principal foodstuffs for Maine's first settlers. Thomas Gorges wrote home to his father: "Hither my diet is beef and pease, butter and cheese, fowl and fish. At winter I intend to get bacon and poultry, so that I cannot see without good judgement the want of anything."[26] As a member of the English aristocracy, Thomas would have been familiar with the traditional sport of fowling, and he was quite excited by the variety of ducks, swans, and geese that could be bagged by a good marksman. Faunal remains at Point Christian are scarce, since the nature of the soil allowed only a few bones to be preserved for almost 350 years. However, the handful of diagnostic bones found there, including the remains of cattle, pig, duck, cod, and smaller fish, support Gorges's written record of his diet. Bones excavated from other seventeenth-century Maine sites confirm a traditional English cooking fare. Most meat came from domestic animals, mostly cow and pig; in addition, the English ate sheep, goat, and fish caught off the coast of Maine. Although fragile fishbones usually decompose rather quickly, fishhooks, lead weights, harpoon tips, and other fishing gear inevitably show up at most Maine sites.[27]

Thomas Gorges noted the palatability of wild game, including raccoon, beaver, otter, moose, deer, and rabbit. Even though the English only occasionally ate wild game, Gorges observed, "The English catch not many of these beasts but they trade with the Indians for them." Bones from wild game and fowl make up a very tiny percentage of excavated remains from English sites. These English settlers were not experienced backwoods frontiersmen. Instead, they were settlers trying to clear the land and make a new England. Their approach to survival in this new land could only be through familiar English pursuits: farming, fishing, trading, and milling. Not until they learned the approaches to those activities practiced by the native Wabanakis would the settlers begin to change, but this was largely a slow process.[28]

Transplanted English culture in early Maine was both rich and varied, as indicated by the spectrum of religious beliefs in early Maine. People came to Maine from all over England to carry out numerous pursuits. The historian David Allen has noted that Massachusetts was settled by a "mixed multitude" of immigrants from diverse corners of England, who brought along a variety of regional cultural values.[29] Current research indicates that Maine, like Massachusetts, was colonized by many different groups of Englishmen. Because of this diversity, it is impossible to stereotype the settlers of Maine. Religion provided a foundation for comfort and familiarity. In his letters home, Thomas Gorges encouraged Sir Ferdinando to allow tolerance of religious practices in the colony in order to attract the greatest number of settlers to the small province of Maine. Although Thomas favored toleration, he nevertheless desired a "moral and godly" community. He demonstrated his concern for traditional community values in one of first duties as deputy governor, when he confronted the Reverend George Burdett about his moral transgressions. The parishioners of Agamenticus had accepted the radical Burdett, despite his Antinomian leanings, because ministers were hard to come by. However, Burdett was convicted of fathering a child by Mary Puddington, the wife of York's tavernkeeper. This incident helped to expose his extremely radical support of "free love," which went well beyond the views of most Antinomians. As a result, Gorges quickly expelled Burdett from the province of Maine.[30]

The first Anglican chapel in New England was built in Agamenticus in 1635, and the charter for the province of Maine called for the establishment of the Church of England. However, with ministers in short supply and potential settlers subscribing to varying beliefs, religious preference was left largely up to the individual. In 1640 when the Reverend John Wheelwright and a band of his Antinomian followers wanted to move to Maine, Deputy Governor Thomas Gorges told him, "We forced no man to the common prayer book or to the ceremonies of the Church of England but allowed the liberties of conscience in this particular."[31] The government of the colony would not force Puritans, Antinomians, or other Protestant sects to participate in the services of the Church of England. They could organize their own church instead.

On hearing this assurance, Wheelwright and his followers began a settlement they called Wells, with a church initially based on Antinomian teachings. Thus, some residents of Maine ardently adhered to Anglican or Puritan tenets and pleaded with authorities for ministers. Thomas Gorges himself had Puritan leanings, although he did not favor separation from the Church of England.[32]

Many generations of Maine historians have subscribed to the long-held belief that most early settlers to Maine came from the West Country of England. Admittedly, as the historian Charles Clark has stated, the "grizzled, horny-handed English sailors from Cornwall, Dorsetshire, Somerset, and Devonshire" were among the first to visit the coast of Maine, and some became residents. Even so, a detailed examination of tax lists and other records of permanent settlers does not indicate a dominance by West Country folk, as one might suppose.[33] If a study of settlers in Agamenticus, as well as on the Saco River, the Kennebec River, and Casco Bay, is representative, then the origins of less than 50 percent of Maine's first generation can be determined with any degree of accuracy. Early records show a West Country presence but certainly not a dominance. When Thomas Gorges arrived in Agamenticus, there appears to have been twenty-eight male heads of households, and only four of these can be reliably traced to the West Country. Others may have come from Lancashire, Buckinghamshire, Essex, Kent, and London.[34]

Kennebec settlers arriving in Maine between 1630 and 1676 hailed from the West Country as well as London, Hertfordshire, Kent, and Lincolnshire. On the lower Saco River only one of the twenty-one male heads of households on the 1636 parish list can be positively traced to the West Country. Another settler is believed to have come from Devon, and Richard Vines apparently had ties to both the West Country and London. Indeed, the London area was definitely the home of two of the settlers, and two others appear to have been from this region. In addition, one settler came from Durham and another from Shrewsbury. Thus it appears that Saco River settlements were much more influenced by Londoners than West Countrymen. In his study of early Casco Bay, Edwin Churchill found a similar mix of settlers from throughout England.[35]

In all three areas, detailed research in English archives might determine the origins of more of these settlers, but in the absence of such data, it would be dangerous to assume that any one region—West County, London, or otherwise—dominated the settling of Maine. Perhaps historians have placed so great an emphasis on Maine's West Country origins because there are so many references to West Country fishermen and vessels in the writings of Thomas Gorges and others. However, much of this contact was due only to seasonal visits by fishermen or to voyages by merchant vessels loaded with goods. Although the West Country's people and economy may have played a very important role in the early colonization of Maine, many of these people were visitors, not settlers.

There is no question that the overwhelming majority of early settlers in Maine came from England, even if their exact origins cannot be determined. A few settlers arrived from other countries, providing further variation to the mix of regional English cultures present in the colony. Some Scotsmen settled several miles upriver from Point Christian in the 1650s, after an unsuccessful royal uprising. Most of these Scots were prisoners, taken at the battles of Dunbar and Worcester. A few other settlers hailed from Ireland, France, Portugal, and Greece, although like the Scots, most of these people arrived in Maine in the 1650s and 1660s. Another unwilling immigrant was the African slave of a Captain Cammock, observed by Thomas Gorges. Although the colony supported few slaves, these individuals nevertheless left at least one poignant reminder of their presence in Maine: a carved ivory effigy, excavated at Pemaquid. Crafted in the style of the Yoruba people of West Africa, it suggests the presence of slaves at Pemaquid or at least indicates that area merchants visited Africa and participated in the slave trade.[36]

Thus, Thomas Gorges administered a colony growing in diversity. As Sir Ferdinando's agent, Thomas Gorges was to try to implement Sir Ferdinando's grand plan for Maine and to occupy the governor's residence, located well up the York River. Built between 1634 and 1635, the residence was known as the manor house of Point Christian. Like medieval English manors, Point Christian would serve as the focus for the area's social and political life. As the seat of the Gorges family, the house would serve as the location for sessions of court, and officials came to Point Christian to meet with Sir Ferdinando's agents.

Arriving in Maine, Thomas Gorges must have expected to find a substantial dwelling, similar to a manor house in England. Instead he found Point Christian in great disrepair. He expressed his dismay in a letter to his father in England: "I found Sir Ferdinando's house much like your barn, only one pretty handsome room and study without glass windows which I reserve for myself. For the household stuff only one crock, two bedsteads and a table board."[37] Born to a wealthy and powerful family, Thomas was used to a life of privilege and luxury. The contrasts must have overwhelmed him as he compared London, the fine capital city he left behind, with his new capital, the small fishing village of Agamenticus.

The archaeological evidence reinforces Thomas Gorges's comparison of Point Christian with a barn. It was a large dwelling, measuring at least twenty feet by thirty feet, at a time when other houses would probably have been quite small. When settlers sailed down the York River past Point Christian, they must have been impressed with the size of the governor's mansion. However, on the inside, the building was much less desirable. Built to a large scale, it nevertheless had an unfinished feel to it. One room was dominated by a large cobblestone hearth measuring ten feet long and four feet deep. With skilled stonemasons in short supply in Maine, the large, finely crafted hearth was an impressive luxury. Likewise, the fifteen-by-twenty-foot cellar, possibly constructed by Thomas Gorges as a beer cellar, was noteworthy. A recently excavated cellar at a contemporary home of a prominent Saco River family measured only six feet by seven feet. However, the Point Christian building was clearly incomplete. For example, the cellar was not made of stone or brick; instead it was lined with wood. Such a cellar would never have been tolerated in an English manor. It probably would have rotted and collapsed within twenty or thirty years. Likewise, several walls of the building had no stone foundation to them; rather, the structural posts of the house were directly anchored into the ground, like a fence post or, in fact, a seventeenth-century barn. Unless vigorously maintained, such a dwelling would rot and fall down after a few decades.[38]

Archaeologists throughout Maine have found several other examples of this type of construction, commonly referred to as "earthfast housing." The James Phips homestead in Woolwich (ca. 1646), the Plymouth Colony trading post at Cushnoc (ca. 1629), and the Saco River home of Richard Hitchcock (ca. 1636–90) are all earthfast (fig. 79). Earthfast dwellings seem to reflect English regionalism. They were a common form of construction in the East Midlands and in southeastern England, areas that contained virtually no building stone.[39]

The full dimensions of Point Christian are unknown, but excavations at the Phips site, Cushnoc, Pemaquid, Arrowsic, and other early Maine house sites have uncovered examples not only of different construction techniques but also of a vast array of types, sizes, and shapes of buildings. Two excavations on the lower Kennebec River have revealed the remains of mid-seventeenth-century "long houses," a building tradition common to the West Country as well as to northern England. The main structure excavated at the Clarke and Lake site on Arrowsic Island is fifteen feet wide and a full sixty feet long. The contemporary homestead of James Phips is of similar proportions, which is not surprising, since the Phips family migrated from the West Country. These structures are evidence of the English regional traditions carried over to Maine.[40]

Perhaps the most interesting of these dwellings is Point Christian, for it would also seem to represent, in microcosm, the story of the province of Maine itself. Point Christian was built as a statement of power, meant to be the manor house of a feudal

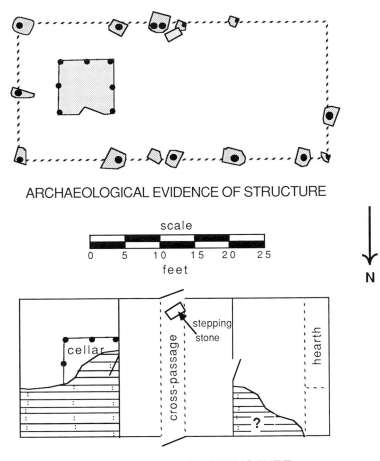

ARCHAEOLOGICAL EVIDENCE OF STRUCTURE

79. Archaeological
evidence and proposed
plan of the Plymouth
Colony trading post
at Cushnoc, ca. 1629.
From Leon E. Cran-
mer, *Cushnoc: The
History and Archae-
ology of Plymouth
Colony Traders on the
Kennebec* (Augusta:
Maine Historic Pres-
ervation Commission,
1990), p. 61.

TENTATIVE PLAN OF STRUCTURE

empire. It was a large building, quickly constructed and only partially finished, and was much more impressive from the outside
than the inside. Thomas Gorges labored to finish the ambitious
building. Archaeological data tell us he installed glass windows.
His letters describe his construction of a beer cellar and his efforts
to fence in the pastures. Still, he left before the job was completed, and indeed, Point Christian would never be completed.
Within a few years, the manor burned down.

Like Point Christian, the province of Maine was an ambitious
but unfinished edifice. In England, Sir Ferdinando dreamed of
a large colony, and he divided this province into eight orderly
counties. In Maine, Thomas found that three counties were more
than enough to organize the few scattered settlers. The county
of Devon would be home to an Anglican bishop and the power-

ful governor of New England, but these offices were never filled. Thomas Gorges never could fully complete the political structure or make it function according to the grand plan. In actuality, the province continued to function as a single political unit. In 1642, when Thomas Gorges learned of the incorporation of Agamenticus as the city of Gorgeana, he wrote to Sir Ferdinando to state that he was not able to make full use of the charter, which needed forty municipal officers. As he pointed out, "If you tie us to it, every man in the plantation must assume offices."[41]

Instead of prospering, the colony was failing. For two decades the economy of New England had been geared toward providing food, supplies, and housing for the continuing wave of immigrants. This Great Migration ended in the early 1640s, when the English Civil Wars began. With no new immigrants for colonists to sell to, prices on livestock, timber, and other products fell. Some settlers abandoned Maine and returned to England or tried their luck in other colonies. In 1642 Thomas complained, "The times are such that many houses lie uninhabited, fields unpaled."[42]

In July 1643, Thomas himself returned to England, a move he had been planning for at least a year. He had decided that although Maine had much to offer, his world was England, not Agamenticus. He returned to accept a commission as a lieutenant colonel in the Parliamentary Cavalry and would later serve in Parliament under the Cromwells and Charles II. Thomas never returned to Maine. He was the last deputy governor of the province of Maine, and the colony was all but forgotten by authorities during the English Civil Wars. When Sir Ferdinando died in 1647, the Gorges family's claim to Maine began to dissolve.[43]

In 1652 Massachusetts annexed Agamenticus and the adjoining townships, thus ending the government of the province of Maine. The Massachusetts authorities even changed the name of Sir Ferdinando's capital, Gorgeana, to York, and the province of Maine became York County. The name change in itself is symbolic. York, England, had been a cathedral city, a Royalist stronghold that had surrendered to Puritan forces several years before. Similarly, the Royalist and Anglican bastion city of Gorgeana fell to Puritan forces from Massachusetts. The Puritans not only incorporated Sir Ferdinando's prize possession into their empire but also rewrote the map, replacing both the native name of Agamenticus and the Anglican name of Gorgeana with the single conquest name of York. Settlers living there took their time adapting to changes in government and titles. As late as 1667, fifteen years after the takeover, no less an authority than the recorder for York County referred to a neighbor as being "of Gorgeana alias York."[44] A few settlers continued to rely on traditional names, perhaps out of habit or to make a political statement, but the usurpation by Massachusetts effectively ended the existence of the province of Maine and Point Christian. The world that Thomas Gorges had known in Agamenticus had permanently changed, and Maine's initial era of settlement drew to a close.

PART FOUR

Victims of a Map

Introduction

Richard D'Abate

The difficulties of life for Europeans in the American wilderness were great, but it is important to remember that like most colonial enterprises, theirs began as an exercise of power and domination. Though strangers in the New World, the Europeans arriving in Norumbega, especially the English, were armed with an inexorable sense of cultural superiority as well as an aggressive confidence in the justness of their own desires. This force, manifested in innumerable ways both violent and systematic, began to push the native inhabitants from the center of their own world to its margins. As their territory was appropriated, the natives increasingly became the strangers in a new American world. In the concluding chapter, the late J. B. Harley examines the role that maps played in this process of dispossession and alienation. "It is in the nature of all maps," Harley noted, "including the 'scientific' maps of our own day, to construct a world in the image of society rather than to hold a mirror to an 'objective' reality." In other words, maps are forms of argument and persuasion about the nature of reality. As Harley shows, in a number of well-known seventeenth-century English maps of the Norumbega region, the most basic cartographical elements—especially the choice of names and the graphic allotment of empty spaces—were tools in the social construction of a satisfying New World image: native-less, uncontested, and ready for the surveyor's chain.

The views Harley expresses are controversial. They stand as an important final word from this major scholar of cartography.

CHAPTER THIRTEEN

New England Cartography and the Native Americans

J. B. Harley

Victims of a Map is the title of a book of poems by the Palestine poet Mahmud Darwish and others.[1] Like the modern tragedy of the dispossessed Palestinian people, the much older tragedy in American history saw the map as an instrument through which power was exercised to destroy an indigenous society. The maps of seventeenth-century New England provide a text for studying the territorial processes by which the Indians were progressively edged off the land. This was not achieved without resistance on the part of the Indians, nor was it a simple process. I do not suggest that maps were the prime movers in the events of territorial appropriation and ethnic alienation. However, as a classic form of power knowledge, maps occupy a crucial place—in both a psychological and a practical sense—among the colonial discourses that had such tragic consequences for the native Americans. By trying to view the place of maps in the encounter and their role as they impinged on Indian affairs, one can add a different dimension to cartographic history.

Hidden Geographies

One of the ironies of the exclusion of the Indians from the map is that the Indians undoubtedly played a significant part in the construction of the first maps by the English of their North American colonies. In a recent essay, James Axtell posed the question, "What would colonial America have been like without the Indians?"[2] What, in particular, would have been the direction of discovery and exploration without Indian guides to the New World? Extending these questions, we can speculate on how the seventeenth-century English maps of America might have looked had the navigators and explorers arrived in an empty land. Beyond the narrow strip of coastal settlement, the details on the maps would undoubtedly have been much sparser. Without Indian contributions to the cartography of the interior, a map of continental scale would have unrolled far more slowly in front of European eyes.

The recognition that early maps are an epitome of the encounter—a set of reciprocal relationships between Native American and European peoples—rather than a chapter in "discovery" history is relatively new. As recently as 1981, the mapping of the New England region was seen as characterized by "an almost complete lack of a cartographic or abstract literacy in Algonquian culture."[3] Today such an opinion may be compared with the following perspective:

> Early colonizers . . . found native North Americans to be proficient cartographers whose geographical knowledge greatly expedited the first European explorations of the region. For a century and a half, information imparted by means of ephemeral maps scratched in the sand or in the cold ashes of an abandoned campfire, sketched with charcoal on bark, or painted on deerskin was incorporated directly into French and English maps, usually enhancing their accuracy.[4]

The cultivation of such an ethnocartographic history involves two initial steps. The first is to accept the existence of an indigenous cartography in many American cultures from the time of Columbus onward. The second is to try to reconstruct the Indian contribution to the "European" maps of the New World. From these steps, we learn that the Indian contribution was a major one.

The fullest evidence of an indigenous cartography as a significant form of local knowledge is found in Middle America. Screen folds and other artifacts, usually manuscripts painted on animal skins, contain major cartographic elements.[5] Elsewhere, in eastern North America, for instance, though there are far fewer artifacts, the notion of a "complete lack of a cartographic . . . literacy" is hardly born out by the record. Gregory Waselkov points out that in the early seventeenth century, the Powhatan Algonquians "spontaneously produced maps on at least three occasions." These ranged "in scope from a simple one showing the course of the James River to an ambitious map depicting their place at the center of a flat world, with England represented by a pile of sticks near the edge" (see fig. 80).[6] Clearly, some if not all the American Indians could draw maps at the time of their first contact with the English.

80. A reconstruction of a model of the world made on the ground by Powhatan Indians in 1607. Courtesy of Brian Harley.

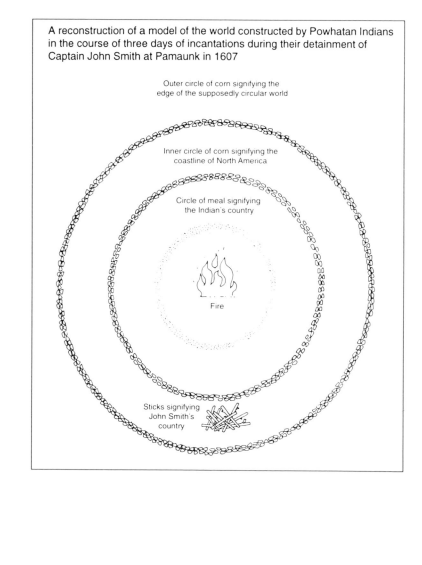

A reconstruction of a model of the world constructed by Powhatan Indians in the course of three days of incantations during their detainment of Captain John Smith at Pamaunk in 1607

Outer circle of corn signifying the edge of the supposedly circular world

Inner circle of corn signifying the coastline of North America

Circle of meal signifying the Indian's country

Fire

Sticks signifying John Smith's country

There is much evidence that geographical knowledge flowed from Indian guides and informants to Europeans and subsequently was incorporated into surviving manuscript or printed maps. Indeed, it may be said that most European maps showing the Americas, from that of Juan de la Cosa (ca. 1500) onward, disguise a hidden stratum of Indian geographical knowledge. During much of the English and French exploration of the coast of North America, the presence of Indian guides—who sometimes made maps—was a matter of routine. In 1607, for example, John Smith noted that when he was some eighteen miles upstream from Jamestown, Virginia, he had met an Indian who offered to draw the James River "with his foote" and who eventually drew with pen on paper "the whole River from Chesseian [Chesapeake] bay to the end of it so far as passadg was for boates."[7] There can be no doubt that Smith's *Map of Virginia* (1612) was fleshed out by several such encounters. The readers of this map were specifically instructed to observe "that as far as you see the little Crosses on rivers, mountaines, or other places, have been discovered; the rest was had by information of the *Savages,* and are set downe according to their instructions."[8] In the key of the map a small Maltese cross appears with the note, "To the crosses have bin discovered what beyond is by relation." If one shades these areas, the extent of the Indian contribution to this particular map becomes clear (fig. 81). Indian geographical knowledge was also filtered into Smith's *Map of Virginia* through other, intermediate documents. On March 12, 1611, Spain's ambassador to England, Don Alonso de Velasco, sent a large manuscript map of northeastern North America to Spain. By comparing the details of the Chesapeake area on this map with Smith's Virginia map, we see that the two maps must have been drawn from a common prototype.[9] Moreover, a gloss on the Velasco map is explicit about its reliance on Indian sources. Of the details shown in the interior, we are told that "al the blue is done by the relations of the Indians,"[10] an admission similar to that of Smith.

Not all printed European maps are as well documented as these, but turning to Smith's map of New England of 1616 (fig. 82), one can hardly doubt that it was similarly underpinned by Indian knowledge. Smith acknowledged that in ranging along the coast, in addition to his crew, "The main assistance next God I had . . . was my acquaintance among the salvages, especially with Dohnannida, one of their greatest lords, who had lived long

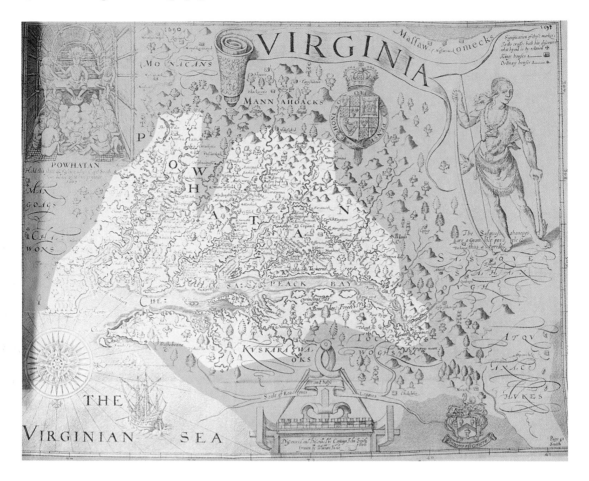

81. John Smith, *Map of Virginia*, 1612, with the area derived from Native American sources shaded. Courtesy of Osher Cartographic Collection, University of Southern Maine.

in England."[11] One may assume, for example, that Indian names to identify places along the coast were supplied by these Indian guides, and the text of Smith's *Description of New England* points to this substratum of knowledge in the map that accompanied the book.[12] Nor was Smith a lone figure in making use of the Indians in this way. Along the New England coast, Bartholomew Gosnold is said to have benefited from a chalk drawing that the local Indians had prepared for him.[13] As he traveled along the coast of Maine and New Hampshire, Samuel de Champlain had Indians with him specifically to serve as guides, and he used their knowledge to compile a map of the coast. He wrote:

> After I had drawn for them with a charcoal the bay and the Island Cape, where we then were, they pictured for me with the same charcoal another bay which they represented as very large. Here they placed six pebbles at equal intervals, giving me thereby to

82. John Smith, *New England Observed*, 1616. Courtesy of University of Southern Maine.

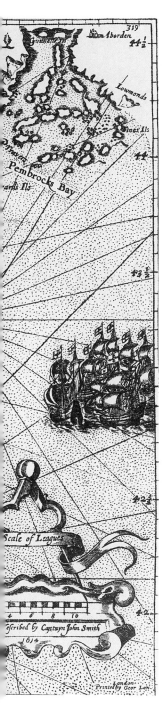

understand that each one of these marks represented that number of chiefs and tribes. Next they represented within the said bay a river which we had passed, which is very long and has shoals.[14]

Champlain's vessel was off Cape Ann at that moment, and the Indians sketched Massachusetts Bay and the Merrimack River and positioned the villages of local Indians on their map by means of pebbles.[15] In yet other cases, Indians were kidnapped and sent back to England to be debriefed in depth about their geographical knowledge.[16] Such events all confirm the vital role of Indian sources of information in the early European mapping of the New England coast.

As the permanent settlements of the English expanded, Indian guides continued to convey geographical information—some of it in map form—from inland journeys.[17] Relating this contribution to individual European maps is a more difficult task, though traces of Indian geography have been identified in some seventeenth-century New England maps. For instance, Malcolm Lewis has suggested that such an influence—even an Indian map—can be detected beyond the limit of English settlement in John Foster's *A Map of New-England* (1677). Winnipesaukee Lake lends the giveaway clues of such a native source: the shape is artificially rounded; the islands are randomly scattered on its surface; and the lake is far too large in size in relation to everything else on the map (fig. 83). Lewis concluded that the English compiler of the map or its prototype may have misunderstood information received from Indian sources.[18] Through such researches, the "intertextual" character of the "English" maps of New England in the seventeenth century—derived from both Indians and settlers—becomes abundantly clear.

Once we accept that Indians made significant contributions to these regional maps, we can also search for shadows of their knowledge in local maps. One such contribution was to maps of land claims and boundary disputes involving Indian territory. So it was with the map of "the Pequids, theire Country," drawn by an unknown draftsman in 1662 and showing part of Connecticut or Rhode Island.[19] As Peter Benes says, "While this is an English document, it shows a characteristic Indian reliance on place names rather than on measured points of reference."[20] Somewhat similar is the map (fig. 84) by the Christianized Indian John Sassamon of Plymouth Colony, giving "the prinsipall names

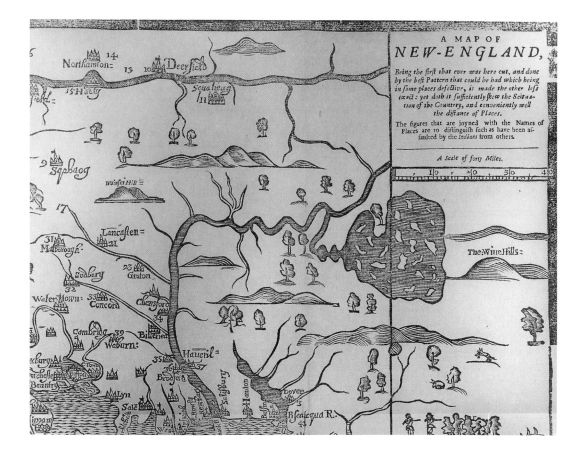

The figures that are joyned with the Names of Places are to distinguish such as have been assaulted by the Indians from others.

83. Detail from John Foster, *A Map of New-England*, 1677. Taken from an 1888 reprint. Courtesy of Dyer Library.

of the land we are now willing should be sold" (1666). This map also relied on the naming of ecological landmarks rather than on geometrical positions or the metes and bounds that had characterized English estate mapping from the beginning of colonization.[21]

It is appropriate to offer some preliminary generalizations about the cartographic encounter and its significance in the wider ideological and political struggle between Indians and whites for the territory of New England. Indian and European maps *were* different, just as their notions of space, territory, and function were often poles apart. As Gregory Waselkov explains, Indian maps often "contain considerable geographical detail," but "their main function was to portray social and political relationships." He continues:

Such a shift in the mapmakers' perspective required a new set of conventions to represent their social world. . . . Social distance

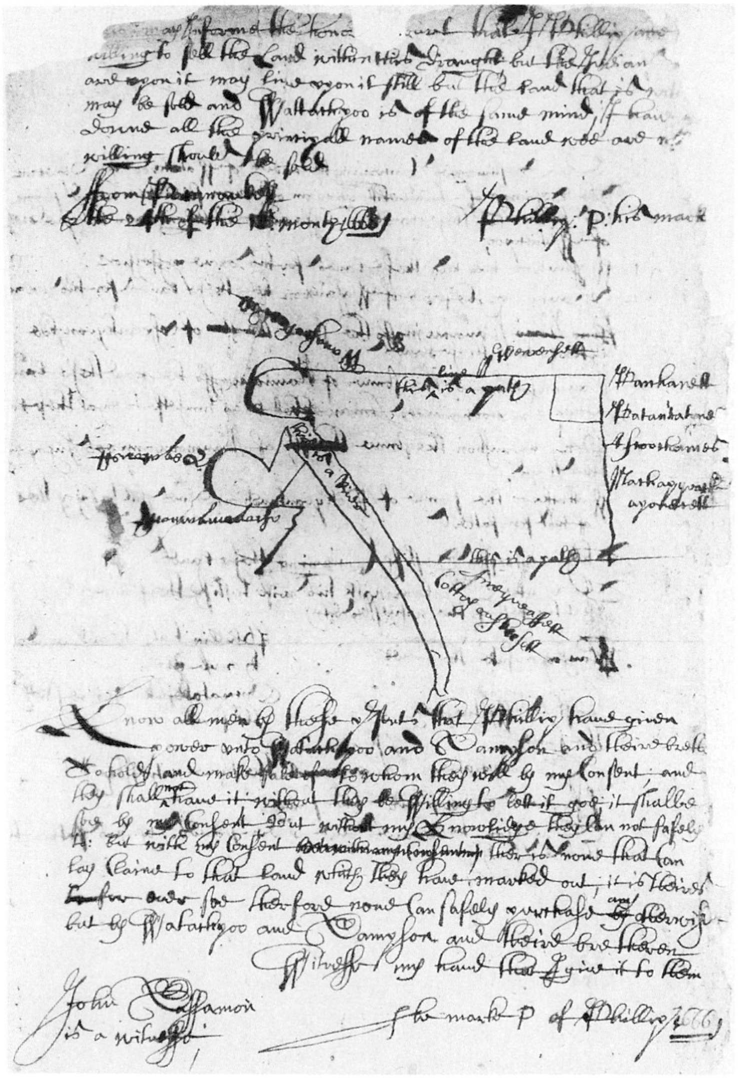

84. Map and deed
for land sold in 1666
by the Wampanoag
sachem King Philip.
The map was prob-
ably drawn by John
Sassamon. In "Indian
Deeds: Treasurer
Accounts; Lists of
Freemen." Courtesy
of Plymouth County
Commissioners.
Photograph courtesy
of Plimoth Plantation.

(based, for example, on the degree of kin relatedness between
social groups) and political distance (the degree of cooperation
between groups, or the extent of control over groups) could be
effectively mapped, but only by replacing absolute measures of
Euclidean distance with a flexible, topological view of space.[22]

It is thus not so much questions of "accuracy" from a European perspective but the historical consequences of such Indian
maps that merit reflection. The fact that English settlers failed
to appreciate the social geometry and the cosmological nuances

of Indian cartography is suggested by their frequent "mistrans-lation" into European maps.[23] Equally significant, in a colonial society where English law and documentary formulas prevailed, the Indians' approach to mapping did not serve them well in re-sisting the colonial appropriation of their lands. In a European culture, where land was conveyed by precise measurement and with a fixing of position by latitude and longitude, the Indians' maps, as we shall see, put them at a technological disadvan-tage. Undoubtedly, some Indians grasped the different geometric principles of the English maps, but they lacked the resources in seventeenth-century New England to develop strategies of re-sistance by adapting European-type maps to their own ends.[24]

Eradicating Place-names

Place-names have always been implicated in the cultural iden-tity of the people who occupy the land. Naming a place anew is a widely documented act of political possession in settlement history.[25] Equally, the taking away of a name is an act of dis-possession. Meron Benvenisti, the historian and former deputy mayor of Jerusalem, has described the process of Hebraizing the names on the ordnance map of Eretz Israel. He wrote, "Like all immigrant societies, we attempted to erase all alien names." Benvenisti added, "The Hebrew map of Israel constitutes one stratum in my consciousness, underlaid by the stratum of the previous Arab map."[26] Or again, if we move back in time and northwestward across space, we reach the scene of Brian Friel's play *Translations*, set in nineteenth-century Ireland. The action is built around the British ordnance surveyors who are making their maps in the Gaelic West. We are told that the cartographer's task "is to take each of the Gaelic names—every hill, stream, rock, even every patch of ground which possessed its own distinctive Irish name—and Anglicize it, either by changing it into approxi-mate English sound or by translating it into English words."[27] As we listen to local Irish people reacting to these changes—and despite the lack of historical realism in some aspects of the dia-logue[28]—we can perhaps experience what it might feel like to be Irish, or Palestinian, or Algonquian and have to learn new names for places previously pronounced in a native tongue. It must be like being written out of history.

The disappearing stratum of ethnic consciousness embodied in the Indian names of Norumbega and those strata on the maps of Ireland and Israel have much in common. In a similar way, maps were important agents in the Anglicization of the toponymy of seventeenth-century New England.[29] They were a medium in a wider colonial discourse for redescribing topography in the language of the dominant society. Yet this was far from a simple process. Not all maps were equally influential, and the pace of adoption of new names varied with both the nature of English settlement and the linguistic geography of the associated Indian groups.[30] Anglicization got off to a slow start. The sixteenth-century voyages of exploration made on behalf of France and Spain, such as those of Giovanni da Verrazzano and Estevan Gomes, left relatively few traces in the regional toponymy of New England.[31] Only when we move from the age of imperial reconnaissance—when the search for a route to the Indies was paramount—to a phase of permanent colonial settlement does the process of renaming the land assume wider significance for the indigenous peoples of America.

In New England the founding document of European colonization, as well as of its modern cartographic and topynymic history, is John Smith's map of 1616. Like Smith's earlier map of Virginia, and Champlain's map of New France, its aim was to encourage permanent colonial settlement with a visible and highly symbolic image of the land to be occupied. In common with planting the flag or raising the cross, rituals of possession were enacted on innumerable occasions along the shores of America. Naming the land was one such baptismal rite for early European colonial societies in the New World. By choosing the name "New England" for the part of America that "hath formerly beene called Norumbega," Smith had in mind to promote English sovereignty in the face of Spanish, French, and Dutch claims in the same region. As he explained, "In this voyage I tooke the description of the coast as well by map as writing, and called it *New-England:* but malicious mindes amongst Sailers and others, drowned that name with the eccho of *Nusconcus, Canaday,* and *Penaquid;* till . . . our most gracious King *Charles,* then Prince of *Wales,* was pleased to confirme it by that title."[32]

New England was thus prominently placed on Smith's map, giving it additional authority and currency. Naming was possessing, at least in part possession. A few years later Sir William Alexander would name "New Scotlande" (Nova Scotia) on his

Mapp of New Englande (1624).[33] Both men doubtless saw the promotional advantages of such toponymic rhetoric in seeking domestic backers for the new colonies, just as the names "New Netherlands," "New France," or "New Spain" made legible the colonial aspirations of those nations in the Americas.[34]

We know that Algonquian place-names had originally been collected by Smith during the exploration that resulted in his map. Such names were later published in his book,[35] but once back in England, the names on the draft map were subjected to an act of intellectual appropriation when the Indian names were struck from the map and replaced by English substitutes. In the older histories of New England this story is reduced to an antiquarian anecdote. It is also, however, an event of considerable ideological significance. Smith himself told how a fair drawing of the map was presented to "our most gracious King Charles, then Prince of Wales." Dismissing the Indians with contemptuous arrogance, Smith continued to address the king, "I heere present your Highness the description in a Map; my humble sute is, you would please to change their Barbarous names, for such English, as Posterity may say, Prince Charles was their Godfather."[36]

Transplanting England in the paper landscape was an easy game to play. The young prince named "Cape James" (Cape Cod) for his father; "Stuart's Bay" (Cape Cod Bay) after the reigning family; "Cape Elizabeth" for his sister; "Cape Anna" after his mother; and "The River Charles" for himself. Smith commemorated his own surname in the Isles of Shoals, which became "Smith Isles." Even the London printer James Reeve would later get into the act by naming a promontory on the Maine coastline "Point Reeves."[37]

Few of these royal inventions survived, but Smith's map became a paradigm for further Anglicization. The Massachusetts Bay Company set up a court that, among other things, decreed the name for each new township in the colony. By the date of the 1635 reissue of Smith's map (fig. 85), a number of new English names—such as South Hampton on the New Hampshire coast and Salem, Charles towne, Water towne, Boston, Dorchester, and Medford—had been added to the copperplate.[38] As previously, this naming process was far more than merely an administrative or legal convenience. In New England as elsewhere, the maps were a means of ideological reproduction as well as practical tools in the history of English colonialism. A roll call of familiar place-names made the unbelievable seem more familiar, the unknown more knowable, and the wilderness less wild. For the English, the map becomes "a narrative of ethnogenesis,"[39] but for the Indians, the reverse was true. They became aliens in their own land. What we still have to tease out of the historical record is the nature of the Indian reaction to this obliteration of the language for their familiar topography. What were the social consequences of the destruction of names preserved through generations of an oral culture and of the redescription of an anciently settled landscape?

Once the process of New England settlement had begun, the record of toponymic colonialism became more complex. In the half century or so between Smith's map and the publication of John Foster's woodcut map in 1677, many more English names were created, and there also seems to have been a hardening of English attitudes, unconsciously or deliberately, toward recognizing an Indian geography in the landscape. Sometimes it was as if renaming was the final act of reprisal against Indian tribes who had tried to resist the English expansion in New England. Thus, after the Pequot massacre at Mystic Fort in May 1637, and after the final dispersal and destruction of the remaining members of the tribe, the very word *Pequot* was wiped from the map. The

85. Detail from John Smith's map *New England Observed*, originally published in 1616, showing new English place-names. The version reproduced is from the 1635 edition of G. Mercator, *Historia Mundi,* courtesy of National Archives of Canada, NMC 55020.

river of that name became the Thames, and the former Pequot village became New London.[40] Even years after their successful persecution of the Pequot War, the United Colonies of New England passed a resolution disallowing the conquered Pequots to be a distinct people or "to retayne the name of Pequatts, or to settle in the Pequatt country."[41] A name could be a potentially dangerous symbol of survival as much as its elimination was public proof of conquest.

Within the main areas of English settlement, the practice of naming may appear more benign or "peaceful," but it was no less thorough in its removal of the traces of earlier Indian culture. Naming the micro features of the New England landscape was an uncoordinated process—part and parcel of the process of agricultural settlement—and it was probably taken for granted by the settlers. Characteristic are the names found on the detailed land surveys that were made of the area around Boston in the mid-seventeenth century. Sometimes simple English generic names were added to landscape features.[42] In other cases (just as with the ordnance survey and the Gaelic names of nineteenth-century Ireland), attempts were made to translate or transliterate Indian names. "Elsabeth River" is thus a corruption of the native "Assebet" to English spelling.[43] Yet in many cases, the Indian population was so sparse that the Algonquian roots of the names of settlements were effectively buried with their former inhabitants. A greater number of Indian names of physical features survive, but for purposes of settlement, their toponymy had been replaced by a distinctive regional category of New England place-names consisting of topographical terms such as *brook, hill, pond, river,* and *swamp*.[44]

Moreover, as William Cronon has noted, even the objectives of English and Indian naming of landscape features were different. Thus, the English "frequently created arbitrary place-names which either recalled localities in their homeland or gave a place the name of its owner," whereas the "Indians used ecological labels to describe how the land could be used."[45] Given such fundamental cultural differences, it is not surprising to discover that only one of all the names on Sassamon's map of Plymouth Colony can be identified on a modern map.[46] These may not have been deliberate acts of cultural genocide, but the fact remains that the land had been effectively redescribed in the vocabulary of the conquerors.

Place-name scholars tend to concentrate on linguistic aspects of the process of naming. Here, however, it is the ideological implications that are stressed. The use of English on the maps—names in an alien language—helped to create a further barrier between the Indians and the settlers. Even where attempts were made to record Indian place-names in maps, this was hardly an innocent expression of scholarly curiosity. As the anthropologist Johannes Fabian stated, "By putting regions on a map and native words on a list, explorers laid the first, and deepest, foundations for colonial power."[47] In French maps, in particular, the recording and mapping of tribal areas and settlements were calculated acts of commercial, political, and religious control.

In New England one reads another variation of this hidden agenda between the lines of William Wood's *New England's Prospect* (1634).[48] The book provides not only a short general glossary of "some of the Natives language" but also geographical lists of "the names of the *Indians* as they be divided into severall Countries," "the names of the noted Habitations," and "at what places be Rivers of note." Some of these names appear in the small map *The South part of New-England, as it is Planted this yeare, 1634* (fig. 86), which was included as a frontispiece to the volume. In this map, partly based on Governor John Winthrop's manuscript map of the Bay Colony plantations of the previous year,[49] Indian and English villages are distinguished by different cartographic signs as well as by place-names. Indian settlements are depicted by small triangles for wigwams (sometimes palisaded) and the Puritans' places with a small circle surmounted by a cross. Thus paganism versus Christianity is inscribed in the coded language of the map, which empowers it with much more than simple locational or record value in the expansion of the frontier. The act of mapping can also be an act of apartheid. By making legible the idea of a separate existence, Wood's map, in its own way, helped, and still helps, perpetuate and legitimate the notion of inferiority and superiority. Once translated into John Eliot's fourteen "praying towns" of Massachusetts Bay, the notion became one of mutually exclusive patterns of occupation on the land.[50]

By 1677, the tendency to eradicate Indian geography had gone yet another stage further. This was the year of publication of William Hubbard's *The Present State of New-England, Being a Narrative of the Troubles with the Indians*.[51] The map that ac-

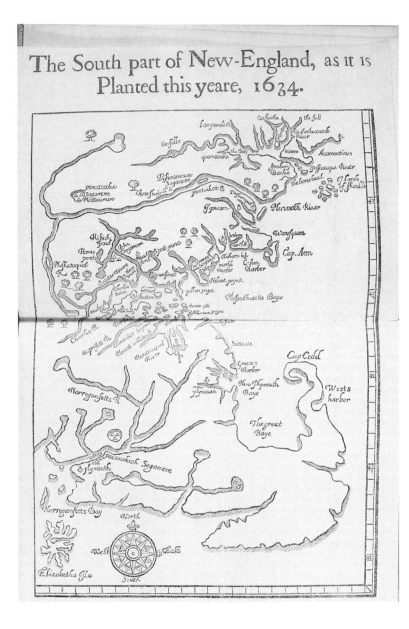

86. William Wood,
*The South part of
New-England, as it is
Planted this yeare, 1634,*
in William Wood,
*New England's Pros-
pect, 1634.* From the
1865 reprint, cour-
tesy of University of
Southern Maine.

companied it—John Foster's woodcut *A Map of New England*—
reduces the Indian presence even further (fig. 87). In the brief
explanation associated with the title of the map, a new twist is
given to the representation of place-names. We read that "the figures joyned with the Names of Places are to distinguish such as
have been assaulted by the Indians" from others. Turning to the
Narrative itself, we find "a Table shewing the Towns and Places
which are inhabited by the English in New England: those that

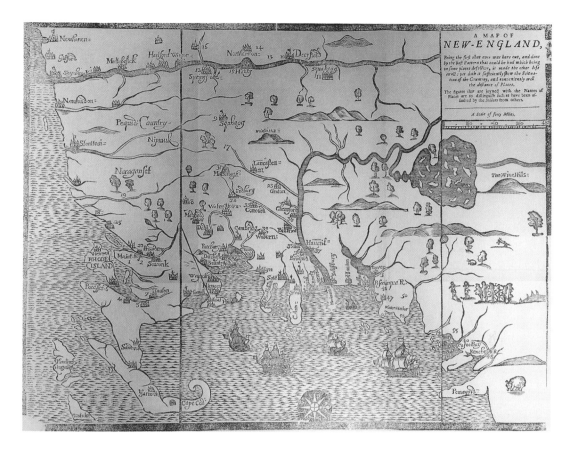

87. John Foster, *A Map of New England*, 1677. Taken from an 1888 reprint. Courtesy of Dyer Library.

are marked with figures, as well as expressed by their names, are such as were assaulted by the Indians, during the late awful Revolutions of Providence."[52]

Linked to the map, and cross-referenced to the fuller account of events in the main text, the message is of "a litany of burned barns, slaughtered stock, and human massacre"[53] for which the Indians are solely responsible. It is not difficult to imagine the propaganda effects of this strident piece of cartographic rhetoric, much like a modern map of a war zone. Foster's map would have further hardened settlers' attitudes toward the Indians. The spotlight plays on the location of assaults. The map gives less emphasis to places that were not attacked, and the record is silent about the colonial violence of the Puritans. The selection of place-names is consciously partial. By declaration, it is a map of "Towns and Places which are inhabited by the English in New England." The scattered trees suggest an English parkland rather than a colonial semiwilderness. The Indian has been made even more marginal. In the heartland of Puritan civilization, the signs for towns and villages are exaggerated. Here there are no wigwams, only church spires, crosses, and the reassuring flag. It has been observed: "It is only across the Merrimack in Maine (from Pascataqua to Pemmaquid) and thus outside the colonial confederation of the Massachusetts Bay, Plymouth, and Connecticut . . . that the cartographer acknowledges the wilds. There the trees are larger, wild animals (rabbit, bear, wolf) evident, and Indians drawn in."[54]

The polemic of cartographic discourse should never surprise us. It is in the nature of all maps, including the "scientific" maps of our own day, to construct a world in the image of society rather than to hold a mirror to an "objective" reality. In Hubbard's map, one observes a religious iconography. The representation affirms the support of the Lord for the Puritan conquest of both the Indians and the wilderness they inhabit. New England can be identified with ancient Israel, and Hubbard's map is not dissimilar to the maps of the Holy Land in the Calvinist Bibles of the same period.[55] It is designed to illustrate, with a belief in literality essential to Puritan thought,[56] the events of a providential history. The maps' progress in plotting New England's geography is a pilgrim's progress,[57] for indeed to some it was the "New English Canaan" that was being represented.[58] The map is a *geographia sacra*, and the names are themselves the habitations of a chosen people. In an age when place-names are recognized as an aspect of cultural survival, and when more Indian names are beginning to be restored to the maps of North America,[59] it is worthwhile to explore some of the historical antecedents and consequences of their original disappearance.

Dividing the "Wilderness"

In Joseph Conrad's Victorian novel *The Heart of Darkness*, the character Marlowe says, "At that time there were many blank spaces on the earth, and when I saw one that looked particularly inviting on a map (but they all look that) I would put my finger on it and say, When I grow up I will go there."[60] The passage is often quoted as an example of how maps stir the geographical imagination. But it also demonstrates the map's double function in colonialism of both opening up and later closing a territory. Conrad's delight in the blank spaces on the map—like that of other writers[61]—is also a symptom of a deeply ingrained colonial mentality that was already entrenched in seventeenth-century New England. In this view the world is full of empty spaces that are ready for taking by Englishmen. America in particular was seen as the "vacant wilderness."[62] In early colonial New England, maps gave much unwitting psychological support to the idea of boundless available land awaiting occupation. The maps also fostered the image of a dehumanized geometrical space—a land without the encumbrance of the Indians—whose places could be controlled by coordinates of latitude and longitude. By the mid-seventeenth century, maps were becoming a necessary device for juridical control of territory. Now, America not only could be desired from afar but also—having been conquered—could be appropriated, bounded, and subdivided. It was as divorced a process as "remote sensing."

We can specifically trace a growing map consciousness among the leaders of the New England colonies. As early as 1641, the General Court of Massachusetts Bay Colony enacted a law requiring every new town within its jurisdiction to have its boundaries surveyed and recorded in a plan.[63] The authority of the map was thus added to the authority of legal treatises, written histories, and the sacred books in sanctioning the taking of the lands of the Indians. The map had become "an epiphenomenon of imperial control."[64]

Consider first the psychological impact of the blank spaces that fill so many of the early printed maps of New England. It could be said that cartographers helped to invent the American wilderness. Take an example chosen almost at random—*A Map of New England*, first published by Robert Morden and William Berry in 1676 (fig. 88).[65] Possibly published to cash in on the newsworthiness of the region just after King Philip's War ("King Philip's Countrey" is shown above the name "Plymouth Colony"), it contains two clearly different images of New England. One portrays a coastal area filled with the huddled villages and towns of the English settlement. The other, beyond and to the northwest, shows an empty map. The presence of America's native inhabitants is denied. The names of a few Indian groups are attached to the land, but "New England" is engraved in large letters forming a great arc over much of the territory. One can interpret this territorial void as a reflection of geographical ignorance or even of scientific probity on the part of the mapmaker, since he avoided including terrain details for which he had no information. But

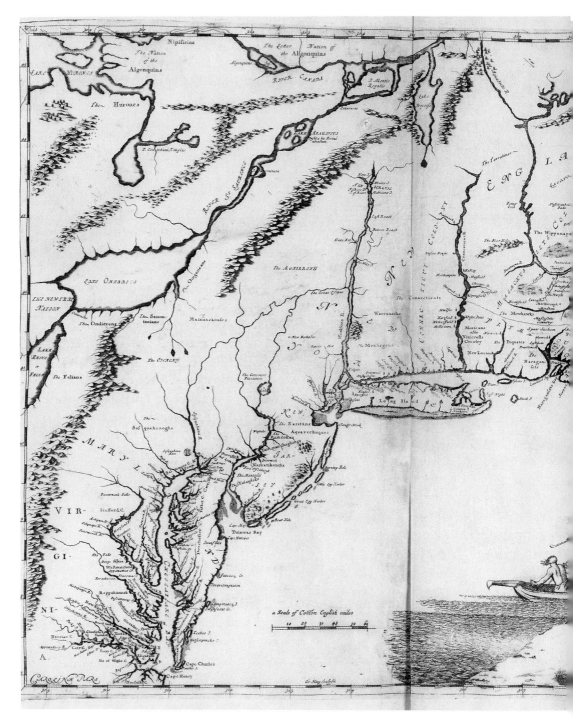

88. Robert Morden
and William Berry, *A
Map of New-England*,
1676. Courtesy of John
Carter Brown Library
at Brown University.

A Map of
New ENGLAND
New YORKE New IERSEY
MARY-LAND & VIRGINIA

*Sould by Robert Morden at y Atlas in
Corn-hill neer y Royal Exchange and by
William Berry at y Globe between York
House & y New Exchange in y Strande
London*

what about the *unintended* consequences of the representation of these vast uninhabited areas? What sort of message did the map send to colonial speculators? How were they received? How far was the map believed, and to what extent did it affect the individual or the group consciousness of the principal actors in England and America?

Answers to such questions must in part lie in the maps themselves. However, the maps have to be seen as part of a wider colonial discourse,[66] one that helped to render Indian peoples invisible in their own land. Cartographers contrived to promote a durable myth of an empty frontier.[67] Maps were yet another form of knowledge — a euphemism for the harshness of control — that allowed the English conveniently to ignore the realities of the Indian societies that they encountered in the New World. They enabled Crown and colonists alike to brush aside evidence they may have had of a well-defined political organization among the northeastern Indians[68] and of a territorial integrity of the Indian nations, an integrity that the French were more willing than the English to accept in their maps.[69] Given the English maps of the period, it became more unlikely that the policymakers would accept, as Francis Jennings put it, that "Indians were as much tied to particular localities as were Europeans."[70] And even if some colonists understood — like Edward Winslow, who had noted in 1624 that every sachem in New England knew "how far the bounds and limits of his own countrey extendeth"[71] — this recognition was not translated into cartography. Maps were largely silent about the Indian territories. Had King Philip been able to see Foster's or Morden's maps of New England, his worst fears about the broken treaties and territorial encroachments of the English would have been confirmed.

Thus cartography and the legal code of New England went hand in hand in the process of exclusion. Both the law and the map were forms of colonial discourse that helped to push the Indian off the land or into the confinement of a reservation system that was already taking shape by the mid-seventeenth century.[72] Maps with their empty spaces can be, and were, read as graphic articulations of the widely held doctrine that colonial expansion was justified when it occurred in "empty" or "unoccupied" land. Sir Thomas More, in the incipient age of English colonialism in North America, had referred to the continent his Utopians colonized whenever their own island became overcrowded. "The natives there," he wrote, "have more land than they can use, so some of it lies fallow." He continued, "Utopians regard a war as just if it is waged to oust a people who refuse to allow vacant land to be used according to the very law of nature."[73] In a similar vein, in 1629, Governor Winthrop of Massachusetts had declared that most land in America "fell under the legal rubric of *vacuum domicilium* because the Indians had not 'subdued' it."[74] The maps would have lent him support, and they would have likewise confirmed the belief of John Cotton, who wrote, "In a vacant soyle, he that taketh possession of it, and bestoweth culture and husbandry upon it, his Right it is."[75] In the words of the title of Samuel Danforth's well-known sermon to the Massachusetts Bay Colony in 1670, the map becomes an icon of an "Errand into the Wilderness."[76] And although a scriptural metaphor was intended, the implications of John Flavel's "Proposition" for the Puritan settlement of lands held by the Indians is unmistakable. "*Husbandmen* divide and separate their lands from other mens, they have their Landmarks and Boundaries by which property is preserved. So are the People of God wonderfully separated, and distinguisht from the People of the earth. It is a special act of Grace, to be inclosed by God out of the Waste Howling Wilderness of the World."[77]

In this passage, the rights of the Puritan cultivator and encloser are given a divine authority greater than the Indian mode of occupation of the land. In the blank spaces of the map, European and Amerindian settlements are also "wonderfully separated."

But if maps were a reinforcing image of a virgin land, they were also the practical documents on which the subdivision and bounding of Indian territories would occur. Because the map was not the territory—and because it was an abstract geometrical space—this was usually an arbitrary process, with little reference to indigenous peoples.[78] In the nineteenth-century "scramble for Africa," native territories were carved up by European powers on maps. Likewise one can talk about an English "scramble" for early-seventeenth-century New England. The attitude of potential "proprietors" was cavalier in the extreme when it came to disposing of the land rights of Indian nations. "Sir Humphrey Gilbert carved (on paper) estates of millions of acres in the vicinity of Narragansett Bay which he had never seen and which, in all probability, had never been sighted by any Englishman."[79] An almost archetypal story of how colonial lands in New England were divided with the help of a map was related by John Smith. The Council for New England had decided in 1623 to procure "new Letters Patent from King James" so that territory could be allocated between a group of twenty prominent colonial speculators. The method adopted was to cut up Smith's map of New England into pieces so that lots could be drawn to divide a "tract of land from the North Sea to the South Sea."[80] Smith's testimony is independently confirmed in another document in which we are told that on June 29, 1623, there was presented to the king at Greenwich

> a plot of all the coasts and lands of New England, divided into twenty parts, each part containing two shares, and twenty lots containing the said double shares, made up in little bales of wax, and the names of twenty patentees by whom these lots were to be drawn. And for that the Lord Duke of Buckingham was then absent, his Majesty was graciously pleased to draw the first lot in his grace's behalf, which contained the eighth number or share. And the rest of the lots were drawn as follows.[81]

The king also drew for two other absent members. There were only eleven patentees present, who drew for themselves. Nine lots were drawn for absent members. In such a way, by means of a partly absentee lottery,[82] the Indian territories were redistributed to an elite in English society. A map of New England recording this process, and listing the names set down in the order they were drawn from the lottery, was published in 1624. It accompanied Sir William Alexander's *Encouragement to Colonies* (fig. 89)[83] and shows the hypothetical territories running back from the coast like the long lots in a French township system.

What is revealing about this incident is the arbitrariness of the mode of division that was executed with the help of a map. As it happened, these arrangements were not implemented,[84] but in one form or another, such a process of bounding and dividing—fragmenting the Indian jurisdictions—was repeated at many different junctures and at scales ranging from the local to the regional in New England colonial history. The map was never far from the action. It is clear, for example, that the colonial patents and charters for the New England colonies were drafted with the help of maps. One could go further and say that they could not have been drafted in the form in which they survived had no maps been available. Maps do not accompany the charters,

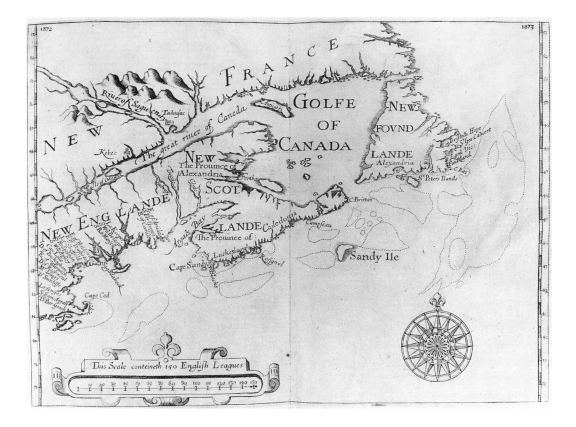

The following labels appear on the map:

FRANCE

NEW FRANCE

Riuer of Segu—
Tadousac

The great riuer of Caneda

Kebec

Ile of Orleans

NEW ENGLANDE

The Prouince of Alexandria

NEW Alexandria

Forthe

SCOT.

LANDE　The Prouince of

Argals Bay

Cape Sandy

Luckeshingon

Rosignol

Caledonia

Campseau

C. Brittan

GOLFE OF CANADA

NEW FOVND LANDE Alexandria

Bristoll Hope
St Geo Calherts
Ant Vic.
Faulkland
C. Ras.
St Peters Ilands

Sandy Ile

Cape Cod

This Scale conteineth 150 English Leagues

10 20 30 40 50 60 70 80 90 100 110 120 130 140 150

89. Sir William Alexander, *A Mapp of New Englande,* in Samuel Purchas, *Purchas his Pilgrimes,* 1625. Courtesy of Osher Cartographic Collection, University of Southern Maine.

but these documents nevertheless define territory in a language of verbal cartography that is unmistakable and presupposes that maps were available to the Privy Council and law officers during the complicated legal process of obtaining a royal charter.[85] In the very first charter of Virginia (1606), for example, that from which the territory of New England would be carved, a demarcation in what was largely terra incognita had to be given in terms of latitude. This presumably was read from a map or globe: "that part of *America* commonly called Virginia . . . situate, lying, and being all along the Sea Coasts, between four and thirty Degrees of *Northerly* Latitude from the Equinoctial Line, and five and forty Degrees of the same Latitude, and in the main Land between the same four and thirty five and forty Degrees . . . or within one Hundred Miles of the Coast thereof."[86]

In this well-known passage, the map is being used to cast a sweeping net of control over a largely unknown land and its people. In the same charter, the Native Americans were already categorized as living "in Darkness and miserable Ignorance of the true Knowledge and Worship of God" and as "Infidels and Savages." This situation, as in Spanish America over a century earlier, became "just" cause, often sanctioned by ecclesiastical and international law, for the appropriation of Indian lands.[87] The Virginia charter went on to permit the establishment of two settlements within this abstract space. One would lie between thirty-four and forty-five degrees north and the other between thirty-eight and forty-five degrees north.[88] Each settlement—irrespective of Indian political organization or the nature of the land—had claims to resources fifty miles north and south and one hundred miles west.

As the maps became more detailed, the language of the charters became geographically more explicit. The better the map, or the more exact the chain and the compass, the better the charters were as instruments of appropriation. Advances in cartography enabled the English settlers to begin to exclude the Indians more definitively from the land and from the resources of the colonial territories. The two Maine charters of 1622 and 1639 point to this process. In the grant to Sir Ferdinando Gorges and Captain John Mason of 1622, the patent was written in terms of latitudes.[89] However, in the grant of Maine by Charles I to Sir Ferdinando Gorges in 1639, it is as if the finger of a lawyer is verbalizing the boundaries of the colony as traced from the best map available to him. To quote only the opening of the passage, Gorges was to receive "all that part . . . of the mainland of New England . . . beginning at the entrance of Passcattaway Harbor and so to pass up the same into the river of Newichewanock, and through the same unto the farthest head thereof, and from there northwestwards till sixty miles be finished, and from Passcattaway Harbor aforesaid northeastwards along the sea coast to Sagadohock."[90]

This is the language of the map. It alone gives the charter its territorial structure. Such indirect evidence for the use of maps as the territorial authority for colonial expansion is reflected in many other New England sources.[91] As new patents were granted, as territories were annexed from the Netherlands and France, as disputes arose about the positioning of particular boundaries between individual colonies,[92] as the Office of Plantations in London sought to impose stronger central control over the American colonies—for example, the proposal to create a "Dominion of New England"[93]—and as land treaties became a way of acquiring Indian tribal lands, maps came to be increasingly used.

Nor was the scale of cartographic influence confined only to the creation of the large political territories of New England. The same symbiosis between cartography and colonialism permeated the creation of local territories in seventeenth-century New England. Many charters of the individual colonies were worded in abstract fashion as if the tabula rasa of the map rather than the land was being divided, and once again, the boundaries had the effect of excluding the Indians while incorporating the English settlers. The power of boundary making, conferring almost feudal power within a Euclidean cage, was comprehensive. Turning again to the grant for the province of Maine in 1639, Sir Ferdinando Gorges was given

> full power and authority to divide all or any part of the territories hereby granted . . . into provinces, counties, cities, towns, hundreds, and parishes, or such other parts of portions as he . . . shall think fit, and in them . . . to appoint and allot out such portions of land for public uses, ecclesiastical and temporal, of what kind soever and to distribute, grant, assign, and set over such particular portions of the said territories, counties, lands, and premises unto such our subjects or the subjects of any other state or prince then in amity with us.[94]

Reading the formulaic language of the charters, we can see that a role for maps is implicit in the mechanism for creating territorial hierarchies and settlements that would structure colonial society. The charters were as much a license for the mapmakers as they were for the landowners, the lawyers, and the politicians. In their Indian policies, all four groups were mapping the common ground of territorial expansion. By the end of the seventeenth century, when New England cartographic history was gathering momentum, maps were being made to describe all tiers of territory, from the individual estate to the colonies as a whole. Even at a local level, they often tended to stress boundaries rather than other features.[95] This is characteristic of a type of European colonial mapping that focused on private property but failed to make legible the usufructuary rights of conquered peoples. Such maps are more than an image of the landscapes of English colonization in New England. They are a discourse of the acquisition and dispossession that lie at the heart of colonialism.

Conclusion

Maps were surely a two-edged weapon in the colonial history of New England. Historiography has tended to look at cartography only from the point of view of the English Crown or settlers, or as an image of the roots of the Anglo-American experience. Indeed, for the colonists, the filling-in of the map was a potent emblem for their own presence on the land. They may have started to appreciate how maps assisted their endeavors in both practical and psychological ways. They would have recognized that maps had become tools of boundary making, of charter framing, of settlement planning, and of strategic value in the war of attrition against the Indians. Not least, and more subtlely, a few would have come to see how maps were the best testimony for the exclusion of the Indians from the territories of New England and how maps were a mirror to God's providence. Documents that enabled the settlers to think territorially were bound to become an integral part of the whole colonial agenda.

But is it also possible to look at New England cartographic history from the Indian point of view? Here the historiography is full of holes. There is no sustained ethnohistorical perspective on maps; one has to read for a geography of absences. It is not known how many Indians saw and understood the English maps of the seventeenth century or how those who saw reacted to the obliteration of their own geography. But at least one can begin to imagine what it was like to be on the wrong side of the map, to see the English place-names advancing across the map, or to feel the sharpness of the boundary as it cut through the ancient territory of an Indian nation. It remains to be seen whether scholars can write a cartographic history that will accommodate both a European and an Indian perspective on the American past.

Notes

General Introduction

1. Fernand Braudel, *The Mediterranean and the Mediterranean World in the Age of Philip II,* 2 vols. (London: Collins, 1972, 1973); Donald W. Meinig, *The Shaping of America: A Geographical Perspective on 500 Years on History,* vol. 1, *Atlantic America, 1492–1800* (New Haven: Yale University Press, 1986).

2. Carl O. Sauer, *Sixteenth Century North America: The Land and the People as Seen by Europeans* (Berkeley: University of California Press, 1971), 11-27.

3. David B. Quinn, *North America from Earliest Discovery to First Settlements: The Norse Voyages to 1612* (New York: Harper and Row, 1977), 110.

4. Quoted in Samuel Eliot Morison, *The European Discovery of America: The Northern Voyages, A.D. 500–1600* (New York: Oxford University Press, 1971), 465.

5. Ibid.

6. Ibid.

7. See discussion and references in ibid., 467-69.

8. Douglas McManis, *Colonial New England: A Historical Geography* (New York: Oxford University Press, 1975), 9.

9. Conrad Heidenreich, "Explorations and Mapping of Samuel de

Champlain, 1603–1632" (Cartographica, Monograph No. 17, 1976), Supplement No. 2 to *Canadian Cartographer* 13 (1976).

10. Bruce G. Trigger, ed., *Handbook of North American Indians* (Washington, D.C.: Smithsonian Institution, 1978), volume 15, labels the inhabitants of the predominant part of Maine as "Eastern Abenaki." A somewhat controversial terminology when first published in 1978, the term has been rejected by many scholars on the basis of subsequent research. Because of this debate, and because the terms tend to exclude the Micmac and the Etchemin (modern-day Maliseet and Passamaquoddy) groups, the labels "Abenaki" and "eastern Abenaki" are generally not used in this book. Instead, the term "Wabanaki" is used as a general reference to the native people of Maine and the Maritimes. Although the label "Wabanaki" is less than ideal, it does not carry the degree of confusion currently associated with the terms "Abenaki" or "eastern Abenaki."

Part I: Introduction

1. Lawrence C. Wroth, *The Voyages of Giovanni da Verrazzano, 1524–1528* (New Haven: Yale University Press, 1970), 133.

Chapter 1, The Indrawing Sea

1. Cited in John Logan Allen, *Passage through the Garden: Lewis and Clark and the Images of the American Northwest* (Urbana: University of Illinois Press, 1975), xix.

2. Cited in ibid., 5.

3. John Kirtland Wright, *Human Nature in Geography* (Cambridge: Harvard University Press, 1966), 66–88, and *"Terrae Incognitae:* The Place of the Imagination in Geography," *Annals of the Association of American Geographers* 37 (1947): 1–15.

4. Ralph Hall Brown, *Mirror for Americans: A Geography of the Atlantic Seaboard* (New York: American Geographical Society, 1952).

5. Strabo, *The Geography of Strabo* (New York: G. P. Putnam's Sons, 1917–32), bk. 1, sec. 1, 8.

6. John L. Allen, "Lands of Myth, Waters of Wonder: The Place of the Imagination in the History of Geographical Exploration," in David Lowenthal and Martyn Bowden, eds., *Geographies of the Mind* (New York: Oxford University Press, 1975), 41–61.

7. See *The Voyages of Captain Luke Foxe and Captain Thomas James,* 1st ser. (London: Hakluyt Society, 1894), 88:35 n. 2.

8. Ibid., 88:32.

9. David Beers Quinn, *England and the Discovery of America* (London: George Allen and Unwin, 1974), 139–42.

10. *Voyages of Captain Luke Foxe* 88:35 n. 10, 22.

11. Ibid.

12. Cf. Justin Winsor, *A Narrative and Critical History of America*, 12 vols. (Boston: Houghton Mifflin and Co., 1889), 1:1–59; John K. Wright, *The Geographical Lore of the Time of the Crusades* (New York: American Geographical Society, 1925), chap. 1.

13. Wright, *Geographical Lore*, 18–19; A. Cary and H. M. Wormington, *Ancient Explorers* (London: Allen and Unwin, 1929), 33–40; Boies Penrose, *Travel and Discovery in the Renaissance* (Cambridge: Harvard University Press, 1952), chap. 1.

14. Wright, *Geographical Lore*, 18–19.

15. E. H. Bunbury, *A History of Ancient Geography*, 2 vols. (London: J. Murray, 1879), 1:xx.; John Fiske, *The Discovery of America*, 2 vols. (Boston: Houghton Mifflin and Co., 1892), 1:250ff.

16. Cary and Wormington, *Ancient Explorers*, 192.

17. Fiske, *Discovery of America* 1:263–65.

18. Tryvgi J. Oleson, *Early Voyages and Northern Approaches* (London: Oxford University Press, 1964), chaps. 3–4 and 14–15; David Beers Quinn, Alison M. Quinn, and Susan Hillier, eds., *New American World: A Documentary History of North America to 1612*, 5 vols. (New York: Arno Press, 1979), vol. 1, chaps. 6–8.

19. Oleson, *Early Voyages*, 91–100; R. A. Skelton, Thomas Marston, and George Painter, *The Vinland Map and the Tartar Relation* (New Haven: Yale University Press, 1965), 160–82.

20. Skelton, Marston, and Painter, *The Vinland Map*, Note B, 179–82.

21. J. A. Williamson, *The Cabot Voyages and Bristol Discovery under Henry VII*, Series II (Cambridge: Hakluyt Society, 1962), 120:14–17; Quinn, *England and the Discovery of America*, 57–58.

22. Quinn, *England and the Discovery of America*, 5–23.

23. Quinn, Quinn, and Hillier, *New American World*, vol. 1, chap. 9; Oleson, *Early Voyages*, chap. 16.

24. Giovanni Ramusio, *Navigationi et Viaggi* (Venice, 1563), cited in Winsor, *Narrative and Critical History* 3:25.

25. Richard Hakluyt, *Principal Voyages of the English Nation*, 1589 edition, cited in Winsor, *Narrative and Critical History* 2:136.

26. Samuel Eliot Morison, *The European Discovery of America*, vol. 1, *The Northern Voyages, A.D. 500–1600* (New York: Oxford University Press, 1971), 213–18. The best source of documents on the Corte-Reals is Quinn, Quinn, and Hillier, *New American World*, vol. 1, chap. 15.

27. Quinn, Quinn, and Hillier, *New American World* 1:150.

28. Quinn, *England and the Discovery of America*, 128.

29. J. Franklin Jameson, *The Northmen, Columbus, and Cabot*, Original Narratives of American History Series (New York: American Historical Society, 1905), 389; Winsor, *Narrative and Critical History* 2:122.

30. Skelton, Marston, and Painter, *The Vinland Map,* 62. The citation is from Peter Martyr's *De Orbe Novo,* Letter of Ponce de Leon to Charles V (1521), cited in Winsor, *Narrative and Critical History* 2:237.

31. Letter of Ponce de Leon to Charles V (1521), cited in Winsor, *Narrative and Critical History* 2:237.

32. Most of what is known of the Verrazzano voyages is derived from his letter to Francis I of France describing his voyage; this was first published in the 1582 edition of Hakluyt's *Principal Voyages* and has since been reprinted in various locations, most recently in Quinn, Quinn, and Hillier, *New American World* 1:281.

33. Quinn, Quinn, and Hillier, *New American World* 1:288.

34. See Allesandro Bacchiani, *Giovanni da Verrazana and His Discoveries in North America Made in 1524,* trans. E. H. Hall in *15th Annual Report of the American Scenic and Historic Preservation Society* (1910), app. A, 135–226, citation from p. 200.

35. Bernard G. Hoffman, *Cabot to Cartier: Sources for a Historical Ethnography of Northeastern North America, 1497–1550* (Toronto: University of Toronto Press, 1961), 112.

36. The citation is from Michael Lok's translation of Martyr's *De Orbe Novo,* entitled (in English) *Decades of the New World* (London, 1612), folio 246.

37. Henry Burrage, ed., *Early English and French Voyages* (New York: Scribner's, 1906), 18.

38. Ibid., 42.

39. Ibid.

40. Ibid., 63.

41. See Allen, *Passage through the Garden,* xxi–xxii.

42. Quinn, Quinn, and Hillier, *New American World* 1:329.

43. Ibid., 135.

44. Quinn, *England and the Discovery of America,* 161–69.

45. Quinn, Quinn, and Hillier, *New American World* 1:168–71. Rastell is quoted on page 169.

46. Quinn, *England and the Discovery of America,* 145–47; Quinn, Quinn, and Hillier, *New American World* 1:172–79.

47. Quinn, Quinn, and Hillier, *New American World* 1:176.

48. Quinn, *England and the Discovery of America,* 178–79.

49. Quinn, Quinn, and Hillier, *New American World* 1:192.

50. Quinn, *England and the Discovery of America,* 172–74.

51. Quinn, Quinn, and Hillier, *New American World* 1:179–80, Thorne quoted on page 180; E. G. R. Taylor, *Tudor Geography, 1485–1583* (New York: Octagon Books, 1968), 45–51.

52. Wright, "The Open Polar Sea," *Human Nature in Geography,* 90–92.

53. Quinn, Quinn, and Hillier, *New American World* 1:187.

54. Taylor, *Tudor Geography*, 45–58; Quinn, Quinn, and Hillier, *New American World* 1:215–16.

55. Quinn, Quinn, and Hillier, *New American World* 1:216.

56. The citation is from the 1589 edition of Hakluyt's *Principal Voyages* as reprinted in Burrage, *Early English and French Voyages*, 106–10.

57. Quinn, Quinn, and Hillier, *New American World* 1:208.

58. Taylor, *Tudor Geography*, 75–102.

59. Ibid., 82.

60. Ibid., 98–99.

61. Morison, *The European Discovery of America*, 497; Quinn, Quinn, and Hillier, *New American World* 4:188–89.

62. Reprinted in Quinn, Quinn, and Hillier, *New American World* 3:5–23.

63. Ibid., 4:14.

64. Ibid., 191.

65. Taylor, *Tudor Geography*, 109.

66. Quinn, Quinn, and Hillier, *New American World* 4:192.

67. The most complete account of the Frobisher voyages is in Richard Collinson, *Three Voyages of Martin Frobisher*, 1st Series (London: Hakluyt Society, 1862); the citations are from p. 72. See also Quinn, Quinn, and Hillier, *New American World* 4:193–227.

68. Oleson, *Early Voyages*, 153.

69. Morison, *The European Discovery of America*, 546.

70. Ibid., 558.

71. Ibid., 586.

72. Quinn, Quinn, and Hillier, *New American World* 4:228.

73. Ibid., 228–51.

74. Ibid., 233.

75. The *Hydrographical Description*, along with other works by Davis, is reprinted in Albert H. Markham, *The Voyages and Works of John Davis, the Navigator*, 1st Series (London: Hakluyt Society, 1880).

76. Cited in Irwin Blacker, ed., *Hakluyt's Voyages* (New York: Viking Press, 1965), 397.

77. For a discussion of Purchas's life and career, see E. G. R. Taylor, *Late Tudor and Early Stuart Geography, 1583–1650* (London: Methuen and Co., 1934), 53–66.

78. Oleson, *Early Voyages*, 161. The account of the Weymouth voyages, along with others of the period, is found in Thomas Rundall, *Narratives of Early Voyages to the Northwest*, 1st Series (London: Hakluyt Society, 1849), 3:62ff.

79. Oleson, *Early Voyages*, 163.

80. Many of the documents and journals of Hudson's four voyages

have been collected in G. M. Asher, *Henry Hudson the Navigator,* 1st Series (London: Hakluyt Society, 1860). The best source for the fourth voyage is the journal of Abacuk Prickett, one of the survivors.

81. Asher, *Henry Hudson the Navigator* 27:188.

82. Ibid., 193–94. A good discussion and many original documents of Hudson's discovery of the bay and subsequent voyages appear in Quinn, Quinn, and Hillier, *New American World* 4:277–98.

83. Ibid., 185.

84. Lawrence Burpee, *The Search for the Western Sea,* 2 vols. (Toronto: Champlain Society, 1935), 1:34.

85. See "Introduction," C. M. Markham, *The Voyages of William Baffin* (London: Hakluyt Society, 1881).

86. *Voyages of Captain Luke Foxe* 88:8.

87. Burpee, *Search for the Western Sea* 1:63.

Chapter 2, The Early Cartography of Maine

1. For the earliest voyages, see D. B. Quinn: *England and the Discovery of America* (New York: Alfred A. Knopf, 1974), 93–144, and *North America from Earliest Discovery to First Settlements: The Norse Voyages to 1612* (New York: Harper and Row, 1977), 108–36.

2. Starting points in Verrazzanian cartography must be William P. Cumming, "The Colonial Charting of the Massachusetts Coast," *Colonial Society of Massachusetts Publications* 70 (1980): 66–118, and W. F. Ganong, *Crucial Maps in the Early Cartography and Place-nomenclature of the Atlantic Coast of Canada,* ed. Theodore E. Layng (Toronto: Toronto University Press, 1964). See also Lawrence C. Wroth, *The Voyages of Giovanni da Verrazzano, 1524–1528* (New Haven: Yale University Press, 1970); Michel Mollat du Jourdain and Jacques Habert, *Giovanni et Girolamo Verrazzano* (Paris: Imprimerie Nationale, 1982); R. A. Skelton, *The Influence of Verrazzano on Sixteenth Century Cartography* (Florence: L. S. Olschki, 1970); and Samuel Elliot Morison, *The European Discovery of America,* vol. 1, *The Northern Voyages, A.D. 500–1600* (New York: Oxford University Press, 1971), 227–325.

3. The major world map by Girolamo da Verrazzano is in the Vatican Library. It dates from 1529 and has thirty names of places between Cape Cod and Cape Breton, as compared with ten on the National Maritime Museum world map. It remains arguable whether all the names on the former were given by Giovanni da Verrazzano himself. His famous "letter" (in Wroth, *Voyages,* in Italian and in translation, 96–143) does not indicate that he examined with any care for detail the thirty-two islands that he mentions.

4. Marcel Destombes, "Nautical Charts Attributed to Verrazzano,"

Imago Mundi 11 (1969): 57–66, with the first reproduction of the National Maritime Museum world map, which he attributes to Girolamo da Verrazzano between 1525 and 1528, with a few additions circa 1540.

5. The Maggiolo map was in Biblioteca Ambrosiana until its destruction in World War II; see Wroth, *Voyages,* pl. 19.

6. On Gomes, see J. T. Medina, *El portugues, Estaban Gómez en el servicio de España* (Santiago, Chile: Elzeviriana, 1908); Louis-André Vigneras, "El viaje de Estaban Gómez a Norte América," *Revista de Indias* 17 (1967): 189–208; "The Voyage of Estaban Gómez from Florida to the Bacallaos," *Terra Incognitae* 2 (1970): 25–28; Morison, *Northern Voyages,* 326–31.

7. The Castiglioni map is in Archivo Marchesi Castiglioni, Mantua, Italy. See L.-A. Vigneras, "The Cartographer Diogo Ribeiro," *Imago Mundi* 16 (1972): 77–82; W. P. Cumming, R. A. Skelton, and D. B. Quinn, *The Discovery of North America* (London: Paul Elek, 1971), fig. 74.

8. Cumming, Skelton, and Quinn, *Discovery of North America,* 104, 106–7, fig. 73, p. 73; Wroth, *Voyages,* 20.

9. I am indebted to Professor William P. Cumming for photocopies of the original in the Real Académia de Historia, Madrid, Spain. See his analysis in his "Colonial Charting," 110–13, forthcoming. Alonso de Chaves, *Espejo de navegantes. Quarto partitu en cosmographia,* ed. Paulino Casteneda, Mariano Cuesta, and Pilar Hernandez (Madrid: Instituto de Historia y Cultura Naval, 1983), 93.

10. See the Madrid copy (in the Académia de Historia), Alonso de Santa Cruz, *Islario de todas las islas del mundo, circa 1540,* ed. Antonio Blásquez (Madrid: Publicaciones de la Real sociedad geografica, 1922), 438–39, figs. 2, 105. One of the two copies in the Hofbibliothek, Vienna, Austria, is in Franz R. Von Wieser, *Die Karten von Amerika den Islario General de Alonso de Santa Cruz* (Innsbruck: Wagner, 1908), pl. 3. The text of the copy in Bibliothèque Publique, Besançon, France, is in Henry Harrisse, *The Discovery of America* (1892; reprint, Amsterdam: N. Izrael, 1961), 234–35, with captions only left for the maps.

11. Jean Fonteneau (Alfonce), *La Côsmographie,* ed. M. Musset (Paris: E. Leroux, 1904).

12. Sigmund Diamond, "Norumbega: New England Xanadu," *American Neptune* 11 (1959): 95–107, is unable to track down the earliest appearance.

13. The first Spanish map of the Americas with some semiofficial status is the world map by Diego Gutiérrez in the British Library, published in 1562, which has "Rio de Gamas" (reproduced in Cumming, Skelton, and Quinn, *Discovery of North America,* 141–43).

14. Facsimile, Ortelius World Map, extract from British Library; B. van t' Hoff, ed., *Gerard Mercator's Map of the World (1569)* (Rotterdam: Publicaties van het Maritiem Museum Prins Hendrik, 1961).

15. John Dee's map of North America, extract from British Library, Cotton MS, Augustus I.i, l, in D. B. Quinn, ed., *Voyages and Colonising Enterprises of Sir Humphrey Gilbert,* 2 vols. (London: Hakluyt Society, 1940), vol. 2; "Sir Humfrey Gilbert Knight his charte" [1552], Free Library of Philadelphia, Elkins collection, no. 42, in Quinn, *Gilbert,* vol. 2; and D. B. Quinn, A. M. Quinn, and S. Hillier, eds., *New American World: A Documentary History of North America to 1612,* 5 vols. (New York: Arno Press, 1979), vol. 3, fig. 90.

16. Quinn, *Gilbert* 2:309–10.

17. Richard Hakluyt, *Divers Voyages Touching the Discoverie of America* (1582; facsimile reprint, Amsterdam: Theatrum Orbis Terraram, 1967).

18. D. B. Quinn, "The Voyage of Etienne Bellenger to the Maritimes in 1583: A New Document," *Canadian Historical Review* 43 (1962): 328–43, Bellenger quoted on page 340, reprinted in D. B. Quinn, *Explorers and Colonies: America, 1500–1625* (London: Hambleden Press, 1990), 285–300.

19. Bibliothèque Nationale, "Les premières euvres de Iaques de Vaulx," Cartes, Reserve Géographie C,4052, Department des Manuscrits, MSS français 150, and 9175, discussed in Quinn, "The Voyage," 337–38.

20. All references to English activities in Maine in 1602–8 are from D. B. Quinn and A. M. Quinn, eds., *The English New England Voyages, 1602–1608,* 2d ser., no. 161 (London: Hakluyt Society, 1983).

21. James Rosier, "A True Relation of the Voyage of Captain George Weymouth," in Henry S. Burrage, ed., *Early English and French Voyages, Chiefly from Hakluyt, 1534–1608* (New York: Charles Scribner's Sons, 1930), 358.

22. Samuel de Champlain, *The Works of Samuel de Champlain,* ed. H. P. Biggar, 6 vols. (1922–36; reprint, Toronto: Toronto University Press, 1971), 1:225–92, comprises the text and coastal charts from *Les Voyages* (Paris, 1613) made between 1603 and 1607.

23. Division of Geography and Maps, Library of Congress, Washington, D.C., facsimile published.

24. Champlain, *Works,* vol. 7 (Portfolio of Maps, etc.).

25. Marc Lescarbot, *Histoire de la Nouvelle France* (Paris, 1609), in *The History of New France,* 3 vols. (Toronto: Champlain Society, 1907–14); see Quinn and Hiller, *New American World,* IV, fig. 126.

26. Simancas, Spain, Archivo General, Estado 2588/25 (MP.y D.1.1); the best reproduction is in Cumming, Skelton, and Quinn, *Discovery of North America,* 264, 266–67; see Quinn and Quinn, *English New England Voyages,* 520–25. William Shackey, *The Historie of Travell into*

Virginia Britania, ed. Louis B. Wright and Virginia Freund (London: Hakluyt Society, 1951), p. 50, stated that in his 1610 New England voyage, Samuel Argall wanted to "make good what Captayne Bartholomew Gosnold, and Captain Weymouth omitted in their discoveryes, observing all along the Coast, and drawing the plotts thereof as he steered homewards into our [Chesapeake] Bay."

27. See Quinn, *North America from Earliest Discovery,* 412–13; Samuel Purchas, *Hakluytus Posthumus or Purchas His Pilgrimes,* vol. 4 (London: W. Stansby for H. Fetherstone, 1625), 1758–62, 1807–9, 1876–91; Lescarbot, *Works* 3:35–72; Lucien Campeau, *La Première Mission d'Acadie (1602–1616)* (Quebec: Presses de l'Universite Laval, 1967), 267–637. See also Henry S. Burrage, *The Beginnings of Colonial Maine, 1602–1658* (Portland: Marks Printing House, 1914), 108, and Marcel Trudel, *The Beginnings of New France, 1524–1663* (Toronto: McClelland and Stewart, 1973), 115.

28. John Smith, *A Description of New England* (1616); *Travels and Works of Captain John Smith,* ed. Edward Arber and A. G. Bradley, 2 vols. (Edinburgh: John Grant, 1910), 2:695–776, Smith quoted on page 703.

29. Ibid., 696.

Chapter 3, On the Meaning of a Name

1. Entries for October 19 and 14, 1492, in *The Log of Christopher Columbus,* trans. Robert H. Fuson (Camden, Maine: International Marine, 1987), 88, 79.

2. Bernard G. Hoffman, *Cabot to Cartier: Sources for a Historical Ethnography of Northeastern North America, 1497–1550* (Toronto: University of Toronto Press, 1961), 101.

3. William Francis Ganong, "Crucial Maps in the Early Cartography and Place Nomenclature of the Atlantic Coast of Canada," parts 1–9, *Proceedings and Transactions of the Royal Society of Canada* 23–31, part 3 (1964): 192.

4. See the concluding chapter by J. B. Harley in this volume.

5. "Translation of the Cellere Codex" [The Letter of Verrazzanno], in Lawrence C. Wroth, *The Voyages of Giovanni da Verrazzanno, 1524–1528* (New Haven: Yale University Press, 1970), 142.

6. Ibid., 138.

7. There is a similar, seemingly naked moment in Columbus's log when the explorer clearly sees that the chief who has entered his cabin to dine is more than equal to any European occasion. See entry for December 18, 1492, *Log of Christopher Columbus,* 139–41.

8. Wroth, *Voyages,* 139.

9. As Wroth points out convincingly, the reference to trees in the

naming of "Arcadia" (Wroth, *Voyages*, 137 n. 9) suggests that the source was Jacopo Sannazaro's *Arcadia* of 1502, a "best seller" throughout the sixteenth century. The discussion of geographical measurements comes at the close of the letter.

10. The issue of just which of the ancient European ancestors the Indians of the New World were descended from became a matter of serious debate in the seventeenth century. See Karen Kupperman, "Were the Indians Alien?" in *Settling with the Indians: The Meeting of English and Indian Cultures in America, 1580–1640* (Totowa, N.J.: Rowman and Littlefield, 1980), 107–40. Not all commentators took the diffusionist approach, however. Marc Lescarbot, who accompanied Champlain to Canada in 1604, adopted what seems like a comparative theory in his *Histoire de la Nouvelle France* (1609); he assumed that American natives and ancient peoples of other parts of the world developed along parallel tracks. In English, see *Nova Francia: A Description of Acadia, 1606*, Book 2, trans. P. Erondelle (London, 1609).

11. See the chapters by Kenneth M. Morrison and James Axtell in this volume for a discussion of how the Indians may have interpreted the moral value of their own social interactions with Europeans in a similar vein.

12. Wroth, *Voyages*, 139.

13. Ibid.

14. "The First Relation of Jaques Carthier of S. Malo, 1534," in Henry Burrage, ed., *Early English and French Voyages* (New York: Scribner's, 1906), 14.

15. John Brereton, *A Brief and True Relation of the Discoverie of the North Part of Virginia* (London, 1602), in David B. Quinn and Alison M. Quinn, eds., *The English New England Voyages, 1602–1608*, 2d ser., no. 161 (London: Hakluyt Society, 1983).

16. Wroth, *Voyages*, 140.

17. Ibid., 155–64.

18. Following Ganong, we can reconstruct the appearance of the name within the time period. "Anorobegua" (Riccardiana Atlas, 1534); "Anorombega" (Gemma Frisius globe, 1537, and the Mercator globe of 1541, which also used "Anorumbega"); "Anoranbegue" (Desliens, 1541); and "Anorobagra" (Harleian, 1542, and Desceliers of 1546). See Ganong, "Crucial Maps," part 4, 157–90.

19. Quoted in Hoffman, *Cabot to Cartier*, 169.

20. Samuel Eliot Morison, *The European Discovery of America*, vol. 1, *The Northern Voyages, A.D. 500–1600* (New York: Oxford University Press, 1971), 465.

21. See Marc Lescarbot's discussion of this moment in *Nova Francia: A Description of Acadia, 1606*, trans. P. Erondelle (1609; reprint, London: Harper and Brothers, 1928), 48–54.

22. Antonello Gerbi, *Nature in the New World*, trans. Jeremy Moyle (Pittsburgh: University of Pittsburgh Press, 1985), 116n.

23. Ganong, "Crucial Maps," part 3, 200–202.

24. Morison, *European Discovery*, 489.

25. There is some question about the actual course sailed by Gomes, whether up the coast from the south or down from the north. In the absence of an account of the journey, the best available evidence for his explorations is in fact the Ribeiro maps. Since the maps incorporate new features north of Cape Cod but simply connect the cape area to already known features along the coast farther to the south, the assumption is that his exploration missed the intervening piece, and the maps followed. See David B. Quinn, *North America from Earliest Discovery to First Settlements: The Norse Voyages to 1612* (New York: Harper and Row, 1977), 160–62. See also Wroth, *Voyages*, 198–200.

26. Wroth, *Voyages*, 139. I am following Wroth's explanation for the discrepancy between the latitude given in the Codex and that of Rome (see 87n).

27. Ganong, "Crucial Maps," part 3, 198–99.

28. Richard Hakluyt, *Divers Voyages Touching the Discoverie of America* (London, 1582), 7.

29. Ibid., 45.

30. See David B. Quinn, ed., "A Discourse Concerning Western Planting" (1584), in David B. Quinn, Alison M. Quinn, and Susan Hillier, eds., *New American World: A Documentary History of North America to 1612*, 5 vols. (New York: Arno Press, 1979).

31. David B. Quinn, *Richard Hakluyt, Editor* (Amsterdam: Theatrum Orbis Terrarum, 1967), 9.

32. Hakluyt, *Divers Voyages*, 53.

33. John Smith, *Advertisements for the Unexperienced Planters of New England . . .* (London, 1631), 13.

34. Morison, *European Discovery*, 489.

Chapter 4, Children of Gluskap

1. Sebastien Rasle, "A Dictionary of the Abenaki Language in North America, [1690–1722]," in John Pickering, ed., *Memoirs of the American Academy of Arts and Sciences*, n.s., 1 (1833): 533. In Rasle's dictionary, the word is spelled *ketakamig8*. According to the orthographic system used by Dr. Frank Siebert of Old Town, Maine, the "correct" Penobscot, eastern Abenaki form is *ktahkamik—*(big land). Siebert notes that the Penobscots used the term to refer to the mainland (Siebert, personal communication).

2. George Popham, Letter to King James I, December 13, 1607, *Collections of the Maine Historical Society* 5 (1857): 359–60. For the notion

that the native peoples in New England thought of their land as part of a larger island, see among others Hendrick Aupamut, *History of the Muh-heakunnuk Indians* (1790), in *Massachusetts Historical Society Collections* 9 (1804): 101; William Wood, *New England's Prospect* (Boston: Publications of the Prince Society, 1865), 2; Edward Winslow, "Winslow's Relation" (1624), in *Massachusetts Historical Society Collections,* 2d ser., 9 (1832): 99.

3. Rasle, "Dictionary," 434; Frank G. Speck, "Penobscot Tales and Religious Beliefs," *Journal of American Folklore* 48 (1935): 4, 18–19. Dr. Frank Siebert suggests that the term *ketchiniweskwe* (great spirit) was invented by Roman Catholic missionaries. In Abenaki, the element *ni-wes* refers to dry seed (of corn), metaphorically expressing the idea of "spirit of life" (Siebert, personal communication).

4. Among others, see Joseph Laurent, *New Familiar Abenakis and English Dialogues, the First Ever Published on the Grammatical System by Jos. Laurent, Abenakis Chief* (Quebec: L. Brousseau, 1884), 46–47.

5. Nicolar, *Life and Traditions,* 7. Note that there are various spellings of the name Gluskap, including *Gloosk-ob, Koluskap,* and *Glooscap.*

6. There is no agreement on the precise etymology or meaning of the name Gluskap. See among others Nicolar, *Life and Traditions,* 12.

7. Frank G. Speck, "Aboriginal Conservators," *Bird-Lore* 40 (1938): 259.

8. Not surprisingly, a limited geographic understanding of territories beyond the immediate region is typical. Compare what Edmund Carpenter observed among the Inuit: "Aivilik men are keen geographers when describing their immediate surroundings. But once they venture to tell of the outer world, geography gives way to cosmography." Edmund Carpenter, Frederick Varley, and Robert Flaherty, *Eskimo* (Toronto: University of Toronto Press, 1959), n.p.

9. For a brief review of Paleo-Indian remains in the region, see among others Arthur E. Spiess and Deborah B. Wilson, *Michaud: A Paleo-indian Site in the New England–Maritimes Region,* Occasional Publications in Maine Archaeology 6 (Augusta: Maine Historical Preservation Commission and the Maine Archaeological Society, 1987), 129–55.

10. David Sanger, *Discovering Maine's Archaeological Heritage* (Augusta: Maine Historical Preservation Commission, 1979), 20; Sanger, "Maritime Adaptations in the Gulf of Maine," *Archaeology of Eastern North America* 18 (1988): 84; and William Cronon, *Changes in the Land: Indians, Colonists, and the Ecology of New England* (New York: Hill and Wang, 1983), 27.

11. "The Description of the Country of Mawooshen," in Samuel Purchas, *Hakluytus Posthumus or Purchas His Pilgrimes, Contayning a History of the World, in Sea Voyages, and Lande-Travells, by Englishmen and Others,* 20 vols. (Glasgow: James MacLehose and Sons, 1906),

19:400. Perhaps forest burning also occurred among the eastern Wabanakis inhabiting Acadia (in particular Nova Scotia and New Brunswick); see Nicolas Denys, *The Description and Natural History of the
Coasts of North America (Acadia)*, ed. and trans. William F. Ganong
(Toronto: Champlain Society, 1908), 377. For evidence of this practice in Massachusetts, see Wood, *New England's Prospect*, 17; see also
Cronon, *Changes*, 48–52, 181–82, and Thomas Morton, *The New English
Canaan, or New Canaan: Containing an Abstract of New England Composed in Three Books* (Boston: Prince Society, 1883).

12. The precontact population estimates remain subject to debate.
Pierre Biard, a French Jesuit missionary active among the eastern
Wabanakis (1611–13), noted in his 1616 treatise *Relation de la Nov-
velle France . . .* that natives informed him "that in the region of the
great river [St. Lawrence], from Newfoundland to Chouacoet [Saco],
there cannot be more than nine or ten thousand people." He added,
"I believe it is the highest number" (Thwaites, *Jesuit Relations* 3:109–
11). In this context it is important to note that Dean R. Snow, in *The
Archaeology of New England* (New York: Academic Press, 1980), 33–34
(reiterated in Dean Snow and Kim M. Lanphear, "European Contact
and Indian Depopulation in the Northeast: The Timing of the First
Epidemics," *Ethnohistory* 35, [1988]: 22–24), erroneously assumes that
these figures are "post-epidemic" with respect to Wabanakis in northern New England. Indeed, Biard's earlier estimates were even lower by
about half (Thwaites, *Jesuit Relations* 2:73). The number of 30,000 presented here is nothing but an educated guess and is relatively low in
comparison with other recent estimates for the region. For instance,
Dean Snow calculated that there were about 10,000 western Wabanakis
(including Penacooks), 11,900 Wabanakis from Saco to the Penobscot
(Armouchiquois and Etchemins), and another 7,600 eastern Wabanakis
(Etchemins) in the St. Croix and St. John river areas. Farther east, he
estimated the pre-epidemic number of Micmacs in the Maritimes at
about 13,000 (Snow, *Archaeology*, 33–34). Snow's total population estimate for the groups here identified as eastern and western Wabanakis is
42,500. In this context, it is of interest to note that Snow's estimate for
the Micmacs is substantially lower than the 35,000 recently suggested
by Virginia Miller (who concluded that this was "not an unlikely minimum figure") in her article "Aboriginal Micmac Population: A Review
of the Evidence," *Ethnohistory* 23 (1976): 117–27. If Miller's figure had
been taken into account, the total population estimate for northern
New England and the Maritimes would have been nearly 75,000.

13. The issue of ethnicity is problematical. For a more detailed dis-
cussion of Wabanaki ethnicity, see Harald Prins, *Tribulations of a Border
Tribe: The Case of the Aroostook Band of Micmacs in Maine* (Ann Arbor:
University Microfilms International, 1988), 152–202.

14. Biard, in Thwaites, *Jesuit Relations* 2:73.

15. "Description of the Country of Mawooshen," in Purchase, *Hakluytus Posthumus* 19:402–3. The orthography of Wabanaki names presents us with difficulties. For instance, Mentaurmet's name (as spelled by the English) was written as *Meteourmite* in Biard's 1612 letter (in Thwaites, *Jesuit Relations* 2:41).

16. Biard, in Thwaites, *Jesuit Relations* 3:89.

17. I am not suggesting that tribal territoriality among the Wabanaki ethnic groups conformed to what has been termed the "riverine model." See also Harald E. L. Prins, "Micmacs and Maliseets in the St. Lawrence River Valley," in W. Cowan, ed., *Actes du 17e Congres des Algonquinistes* (Ottawa: Carleton University, 1986), 263–78; Prins, *Tribulations,* 274–76.

18. This section on material culture draws on a variety of sources, including accounts by Biard, Morton, Wood, and Denys. Other important sources include Samuel de Champlain, *The Works of Samuel de Champlain,* ed. H. P. Biggar, 6 vols. (Toronto: Champlain Society, 1922–36); James Rosier, "A True Relation of the Most Prosperous Voyage Made This Present Yeare 1605, by Captain G. Weymouth, in the Discovery of the Land Virginia," in Henry S. Burrage, ed., *Rosier's Relation of Weymouth's Voyage to the Coast of Maine, 1605* (Portland: Gorges Society, 1887), 38–75; Marc Lescarbot, *The History of New France,* 3 vols. (Toronto: Champlain Society, 1907–14); John Josselyn, "An Account of Two Voyages to New England," *Massachusetts Historical Society Collections,* 3d ser., 3 (1833): 211–396.

19. Sebastien Rasle, Letter from Norridgewock (October 12, 1723), *Collections and Proceedings of the Maine Historical Society* 4 (1893): 267. According to Champlain (*Works* 2:15), "From Saco along the whole coast as far as Tadoussac [these birch bark canoes] are all alike." These Wabanaki hunting canoes, often no more than ten feet long, usually carried only about four to six individuals. Larger ocean-going canoes could measure more than twenty feet, carrying a fairly large number of people. Also note that Champlain (*Works* 1:338) observed that the wooden dugouts, not reported among the Wabanakis, were used south of Cape Ann, in Massachusetts and beyond.

20. Denys, *Description and Natural History,* 422; Morton, *New English Canaan,* 186.

21. Josselyn, "Account of Two Voyages," 297–98.

22. Rasle, Letter from Norridgewock, 266; Charles G. Willoughby, "Homes and Gardens of New England Indians," *American Anthropologist* 8 (1906): 116. The quote is from Biard, in Thwaites, *Jesuit Relations* 2:41.

23. Josselyn, "Account of Two Voyages," 307.

24. See among others Jesse D. Jennings, *Prehistory of North America* (Mountain View, Calif.: Mayfield Publishing Co., 1989), 258–60.

25. For a general overview, see K. M. Bennett, "The Food Economy of the New England Indians," *Journal of Political Economy* 63 (1955): 369-97. See also Harald Prins, "Cornplanters at Meductic: Ethnic and Territorial Reconfigurations in Colonial Acadia," *Man in the Northeast* no. 44 (1992): 55-72.

26. Biard, in Thwaites, *Jesuit Relations* 2:73.

27. Denys, *Description and Natural History,* 349.

28. Lescarbot, in Thwaites, *Jesuit Relations* 2:185. See also Rosier, who wrote that Wabanaki tribesmen on the central Maine coast hunted whales "with a multitude of their boats" (Rosier, "True Relation," 158).

29. Denys, *Description and Natural History,* 359, 171; see also Wood, *New England's Prospect,* 40, 75, 108.

30. Morton, *New English Canaan,* 39, 107, 226.

31. Denys, *Description and Natural History,* 435-37.

32. Ibid., 380, 381; Wood, *New England's Prospect,* 75; for wild rice gathering, see also Frank G. Speck, *Penobscot Man: The Life History of a Forest Tribe in Maine* (Philadelphia: University of Pennsylvania Press, 1940), 92. Frank G. Speck, "Medicine Practices on the Northeastern Algonquians," *International Congress of Americanists Proceedings* 19 (1915): 303-21.

33. Biard, in Thwaites, *Jesuit Relations* 2:77.

34. Thwaites, *Jesuit Relations* 2:49, 167, 249, 3:225. *Kenduskeag* is sometimes also referred to as *Kadesquit.* See also Thwaites, *Jesuit Relations* 2:49, 3:225, and Snow, *Archaeology,* 33-47.

35. Based on Louis Paul (personal communication, 1985). Earlier, a Canadian missionary, J. A. Maurault, in *Histoire des Abenakis, depuis 1605 jusqu'a nos jours* (Sorel, Quebec, Canada: L'Atelier Typographique de la Gazette de Sorel, 1866), suggested that the term referred to "land of the little dogs." See also Prins, *Tribulations,* 162.

36. Peter Thomas, "Contrastive Subsistence Strategies and Land Use as Factors for Understanding Indian-White Relations in New England," *Ethnohistory* 23, (1976): 6-13, quotation on page 13; Howard S. Russell, *Indian New England before the Mayflower* (Hanover, N.H.: University Press of New England, 1980), 150-51; James Petersen (personal communication, 1989).

37. See among others Champlain, *Works* 1:327-30, 3:374-75; Lescarbot, *History of New France* 1:195; Wood, *New England's Prospect,* 106; Rasle, Letter from Norridgewock, 269; Morton, *New English Canaan,* 160; Russell, *Indian New England,* 168.

38. Wood, *New England's Prospect,* 75-77, quotation on page 75; Morton, *New English Canaan,* 205-10; Denys, *Description and Natural History,* 356-57.

39. Samuel de Champlain, *Voyages of Samuel de Champlain, 1604-1618,* ed. W. L. Grant (New York: Charles Scribner's Sons, 1907), 61-63.

40. Wood, *New England's Prospect,* 102.

41. Lescarbot, *History of New France* 2:324.

42. Wood, *New England's Prospect*, 69 (quotation), 79; Morton, *New English Canaan*, 201; B. F. De Costa, *Ancient Norumbega, or the Voyages of Simon Ferdinando and John Walker to the Penobscot River, 1579–1580* (Albany, N.Y.: Joel Munsell's Sons, 1890), 7. Regarding the intertribal trade in moose hides, it should be noted that similar networks existed in the St. Lawrence River valley, for example, where horticultural Hurons acquired hides from Montagnais hunters in exchange for surplus corn.

43. In Thwaites, *Jesuit Relations* 2:73, 3:75. For a good overview, see also Charles G. Willoughby, "Dress and Ornament of the New England Indians," *American Anthropologist* 7 (1905): 499–508.

44. Wood, *New England's Prospect*, 70.

45. Biard, in Thwaites, *Jesuit Relations* 3:117.

46. Ibid., 75.

47. For a good overview, see also Ruth H. Whitehead, "Every Thing They Make and Wear," unpublished manuscript, n.d., Provincial Museum of Nova Scotia, Halifax.

48. Lescarbot, *History of New France* 3:133–34.

49. Champlain, *Works* 1:444–45; generally, according to Lescarbot (*History of New France* 3:133), eastern Wabanaki groups such as the Micmacs did not fancy these decorative elements. However, when Jacques Cartier encountered tribespeople (who could have been Micmacs) in the Gulf of St. Lawrence in 1532, he described them as having topknots in which they wove "a few bird's feathers." In H. P. Biggar, *The Voyages of Jacques Cartier* (Ottawa: Public Archives of Canada, 1924), 22–23.

50. Denys, *Description and Natural History*, 414.

51. Champlain, *Voyages* (New York: Charles Scribner's Sons, 1907), 61–63; Lescarbot, *History of New France* 3:135.

52. John Brereton, "A Briefe and True Relation of the Discoverie of the North Part of Virginia . . . Made This Present Yeere 1602," in L. B. Wright, ed., *The Elizabethan's America: A Collection of Early Reports by Englishmen on the New World* (Cambridge: Harvard University Press, 1965), 143; Daniel Gookin, *Historical Collections of the Indians in New England*, in *Massachusetts Historical Society Collections*, 1st ser., 1 (1806): 153; Wood, *New England's Prospect*, 71–72. The Wampanoags in southern Massachusetts were described as wearing "on their heads long hair to the shoulders, only cut before [and] some trussed up before with a feather, broad-wise, like a fan; another a fox tail hanging out." William Bradford, cited in H. C. Porter, *The Inconstant Savage: England and the North American Indian, 1500–1660* (London: Duckworth, 1979), 429.

53. Morton, *New English Canaan*, 197; Wood, *New England's Prospect*, 31, 74. The Micmac chieftain Membertou was described as "bearded like a Frenchman" (Thwaites, *Jesuit Relations* 2:23; see also

Lescarbot, *History of New France* 3:140). Elsewhere, tribesmen were described as "thin-bearded," and some even sported false beards fashioned "of the hair of beasts" (Brereton, in Porter, *Inconstant Savage,* 268).

54. Denys, *Description and Natural History,* 414.

55. Wood, *New England's Prospect,* 74; see also Denys, *Description and Natural History* 414; J. P. Baxter, ed., *Documentary History of the State of Maine,* vol. 10 (Portland: Maine Historical Society, 1910), 463.

56. Wood, *New England's Prospect,* 95.

57. Rosier, in Porter, *Inconstant Savage,* 270; see also Josselyn, "Account of Two Voyages," 297–98.

58. Brereton, in Wright, *Elizabethan's America,* 137–38.

59. Abbe S. Maillard, *An Account of the Customs and Manners of the Micmakis and Maricheets Savage Nations, Now Dependent on the Government of Cape Breton* (London: S. Hooper and A. Morley, 1758), 55; Sieur N. de Diereville, *Relation of the Voyage to Port Royal in Acadia or New France,* ed. J. C. Webster (Toronto: Champlain Society, 1933), 169–70. The quote is from Wood, *New England's Prospect,* 74.

60. The quotations are from Denys, *Descriptions and Natural History,* 407, 411; Biard, in Thwaites, *Jesuit Relations* 3:75; see also Wood, *New England's Prospect,* 101.

61. Rosier, "True Relation," 121. This red copper may have been mined locally, since the eastern Wabanakis were familiar with various mines on the coast of the Bay of Fundy. Early French explorers, including Champlain, refer to these mines (see also Thwaites, *Jesuit Relations* 3:296); a leather belt found at Merriconeag Sound, Maine, included some four hundred red copper pieces of varied size, attached to each other with soft leather strings (in *Historical Magazine* [1869], 247).

62. Denys, *Description and Natural History,* 411; see also Wood, *New England's Prospect,* 108; Morton, *New English Canaan,* 201.

63. Denys, *Description and Natural History,* 370, 407, 411, 413; Wood, *New England's Prospect,* 73, 108; Morton, *New English Canaan,* 201, 207, 209, 210; see also Biard, in Thwaites, *Jesuit Relations* 3:75.

64. For the etymology of native place-names in Maine, see especially Fanny H. Eckstorm, *Indian Place Names of the Penobscot Valley and the Maine Coast* (1941; reprint, Orono: University of Maine at Orono Press, 1978).

65. Cronon, *Changes,* 65.

66. The meaning of *Mawooshen* remains unclear. Frank Siebert (personal communication, 1988) suggests that it refers to the Mousam River. In this context, it is of interest to note that Eckstorm (*Indian Place Names,* 101) "discovered that many place names which Penobscot Indians could not translate were easily interpreted by Passamaquoddy and Micmac Indians." Recently, a Maliseet speaker, Louis Paul of Woodstock Reserve, New Brunswick, suggested that *mawoossan* refers

to "a bunch of people walking or acting together" — *mawe* referring to a "coming together" of more than two people.

67. Captain George Popham, Letter to King James I (written from Fort St. George, December 13, 1607), in *Collections of the Maine Historical Society* 5 (1857): 359–60. Samuel Purchas, *Purchas, His Pilgrimage, or Relations of the World and the Religions Observed in All Ages and Places Discovered, from the Creation unto This Present,* 3d ed. (London: Printed by William Stansby for H. Fetherstone, 1617), 939–41.

68. Nicolar, *Life and Traditions,* 5.

69. Frank G. Speck, "Penobscot Tales," 42.

70. Speck, "Penobscot Tales," 42–45; see also Eckstorm, *Indian Place Names,* 200–201.

71. Among others, see Garrick Mallery, "Petroglyphs in North America," *Tenth Annual Report of the Bureau of Ethnology to the Secretary of the Smithsonian Institution, 1888–1889* (Washington, D.C.: Government Printing Office, 1893).

72. Rasle, Letter from Norridgewock, 300.

73. Chrestien Le Clercq, *New Relation of Gaspesia, with the Customs and Religion of the Gaspesian Indians,* trans. and ed. William F. Ganong (Toronto: Champlain Society, 1910), 136; see also Wilson D. Wallis and Ruth S. Wallis, *The Micmac Indians and Eastern Canada* (Minneapolis: University of Minnesota Press, 1955), 54–56.

74. See among others Mark Hedden, "Form of the Cosmos in the Body of the Shaman," *Maine Archaeological Society Bulletin* 27 (Spring 1987): ii–iv; Marc Hedden, "Prehistoric Maine Petroglyphs" (a videoscript), *Maine Archaeological Society Bulletin* 28 (1988). The quotation is by Father Michael Ch. O'Brien, in Eckstorm, *Indian Place Names,* 66.

75. Joseph Nicolar, alias "Young Sebattis," in the *Old Town Herald* (1887?), reprinted in Eckstorm, *Indian Place Names,* 239–41, see also 65–66. Note that this place-name was originally spelled *Arquar-har-see-dek* by Nicolar.

76. In Mallery, "Petroglyphs," 83. (Note that Birch Point is also referred to as Clarks Point.)

77. Lescarbot, *History of New France* 3:21.

78. *Wenooch,* also spelled *Waunnuxuk* or *a8enn8tsak,* is derived from *awaun - ewo* (who is that?) (plural *tsak*): Rasle, "Dictionary," 458; Trumbull, note 1 in Morton, "New English Canaan," 254; Roger Williams, *Key into the Language of the Indians of New England* (1643), in *Massachusetts Historical Society Collections,* 1st ser., 3 (1794): 89. When the eastern Wabanakis became more familiar with early Europeans on their coasts, they learned to communicate in pidgin with the strangers, referring to the English as "Ingres," to the French generally as "Normans," to those from St. Malo as "Samaricois," and to Basques as "Bascua" (Biard, in Thwaites, *Jesuit Relations* 1:163).

79. Cornelius Jaenen, "Amerindian Views of French Culture in the Seventeenth Century," *Canadian Historical Review* 60 (1974): 271, 272; see also Biard, in Thwaites, *Jesuit Relations* 3:22, 75.

80. Biard, in Thwaites, *Jesuit Relations* 1:175; Francois Du Creux, *The History of Canada or New France*, ed. J. B. Conacher, 2 vols. (Toronto: Champlain Society, 1952), 1:160.

81. Cited in LeClerq, *New Relation*, 104.

82. Gabriel Archer, in *Massachusetts Historical Society Collections*, 3d ser., 8 (1843): 73–74.

83. Ferdinando Gorges, *A Briefe Narration of the Originall Undertakings of the Advancement of Plantations into the Parts of America, Especially, Shewing the Beginning, Progress and Continuance of That of New England* (Boston: Publications of the Prince Society, 1890), 2:10.

84. [Samuel de Champlain], *The Voyages and Explorations of Samuel de Champlain, 1604–1616, Narrated by Himself, together with the Voyage of 1603*, trans. Annie N. Bourne, ed. Edward G. Bourne, 2 vols. (New York: Allerton Book Co., 1922), 1:106, 110.

85. Joseph Chadwick, "Survey of Routes to Canada, from Fort Pownal on the Penobscot to Quebec," manuscript, 1764, State Archives, Massachusetts State Library, Boston. Segments of this manuscript are cited in Eva L. Butler and Wendell S. Hadlock, "A Preliminary Survey of the Munsungan-Allagash Waterways," *Robert Abbe Museum Bulletin* 8 (1962): 17. Colonel Montresor, in *Maine Historical Society Collections* 1 (1831): 354.

86. According to Butler and Hadlock, "[Chadwick] was allowed to keep no books and make no maps at the time, but later made a fairly accurate map and well documented account of his trip despite the difficulties he encountered" ("Preliminary Survey," 17).

87. Nicolar, *Life and Traditions*, 64.

88. Silas T. Rand, *Legends of the Micmas* (1894; reprint, New York and London: Johnson Reprint Corp., 1971), 156.

Chapter 5, Mapping Otherness

1. The literature on Europeans is enormous. See, for example, James Axtell, *The European and the Indian: Essays in the Ethnohistory of Colonial North America* (New York: Oxford University Press, 1981); idem, *The Invasion Within: The Contest of Cultures in Colonial North America* (New York: Oxford University Press, 1985); idem, *After Columbus: Essays in the Ethnohistory of Colonial North America* (New York: Oxford University Press, 1988); Robert F. Berkhofer, Jr., *The White Man's Indian: Images of the American Indian from Columbus to Present* (New York: Knopf, 1978); Fredi Chiappeli, ed., *First Images of America: The Impact of the New World on the Old*, 2 vols. (Berkeley: University of California

Press, 1976); Olive Patricia Dickason, *The Myth of the Savage and the Beginnings of French Colonialism in the Americas* (Edmonton: University of Alberta Press, 1984); Cornelius Jaenen, *The French Relationship with the Native People of New France and Acadia* (Ottawa: Indian and Northern Affairs, 1984); Francis Jennings, *The Invasion of America: Indians, Colonialism, and the Cant of Conquest* (Chapel Hill: University of North Carolina Press, 1975); and Bernard W. Sheehan, *Savagism and Civility: Indians and Englishmen in Colonial Virginia* (Cambridge: Cambridge University Press), 1980.

For one outstanding exception to the overlooked Native American response, see LaVerne Harrell Clark, *They Sang for Horses: The Impact of the Horse on Navajo and Apache Folklore* (Tucson: University of Arizona Press, 1966). This book examines the ways in which the Navajos and the Apaches reinterpreted their cosmogonic traditions to account for the existence of horses and Europeans. Another example can be seen in the materials on the Hopi "great other" Maasaw, who oversaw the ways in which various ethnic and racial identities came into being. See Ekkehart Malotki and Michael Lomatuway'ma, *Maasaw: Profile of a Hopi God* (Lincoln: University of Nebraska Press, 1987), and Gordon Brotherston, *Image of the New World: The American Continent Portrayed in Native Texts,* trans. Ed Dorm (London: Thames and Hudson, 1979).

2. See, as examples, Richard Bauman and Joel Sherzer, eds., *Explorations in the Ethnography of Speaking* (New York: Columbia University Press, 1974); James A. Boon, *Other Tribes, Other Scribes: Symbolic Anthropology in the Comparative Study of Cultures, Histories, Religions, and Texts* (New York: Cambridge, 1982); James Clifford and George E. Marcus, eds., *Writing Culture: The Poetics and Politics of Ethnography* (Berkeley: University of California Press, 1986); Vine Deloria, Jr., *God Is Red* (New York: Dell, 1973); Sam D. Gill, *Beyond the "Primitive": The Religions of Nonliterate Peoples* (Englewood Cliffs, N.J.: Prentice Hall, 1982); idem, *Native American Religions* (Belmont, Calif.: Wadsworth Publishing Company, 1982); Jonathan D. Hill, ed., *Rethinking Myth and History: Indigenous South American Perspectives on the Past* (Urbana: University of Illinois Press, 1988); George Lakoff and Mark Johnson, *Metaphors We Live By* (Chicago: University of Chicago Press, 1980); William H. McNeill, *Mythistory and Other Essays* (Chicago: University of Chicago Press, 1986), 3–22; Alfonso Ortiz, "Some Concerns Central to the Writing of 'Indian' History," *Indian Historian* 10 (1977): 17–22; Dennis Tedlock, "The Spoken Word and the Work of Interpretation in American Indian Religion," in Alan M. Olson, ed., *Myth Symbol and Reality* (Notre Dame: University of Notre Dame Press, 1980), 129–44; idem, *The Spoken Word and the Work of Interpretation* (Philadelphia: University of Pennsylvania Press, 1983); Tzetvan Todorov, *The Conquest*

of America: The Question of the Other, trans. Richard Howard (New York: Harper and Row, 1984); Victor Turner, *The Ritual Process: Structure and Anti-Structure* (Ithaca, N.Y.: Cornell University Press, 1969); idem, *The Anthropology of Performance* (New York: PAJ Publications, 1987); and Jan Vansina, *Oral Tradition as History* (Madison: University of Wisconsin Press, 1985).

3. Thomas C. Blackburn, *December's Child: A Book of Chumash Oral Narratives* (Berkeley: University of California Press, 1975).

4. Jonathan Z. Smith, *Map Is Not Territory* (Leiden, Netherlands: E. J. Brill, 1979).

5. See, as examples, Dan Ben-Amos and Kenneth S. Goldstein, eds., *Folklore: Performance and Communication* (The Hague: Mouton, 1975); Blackburn, *December's Child;* Percy S. Cohen, "Theories of Myth," *Man* 4 (1969): 337–54; William G. Doty, *Mythography: The Study of Myths and Rituals* (University: University of Alabama Press, 1986); Alan Dundes, "Folk Ideas as Units of Worldview," in America Paredes and Richard Bauman, eds., *Toward New Perspectives in Folklore* (Austin: University of Texas Press, 1972); Walter R. Fisher, *Human Communication as Narration: Toward a Philosophy of Reason, Value, and Action* (Columbia: University of South Carolina Press, 1987); Robert A. Georges, "Toward an Understanding of Storytelling Events," *Journal of American Folklore* 82 (1969): 313–28; Dell Hymes, "The Grounding of Performance and Text in a Narrative View of Life," *Alcheringa* 4 (1978): 137–39; Edward L. Schieffelin, "Performance and the Cultural Construction of Reality," *American Ethnologist* 12 (1985): 707–24; Katherine Spencer, *Mythology and Values: An Analysis of Navajo Chantway Myths* (Philadelphia: American Folklore Society, 1957); and Christopher Vecsey, *Imagine Ourselves Richly: Mythic Narratives of North American Indians* (New York: Crossroad, 1988).

6. Barbara C. Sproul, *Primal Myths: Creating the World* (New York: Harper and Row, 1979).

7. N. Ross Crumrine and Marjorie Halpin, eds., *The Power of Symbols: Masks and Masquerade in the Americas* (Vancouver: University of British Columbia Press, 1983); Doty, *Mythography;* Clifford Geertz, *The Interpretation of Cultures* (New York: Basic Books, 1973), 87–141; Gill, *Beyond the "Primitive";* Gill, *Native American Religions;* Georges, "Toward an Understanding"; Tedlock, "Spoken Word"; Tedlock, *Spoken Word;* Spencer, *Mythology and Values.*

8. Kenneth M. Morrison, "Towards a History of Intimate Encounters: Algonkian Folklore, Jesuit Missionaries, and Kiwakwe, the Cannibal Giant," *American Indian Culture and Research Journal* 3 (1979): 51–80; idem, "The Mythological Sources of Abenaki Catholicism: A Case Study of the Social History of Power," *Religion* 11 (1981): 235–63.

9. Charles G. Leland, *The Algonquin Legends of New England; or, Myths and Folklore of the Micmac, Passamaquoddy, and Penobscot Tribes* (Boston: Houghton, Mifflin and Co., 1894), 15–17.

10. Frank G. Speck, "Penobscot Transformer Tales, dictated by Newell Lion," *International Journal of American Linguistics* 1 (1918): 184–94; Frank G. Speck, "Penobscot Tales and Religious Beliefs," *Journal of American Folklore* 48 (1935): 6.

11. Leland, *Algonquian Legends*, 60; John Dyneley Prince, *Passamaquoddy Texts*, vol. 10 of *Publications of the American Ethnological Society* (New York: American Ethnological Society, 1931), 31.

12. Frank G. Speck, *Penobscot Man* (Philadelphia: University of Pennsylvania Press, 1940), 203; idem, "Penobscot Shamanism," *Memoirs of the American Anthropological Association* 6 (1919): 240.

13. Joseph Nicolar, *Life and Traditions of the Red Man* (1893; reprint, Fredericton, New Brunswick, Canada: St. Anne's Point Press, 1979), 83.

14. Lou Marano, "Windigo Psychosis: The Anatomy of an Emic-Etic Confusion," *Current Anthropology* 23 (1982): 385–412; Morrison, "Towards a History."

15. Bruce J. Bourque and Ruth Holmes Whitehead, "Tarrentines and the Introduction of European Trade Goods in the Gulf of Maine," *Ethnohistory* 32 (1985): 327–41.

16. Kenneth M. Morrison, *The Embattled Northeast: The Elusive Ideal of Alliance in Abenaki-Euramerican Relations* (Berkeley: University of California Press, 1984), 60–71.

17. Kenneth M. Morrison, "The People of the Dawn: The Abenaki and Their Relations with New England and New France, 1600–1727" (Ph.D. diss., University of Maine, 1975), 51–55.

18. Henry S. Burrage, ed., *Early English and French Voyages* (New York: Scribner's, 1906), 347, 368, 372–73, 376.

19. Ibid., 371–79.

20. Henry O. Thayer, ed., *The Sagadahoc Colony* (Portland: Gorges Society, 1892), 56–80, quotation; Burrage, *Early English and French Voyages*, 399–419; Henry S. Burrage, *Gorges and the Grant of the Province of Maine, 1622* (Augusta, Maine: Printed for the State, 1923), 79–98.

21. Lucien Campeau, ed., *Monumenta Novae Franciae. I. La Premiere Mission d'Acadie (1602–1616)* (Quebec: Les Presses de l'Universite Laval, 1967), 246; Reuben Gold Thwaites, ed., *The Jesuit Relations and Allied Documents*, 73 vols. (1896–1901; reprint, New York: Pageant Book Co., 1959), 2:45–47.

22. Nicolar, *Life and Traditions*, 83.

23. George P. Winship, ed., *Sailors' Narratives of Voyages along the New England Coast, 1524–1624* (Boston: Houghton, Mifflin and Co., 1905), 181–82.

24. Thwaites, *Jesuit Relations* 2:79, 3:109.

25. Marc Lescarbot, *The History of New France*, 3 vols. (Toronto: Champlain Society, 1907–14), 2:104, 3:125; Chrestien Le Clercq, *New Relation of Gaspesia, with the Customs and Religion of the Gaspesian Indians*, trans. and ed. William F. Ganong (Toronto: Champlain Society, 1910), 246; Thwaites, *Jesuit Relations* 1:177, 2:125, 3:73, 75, 109, 123, 213.

26. Peter Paul (personal communication).

27. Frank G. Speck, "Some Micmac Tales from Cape Breton Island," *Journal of American Folklore* 28 (1915): 60–61; idem, "Wawenock Myth Texts from Maine," *43rd Annual Report of the Bureau of American Ethnology* (Washington, D.C.: Bureau of American Ethnology, 1928), 180–81, 186.

Chapter 6, Trade and Alliances in the Contact Period

1. John Brereton, "A Brief and True Relation of the Discovery of the North Part of Virginia, 1602," in Henry S. Burrage, ed., *Early English and French Voyages* (New York: Scribner's, 1906), 337.

2. Martin Pring, "A Voyage Set out from the Citie of Bristol, 1603," in Burrage, *English and French Voyages*, 347.

3. Brereton, "Brief and True Relation," 330–31. The "baske" or "Biscay shallop" was a style of boat originally developed during the sixteenth century by the Basques for whaling but later widely adopted by seafarers of other nationalities for a variety of uses. See William A. Baker, *Sloops and Shallops* (Barre, Mass.: Barre Publishing Company, 1966), 12–19.

4. Samuel Eliot Morison, *The European Discovery of America*, vol. 1, *The Northern Voyages, A.D. 500–1600* (New York: Oxford University Press, 1971), 469.

5. David B. Quinn, *North America from Earliest Discovery to First Settlement: The Norse Voyages to 1612* (New York: Harper and Row, 1977), 387.

6. See chapter 2 of this volume for details on the specific voyages to the Gulf of Maine in the sixteenth century.

7. Benjamin F. Decosta, *Ancient Norumbega, or the Voyages of Simon Ferdinando and John Walker to the Penobscot River, 1479–1580* (Albany: Joel Munsell's Sons, 1890), 5–7, quotation on page 7.

8. Frank T. Siebert, Jr., "The Identity of the Tarrentines, with an Etymology," *Studies in Linguistics* 23 (1973): 69–76; Dean R. Snow, *The Archaeology of New England* (New York: Academic Press, 1980), 32; Harold A. Innis, *The Cod Fisheries: The History of an International Economy* (New Haven: Yale University Press, 1940), 24–26, 38, 47; Morison, *European Discovery of America*, 228–33, 248–49, 480–81; Bernard G. Hoffman, *Cabot to Cartier: Sources for a Historical Ethnography of Northeastern North America, 1497–1550* (Toronto: University of Toronto Press, 1961), 35; and Henry P. Biggar, ed., *The Precursors of Jacques Cartier,*

1497–1534, Canadian Archives Publications No. 5 (Ottawa: Government Printing Bureau, 1911), 195–97.

9. Edwin A. Churchill, "The Founding of Maine, 1600–1640: A Revisionist Interpretation," *Maine Historical Society Quarterly* 18 (1978): 25.

10. James Rosier, "A True Relation of the Most Prosperous Voyage Made This Present Year 1605, by Captain George Weymouth, in the Discovery of the Land of Virginia," in Charles H. Levermore, ed., *Forerunners and Competitors of the Pilgrims and Puritans,* 2 vols. (Brooklyn: New England Society, 1912), 1:348.

11. Churchill, "Founding of Maine," 25.

12. Quinn, *North America from Earliest Discovery,* 189–91, 241–42.

13. Churchill, "Founding of Maine," 26.

14. "The Voyages of the Sieur de Champlain, Book I, 1604–1607" in Samuel de Champlain, *The Works of Samuel de Champlain,* ed. Henry P. Biggar, 6 vols. (Toronto: Champlain Society, 1922–36), 1:365.

15. Rosier, "True Relation," 342.

16. "Voyages of the Sieur de Champlain" 1:294.

17. Champlain, *Works* 2:263–327; A. P. Sevigny, *Les Abenaquis: Habitat et Migrations (17e et 18e siecles)* (Montreal: Les Editions Bellarmin, 1976), 46–49.

18. "Des Sauvages, or the Voyage Samuel Champlain Made to New France in the Year 1603," in *Works* 1:103, 166–67.

19. Hoffman, *Cabot to Cartier,* 202–3; see also Bruce Trigger, "Hochelaga: History and Ethnohistory," in James F. Pendergast and Bruce G. Trigger, eds., *Cartier's Hochelaga and the Dawson Site* (Montreal: McGill-Queen's University Press, 1972), 72–93.

20. "Des Sauvages" 1:166–67.

21. "The Description of the Country of Mawooshen Discovered by the English in the Yeere 1602," in Samuel Purchas, *Hakluytus Posthumus or Purchas His Pilgrimes,* 20 vols. (Glasgow: James MacLehose and Sons, 1906), 19:400–405, quotation on page 401.

22. "Voyages of the Sieur de Champlain" 1:312, 325; Sevigny, *Les Abenaquis,* 47–48.

23. Gabriel Archer, "The Relation of Captain Gosnold's Voyage to the North Part of Virginia, 1602," *Massachusetts Historical Society Collections,* 3d ser, 7 (1843): 73.

24. Alfred G. Bailey, *The Conflict of European and Eastern Algonkian Cultures, 1504–1700: A Study in Canadian Civilization* (Toronto: University of Toronto Press, 1969), 19.

25. Marc Lescarbot, *The History of New France,* 3 vols. (Toronto: Champlain Society, 1907–14), 2:24.

26. Quinn, *North America from Earliest Discovery,* 392.

27. Lescarbot, *History of New France* 2:309.

28. Champlain, *Works* 2:394. We have known from other sources, in-

cluding Lescarbot, that Messamouet was a Souriquois from La Have, on Nova Scotia's southeastern coast, and that Secoudon was an Etchemin sagamore from Ouigoudi, at the mouth of the St. John River. See Lescarbot, *History of New France* 2:323.

29. Lescarbot, *History of New France* 2:324.

30. Alvin Morrison, "Membertou's Raid on the Chouacoet Almouchiquois: The Micmac Sack of Saco in 1607," in William Cowan, ed., *Proceedings of the 6th Algonkian Conference, 1974* (Ottawa: Canadian Ethnology Service, Merchury Series, 1975), 141–58. Messamouet's visit to France must have occurred before or shortly after de Grandmont's death in 1580 (Lescarbot, *History of New France* 2:324; Harald Prins, personal communication). He may have been one of the first natives from Acadia to visit France, but he was not the last. A man "from the coast of Acadia" went with Jean Sarcel De Prevert in 1603 (see "Des Sauvages" 1:188). A Souriquois from southern Nova Scotia named Cacagous (the Micmac word for "crow") not only visited France but also was baptized in Bayonne before 1611 (see Reuben G. Thwaites, ed., *The Jesuit Relations and Allied Documents: Travels and Explorations of the Jesuit Missionaries in New France, 1610–1791,* 73 vols. [Cleveland: Burrows Brothers, 1896–1901], 1:163, and S. T. Rand, *Dictionary of the Language of the Micmac Indians Who Reside in Nova Scotia, New Brunswick, Prince Edward Island, Cape Breton, and Newfoundland* [1888; reprint, New York: Johnson Reprint Co., 1972], 73). These natives were probably invited to visit France in order to forge closer French-Indian trade relationships and to increase native cooperation with French fur traders operating in the Gulf of St. Lawrence.

31. "Voyages of the Sieur de Champlain" 1:442–43.

32. Lescarbot, *History of New France* 3:448.

33. Ibid., 507–8.

34. James Davies, "Relation of a Voyage to Sagadahoc," in Burrage, *Early Voyages,* 402–3.

35. Siebert, "Identity of the Tarrentines."

36. Robert Juet, "The Third Voyage of Master Henry Hudson toward Nova Zambia . . . ," in Purchas, *Hakluytus Posthumus* 13:346.

37. Ibid., 347–48.

38. Bruce Trigger, *The Children of Aataentsic* (Montreal: McGill-Queen's University Press, 1976), 362; Quinn, *North America from Earliest Discovery,* 392; L. Turgeon, "Pecheurs Basques et Indiens des Cotes du Saint-Laurent au XVIe Siecle: Perspectives de Recherches," *Etudes Canadians: Le Canada Atlantique, Acts de Colloque de Nantes* 13 (1982): 11.

39. Baker, *Sloops and Shallops,* 20–28.

40. Thwaites, *Jesuit Relations* 47:223–29, quotation on page 223.

41. Lescarbot, *History of New France* 3:60; D. S. Davis, Nova Scotia Museum, personal communications.

42. Trigger, *Children of Aataentsic*, 208; Neal Salisbury, *Manitou and Providence: Indians, Europeans, and the Making of New England, 1500–1643* (New York: Oxford University Press, 1982), 67–68.

43. "Des Sauvages" 1:166–67.

44. Lescarbot, *History of New France* 2:323–24.

45. Ibid., 1:324.

46. Bailey, *The Conflict*, 35.

47. "Voyages of the Sieur de Champlain," 1:338–39.

48. Ibid., 295.

49. Ferdinando Gorges, "A Brief Narration of the Original Undertakings of the Advancement of Plantations into the Parts of America, Showing the Beginning, Progress and Continuance of that of New England," in James P. Baxter, ed., *Sir Ferdinando Gorges and His Province of Maine*, vol. 2 (Boston: Prince Society, 1890), 75–76.

50. Bailey, *The Conflict*, 34–35.

51. Lescarbot, *History of New France* 3:55; Thwaites, *Jesuit Relations* 3:199–201; "Voyages of the Sieur de Champlain" 4:21.

52. John Smith, "A Description of New England," *Travels and Works of Captain John Smith*, ed. Edward Arber, 2 vols. (Edinburgh: John Grant, 1910), 1:188, 205.

53. Snow, *Archaeology of New England*, 38.

54. Thwaites, *Jesuit Relations* 3:110.

55. Ibid.

56. Lescarbot, *History of New France* 1:195.

57. Thwaites, *Jesuit Relations* 1:177.

58. Ibid., 131.

59. John Winthrop, *The History of New England from 1630–1649*, ed. J. Savage, 2 vols. (Boston: Little, Brown, 1853), 1:72; Harald Prins, personal communication.

60. Trigger, *Children of Aataentsic*, 213–17; Eric R. Wolf, *Europe and the People without History* (Berkeley: University of California Press, 1982), 174.

61. Bailey, *The Conflict*, 34–35; Trigger, *Children of Aataentsic*, 213.

Chapter 7, The Exploration of Norumbega

1. Charles Horton Cooley, *Life and the Student* (New York: Alfred A. Knopf, 1927), 201–2.

2. William S. Simmons, *Spirit of the New England Tribes: Indian History and Folklore, 1620–1984* (Hanover, N.H.: University Press of New England, 1986), 65.

3. Sebastien Rasle, "A Dictionary of the Abenaki Language in North America," in John Pickering, ed., *Memoirs of the American Academy of*

Arts and Sciences, n.s., 1 (1833): 539 ("Englishmen" here is used in a generic sense for Europeans).

4. William Wood, *New England's Prospect,* ed. Alden T. Vaughan (Amherst: University of Massachusetts Press, 1977), 95–96; Roger Williams, *A Key into the Language of America* (London, 1643), 59. In 1869 the Micmacs remembered that the first white men they had seen arrived on a small floating island with tall trees. The next day they awoke to find a number of bears crawling about the tree limbs. Grabbing weapons, they rushed to hunt them but found men instead. See Silas Tertius Rand, *Legends of the Micmacs* (New York: Longman's Green, 1894), 225–26.

5. J. Franklin Jameson, ed., *Johnson's Wonder-Working Providence, 1628–1651* (New York: Charles Scribner's Sons, 1910), 39–40.

6. John Smith, *The Complete Works of Captain John Smith,* ed. Philip L. Barbour, 3 vols. (Chapel Hill: University of North Carolina Press, 1986), 1:324, 340, 381.

7. Ibid., 381, 402; James W. Bradley, "Native Exchange and European Trade: Cross-Cultural Dynamics in the Sixteenth Century," *Man in the Northeast* 33 (Spring 1987): 37–38; Samuel Purchas, *Hakluytus Posthumus or Purchas His Pilgrimes,* 20 vols. (Glasgow: James MacLehose and Sons, 1906), 13:347.

8. David B. Quinn, Alison M. Quinn, and Susan Hillier, eds., *New American World: A Documentary History of North America to 1612,* 5 vols. (New York: Arno Press 1979), 1:148–51.

9. Ibid., 273–79.

10. Ibid., 274, 277.

11. Ibid., 273, 279.

12. Ibid., 149, 151.

13. Lawrence C. Wroth, *The Voyages of Giovanni da Verrazzano, 1524–1528* (New Haven: Yale University Press, 1970), 137–39.

14. Ibid., 138.

15. Ibid., 139–40.

16. Ibid., 140–41.

17. Ibid.

18. Quinn, Quinn, and Hillier, *New American World* 4:304, 306–8; Bruce J. Bourque and Ruth Holmes Whitehead, "Tarrentines and the Introduction of European Trade Goods in the Gulf of Maine," *Ethnohistory* 32 (1985): 327–41.

19. David B. Quinn and Alison M. Quinn, eds., *The English New England Voyages, 1602–1608,* Hakluyt Society Publications 2d ser., no. 161 (London: Hakluyt Society, 1983), 117–18.

20. Ibid., 125, 127, 131, 134, 154.

21. Ibid., 130, 133–36, 154, 158.

22. Ibid., 221, 222, 227.

23. Ibid., 267–68, 269.

24. Ibid., 270, 272–73, 275.

25. Ibid., 270. See Quinn, Quinn, and Hillier, *New American World* 2:349, 4:62.

26. Quinn and Quinn, *English New England Voyages,* 273; James Axtell, "The Power of Print in the Eastern Woodlands," *William and Mary Quarterly,* 3d ser., 44 (1987): 300–309.

27. Quinn and Quinn, *English New England Voyages,* 274.

28. Ibid., 277–78, 278 n. 2.

29. Ibid., 279–81.

30. Ibid., 282–85, 287–88, 293–95, 303.

31. Ibid., 349–50, 351, 413.

32. Ibid., 344, 438–39, 455–56, 476.

33. Ibid., 409–12.

Chapter 8, Political Definitions

1. Sir Edmund Andros to King James II, July 9, 1688, Great Britain, Public Record Office (hereafter PRO), CO1/65, No. 20.

2. Marcel Trudel, *The Beginnings of New France, 1524–1663* (Toronto: McClelland and Stewart, 1973), 56–57.

3. [Sir Ferdinando Gorges], "A Brief Relation of the Discovery and Plantation of New England," in Henry Sweetser Burrage, ed., *Gorges and the Grant of the Province of Maine* (Portland: State of Maine, 1923), 142.

4. On these early French and English initiatives, see John G. Reid, *Acadia, Maine, and New Scotland: Marginal Colonies in the Seventeenth Century* (Toronto: University of Toronto Press, 1981), 14–20.

5. Reuben Gold Thwaites, ed., *The Jesuit Relations and Allied Documents: Travels and Explorations of the Jesuit Missionaries in New France, 1610–1791,* 73 vols. (Cleveland: Burrows Brothers, 1896–1901), 3:223.

6. See Kenneth M. Morrison, *The Embattled Northeast: The Elusive Ideal of Alliance in Abenaki-Euramerican Relations* (Berkeley: University of California Press, 1984), 124–25.

7. Abraham Shurt to John Winthrop, June 28, 1636, "Winthrop Papers," *Massachusetts Historical Society Collections,* 4th ser., 6–7, 5th ser., 1 (1863–71), 6:570–71.

8. James Kendall Hosmer, ed., *Winthrop's Journal,* 2 vols. (New York: Barnes and Noble, 1908), 1:201.

9. Alaric Faulkner and Gretchen Fearon Faulkner, *The French at Pentagoet, 1635–1674: An Archaeological Portrait of the Acadian Frontier* (Augusta, Maine, and Saint John, N.B.: Maine Historic Preservation Commission and New Brunswick Museum, 1987), 16–20; Reid, *Acadia, Maine, and New Scotland,* 84–87.

10. Great Patent of New England, November 3, 1620, in Mary Frances Farnham, ed., "Documentary History of the State of Maine," *Maine Historical Society Collections,* series 2, 7 (1901), 26.

11. Charter of the Province of Maine, April 3, 1639, in Farnham, "Documentary History" 7:223–43. See also Charles E. Clark, *The Eastern Frontier: The Settlement of Northern New England, 1610–1763* (New York: Alfred A. Knopf, 1970), 16–20; John G. Reid, *Maine, Charles II, and Massachusetts: Governmental Relationships in Early Northern New England* (Portland: Maine Historical Society, 1977), 6–8.

12. For examples of early women settlers, see E. A. Churchill, "A Most Ordinary Lot of Men: The Fishermen at Richmond Island, Maine, in the Early Seventeenth Century," *New England Quarterly* 57 (1984): 191–92, 201–3.

13. John Josselyn, "An Account of Two Voyages to New England," *Massachusetts Historical Society Collections,* 3d ser., 3 (1833): 226.

14. Thomas Gorges to Sir Ferdinando Gorges, September 22, 1640, in Robert E. Moody, ed., *The Letters of Thomas Gorges: Deputy Governor of the Province of Maine, 1640–1643* (Portland: Maine Historical Society, 1978), 14; Thomas Gorges to Richard Bernard, October 9, 1640, in ibid., 17. On the proprietary structures of the province of Maine, see Reid, *Acadia, Maine, and New Scotland,* 54–55, 104–5.

15. Charles Thornton Libby, Robert E. Moody, and Neal W. Allen, eds., *Province and Court Records of Maine, 1636–1727,* 6 vols. (Portland: Maine Historical Society, 1928–75), 1:171. On the expulsion of Wheelwright and his followers from Massachusetts, see David E. Van Deventer, *The Emergence of Provincial New Hampshire, 1623–1741* (Baltimore: Johns Hopkins University Press, 1976), 6–8.

16. Libby, Moody, and Allen, *Province and Court Records* 1:133–34. See also Edwin Arnold Churchill, "Too Great the Challenge: The Birth and Death of Falmouth, Maine, 1624–1676" (Ph.D. diss., University of Maine, 1979), 166–98; Richard Arthur Preston, *Gorges of Plymouth Fort: A Life of Sir Ferdinando Gorges, Captain of Plymouth Fort, Governor of New England, and Lord of the Province of Maine* (Toronto: University of Toronto Press, 1953), 341–45; Reid, *Acadia, Maine, and New Scotland,* 114–24.

17. Reid, *Acadia, Maine, and New Scotland,* 131–35.

18. Report of Committee for Trade and Plantations, June 19, 1679, PRO, CO391/3, No. 21.

19. Grant of the Council for New England, April 22, 1635, PRO, CO1/8, No. 56. See also George Pratt Insh, *Scottish Colonial Schemes, 1620–1686* (Glasgow: Maclehose, Jackson, and Co., 1922), 89–90. The initial grant to William, Lord Alexander, in 1635 had excluded an area between Pemaquid and the Kennebec, which was to be divided among other members of the Council for New England, but the regrant to

Alexander's father in 1638 included this territory. See "Records of the Council for New England," *Proceedings of the American Antiquarian Society, 1867* (Cambridge, Mass.: John Wilson, 1867), 130-31.

20. Warrant, July 14, 1656, PRO, CO1/13, No. 4; Patent, August 9, 1656, PRO, CO1/13, No. 11; Faulkner and Faulkner, *The French at Pentagoet*, 21-22; Reid, *Acadia, Maine, and New Scotland*, 137-38.

21. Bounds of Sir Thomas Temple's Patent of Nova Scotia, July 1662, PRO, CO1/16, No. 86; Patent of the Duke of York, Massachusetts Archives, 3, ff. 303-5.

22. Samuel Maverick, "A Briefe Description of New England," British Library, Egerton MSS, 2395, 397; Josselyn, "Two Voyages," 345. Although exact population numbers are impossible to extract from surviving sources, Robert Earle Moody's estimate of some 775 English settlers in the Kennebec-Penobscot territory by 1675 is generally convincing. This compares with the same author's figure, based on militia records, of 3,500 between the Piscataqua and the Kennebec. Robert Earle Moody, "The Maine Frontier, 1607 to 1763" (Ph.D. diss., Yale University, 1933), 259-60.

23. Charles II to Sir Thomas Temple, December 31, 1667, PRO, CO1/21, No. 168.

24. Report of Grandfontaine, [1671], C11D, I, 139, and Jean Talon to Jean-Baptiste Colbert, November 2, 11, 1671, C11A, III, 161, 187-88, both in France, Archives des Colonies.

25. New York council minutes, June 9, 1677, in Franklin B. Hough, ed., "Pemaquid Papers," *Maine Historical Society Collections*, series 1, 5 (1857), 14-15.

26. Edward Randolph to Sir Leoline Jenkins, April 30, 1681, PRO, CO1/46, No. 130; see also Reid, *Maine, Charles II, and Massachusetts*, 184-94.

27. Reid, *Maine, Charles II, and Massachusetts*, 194-204.

28. Faulkner and Faulkner, *The French at Pentagoet*, 25-29.

29. Anthony Brockholst to Henry Jocelyn, August 24, 1682, in Hough, "Pemaquid Papers," 58-59. On John Nelson, see Richard R. Johnson, *John Nelson, Merchant Adventurer: A Life between Empires* (New York: Oxford University Press, 1991), esp. 24-27.

30. Edward Randolph to John Povey, June 21, 1688, in Robert Noxon Toppan and Alfred Thomas Scrope Goodrick, eds., *Edward Randolph; Including His Letters and Official Papers from the New England, Middle, and Southern Colonies in America, with Other Documents Relating Chiefly to the Vacating of the Royal Charter of the Colony of Massachusetts Bay, 1676-1703*, 7 vols. (Boston: Prince Society, 1898-1909), 4:224-25. On Saint-Castin and the Penobscots, see Morrison, *The Embattled Northeast*, 120-22, and Robert Le Blant, *Le Baron de St-Castin: Une figure légendaire de l'histoire Acadienne* (Dax, France: P. Pradeu, 1934), 41-73.

31. Thomas Gorges to Sir Ferdinando Gorges, September 19, 1642, in Moody, *Letters of Thomas Gorges,* 120; Petition of Scarborough and Falmouth, [1660], Scarboro Papers, principally from the Maybery estate, 1640–1818, Maine Historical Society Archives.

32. Morrison, *The Embattled Northeast,* 111.

33. Ibid., 113–16.

34. See David S. Lovejoy, *The Glorious Revolution in America* (New York: Harper and Row, 1972).

35. Morrison, *The Embattled Northeast,* 124–25.

36. Ibid., 128–37.

Chapter 9, "Wee Tooke Great Store of Cod-fish"

1. Harold Innis, *The Cod Fisheries: The History of an International Economy* (Toronto: University of Toronto Press, 1940); Charles L. Woodbury, *The Relation of the Fisheries to the Discovery and Settlement of North America* (Boston: Alfred Mudge and Son, 1880); Raymond McFarland, *A History of the New England Fisheries* (New York: D. Appleton and Co., 1911); Edwin A. Churchill, "Too Great the Challenge: The Birth and Death of Falmouth, Maine, 1624–1676" (Ph.D. diss., University of Maine, 1979); idem, "The Founding of Maine, 1600–1640: A Revisionist Interpretation," *Maine Historical Society Quarterly* 18 (1978): 21–54; Alaric Faulkner, "Archaeology of the Cod Fishery: Damariscove Island," *Historical Archaeology* 19 (1985): 57–86; Faith Harrington, "Sea Tenure in Seventeenth-Century New England: Native Americans and Englishmen in the Sphere of Marine Resources" (Ph.D. diss., University of California, Berkeley, 1985); idem, "Archaeology at the Isles of Shoals," *Context* 6 (1988); and idem, "The Dynamics of the Fishing Community at the Isles of Shoals," in Anne Yentsch and Mary Beaudry, eds., *The Art and Mystery of Historical Archaeology* (West Caldwell, N.J.: Telford Press, forthcoming).

2. John Smith, *A Description of New England* (1616) and *New England Trials* (1622), in Samuel Purchas, *Hakluytus Posthumus or Purchas His Pilgrimes,* 20 vols. (Glasgow: James MacLehose and Sons, 1906); William Wood, *New England's Prospect* (1634; reprint, Boston: E. M. Boynton, 1897).

3. Sources are divided over the location of the encounter; D. B. Quinn believes Gosnold's "Savage Rock" was Cape Elizabeth, whereas other authors state that it was near Nahant, Massachusetts. However, the majority follow S. E. Morison, who believes it was near Cape Neddick, Maine. See Purchas, *Hakluytus Posthumus,* 303–4, for Archer's description as quoted here. See also Bruce Bourque and Ruth Whitehead's description of this event in chapter 6 of this volume.

4. N. Salisbury, *Manitou and Providence: Indians, Europeans, and the*

Making of New England, 1500–1643 (New York: Oxford University Press, 1982), 55; Bruce Bourque and Ruth Whitehead, "Tarrentines and the Introduction of European Trade Goods in the Gulf of Maine," *Ethnohistory* 32 (1985): 327.

5. Purchas, *Hakluytus Posthumus*, 4–5.

6. Churchill, "Founding of Maine," 25.

7. Purchas, *Hakluytus Posthumus*, 305.

8. Charles H. Levermore, ed., *Forerunners and Competitors of the Pilgrims and Puritans* (Brooklyn: New England Society, 1912), 61.

9. Salisbury, *Manitou and Providence*, 90.

10. Quoted in Henry S. Burrage, *Rosier's Relation of Weymouth's Voyage to the Coast of Maine, 1605* (Portland: Gorges Society, 1887), 94–154, quotation on page 129.

11. In ibid., 129–54, quotation on page 134.

12. Champlain's *General Map of 1612* was published as Book Two of Samuel de Champlain, *The Works of Samuel de Champlain*, ed. H. P. Biggar, 6 vols. (Toronto: Champlain Society, 1922–36).

13. Leo Bonfanti, *The Massachusetts Bay Colony*, vol. 1, *Plymouth Colony to 1623* (Wakefield, Mass.: Pride Publications, 1974).

14. *Maine Historical Society Collections* 3 (1853): 294n.

15. Levermore, *Forerunners and Competitors*, 365.

16. Biard quoted in Reuben G. Thwaites, ed., *The Jesuit Relations and Allied Documents*, 73 vols. (1896–1901; reprint, New York: Pageant Book Co., 1959), 2:223.

17. Thwaites, *Jesuit Relations* 2:253.

18. Charles M. Andrews, *The Colonial Period of American History*, vol. 1, *The Settlements* (New Haven: Yale University Press, 1934), 98–100.

19. Robert F. Berkhofer, *The White Man's Indian: Images of the American Indians from Columbus to the Present* (New York: Vintage, 1978), 18.

20. Purchas, *Hakluytus Posthumus*, 78.

21. Quoted in James Wharton, *The Bounty of the Chesapeake: Fishing in Colonial Virginia* (Charlottesville: University Press of Virginia, 1957), 18.

22. Wharton, *Bounty of the Chesapeake*, 19.

23. Ibid., 25.

24. Sources for chart in figure 59 include Argall, in Purchas, *Hakluytus Posthumus*, 78; Biard, in Thwaites, *Jesuit Relations* 2:253; Charles F. Jenney, *The Fortunate Island of Monhegan* (Worcester, Mass.: Proceedings of the American Antiquity Society, 1921); Richard Preston, "Fishing and Plantation: New England in the Parliament of 1621," *American Historical Review* 65 (1939): 34; Edward Winslow, "Good Newes from New England or a True Relation of Things Very Remarkable at the Plantation of Plimoth in New England . . . 1624," in Alexander Young, ed., *Chronicles of the Pilgrim Fathers of the Colony of Plymouth, from 1602*

to 1625 (Boston: C. C. Little and J. Brown, 1841), 292–93; Smith, in Purchas, *Hakluytus Posthumus;* John Smith, *Advertisements for the Unexperienced Planters,* in *Massachusetts Historical Society Collections,* ser. 3, 3 (1833): 27; Christopher Levett, *A Voyage into New England, Begun in 1623 and Ended in 1624,* in *Maine Historical Society Collections* 2 (1847); and Sir William Alexander, *Encouragement to Colonies* (London, 1630), quoted in Innis, *Cod Fisheries,* 72.

25. Samuel E. Morison, *The Maritime History of Massachusetts, 1783–1860* (Boston: Houghton Mifflin Co., 1921); Innis, *Cod Fisheries,* 72; John Smith, *Description of New England,* in *Massachusetts Historical Society Collections,* ser. 3, 6 (1837): 103.

26. Smith, in Purchas, *Hakluytus Posthumus,* 300.

27. Levermore, *Forerunners and Competitors;* Henry S. Burrage, *George Folsom, John A. Poor, and a Century of Historical Research with Reference to Colonial Maine* (Portland: Maine Historical Society, 1926); Charles K. Bolton, *The Real Founders of New England: Stories of Their Life along the Coast, 1602–1628* (Boston: F. W. Faxon Co., 1929).

28. Jenney, *Fortunate Island.*

29. Wharton, *Bounty of the Chesapeake,* 22.

30. See Purchas, *Hakluytus Posthumus,* 301; Levermore, *Forerunners and Competitors,* 22; Jenney, *Fortunate Island;* Bolton, *Real Founders;* and Innis, *Cod Fisheries.*

31. Smith, in Purchas, *Hakluytus Posthumus,* 301.

32. Ibid.

33. Ibid.

34. Ibid.

35. Smith, *Advertisements,* 25; Preston, *Fishing and Plantation,* 34; Innis, *Cod Fisheries,* 72.

36. Smith, *Advertisements,* 25.

37. Smith in Purchas, *Hakluytus Posthumus,* 304.

38. Preston, "Fishing and Plantation," 34.

39. Smith, *Advertisements,* 27.

40. Ibid., 26.

41. Ibid., 27.

42. Winslow, "Good Newes," 292–93.

43. Sydney V. James, ed., *Three Visitors to Early Plymouth* (Plymouth, Mass.: Plimouth Plantation, 1963), 25.

44. Churchill, "Founding of Maine," 45.

45. This discussion, for example, will not focus on the prominent Plymouth Plantation or the lesser-known Cushnoc trading post, since these did not operate solely as fisheries.

46. Burrage, *Rosier's Relation,* 95.

47. At least this is Smith's version in his *Travels and Works, I,* ed. E. Arber (Edinburgh: John Grant, 1910), 187, 240, and in his *Descrip-*

tion of New England, 103. In his *Advertisements,* 307, he describes the episode somewhat differently and says his fifteen men, or eighteen at the most, took more than sixty thousand cod in less than a month, thus cutting down two variables (the number of men and the amount of time it took to catch the fish) and amplifying the amount of fish caught and processed.

48. Bolton, *Real Founders,* 29; and Jenney, *Fortunate Island,* 321.

49. William Bradford, *Of Plymouth Plantation, 1620–1647,* ed. Samuel E. Morison (New York: Knopf, 1952).

50. Edwin A. Churchill, "Introduction: Colonial Pemaquid," in Helen B. Camp, *Archaeological Excavations at Pemaquid, Maine, 1965–1974* (Augusta: Maine State Museum, 1975), p. ix.

51. Excavations at Pemaquid were directed by Helen Camp from 1965 to 1974 and by Dr. Robert Bradley from 1978 to 1982.

52. James, *Three Visitors,* 15–16.

53. Ibid.

54. Bradford, *Of Plymouth Plantation,* 99.

55. Gretchen F. Faulkner, "The Archaeological and Historical Documentation of the Cod Fishery on Damariscove Island" (unpublished ms. in possession of the author), 4.

56. Ibid., 5.

57. During the summers of 1979 and 1980, Alaric Faulkner, of the University of Maine, directed a summer field school in historical archaeology that focused on the history and land use of Damariscove Island and particularly on locating Gorges's early fishing station; see Faulkner, "Archaeology of the Cod Fishery," 57–86.

58. *Massachusetts Historical Society Collections* 2 (1902): 79.

59. *York Deeds* (Portland: B. Thurston and Co., 1887), book II, folio 4.

60. Smith, *Description of New England,* 103.

61. Thomas Johnson, "The William Pepperrell Site on Appledore Island, Isles of Shoals: The Architectural Debris and Its Analysis" (unpublished ms., 1989, in possession of the author), 28; Abbott Lowell Cummings, *The Framed Houses of Massachusetts Bay, 1625–1725* (Cambridge: Harvard University Press, 1979), 153.

62. Wilbur D. Spencer, *Pioneers on Maine Rivers* (Portland, Maine: Lakeside Printing, 1930), 54.

63. Harrington, "Sea Tenure," 131; Richard M. Candee, "Wooden Buildings in Early Maine and New Hampshire: A Technological and Cultural History, 1600–1720" (Ph.D. diss., University of Pennsylvania, 1976), 14, 82, 83; John W. Durel, "From Strawberry Banke to Puddle Dock: The Evolution of a Neighborhood, 1630–1850" (Ph.D. diss., University of New Hampshire, 1984), 16.

64. Jere R. Daniell, *Colonial New Hampshire* (Millwood, N.Y.: KTO Press, 1981), 26.

65. Military construction during World War II has probably had a severe destructive impact on the archaeology of Odiorne's Point, but this needs to be borne out by testing. See "State Coastal Properties Project: Part II, Fort Dearborn at Odiorne Point," (unpublished report, 1982, in possession of the author), compiled by the Thoresen Group for the state of New Hampshire, with archaeological research and recommendations by author.

66. Bradford, *Of Plymouth Plantation,* 146.

67. Ibid., 149.

68. Wallace Notestein, *The English People on the Eve of Colonization* (New York: Harper and Row, 1962), 263–64.

Chapter 10, Fort Pentagoet and Castin's Habitation

1. Jacob W. Gruber, "The French Settlements on St. Croix Island, Maine: Excavations for the National Park Service, 1968–69," (1972), ms. on file, Historical Archaeology Laboratory, University of Maine, Orono; John L. Cotter, "Premier établissement français en Acadia: Sainte-Croix," *Dossiers de l'archéologie* 27 (1974): 60–71; Norman F. Barka, "Historic Sites Archaeology at Portland Point, New Brunswick, Canada, 1631–c. 1850 A.D." (Ph.D. diss., Harvard University, 1965).

2. G. W. Brown et al., eds., *Dictionary of Canadian Biography* (Toronto: University of Toronto Press, 1966), 1:505.

3. Samuel Adams Drake, *Nooks and Corners of the New England Coast* (1875; reprint, Detroit: Singing Tree Press, 1969), 75–76.

4. M. A. MacDonald, *Fortune and La Tour* (Toronto: Methuen 1983); John G. Reid, *Acadia, Maine, and New Scotland: Marginal Colonies in the Seventeenth Century* (Toronto: University of Toronto Press, 1981).

5. Brown et al., *Dictionary of Canadian Biography,* 1:504; M. Delafosse, "La Rochelle et le Canada au XVIIe Siècle," *Revue d'histoire de L'Amérique Française* 4 (1951): 473.

6. G. Debien, "Engagés pour le Canada au XVIIe Siècle vus de La Rochelle," *Revue d'histoire de L'Amérique Française* 6, no. 2 (1952): 177–233, and 6, no. 3 (1952): 374–407.

7. M. Delafosse, "La Rochelle et le Canada," 471.

8. Myra Stanbury, *Batavia* (exhibition catalogue) (Perth: Department of Maritime Archaeology, Western Australian Museum, n.d.); C. L. van der Pijl-Ketl, ed., *The Ceramic Load of the "Witte Leeuw," 1613* (Amsterdam: Rijksmuseum, n.d.), 246.

9. Alaric Faulkner and Gretchen F. Faulkner, *The French at Pentagoet, 1635–1674: An Archaeological Portrait of the Acadian Frontier* (Augusta, Maine, and Saint John, N.B.: Maine Historic Preservation Commission and New Brunswick Museum, (1987), 145–51.

10. Norman F. Barka, "Historic Sites Archaeology at Portland Point,

New Brunswick, Canada, 1631-c. 1850 A.D." (Ph.D. diss., Harvard University, 1965), 450-51.

11. James K. Hosmer, *Winthrop's Journal: History of New England, 1630-1649* (New York: Charles Scribner's Sons, 1908), 178; "Commission of Peter Mutton, Master of a Trading Vessel, for Charles d'Aulnay" (1643), Massachusetts Archives, vol. 2, fol. 477a.

12. William Bradford, *Of Plymouth Plantation, 1620-1647*, ed. Samuel E. Morison (New York: A. Knopf, 1952), 279.

13. Jean Chapelot et al., *Potiers de Santonge—Huit Siècles d'Artisinat Rural* (exhibition catalogue) (Paris: Musée National des Arts et Traditions Populaires, 1975), 119-21.

14. Geneviève Massignon, "La Seigneurie de Charles de Menou d'Aulnay, Gouverneur de l'Acadie, 1635-50," *Revue d'Histoire de l'Amérique Française* 16 (1962-63): 496, 500, 501. Massignon reproduces the d'Aulnay crest from a stained glass window of the church St-Sulpice d'Aulnay, in the town of d'Aulnay's mother's family in France. It has in common with the badge a central cross surrounded by an oak leaf cluster.

15. Pierre Goubert, *The Ancien Régime: French Society, 1600–1750* (New York: Harper and Row, 1973), 162.

16. C.f. Ivor Noel Hume, *Martin's Hundred* (New York: Knopf, 1982), 85.

17. Ibid., 60.

18. Goubert, *The Ancien Régime*, 166.

19. Faulkner and Faulkner, *The French at Pentagoet*, 135-61.

20. Wm. F. Ganong, ed. and trans., *The Description and Natural History of the Coasts of North America by Nicholas Denys* (Toronto: Champlain Society, 1908), 154, 109.

21. *Collection de manuscrits contenant lettres, memoires, et autres documents historiques relatifs à la Nouvelle-France*, vol. 1 (Québec: A Coté and Co., 1883), 191-94.

22. James Phinney Baxter, ed., *Documentary History of the State of Maine*, vol. 10 (Portland: Maine Historical Society, 1907), 29.

23. Faulkner and Faulkner, *The French at Pentagoet*, 222-24 (analysis after Arthur Spiess).

24. Ganong, *Coasts of North America*, 154.

25. Faulkner and Faulkner, *The French at Pentagoet*, 226 (analysis after Catherine Carlson).

26. Jorge Barrera, personal communication, March 1985.

27. Iain C. Walker, "Clay Tobacco Pipes, with Particular Reference to the Bristol Industry," *History and Archaeology* 11 (1977): 1420; Adrian Oswald, "Clay Pipes for the Archaeologist," *British Archaeology Reports* 14 (1975): 152.

28. Oswald, "Clay Pipes," 117–18, fig. 22, no. 14; Helen B. Camp, *Archaeological Excavations at Pemaquid, Maine, 1965–1974* (Augusta: Maine State Museum, 1975), 57, 59, 78; idem, "White Clay Tobacco Pipes," *Maine Archaeological Society Bulletin* 22 (1982): 24, 33, fig. 4.

29. Robert Le Blant, *Le Baron de St-Castin: Une figure légendaire de l'histoire Acadienne* (Dax, France: P. Pradeu, 1934), 157–60.

30. Wm. Inglis Morse, ed., "General Census of Acadia by Gargas, 1687–1688," *Acadiensia Nova* (1934), 149, 151.

31. Lise Boily and Jean-François Blanchette, *The Bread Ovens of Québec* (Ottawa: National Museum of Man, 1979).

32. David Christianson, "Acadian Archaeological Research at Belle-isle Nova Scotia," *The Occasional: An Occasional Journal for Nova Scotia* 8 (1984): 17–21; idem, "Belleisle 1983: Excavations at a Pre-Expulsion Acadian Site," *Nova Scotia Museum Curatorial Report Number 48* (Halifax: Nova Scotia Department of Education, 1984).

33. Oswald, "Clay Pipes," 152. Although known pipe makers number more than six thousand, relatively few exported their products to the New World in quantity during the colonial period. In this case the pipe makers are listed on the "Freedom Rolls" of Bristol in the years mentioned, marking the completion of their apprenticeship under a master pipe maker. Once free to work on their own, these individuals often marked the stem, heel, or bowl of their pipes with their initials. The Evans and Tippett families are well-known exporters of tobacco pipes to New England, and their products show up frequently on late-seventeenth-century sites.

34. Le Blant, *Le Baron de St-Castin*, 131–32. The English merchant, John Nelson, was a nephew of Sir Thomas Temple, who controlled Acadia for most of the English interregnum from 1654 to 1670. Nelson's consignment of wine for Saint-Castin was actually Spanish, coming from Malaga aboard the English vessel *Jane*. See extract from "The Memorials of the English and French Commissaries Concerning the Limits of Nova Scotia or Acadia," quoted in George A. Wheeler, *History of Castine, Penobscot, and Brooksville, Me.* (Bangor: Burr and Robinson, 1875), 225.

35. Le Blant, *Le Baron de St-Castin*, 82–83.

36. Beads from Saint-Castin's Habitation are principally of types IIa37 (aqua blue), IIa14 (white), and IIa7 (black), whereas those from seventeenth-century contexts at Pentagoet are predominantly of a larger IIa46 (blue) variety. Kenneth Kidd and Martha Ann Kidd, "A Classification System for Glass Beads for the Use of Field Archaeologists," *Canadian Historic Sites: Occasional Papers in Archaeology and History 1* (Ottawa: Parks Canada, 1974), 56.

37. Camp, *Archaeological Excavations at Pemaquid*, 47, 66, 69; Emer-

son W. Baker, *The Clarke and Lake Company: The Historical Archaeology of a Seventeenth-Century Maine Settlement* (Augusta: Maine Historic Preservation Commission, 1985), 35–37.

38. George A. Wheeler, *Castine Past and Present* (Boston: Rockwell and Churchill Press, 1896), 81. Additional religious artifacts including a beaver effigy and a cross, both cast in lead, and an "IHS" ring were recovered from Castin's Habitation in 1992.

39. Faulkner and Faulkner, *The French at Pentagoet*, 28.

40. Kenneth E. Lewis, *The American Frontier: An Archaeological Study of Settlement Pattern and Process,* Studies in Historical Archaeology (Orlando: Academic Press, 1984), 16–18.

41. Bradford, *Of Plymouth Plantation,* 279.

42. "Lettre de Talon du Ministre Colbert, November 11, 1671," *Rapport de l'Archiviste de la Province de Québec, 1930–31* (Québec: Rédempti Paradis, 1931), 163.

43. *Collection de manuscrits* 1:224; Brown et al., *Dictionary of Canadian Biography* 1:63.

44. James Deetz, *In Small Things Forgotten* (New York: Anchor Doubleday, 1977), 36–37.

45. Goubert, *The Ancien Régime,* 53, 153.

46. Ibid., 53–56.

47. Ibid., 153, 163, 166.

Chapter 11, Mid-Seventeenth-Century Maine

1. W. Noel Sainsbury, ed., "Minutes of the Council for Foreign Plantations, June 21, 1671," vol. 7, no. 566, and "Account of the Militia in the Province of Maine, February 16, 1672," vol. 7, no. 762, both in *Calendar of State Papers, Colonial Series,* 46 vols. to date (London: various publishers, 1860–); Evarts B. Greene and Virginia D. Harrington, *American Population before the Federal Census of 1790* (New York: Columbia University Press, 1932), xxiii.

2. Alaric Faulkner and Gretchen Faulkner, *The French at Pentagoet, 1635–1674: An Archaeological Portrait of the Acadian Frontier* (Augusta: Maine Historic Preservation Commission, 1987), 3, 16–29. See also George A. Wheeler, *History of Castine, Penobscot, and Brooksville, Maine* (Cornwall, N.Y.: privately printed, 1923), 14–31.

3. Edwin A. Churchill, "The Founding of Maine, 1600–1640: A Revisionist Interpretation," *Maine Historical Society Quarterly* 18 (1978): 30, 48–49; Edwin A. Churchill, "Early Settlement," in Gerald E. Morris, ed., *The Maine Bicentennial Atlas: An Historical Survey* (Portland: Maine Historical Society, 1976), 2–3, pl. 5.

4. Edwin A. Churchill, "Too Great the Challenge: The Birth and Death of Falmouth, Maine, 1624–1676" (Ph.D. diss., University of

Maine, 1979), 108, 260–63. The same pattern was noticed in Gary T. Lord, "The Politics and Social Structures of Seventeenth Century Portsmouth, New Hampshire" (Ph.D. diss., University of Virginia, 1976), 18, and Emerson W. Baker, "Trouble to the Eastward: The Failure of Anglo-Indian Relations in Early Maine" (Ph.D. diss., College of William and Mary, 1986), 73–74, 79, 86, 92.

5. Charles E. Clark, *The Eastern Frontier: The Settlement of Northern New England, 1610–1763* (New York: Alfred A. Knopf, 1970), 65–66; Churchill, "Founding of Maine," 30–31; William Hubbard, *The History of the Indian Wars in New England*, ed. Samuel G. Drake, 2 vols. (Roxbury, Mass.: W. Elliot Woodward, 1865), 2:76; John Josselyn, "An Account of Two Voyages to New England," *Massachusetts Historical Society Collections*, 3d ser., 3 (1833): 345; Samuel Maverick, "A Brief Description of New England and the Several Towns Therein, Together with the Present Government Thereof," *Massachusetts Historical Society Proceedings*, 2d ser., 1 (1884–85): 231–32; Chevalier de Grandfontaine, "The River and Country of Pentagoet and Other Surrounding Places," in Faulkner and Faulkner, *The French at Pentagoet*, 280.

6. John Smith, "A Description of New England," *Travels and Works of Captain John Smith*, ed. Edward Arber, 2 vols. (Edinburgh: John Grant, 1910), 203.

7. Substantial road-related information is contained in Charles T. Libby, Robert E. Moody, and Neal W. Allen, eds., *Province and Court Records of Maine, 1636–1727*, 6 vols. (Portland: Maine Historical Society, 1928–75). The following items from volume 2 are typical: "Order for the Repair of Roads from Kittery to York, June 30, 1653," 14–15; "Order for Ferry over Cape Porpus River, July 5, 1664," 158.

8. Faulkner and Faulkner, *The French at Pentagoet*, 160, 251.

9. Michael Wigglesworth, "God's Controversy with New England . . . 1662," in *Massachusetts Historical Society Proceedings* 12 (1871): 83–84; Howard Mumford Jones, *O Strange New World American Culture: The Formative Years* (New York: Viking Press, 1964), 55–61; Roderick Nash, *Wilderness and the American Mind* (New Haven: Yale University Press, 1967), 1–3, 28–29, 39; John R. Stilgoe, *Common Landscapes of America, 1580–1845* (New Haven: Yale University Press, 1982), 7–12.

10. John Winter to Robert Trelawny, June 18, 1634, in James P. Baxter, ed., *The Trelawny Papers* (Portland, Maine: Hoyt, Fogg, and Donham, 1884), 26–27; Edwin A. Churchill, "Introduction: Colonial Pemaquid," in Helen B. Camp, *Archaeological Excavations at Pemaquid, Maine, 1965–1974* (Augusta: Maine State Museum, 1975), xi–xii, xviii; Franklin B. Hough, ed., "Papers Relating to Pemaquid and Parts Adjacent in the Present State of Maine . . . ," *Maine Historical Society Collections*, 1st ser., 5 (1857): 18–23.

11. Faulkner and Faulkner, *The French at Pentagoet*, 3, 29, 38, 268–

69; Georges Cerbeland Salagnac, "Abbadie de Saint-Castin, Jean-Vincent 'P,'" *Dictionary of Canadian Biography*, vol. 2 (Toronto: University of Toronto Press, 1969), 4–7.

12. Thomas Gorges to Sir Ferdinando Gorges, September 19, 1642, in Robert E. Moody, ed., *The Letters of Thomas Gorges: Deputy Governor of the Province of Maine, 1640–1643* (Portland: Maine Historical Society, 1978), 120–22. Harald E. L. Prins, "Turmoil on the Wabnaki Frontier: 1524–1678" (manuscript chapter for a forthcoming Maine history text); Harald E. L. Prins and Bruce J. Bourque, "Norridgewock: Village Translocation on the New England–Acadian Frontier," *Man in the Northeast*, no. 33 (1987): 141–42.

13. Nash, *Wilderness*, 2, 29–30.

14. Churchill, "Founding of Maine," 35–41; "Proceedings against Gregory Cassell, 1654," *Records of the Court of Assistant of the Colony of Massachusetts Bay, 1630–1692*, 3 vols. (Boston: County of Suffolk, 1901–28), 3:59–63.

15. This and the following two paragraphs are based on Churchill, "Falmouth," 142–48. More recently, Karen O. Kupperman provided a highly detailed study on the subject "Climate and Mastery of the Wilderness in Seventeenth Century New England," in *Seventeenth Century New England* (Boston: Colonial Society of Massachusetts, 1984), 3–38.

16. Arnold Toynbee was thoroughly impressed with the area's environmental harshness, in 1930 stating that Maine was "a relic of seventeenth century New England . . . still inhabited by woodmen and watermen and hunters," earning scant livings caring for tourists. Arnold J. Toynbee, *A Study of History*, vol. 2 (London: Oxford, 1939), 294–96. It might be suggested that he overstated the case a bit.

17. Churchill, "Falmouth," 149–52; Howard S. Russell, *A Long Deep Furrow: Three Centuries of Farming in New England* (Hanover, N.H.: University Press of New England, 1976); Clarence A. Day, *A History of Maine Agriculture, 1609–1860* (Orono: University of Maine Press, 1954), 38–39.

18. Churchill, "Falmouth," 152–55; see also William Cronon, *Changes in the Land: Indians, Colonists, and the Ecology of New England* (New York: Hill and Wang, 1983), 132–34, 199–200.

19. Churchill, "Falmouth," 236–65, 277–80; Baker, "Trouble to the Eastward," 79; Robert E. Moody, "The Maine Frontier 1607 to 1760" (Ph.D. diss., Yale University, 1933), 261.

20. Churchill, "Falmouth," 157–61; Camp, *Pemaquid*, 7–9, 28, 37, 44–45, 47, 49. Similar patterns were found at the Clarke and Lake settlement at Arrowsic, Maine. See James Leaman, "Archaeological Report on the Clarke and Lake Settlement, Arrowsic, Maine, for 1970–1975" (typescript, Maine State Museum, 1975).

21. Faulkner and Faulkner, *The French at Pentagoet*, 196–97, 223–24, 228, 237, 249–54, 267–68. Decreasing availability of wild game because of overhunting was discussed by Cronon (*Changes in the Land*, 99–105), although he emphasized patterns in southern and central New England. The lack of wild game faunal remains at the 1658–76 Clarke and Lake site at Arrowsic, along with the evidence from Pentagoet, suggests a similar pattern farther north. See Emerson W. Baker, *The Clarke and Lake Company: The Historical Archaeology of a Seventeenth-Century Maine Settlement* (Augusta: Maine Historical Preservation Commission, 1985).

22. "Depositions regarding Robert Nash, June–July, 1645," in James P. Baxter, ed., *The Baxter Manuscripts*, vols. 4–6, 9–24 of *The Documentary History of the State of Maine*, 24 vols. (Portland, Maine: various publishers, 1889–1916), 4:5–8.

23. Faulkner and Faulkner, *The French at Pentagoet*, 20, 28, 107, quotation on page 20; John G. Reid, *Acadia, Maine, and New Scotland: Marginal Colonies in the Seventeenth Century* (Toronto: University of Toronto Press, 1981), 135–36, 161–62; George A. Rawlyk, *Nova Scotia's Massachusetts: A Study of Massachusetts–Nova Scotia Relations, 1630–1784* (Montreal: McGill-Queens Press, 1973), 21–25, 37–39; William I. Roberts III, "The Fur Trade of New England in the Seventeenth Century" (Ph.D. diss., University of Pennsylvania, 1958), 179–80, 203–6.

24. Charles E. Banks, *History of York*, 2 vols. (Boston: Murray Printing Co., 1931–35) 2:210–11; "Presentments of Maine Towns for Not Providing Powder and Bullets, July 2, 1672," in Libby, Moody, and Allen, *Province and Court Records* 2:242.

25. "Account of the Militia in the Province of Maine, February 16, 1672," *Calendar of State Papers*, vol. 7, no. 762.

26. "Order for the Purchase of Powder & Shott for Ye Traine Bandes, April 12, 1677," Biddeford Town Records from 1653 to 1773, transcribed by Ida F. Twombley (typescript, microfilm copy), Maine State Archives, Augusta; "Order for the Ordering of Troops at Saco, Wells and Cape Porpus, July 5, 1653," Baxter, *Documentary History* 4:91; "Presentment of Nathaniel Cloyce and Abigal Williams, October 1, 1667," in Libby, Moody, and Allen, *Province and Court Records* 1:335–36; Hubbard, *Indian Wars* 2:145; Richard M. Candee, "Wooden Buildings in Early Maine and New Hampshire: A Technological and Cultural History, 1600–1720" (Ph.D. diss., University of Pennsylvania, 1976), 260–64.

27. This information was derived from the analysis of 218 Maine inventories dating from 1635 to 1700, found in Libby, Moody, and Allen, *Province and Court Records*, vols. 1 and 2; *York Deeds*, 18 vols., various eds. (Portland [vols. 1–5] and Bethel [vols. 12–17]: various publishers, 1887–1910), vol. 5; and York County Registry of Probate, Alfred, Maine, vols. 1 and 2.

28. William Hubbard, "A General History of New England," *Massachusetts Historical Society Collections*, 2d ser., 6 (1815): 545; David Grayson Allen, "*Vacuum Domicilium:* The Social and Cultural Landscape of Seventeenth-Century New England," in Jonathan L. Fairbanks and Robert F. Trent, eds., *New England Begins: The Seventeenth Century*, 3 vols. (Boston: Museum of Fine Arts, 1982), 1:1–2, 49. Emerson Baker noted in a personal communication that some of the English place-names were introduced not by the first settlers but by Massachusetts when it annexed Maine. Further investigation revealed four major examples. In two—the replacement of the earlier English names of Gorgeana and Somersetshire by the town and county names of York respectively—Bay Colony leadership was clearly erasing references to Sir Ferdinando Gorges, their arch-rival for the region. The other two instances, Scarborough and Falmouth, were new names for new entities made up of several earlier, smaller units. For example, Scarborough, established in 1658, encompassed the older communities of Black Point, Blue Point, Dunstan, West Spurwink, and Stratton's Island. The earlier names of other Maine towns were unchanged by the Massachusetts takeover. Information from *Letters of Thomas Gorges;* Libby, Moody, and Allen, *Province and Court Records*, vols. 1 and 2; *York Deeds* 1; and Sybil Noyes, Charles T. Libby, and Walter G. Davis, *Genealogical Dictionary of Maine and New Hampshire* (1928–39; reprint, Baltimore: Genealogical Publishing Co., 1972).

29. Thomas Gorges to Richard Bernard, October 9, 1640, in *Letters of Thomas Gorges*, 17.

30. Churchill, "Falmouth," 117–21, 176–78; Thomas Gorges to John Winter, October 1640, in *Letters of Thomas Gorges*, 20–21.

31. Churchill, "Falmouth," 121–24, 274–86, 309–15. The tie between individual status and land grants is also considered in Sumner Chilton Powell, *Puritan Village: The Formation of a New England Town* (Garden City, N.Y.: Doubleday and Co., 1965), 118, 172–75; Darrett B. Rutman, *Winthrop's Boston: Portrait of a Puritan Town, 1630–1649* (Chapel Hill: University of North Carolina Press, 1965), 72–82; and Kenneth A. Lockridge, *A New England Town: The First Hundred Years, Dedham, Massachusetts, 1626–1736* (New York: W. W. Norton and Co., 1970), 10–12.

32. See especially Camp, *Pemaquid,* and Baker, *Clarke and Lake.*

33. Faulkner and Faulkner, *The French at Pentagoet*, 196–97, 237, 249–54, 261, 267–68.

34. The history of seventeenth-century Maine religion has yet to be written. Jonathan Greenleaf's 1821 *Sketches of the Ecclesiastical History of the State of Maine* is both fragmented and incomplete. A number of denominational studies provide substantial information, including Calvin Clark, *History of the Congregational Churches of Maine*, vol. 2 (Portland: Congregational Christian Conference of Maine, 1935), 1–70;

Henry Burrage, *History of the Baptists in Maine* (Portland: Marks Printing House, 1904), 1–27; Jonathan M. Chu, "The Social and Political Context of Heterodoxy: Quakerism in Seventeenth Century Kittery," *New England Quarterly* 54 (1981): 365–84. Also, mention can be found in Clark, *Eastern Frontier*, 37–49, 79–89. The information in the text on early Anglo-Maine religion derives partly from these and a number of other minor secondary sources but reflects more basically several primary sources consulted for sections in Churchill, "Falmouth," 128–30, 302–9, and Edwin A. Churchill, "English Beachheads in Seventeenth Century Maine" (manuscript chapter for a forthcoming Maine history text). These sources include Libby, Moody, and Allen, *Province and Court Records*, "Biddeford Town Records," and "Kittery Town Records, 1648–1709" (manuscript, microfilm copy, Maine State Archives, Augusta). Also of great utility was Noyes, Libby, and Davis, *Genealogical Dictionary of Maine and New Hampshire*.

35. Faulkner and Faulkner, *The French at Pentagoet*, 18, 24, 43, 74, 172. More religious activity than indicated by Faulkner and Faulkner is suggested by Wheeler, *History of Castine*, 96. One gets a similar impression from G.-M. Dumas, "Leonard de Chartes," in G. W. Brown et al., eds., *Dictionary of Canadian Biography* (Toronto: University of Toronto Press, 1966), 1:468–69.

36. Josselyn, "Two Voyages," 344–45; Hubbard, *Indian Wars* 2:73.

37. Churchill, "Founding of Maine," 31–49; T. H. Breen and Stephen Foster, "Moving to the New World: The Character of Early Massachusetts Immigration," *William and Mary Quarterly*, 3d ser., 30 (1973): 216–17.

38. Churchill, "Falmouth," 148–49; Russell, *Long Deep Furrow*, 10–11, 39, 47, 54; Darrett Rutman, *Husbandmen of Plymouth: Farms and Villages in the Old Colony, 1620–1692* (Boston: Beacon Press, 1967), 5, 42–43; Stephen Taber, "The Mechanics of Frost Heaving," *Journal of Geology* 33 (1930): 303–7.

39. Hubbard, *Indian Wars* 2:72–75; Josselyn, "Two Voyages," 344; Maverick, "Brief Description of New England," 232.

40. Maverick, "Brief Description of New England," 232; Josselyn, "Two Voyages," 347.

41. Hubbard, *Indian Wars* 2:75.

42. Richard M. Candee, "Merchant and Millwright," *Old-Time New England* 60 (1969–70): 145–47; Hubbard, *Indian Wars* 2:223–24.

43. Churchill, "Falmouth," 264–65; Moody, "Maine Frontier," 263.

44. For this and the following three paragraphs, see Laurel T. Ulrich, *Good Wives: Image and Reality in the Lives of Women in Northern New England, 1650–1750* (New York: Oxford University Press, 1980), 20–24, 27–32, 43–44. A brief summary of women's activities at the 1630s fishing station at Richmond Island, Maine, is provided in Edwin A. Churchill,

"A Most Ordinary Lot of Men: The Fishermen at Richmond Island, Maine, in the Early Seventeenth Century," *New England Quarterly* 57 (1984): 191–92. The mid-seventeenth-century Falmouth population profile is considered in Churchill, "Falmouth," 262–65, 367–409, and educational practices in the community are discussed on 139–40.

45. Ulrich, *Good Wives*, 13.

46. Ibid., 35–50 (quote on 37–38).

47. The propensity for rapid remarriage was repeatedly demonstrated in Falmouth from 1640 to 1675 (see Churchill, "Falmouth," 367–409).

48. Barbara McLean Ward, "Women's Property and Family Continuity in Eighteenth Century Connecticut," in Peter Benes, ed., *Early American Probate Inventories* (Boston: Boston University, 1989), 74–85.

49. Bruce Bourque and Ruth Whitehead, "Tarrentines and the Introduction of European Trade Goods in the Gulf of Maine," *Ethnohistory* 32 (1985): 327–41; Baker, *Clarke and Lake*, 7–14; Churchill, "Colonial Pemaquid," ix–xi.

50. Faulkner and Faulkner, *The French at Pentagoet*, 1, 3, 14–23, 28; Rawlyk, *Nova Scotia's Massachusetts*, 25.

51. James Truslow Adams, "Morton, Thomas," *Dictionary of American Biography*, vol. 13, ed. Dumas Malone (New York: Charles Scribner's Sons, 1934), 267; Salagnac, "Saint-Castine," 4–7; Churchill, "Colonial Pemaquid," xi, xviii. Concerning trading guns to the Indians, see Roberts, "Fur Trade," 53–62, and William Bradford, *Of Plymouth Plantation* (New York: Alfred A. Knopf, 1952), 279. Baker ("Trouble to the Eastward," 124–30) notes a real basis for the anxieties in the less than stellar character of many of those Europeans on the frontier carrying out the actual trade with the Indians.

52. Josselyn, "Two Voyages," 349; Churchill, "Falmouth," 155; Moody, "Maine Frontier," 267–70.

53. Candee, "Merchant and Millwright," 133; Churchill, "Falmouth," 291–96.

54. William D. Williamson, *The History of Maine*, 2 vols. (Hallowell: Glazier, Masters and Co., 1832), vol. 1, chaps. 21–23, and vol. 2, chaps. 11–13; Moody, "Maine Frontier," section 1, 182–89, and chaps. 6–7, and section 2, chaps. 1–3, 8; Edwin A. Churchill, "Colonial Wars," in Morris, *Maine Bicentennial Atlas*, 6–7, pls. 11, 13. See also John Noble, "King Philip's War in Maine" (Master's thesis, University of Maine, 1970), and Richard M. Gaffney, "Lovewell's War in Maine, 1722–1725" (Master's thesis, University of Maine, 1961).

55. Reid, *Acadia, Maine, and New Scotland*, chap. 8; Rawlyk, *Nova Scotia's Massachusetts*, chaps. 3–7; Roberts, "Fur Trade," 203–12; Wheeler, *Castine*, 17–29.

Chapter 12, The World of Thomas Gorges

1. Research on Thomas Gorges is possible only through the extensive editorial work and research of Robert Moody, who transcribed Gorges's surviving letterbooks. See Robert E. Moody, ed., *The Letters of Thomas Gorges: Deputy Governor of the Province of Maine, 1640–1643* (Portland: Maine Historical Society, 1978); Robert E. Moody, "Thomas Gorges, Proprietary Governor of Maine, 1640–1643," *Massachusetts Historical Society Proceedings* 75 (1963): 10–26. The word *Wabanaki* is used in this chapter as a generic term for the native people of the region and for groups and individuals whose specific tribal identity is unknown.

2. Cotton Mather, *Magnalia Christi Americana,* 2 vols. (Hartford: S. Andrus, 1820), 2:573.

3. Charles E. Banks, *History of York, Maine* (Boston: Calkins Press, 1931), 59.

4. Henry Burrage, *The Beginnings of Colonial Maine, 1602–1658* (Portland: Marks Printing House, 1914), 317–21; Banks, *History of York,* 120–30; Charles E. Clark, *The Eastern Frontier: The Settlement of Northern New England, 1610–1763* (New York: Alfred A. Knopf, 1970), 16–20.

5. Paul J. Lindholt, ed., *John Josselyn, Colonial Traveler: A Critical Edition of Two Voyages to New England* (Hanover: University Press of New England, 1988), 19.

6. Moody, *Letters of Thomas Gorges,* 7.

7. Ibid., 6, xi.

8. Ibid., 45.

9. For comparative data on New England and southern families, see Lorena S. Walsh, "'Till Death Us Do Part': Marriage and Family in Seventeenth-Century Maryland," in Thad W. Tate and David L. Ammerman, eds., *The Chesapeake in the Seventeenth Century: Essays on Anglo-American Society and Politics* (New York: W. W. Norton and Co., 1979), 126–29; Gary B. Nash, "Social Development," in Jack P. Greene and J. R. Pole, eds., *Colonial British America: Essays in the New History of the Early Modern Era* (Baltimore: Genealogical Publishing Co., 1984), 235–45; Banks, *History of York,* 191; and Moody, *Letters of Thomas Gorges,* 23, 24, 92–93, 96.

10. Perhaps the best known of these ships was the *Angel Gabriel,* which sank in a hurricane while anchored at Pemaquid on August 15, 1635. Edwin A. Churchill, "Introduction: Colonial Pemaquid," in Helen B. Camp, *Archaeological Excavations at Pemaquid, Maine, 1965–1974* (Augusta: Maine State Museum, 1975), 12. A twenty-two-foot-long dugout canoe, carved out of one tree and probably used by seventeenth-century fishermen, was excavated in 1986 from the sands of Biddeford Pool. Emerson W. Baker, "The Biddeford Dugout Canoe" (manuscript, 1988, in possession of the author).

11. Moody, *Letters of Thomas Gorges*, 45.

12. Ibid.; Alaric Faulkner, "Archaeology of the Cod Fishery: Damariscove Island," *Historical Archaeology* 19 (1985): 60–61. For the growth of Boston, see Bernard Bailyn, *The New England Merchants in the Seventeenth Century* (Cambridge: Harvard University Press, 1955), 95–98.

13. Moody, *Letters of Thomas Gorges*, 24–25, 45, 63, 92, 97, 99–100; Christopher Levett, "A Voyage unto New England," in *Maine and the Age of Discovery* (Portland: Maine Historical Society, 1988), 44; Emerson W. Baker, "I Found Sir Ferdinando's House Much Like Your Barn: Excavations at Maine's First Governor's Residence (1634–1643)" (paper presented at the Council for Northeast Historical Archaeology annual meeting, 1987). For examples of North Devon ceramics and Bristol pipes, see Helen Camp, *Investigations at Pemaquid*, 57–65; Emerson W. Baker, *The Clarke and Lake Company: The Historical Archaeology of a Seventeenth-Century Maine Settlement* (Augusta: Maine Historic Preservation Commission, 1985), 23, 27; and Leon E. Cranmer, *Cushnoc: The History and Archaeology of Plymouth Colony Traders on the Kennebec* (Augusta: Maine Historic Preservation Commission, 1990), 82–86. North Devon ceramics are also found in other American colonial sites. The West Country ports appear to have also had a particularly strong trade relationship with Virginia and Maryland. See Alison Grant, *North Devon Pottery: The Seventeenth Century* (Exeter: University of Exeter, 1983), 114–30.

14. Bruce Bourque and Ruth Whitehead, "Tarrentines and the Introduction of European Trade Goods in the Gulf of Maine," *Ethnohistory* 32 (1985): 327–41.

15. For a discussion of trade goods in Maine, see Emerson W. Baker, "Trouble to the Eastward: The Failure of Anglo-Indian Relations in Early Maine" (Ph.D. diss., College of William and Mary, 1986), 132–43, and Susan Gibson, ed., *Burr's Hill: A Seventeenth-Century Wampanoag Burial Ground in Warren, Rhode Island* (Providence, R.I.: Brown University, 1980).

16. Levett, "Voyage unto New England," 39.

17. Neal Salisbury, *Manitou and Providence: Indians, Europeans, and the Making of New England, 1500–1643* (New York: Oxford University Press, 1982), 69–71, 101–6; Kenneth M. Morrison, *The Embattled Northeast: The Elusive Ideal of Alliance in Abenaki-Euramerican Relations* (Berkeley: University of California Press, 1984), 30–36; James P. Baxter, ed., *The Trelawney Papers*, vol. 3 of *The Documentary History of the State of Maine* (Portland: Maine Historical Society, 1884), 461.

18. Moody, *Letters of Thomas Gorges*, 98.

19. Ibid., 91.

20. Ibid., 2; Levett, "Voyage unto New England," 49.

21. Levett, "Voyage unto New England," 47–50.

22. Moody, *Letters of Thomas Gorges,* 110.

23. Alvin H. Morrison, "Membertou's Raid on the Chouacoet Armouchiquois: The Micmac Saco of Saco in 1607," and Marc Lescarbot, "The Defeat of the Armouchiquois Savages by Chief Membertou and his Savage Allies," trans. Thomas Goetz, in William Cowan, ed., *Papers of the Sixth Algonquian Conference, 1974* (Ottawa: Carleton University, 1975), 141–79. Samuel de Champlain, *The Works of Samuel de Champlain,* ed. H. P. Biggar, 6 vols. (1922–36; reprint, Toronto: University of Toronto Press, 1971), 324–28. Vines's journal of the trip does not survive, but Sir Ferdinando Gorges later wrote an account based on the journal. See James Phinney Baxter, ed., *Sir Ferdinando Gorges and His Province of Maine,* 3 vols. (Boston: Prince Society, 1890), 2:19.

24. Charles F. Carroll, *The Timber Economy of Puritan New England* (Providence: Brown University Press, 1973), 104–9; Paul E. Rivard, *Maine Sawmills: A History* (Augusta: Maine State Museum, 1990), 15–20; Moody, *Letters of Thomas Gorges,* 2, 52, 91, 100.

25. Moody, *Letters of Thomas Gorges,* 1, 52, 57, 66, 81, 91, 100–101, 124–25.

26. Ibid., 1 (quotation), 13, 92, 124–25.

27. Ibid., 48; Baker, *Clarke and Lake Company,* 36–38; Camp, *Investigations at Pemaquid,* 33, 68.

28. Moody, *Letters of Thomas Gorges,* 48.

29. David Grayson Allen, *In English Ways: The Movement of Societies and the Transferral of English Local Law and Custom to Massachusetts Bay in the Seventeenth-Century* (Chapel Hill: University of North Carolina Press, 1981), 3–18.

30. Moody, *Letters of Thomas Gorges,* 5, 6, 9, 11, 13; Sybil Noyes, Charles T. Libby, and Walter G. Davis, *Genealogical Dictionary of Maine and New Hampshire* (1928–39; reprint, Baltimore: Genealogical Publishing Co., 1972), 119–20; Banks, *History of York,* 113–19.

31. Moody, *Letters of Thomas Gorges,* 17.

32. Clark, *Eastern Frontier,* 36, 47–49; Wilbur D. Spencer, *Pioneers on Maine Rivers* (1930; reprint, Baltimore: Genealogical Publishing Co., 1973), 131; Edwin A. Churchill, "The Founding of Maine, 1600–1640: A Revisionist Interpretation," *Maine Historical Society Quarterly* 18 (1978): 34; John G. Reid, *Acadia, Maine, and New Scotland: Marginal Colonies in the Seventeenth Century* (Toronto: University of Toronto Press, 1981), 120–21.

33. For an example of the stereotypical view of Maine, see Charles M. Andrews, *The Colonial Period of American History,* vol. 1, *The Settlements* (New Haven: Yale University Press, 1934), 428. For references to others making this assumption, see Edwin A. Churchill, "Too Great

the Challenge: The Birth and Death of Falmouth, Maine, 1624–1676"
(Ph.D. diss., University of Maine, 1979), 106–8. The quote is from
Clark, *Eastern Frontier,* 14.

34. The author has studied immigrant origins from several early
Maine communities. The most comprehensive study was undertaken
on all immigrants into the Kennebec River region between 1654 and
1676. In Saco, the settlers listed on the 1636 tax list (the earliest list
of settlers for the community) was utilized, and in York, a list of all
settlers from 1630 to 1640 was made and examined. The principal references used for genealogical data were Banks, *History of York,* and
Noyes, Libby, and Davis, *Genealogical Dictionary.*

35. The evidence from Saco is unpublished data of the author's, collected principally from Noyes, Libby, and Davis, *Genealogical Dictionary.* For the Kennebec data, see Emerson W. Baker, "Trouble to the
Eastward," 86–92, 231–36, and Churchill, "Too Great the Challenge,"
106–8, 260–63. Gary Lord made similar findings just over the provincial
boundary in Portsmouth. See Gary T. Lord, "Politics and Social Structures of Seventeenth-Century Portsmouth, New Hampshire" (Ph.D.
diss., University of Virginia, 1976), 18.

36. Clark, *Eastern Frontier,* 84, 87; Banks, *History of York,* 206–12. At
least a dozen Scots ended up in York, forming the settlement of "Scot-
land." For references to other nationalities in Maine, see Charles T.
Libby, Robert E. Moody, and Neal W. Allen, eds., *Province and Court
Records of Maine, 1636–1727,* 6 vols., 2:106, 114, 237, 292, 458, 484; Moody,
Letters of Thomas Gorges, 55; and Neill DePaoli, "Pemaquid, Maine:
Preliminary Reconstruction of a Seventeenth-Century Coastal Com-
munity's Domestic and International Trade Connections" (paper pre-
sented at the annual meeting of the Society for Historical Archaeology,
Philadelphia, 1982).

37. Moody, *Letters of Thomas Gorges,* 1.

38. Baker, "I Found Sir Ferdinando's House."

39. Robert L. Bradley, "Was the Plantation Despicable? The Archaeology of the Phips Site, ca. 1646–1676," *Kennebec Proprietor* 6 (1990):
11–17; Cranmer, *Cushnoc,* 51–62. Information on the Richard Hitchcock
home is unpublished data in possession of the author.

40. Baker, *Clarke and Lake Company,* 51–57; Bradley, "Was the Plantation Despicable?" 11–17. The term *long house* refers to form rather than
function. In England, a long house was a dual-purpose building, in the
medieval tradition, that housed people in one end and their livestock
in the other. R. J. Brown, *English Farmhouses* (London: Robert Hale,
1982), 90–106.

41. Moody, *Letters of Thomas Gorges,* 89, 115.

42. Ibid., 94.

43. Ibid., 6; Reid, *Acadia, Maine, and New Scotland*, 111–14.

44. Banks, *History of York*, 192.

Chapter 13, New England Cartography

1. Mahmud Darwish, Samid al-Qasim, and Adonis, *Victims of a Map*, trans. Abdullah al-Udhari (London: Al Saqi Books, 1984).

2. James Axtell, "Colonial America without the Indians: A Counterfactual Scenario," in Frederick E. Hoxie, ed., *Indians in American History: An Introduction* (Arlington Heights, Ill.: Harlan Davidson, 1988), 47–65.

3. Peter Benes, *New England Prospect: A Loan Exhibition of Maps at the Currier Gallery of Art, Manchester, New Hampshire* (Boston: Boston University for the Dublin Seminar for New England Folklife, 1981), 76.

4. Gregory A. Waselkov, "Indian Maps of the Colonial Southeast," in Peter H. Wood, Gregory A. Waselkov, and M. Thomas Hatley, eds., *Powhatan's Mantle: Indians in the Colonial Southeast* (Lincoln: University of Nebraska Press, 1989), 292–343, quotation on page 292. This had also been noted earlier. See, for example, Louis De Vorsey, "Amerindian contributions to the mapping of North America: A Preliminary View," *Imago Mundi* 30 (1978): 71–78, in which DeVorsey wrote, "It is clear from the narratives and journals of scores of explorers, from Columbus onward, that Amerindian cartographers and guides in every region of the continent contributed significantly to the outlining and filling up of the North American map" (71).

5. Donald Robertson, *Mexican Manuscript Painting of the Early Colonial Period* (New Haven: Yale University Press, 1959); Donald Robertson, "The Pinturas (Maps) of the Relaciones Geográficas, with a Catalog," in *Handbook of Middle American Indians*, vol. 12, *Guide to Ethnohistorical Sources*, part 1, ed. H. F. Cline (Austin: University of Texas Press, 1972), 243–78; Mary Elizabeth Smith, *Picture Writing from Ancient Southern Mexico: Mixtec Place Signs and Maps* (Norman: University of Oklahoma Press, 1973). Some examples in the context of the Columbian encounter are given in J. B. Harley, *Maps and the Columbian Encounter: An Interpretive Guide to the Travelling Exhibition* (Milwaukee: Golda Meir Library, 1990).

6. Waselkov, "Indian Maps," 292. For the source of the cosmological map, see Philip L. Barbour, ed., *The Jamestown Voyages under the First Charter, 1606–1609*, Hakluyt Society, 2d. ser. 136–37 (Cambridge: Cambridge University Press for the Society, 1969), 82; for a graphic reconstruction, see G. Malcolm Lewis, "The Indigenous Maps and Mapping of North American Indians," *Map Collector* 9 (1979): 25–32.

7. Barbour, *Jamestown Voyages*, 82.

8. See [John Smith], "A Map of Virginia, with a Description of the Country, by Captain Smith . . ." in *The Complete Works of Captain John Smith*, ed. Philip L. Barbour, 3 vols. (Chapel Hill: University of North Carolina Press, 1986), 1:140–41, for a reproduction of the map.

9. Barbour, *Complete Works of Captain John Smith* 1:123.

10. Don Alonso De Velasco (1611), Untitled map of the east coast of North America, MS, Estado., Log. 2588, fol. 22, Archivo General de Simancas, Simancas, Spain. This is reproduced in part in G. Malcolm Lewis, "Indicators of Unacknowledged Assimilations from Amerindian *Maps* on Euro-American Maps of North America: Some General Principles Arising from a Study of La Verendyre's Composite Map, 1728–29," *Imago Mundi* 38 (1986): 9–34, where the possible Indian content of the map is discussed.

11. [John Smith], "A Description of New England; or, Observations and Discoveries in North America, 1616," in Smith, *Complete Works* 1:351. I am grateful to Harald E. L. Prins for this reference.

12. Ibid., 1:291–370.

13. Gabriel Archer, "The Relation of Captaine Gosnols Voyage to the North Part of Virginia . . . 1602," in Samuel Purchas, *Hakluytus Posthumus or Purchas His Pilgrimes*, 20 vols. (1906; reprint, New York: AMS Press, 1965), 18:304.

14. Samuel de Champlain, *The Works of Samuel de Champlain*, ed. H. P. Biggar, 6 vols. (Toronto: Champlain Society, 1922–36), 1:335–36.

15. G. Malcolm Lewis, "Native North Americans' Cosmological Ideas and Geographical Awareness," in John L. Allen, ed., *North American Exploration* (Lincoln: University of Nebraska Press, forthcoming).

16. George Weymouth was serving the interests of Ferdinando Gorges, later lord proprietor of Maine. Once in England, the Indians were imprisoned in Somerset Castle for a "full three years," and Weymouth was able to learn from them of their homeland with its "goodly Rivers, stately Islands, and safe harbours." Furthermore, he got them to set "downe what great Rivers ran up into the Land, what Men of note were seated on them, what power they were of, how allyed [and] what enemies they had." Ferdinando Gorges, *A Briefe Narration of the Original Undertakings of the Advancement of Plantations into the Parts of America* (London: Printed by E. Brudenell, 1658), 4. The Indians were later returned to New England to act as guides and interpreters. Quoted by Lewis, "Native North Americans."

17. The use of Indian geographical knowledge is implied in William Wood, *New England's Prospect* (1634; reprint, Boston: Publications of the Prince Society, 1865), 1–2, where, in describing "the Situation, Bayes, Havens, and Inlets," Wood noted that New England is "surrounded on the North-side with the spacious River *Canada*, and on the South with *Hudsons River* . . . these two Rivers . . . having their rise

from the great Lakes which are not farre off one another, as the *Indians* doe certainely informe us."

18. Lewis, "Unacknowledged Assimilations," 28. Lewis also discussed distortions in European colonial maps as being related to their misunderstanding of information supplied by Indians. G. Malcolm Lewis, "Misinterpretation of Amerindian Information as a Source of Error on Euro-American Maps," *Annals of the Association of American Geographers* 77 (1987): 542–63.

19. Benes, *New England Prospect,* 27–28.

20. Ibid., 28.

21. Ibid., 75–76.

22. Waselkov, "Indian Maps," 300.

23. For examples, see Lewis, "Unacknowledged Assimilations."

24. See Michel de Certeau, *The Practice of Everyday Life,* trans. Steven Rendall (Berkeley: University of California Press, 1984), xiii, who wrote of the Indians in New Spain: "Submissive, and even consenting to their subjection, the Indians nevertheless often *made* of the rituals, representations, and laws imposed on them something quite different from what their conquerors had in mind; they subverted them not by rejecting or altering them, but by using them with respect to ends and references foreign to the system they had no choice but to accept." An example in cartographic history of such a subversion would be the "Mapa Mundi" of Felipe Guamán Poma de Ayala in the *Nueva Corónica y Buen Gobierno,* 1615. See Rolena Adorno, *Guaman Poma: Writing and Resistance in Colonial Peru* (Austin: University of Texas Press, 1986), and Gordon Brotherston, *The Image of the New World: The American Continent Portrayed in Native Texts,* translations prepared in collaboration with Ed Dorn (London: Thames and Hudson, 1979).

25. F. J. Ormeling, *Minority Toponyms on Maps: The Rendering of Linguistic Minority Toponyms on Topographic Maps of Western Europe* (Utrecht: Drukkerij Elinkwijk Bu, 1983).

26. Meron Benvenisti, *Conflicts and Contradictions* (New York: Villard Books, 1986), epilogue, 191–202.

27. Brian Friel, *Translations* (London: Faber and Faber, 1981), 34.

28. For a critique of Friel's *Translations* as an authentic historical document, as opposed to creative fiction, see John Andrews, "The Playwright as Historian," in *Essays for Brian Friel* (forthcoming).

29. Justin Winsor, "Early Maps of New England," in Justin Winsor, ed., *Narrative and Critical History of America,* 8 vols. (Boston: Houghton Mifflin, 1884), 3:381–84; Clarice E. Tyler, "Topographical Terms in the Seventeenth-Century Records of Connecticut and Rhode Island," *New England Quarterly* 2 (1929): 382–401.

30. For some of its complexities, in a study making systematic use of manuscript and printed maps, see Arthur J. Krim, "Acculturation of

the New England Landscape: Native and English Toponymy of East-ern Massachusetts," in Peter Benes, ed., *New England Prospect: Maps, Place Names, and the Historical Landscape* (Boston: Boston University, 1980), 69–88.

31. Justin Winsor, "The Earliest Maps of Massachusetts Bay and Boston Harbor," in Justin Winsor, ed., *Memorial History of Boston*, 4 vols. (Boston: James E. Osgood, 1888), 1:39–61. The most authori-tative modern summary of the early mapping of New England is William P. Cumming, "The Colonial Charting of the Massachusetts Coast," in *Seafaring in Colonial Massachusetts: A Conference Held by the Colonial Society of Massachusetts, November 21 and 22, 1975* (Boston: Colonial Society of Massachusetts, 1980).

32. Barbour, *Complete Works of Captain John Smith* 3:278.

33. William Alexander, *The Map and Description of New England* (London, 1624).

34. Smith, in Barbour, *Complete Works of Captain John Smith* 2:440, 442, tells us how he spent the summer of 1616 visiting the towns and gentry in Devon and Cornwall, "giving them Bookes and Maps." He also presented "one thousand with a great many maps, both of Virginia and New England . . . to thirty of the Chief Companies in London at their halls." For examples of the later use of maps in colonial promo-tion, see Jeannette D. Black, "Mapping the English Colonies in North America: The Beginnings," in Norman J. W. Thrower, ed., *The Com-pleat Plattmaker: Essays on Chart, Map, and Globe Making in England in the Seventeenth and Eighteenth Centuries* (Berkeley: University of Cali-fornia Press, 1978), 101–25, esp. 115–18.

35. The old and new names are tabulated by Smith in a leaf inserted in some copies of *A Description of New England* in Barbour, *Complete Works of Captain John Smith* 1:319.

36. Ibid., dedication "To the High Hopeful Charles, Prince of Great Britaine," 1:309. The story is garbled in some popular histories of American cartography. See Seymour I. Schwartz and Ralph E. Ehren-berg, *The Mapping of America* (New York: Harry N. Abrams, 1980), 96, where it is stated that the place-names were "demanded by the fifteen-year-old Prince Charles of Scotland."

37. Benes, *New England Prospect: A Loan Exhibition of Maps*, 5–6.

38. Winsor, "Earliest Maps of Massachusetts Bay" 1:52–56.

39. The phrase is that of William Boelhower, "Inventing America: The Culture of the Map," *Revue Française D'Etudes Americaines* 36 (1988): 211–24.

40. Ronald Sanders, *Lost Tribes and Promised Lands: The Origins of American Racism* (Boston: Little, Brown and Co., 1978), 339–40.

41. Benes, *New England Prospect: A Loan Exhibition of Maps*, 27.

42. Krim, "Acculturation of the New England Landscape," 75–78.

43. Ibid., 79.

44. Wilbur Zelinsky, "Some Problems in the Distribution of Generic Terms in the Place-Names of the Northeastern United States," *Annals of the Association of American Geographers* 45 (1955): 319–49.

45. William Cronon, *Changes in the Land: Indians, Colonists, and the Ecology of New England* (New York: Hill and Wang, 1983), 66.

46. Benes, *New England Prospect: A Loan Exhibition of Maps,* 76.

47. Johannes Fabian, *Language and Colonial Power: The Appropriation of Swahili in the Former Belgian Congo, 1880–1938* (Cambridge: Cambridge University Press, 1986), 27.

48. Wood, *New England's Prospect.* For a modern edition, see William Wood, *New England's Prospect,* ed. Alden T. Vaughan (Amherst: University of Massachusetts Press, 1977).

49. Or on a common prototype. On the map, see Justin Winsor, "The Winthrop Map," in *Narrative and Critical History,* vol. 3, after p. 380, and Judge Chamberlain, "Early Map of Eastern Massachusetts," *Massachusetts Historical Society Proceedings,* 2d ser., 1 (1884): 211–14.

50. William Hubbard, *The Present State of New-England, Being a Narrative of the Troubles with the Indians 1677* (New York: York Mail-Print, 1972). On the "praying towns," see Neal Salisbury, "Red Puritans: The 'Praying Indians' of Massachusetts Bay and John Eliot," *William and Mary Quarterly* 31 (1974): 27–54. On the policy of breaking up tribal units and confining them to artificially established plantations or reservations, see also Yasu Kawashima, "Jurisdiction of the Colonial Courts over the Indians in Massachusetts, 1689–1763," *New England Quarterly* 42 (1969): 532–50.

51. Hubbard, *The Present State.* The "Table" is printed on seven pages of the original text following p. 131.

52. Ibid., xv.

53. Ibid., xiii.

54. Cecelia Tichi, introduction to Hubbard, *The Present State,* xiii.

55. See Catherine Delano Smith, "Maps in Bibles in the Sixteenth Century," *Map Collector* 39 (1987): 2–14; also Catherine Delano Smith and Elizabeth M. Ingram, *Maps in Bibles, 1500–1600: An Illustrated Catalogue* (Geneva: Librarie Droz, 1991).

56. Hubbard, *The Present State,* vii, clearly regarded a realistic geographical framework as important to his narrative, believing that truth suffered when events occurred in amorphous space undefined by familiar landmarks. He wrote, "For our Souldiers in the pursuit of their Enemies being drawn into many desert places, inaccessible Woods, and unknown Paths, which no Geographers hand ever measured, scarce any Vultures eye had ever seen, there was a necessity to take up many things in reference thereunto upon no better credit sometimes than common Report."

57. I adopt this sentence from Boelhower, "Inventing America."

58. Thomas Morton, *The New English Canaan, or New Canaan: Containing an Abstract of New England Composed in Three Books* (Boston: Prince Society, 1883). For the broader context of these attitudes toward the territory, see Mason I. Lowance, Jr., *The Language of Canaan: Metaphor and Symbol in New England from the Puritans to the Transcendentalists* (Cambridge: Harvard University Press, 1980.).

59. See, for example, "What's in a Name? For Indians, Cultural Survival," *New York Times,* August 4, 1988 (the restoration of Apache names in an Arizona reservation), or "NWT Natives Seek to Put Own Stamp on Map of North," *Globe and Mail* (Toronto), October 12, 1987 (on the restoration of traditional Indian and Inuit names to the Northwest Territories, Canada), and "A Town with a History, but Whose?" *New York Times International,* April 20, 1991 (the debate about restoring the Indian name *Aquinnah* to the town of Gay Head on Martha's Vineyard, Massachusetts).

60. Joseph Conrad, *Heart of Darkness: An Authoritative Text, Backgrounds and Sources, Criticism,* ed. Robert Kimbarough (New York: W. W. Norton and Co., 1971), 8; for Conrad's other writing on geography and maps, see also pp. 99–104.

61. See also Sir Richard Burton, *Personal Narrative of Pilgrimage to Al-Medinah and Meccah,* 2 vols. (New York: Dover, 1964), 1:1, where he wrote of "that opprobrium to modern adventure, the huge white blot which in our maps still notes the Eastern and the Central regions of Arabia," with the implication that it is the duty of the European explorer to fill it.

62. Even allowing for the fact that the local Indian populations had been greatly reduced by disease by the time the Puritan settlers arrived, the notion of "emptiness" is as exaggerated as it is deeply ingrained in American historiography. Perry Miller, *Errand into the Wilderness* (Cambridge: Harvard University Press, 1964), vii, wrote of "the massive narrative of the movement of European culture into the vacant wilderness of America." See the discussion in Jane Tompkins, "'Indians': Textualism, Morality, and the Problem of History," *Critical Inquiry* 13 (1986): 101–19.

63. Benes, *New England Prospect: A Loan Exhibition of Maps,* 36.

64. Lewis Pyenson, "Cultural Imperialism and Exact Science: German Expansion Overseas, 1900–1930," *History of Science* 20 (1982): 1–43.

65. For a description, see Jeannette D. Black, *The Blathwayt Atlas,* vol. 2, *Commentary* (Providence: Brown University Press, 1970–75), map 11, 82–85.

66. For this wider discourse, which could have been written with seventeenth-century maps in mind, see especially "Bounding the Land," chapter 4 in Cronon, *Changes in the Land,* 54–81.

67. For its present-day survival, see James Axtell, "Europeans, Indians, and the Age of Discovery in the American History Textbooks," *American Historical Review* 92 (1987): 621–32.

68. For the evidence for this organization, see Anthony F. C. Wallace, "Political Organization and Land Tenure among the Northeastern Indians, 1600–1830," *Southwestern Journal of Anthropology* 13 (1957): 301–21. Early European accounts demonstrate that tribal territories were clearly delimited by natural features such as rivers, lakes, and watershed lines. For example, see "The Description of the Country of Mawooshen," (an eastern Abenaki account recorded in 1605) in David B. Quinn and Alison M. Quinn, eds., *The English New England Voyages, 1602–1608*, 2d ser., no. 161 (London: Hakluyt Society, 1983), 469–76. The description was obtained from one of the Indians captured by Weymouth and taken back to England (see note 16 above).

69. On the background to French representation of Indian territories on maps, see Cornelius J. Jaenen, "Characteristics of French-Amerindian Contact in New France," in Stanley H. Palmer and Dennis Reinhartz, eds., *Essays on the History of North American Discovery and Exploration* (College Station: Texas A&M University Press, 1988), 79–101.

70. Francis Jennings, *The Invasion of America: Indians, Colonialism, and the Cant of Conquest* (New York: W. W. Norton and Co., 1976), 67.

71. Ibid., 67, quoting Edward Winslow, "Good Newes from New England . . . ," in Alexander Young, ed., *Chronicles of the Pilgrim Fathers of the Colony of Plymouth from 1602 to 1625* (Boston: C. C. Little and J. Brown, 1841), 361.

72. On the origins of the reservation system in New England, see Yasu Kawashima, "Legal Origins of the Indian Reservation in Colonial Massachusetts," in Bruce A. Glasrud and Alan M. Smith, eds., *Race Relations in British North America, 1607–1783* (Chicago: Nelson-Hall, 1982), 65–83.

73. *The Essential Thomas More*, ed. and trans. James J. Greene and John P. Dolan (New York, 1967), 61, quoted in Sanders, *Lost Tribes and Promised Lands*, 327.

74. John Winthrop, Sr., "General Considerations for the Plantation in New England, with an Answer to Several Objections," *Winthrop Papers* 2:120, in Jennings, *Invasion of America*, 82.

75. Quoted in Cronon, *Changes in the Land*, 56–57.

76. Quoted in Lowance, *The Language of Canaan*, 57, from Samuel Danforth, *A Briefe Recognition of New England's Errand into the Wilderness* (Boston, 1670).

77. Ibid., 71, quoting John Flavel, *Husbandry Spiritualized* (Boston, 1709).

78. Robert David Sack, *Human Territoriality: Its Theory and History*

(Cambridge: Cambridge University Press, 1986), 134; see also D. W. Meinig, *The Shaping of America: A Geographical Perspective on 500 Years of History*, vol. 1, *Atlantic America, 1492–1800* (New Haven: Yale University Press, 1986), 232–33.

79. W. P. Cumming, R. A. Skelton, and D. B. Quinn, *The Discovery of North America* (London: Paul Elek, 1971), 21.

80. John Smith, "The True Travels, Adventures, and Observations of Captaine John Smith," 892, and "Advertisements; or, The Path-way to Experience to Erect a Plantation," 946–47, in Smith, *Complete Works* 3:222, 286.

81. J. P. Baxter, ed., *Documentary History of the State of Maine*, 24 vols., 2d ser. (Portland: Various Publishers, 1869–1916), 7:73–75.

82. The method of dividing land by lottery was also used to allocate land at the township level in New England. See, for example, John Smith, "The Generall Historie of Virginia, New England, and the Summer Isles, 1624," in Smith, *Complete Works* 2:776. He wrote of the first New England plantation, "So in the afternoone we went to measure out the grounds, and divided our company into 19 families, alotting to every person a poule in bredth and three in length: and so we cast lots where euery man should lie, which we staked out."

83. Alexander, *Description of New England*.

84. Winsor, *Narrative and Critical History* 3:307.

85. For a description of this process, see W. Keith Kavenagh, ed., *Foundations of Colonial America: A Documentary History*, vol. 1, *Northeastern Colonies* (New York: Chelsea House Publishers and R. R. Bowker Co., 1973), 5–6, which does not, however, mention maps. Independent confirmation of the use of maps in this process is suggested by the map collections of English royalty and statesmen in this period.

86. F. N. Thorpe, ed., *The Federal and State Constitutions, Colonial Charters, and Other Organic Laws of the United States*, 7 vols. (Washington, D.C.: Government Printing Office, 1909), 7:3783, quoted in Sack, *Human Territoriality*, 134.

87. Ibid., 3784. For the wider legal background to this doctrine, see Olive Patricia Dickason, "Old World Law, New World Peoples, and Concepts of Sovereignty," in Palmer and Reinhartz, *North American Discovery and Exploration*, 52–78, note 43.

88. Thorpe, *Federal and State Constitutions* 7:3783–84.

89. Kavenagh, *Foundations of Colonial America* 1:40–44.

90. Ibid., 90–92.

91. See especially Benes, *New England Prospect: A Loan Exhibition of Maps*.

92. Richard M. Candee, "Land Surveys of William and John Godsoe of Kittery, Maine: 1689–1769," in Benes, *New England Prospect: Maps, Place Names*, 12.

93. See Viola Barnes, *The Dominion of New England* (New Haven: Yale University Press, 1923). A map associated with this proposal is described by Jeanette Black, *The Blathwayt Atlas,* Vol. II, Map 12, 86–87.

94. Kavenagh, *Foundations of Colonial America* 1:96–107.

95. The examples reproduced in Benes, *New England Prospect: A Loan Exhibition of Maps,* bear this out.

Notes on the Contributors

John L. Allen is Professor of Geography at the University of Connecticut.

James Axtell is the William R. Kenan, Jr., Professor of Humanities at the College of William and Mary.

Emerson W. Baker is Assistant Professor of History at Salem State College, Salem, Massachusetts, and has served as Managing Editor of *American Beginnings: Exploration, Culture, and Cartography in the Land of Norumbega.*

Bruce J. Bourque is Archaeologist at the Maine State Museum and teaches anthropology at Bates College, Lewiston, Maine.

Edwin A. Churchill is Chief Curator at the Maine State Museum.

Richard D'Abate is Associate Director of the Maine Humanities Council.

Alaric Faulkner is Professor of Anthropology at the University of Maine.

Gretchen F. Faulkner is Development Officer for the Hudson Museum at the University of Maine.

The late *J. B. Harley* was Professor of Geography at the University of Wisconsin at Milwaukee.

Faith Harrington is Research Fellow in New England Studies and Geography-Anthropology at the University of Southern Maine.

Kristine L. Jones is an ethnohistorian and independent scholar who has served as Managing Editor of *American Beginnings: Exploration, Culture, and Cartography in the Land of Norumbega.*

Victor A. Konrad is Executive Director of the Foundation for Educational Exchange between Canada and the United States of America and is Professor of Geography at Carleton University.

Kenneth M. Morrison is Associate Professor of Religious Studies at Arizona State University.

Harald E. L. Prins is Associate Professor of Anthropology at Kansas State University.

David B. Quinn is Emeritus Professor of Modern History at the University of Liverpool.

John G. Reid is Professor of History at Saint Mary's University, Halifax, Nova Scotia.

Ruth H. Whitehead is Assistant Curator in History and staff ethnologist at the Nova Scotia Museum.

Index

Page numbers in italics indicate illustrations.